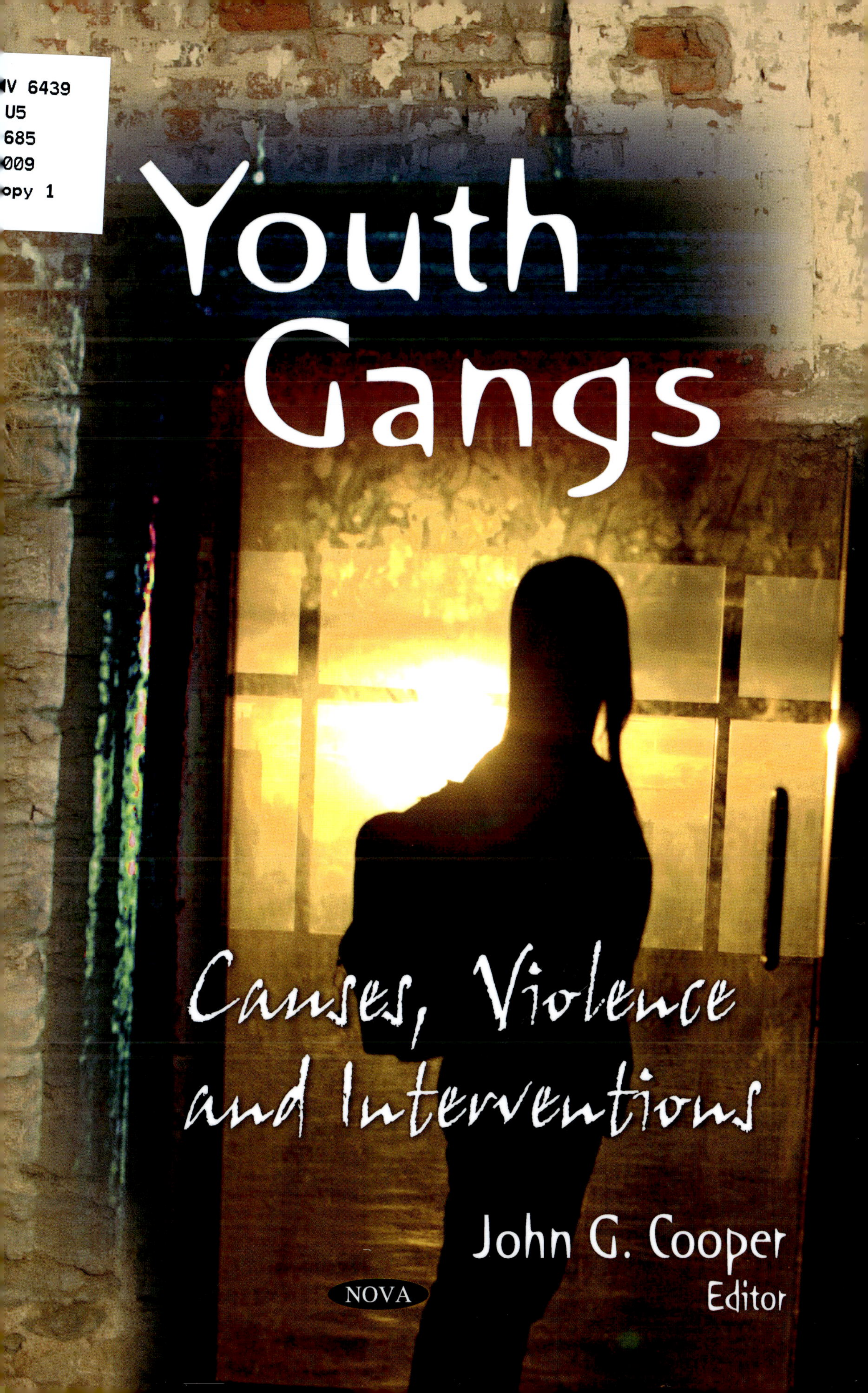

Youth Gangs

Causes, Violence and Interventions

John G. Cooper
Editor

NOVA

YOUTH GANGS: CAUSES, VIOLENCE AND INTERVENTIONS

YOUTH GANGS: CAUSES, VIOLENCE AND INTERVENTIONS

JOHN G. COOPER
EDITOR

Nova Science Publishers, Inc.
New York

For permission to use material from this book please contact us:
Telephone 631-231-7269; Fax 631-231-8175
Web Site: http://www.novapublishers.com

LIBRARY OF CONGRESS CATALOGING-IN-PUBLICATION DATA

Available Upon Request

ISBN: 978-1-60692-547-8

Published by Nova Science Publishers, Inc. ✦ New York

CONTENTS

Preface		**vii**
Chapter 1	**Youth Gangs: Background, Legislation, and Issues** *Celinda Franco*	**1**
Chapter 2	**Making Communities Safer: Youth Violence and Gang Interventions that Work** *United States Government Printing Office*	**45**
Chapter 3	**Protecting Our Youth: Paths to Gang Prevention in Our Communities** *Unites States Government Printing Office*	**177**
Index		**243**

PREFACE

Gang activity and related violence threaten public order in a diverse range of communities in the United States today. Congress has long recognized that this problem affects a number of issues of federal concern, and federal legislation has been introduced in the 110th Congress to address some aspects of the issue. Youth gangs have been an endemic feature of American urban life. They are well attested as early as the 18th century and have been a recurrent subject of concern since then. Contemporary views of the problem have been formed against the background of a significant adverse secular trend in gang activity during the last four decades. In particular, the rapid growth of gang membership, geographical dispersion, and criminal involvement during the violent crime epidemic — associated with the emergence of the crack cocaine market during the mid-1980s to the early 1990s — have intensified current concerns. The experience of those years continues to mark both patterns of gang activity and public policy responses toward them. Policy development and implementation in this area are bedeviled by discrepant uses of the term "gang" and the absence of uniform standards of statistical reporting. There are reasons for special care in the use of data on gangs and their activity. Without a standardized definition of what is meant by "gang," such as the age group or activities engaged in by its members, or standardized reporting among the state, local, tribal, and federal levels of government, it is difficult to target anti-gang initiatives and evaluate their effectiveness. According to a national gang survey, the most recent estimate indicates that there were about 760,000 gang members in 24,000 gangs in the United States in 2004.

This book provides background information on the issue of youth gangs, including data on gangs and gang crime. It reviews existing anti-gang initiatives at the federal, state, and local levels, and describes some of the legislation proposed during the 110th Congress to address the gang problem, as well as some of the issues raised by those bills.

In: Youth Gangs: Causes, Violence and Interventions
Editor: John G. Cooper
ISBN: 978-1-60692-547-8

Chapter 1

YOUTH GANGS: BACKGROUND, LEGISLATION, AND ISSUES*

Celinda Franco

ABSTRACT

Gang activity and related violence threaten public order in a diverse range of communities in the United States today. Congress has long recognized that this problem affects a number of issues of federal concern, and federal legislation has been introduced in the 110th Congress to address some aspects of the issue.

Youth gangs have been an endemic feature of American urban life. They are well attested as early as the 18th century and have been a recurrent subject of concern since then. Contemporary views of the problem have been formed against the background of a significant adverse secular trend in gang activity during the last four decades. In particular, the rapid growth of gang membership, geographical dispersion, and criminal involvement during the violent crime epidemic — associated with the emergence of the crack cocaine market during the mid-1980s to the early 1990s — have intensified current concerns. The experience of those years continues to mark both patterns of gang activity and public policy responses toward them. Reports about the increased activity and recent migration of a violent California-based gang, the Mara Salvatrucha (MS-13), have heightened concerns about gangs in certain areas of the country.

Policy development and implementation in this area are bedeviled bydiscrepant uses of the term "gang" and the absence of uniform standards of statistical reporting. There are reasons for special care in the use of data on gangs and their activity. Without a standardized definition of what is meant by "gang," such as the age group or activities engaged in by its members, or standardized reporting among the state, local, tribal, and federal levels of government, it is difficult to target anti-gang initiatives and evaluate their effectiveness. According to a national gang survey, the most recent estimate indicates that there were about 760,000 gang members in 24,000 gangs in the United States in 2004.

In the 110th Congress, several bills have been introduced that would address various aspects of the gang problem. Some of the bills would address the problem through comprehensive gang prevention initiatives, such as H.R. 3846. Other bills address the

---

* Excerpted from CRS Report Order Code RL33400, dated January 25, 2008.

gang problem through combinations of criminal penalty enhancements, targeted prosecutorial efforts and anti-gang task forces, and gang prevention provisions. These anti-gang proposals include H.R. 880, H.R. 1582, H.R. 3547, H.R. 3922, S. 456, S. 990, and S. 2237.

This report provides background information on the issue of youth gangs, including data on gangs and gang crime. It reviews existing anti-gang initiatives at the federal, state, and local levels, and describes some of the legislation proposed during the 110th Congress to address the gang problem, as well as some of the issues raised by those bills. This report will be updated in response to significant legislative activity in the 110th Congress.

INTRODUCTION

Organized youth gangs[1] and the criminal activity they engage in have long been a concern to policy makers. National attention on gangs reached a high point in the mid-1980s and early 1990s as the violent crime rate reached unprecedented numbers. Although concerns about gangs and gang-related violence during these years were essentially isolated to inner-city urban areas, today the concern has shifted to include violent gang activities that have more recently proliferated into rural and suburban areas. Growing concerns about the number and geographic migration of certain violent Latino gangs into new areas, both rural and suburban, brought the issue before Congress. In addition, concerns about the potential threat gangs pose to domestic security, along with longstanding concerns about the prevalence of gangs in urban areas and the proliferation of gangs in rural areas, continue to fuel congressional interest.

For the most part, gangs and gang crime have been a state and local law enforcement issue. Until recently, the federal role in stemming illegal gang activity was largely limited to grant programs to state and local law enforcement and community-based agencies. As gangs became more sophisticated and expanded the types of illegal activities they engaged in (i.e., money laundering, drug enterprise, etc.), Congress and the Administration began to take note. Although federal laws already existed for prosecuting the types of crimes committed by gang members at the federal level, Congress began to specifically address the gang problem and gang-related violence linked to the "crack" cocaine epidemic of the late 1980s through the Anti-Drug Abuse Acts of 1986 and 1988 (P.L. 99-570 and P.L. 100-690).[2] Further congressional action on gangs did not occur until 1994, when Congress passed legislation designed to address the gang problem through more comprehensive approaches.[3]

This report provides background information on the issue of youth gangs, including data on gangs and gang crime. It reviews existing anti-gang initiatives at the federal, state, and local levels and describes proposed federal legislation designed to address the problem, as well as some of the issues raised by these proposals. The report then briefly discusses policy options for dealing with the gang problem.

BACKGROUND

Gang activity in the United States has been traced back to the late 18th century, in the years following the end of the American Revolution.[4] The earliest identifiable gangs were recorded living in the slums of New York City in 1783.[5] It has been estimated that in 1855, New York City alone had more than 30,000 gang members.[6] The emergence of youth gangs in the U.S. is thought by some to be connected to immigration patterns, forming as a collective response to urban conditions in many of the large cities populated by recent immigrants as they struggled to make economic, social, and cultural adjustments. One of the earliest researchers on youth gangs, Frederic M. Thrasher, wrote in 1927 that the gangs he studied in Chicago may have emerged from "play groups" in immigrant neighborhoods.[7]

Early in American history, gangs were made up of specific ethnic groups, such as Irish, Italian, Jewish, Slavic, and other ethnic groups who immigrated to the United States and were drawn to the first large cities of New York, Boston, and Philadelphia. Most gang researchers agree that waves of immigration played a major role in the formation and spread of gangs in the United States. For many immigrant groups, gangs have historically provided a way of developing economic or social advantages in a strange country. In more recent history, the past 35 years have brought waves of immigrant groups of Asians (Cambodians, Filipinos, Koreans, Samoans, Thais, and others) and Latin Americans (Colombians, Cubans, Dominicans, Ecuadorians, Mexicans, Panamanians, Puerto Ricans, and many others) into urban areas across the country where many of the same language and cultural barriers have led to the formation of gangs among these groups.[8]

Most of the research on youth gangs has traditionally been based on sociological, ethnographic, and psychological methods. Using the methodological constructs of these disciplines, the majority of the research focuses on how the socioeconomic and environmental factors work to foster youth gangs. Poverty, poor educational opportunities, joblessness, and unstable family structures are among the social structures identified that can influence *at-risk* youth to join and to remain in gangs. Gangs are found in urban and suburban neighborhoods or rural areas where disaffected youths or migrant populations face poverty, poor schools, and joblessness. Researchers have also identified many factors that contribute to heighten a juvenile's risk of joining a gang, including familial and individual problems, such as juveniles growing up with little or no parental involvement (no parents, single parents, or both parents working) or juveniles with behavioral problems (see table 1). According to gang researchers, such *at-risk* juveniles would be more likely to look to gangs to find acceptance, stability, companionship, and a sense of identity, particularly when their communities or the larger society is not perceived to provide opportunities for integration and acceptance.

Table 1. Selected Risk Factors For Youth Gang Membership

Community	Poverty, social disorganization Gangs in the neighborhood Availability of firearms Availability of drugs High crime
Family	Broken home, parental drug/alcohol use Lack of parental role models Low socioeconomic status Family violence
Individual	Prior delinquency Deviant attitudes Aggression Behavioral problems Victimization

Source: Phelan A. Wyrick and James C. Howell, "Strategic Risk-Based Response to Youth Gangs," *Juvenile Justice Journal*, vol. IX, no. 1 (September 2004).

Gang membership is also influenced by socioeconomic and class distinctions that often stem from prejudice, racism, and alienation from many of society's institutions. Gangs provide affiliation with others who have certain characteristics in common to one another but who may be considered as outsiders in the larger society, often providing income to those with few prospects of finding a job or making a living. Gang membership has not always been associated with serious criminal activity, although research indicates that joining a gang does increase an individual's risk of involvement in crime. Gangs often fight other rival gangs over *turf* issues and often are involved in petty crimes and misdemeanors. More highly organized gangs are often involved in more serious crimes such as drug trafficking, violence, and illegal possession of firearms.

Definition of a Youth Gang

Academics and other experts on gangs continue to debate the formal definition of the term "gang" and the types of individuals included in gangs. Does a gang consist of members of certain ages? Are gangs always involved in crime? Do gangs vary in composition and organization from community to community, or do they all have some common elements in their organization, activities, and cultures? Despite decades and mountains of research there is still not a common definition of "gang" that is accepted by police, schools, academics, and communities across the nation.

Generally, there is agreement that gangs usually have a name and some sense of identity that can sometimes be indicated by symbols such as clothing, graffiti, and hand signs that are unique to the gang. Typically, gangs tend to have some degree of permanence and organization and are generally, to some degree, involved in delinquent or criminal activity. The criminal activities of gangs can range widely from graffiti, vandalism, petty theft, robbery, and assaults, to more serious criminal activities such as drug trafficking, drug smuggling, money laundering, alien smuggling, extortion, home invasion, murder, and other violent felonies. Some of the characteristics that are used to identify gang membership, often in combination with self-identification, are symbols or symbolic behavior, the association with known gang members, participation in certain criminal behavior, the individual's location or residence, identification by a police informant, or direct observation of certain symbols or symbolic behavior by law enforcement officers.[9]

Gang definitions vary widely and have changed over time. Early in the twentieth century, gangs could be seen by some as benign groups of friends from the same neighborhood providing social support and a sense of community, sometimes bound by kinship, and not established to commit delinquent acts. Gang members could be perceived as providing a protective function for their communities by attacking or driving out unwanted interlopers. However, today gangs are most often seen as juvenile delinquents and criminals who are more likely to be a threat to communities and public order, frequently as drug traffickers and violent criminals. Although this may not be true of all gang members, it is certainly clear that popular images in the media often portray gang members as criminals, and they are widely perceived as such by many.

The Department of Justice (DOJ) Office of Juvenile Justice and Delinquency Prevention (OJJDP), relying on several definitions offered by "leading theorists and researchers," defines a youth gang as a group that is involved in a pattern of criminal acts, typically composed only of juveniles, but may include young adults in their membership. Prison gangs, ideological gangs, hate groups, motorcycle gangs, and gangs whose membership is restricted to adults and that do not have the characteristics of youth gangs are excluded. The DOJ National Criminal Justice Reference Service (NCJRS), while acknowledging that gangs are defined in many ways, provides a common definition of a gang as a group of three or more individuals who engage in criminal activity and identify themselves with a common name or sign.

Gangs are also defined in current federal law. The U.S. Criminal Code defines a "criminal street gang" as:

> an ongoing group, club, organization, or association of 5 or more persons — (A) that has as 1 of its primary purposes the commission of 1 or more of the criminal offenses described in subsection (c); (B) the members of which engage, or have engaged within the past 5 years, in a continuing series of offenses described in subsection (c); and (C) the activities of which affect interstate or foreign commerce.[10]

The criminal offenses ascribed to a *criminal street gang* in subsection (c) include certain federal felonies that involve a controlled substance with a maximum penalty of five or more years of imprisonment; a federal felony that involves violence, or attempted violence, against another person; or, aconspiracyto commit either of these types of federal felonies.[11]

Several of the broad anti-gang bills introduced in the 110th Congress would modify the federal criminal code definition[12] of a *criminal street gang* as groups, associations, organizations, etc., consisting of *three* or more (instead of five or more) persons. In addition, most of these anti-gang bills would increase the penalties applied to *criminal street gang* crime and specified a number of violent crimes that would be punishable under the bills. Introduced in the 110th Congress, S. 456, H.R. 1582, H.R. 880, S. 990, and H.R. 1692 contain some version of this type of provision (see discussion below).

For most of the history of the research on gangs, the definition of gang membership relied on most by researchers has been self-identification by gang members themselves. Law enforcement officers, too, most often rely on a suspect's willingness to self-identify or "claim"gangmembership for police identification and reporting purposes. For policy makers, how the term "gang" is defined and who is a gang member are important concepts for gauging the extent and nature of the problem, as well as for developing appropriate policy and program responses. The continued absence of a standard definition limits the utility of data collection for research purposes and for criminal reporting. It also limits the ability to quantify and understand the extent of the gangproblem and complicates any national public policy response.

PREVALENCE OF THE PROBLEM

To establish a framework for considering federal gang policy, it is important to consider the data sources that indicate the pervasiveness of the gang problem. National estimates of gangs and gang members are provided through an annual survey administered by the National Youth Gang Center and funded through grants from the Office of Justice Programs (OJP). The 2004 NYGC survey is discussed below along with a brief look at data trends since the survey began in 1995. In addition, this section will provide an overview of the latest blended-year analysis from the NYGC of the 2002-2003 surveys, which elicited responses to slightly different questions than are included in the standard annual survey. These two surveys provide the only national estimates of how widespread the gang problem is and the extent of gang involvement in certain types of criminal victimization.

National Youth Gang Survey

Since 1995, the National Youth Gang Center (NYGC) has conducted an annual survey of a selected sample of law enforcement agencies on the characteristics of youth gangs. The NYGC survey is federally initiated by the Office of Juvenile Justice and Delinquency Prevention (OJJDP) and administered by the Institute for Intergovernmental Research. The NYGC survey provides the *only* national estimates of gang membership and activity. The survey is based on responses of a nationally representative sample of law enforcement agencies taken from the U.S. Census Bureau and the Federal Bureau of Investigation (FBI) data. The information reported in the survey concerns solely youth gangs, defined for purposes of the survey as "a group of youths or young adults in your jurisdiction that you or other responsible persons in your agency or community are willing to identify as a 'gang' member." The survey specifically excludes motorcycle gangs, hate or ideology groups, prison gangs,[13] and exclusively adult gangs.

The 2004 NYGC Survey

The 2004 NYGC survey, released April 2006, examined the prevalence of gangs and their illegal activities.[14] According to the survey results, youth gangs were active in more than 2,900 jurisdictions that city and county law enforcement agencies served in 2004. The survey also estimated that approximately 760,000 gang members and 24,000 gangs were active in the United States in 2004. The estimated number of gang members between 1996 and 2002 increased 14%. As figure 1 indicates, in the larger cities the number of respondents reporting a gang problem dropped slightly for the period 1999-2001 and began to rise slightly for the 2002-2004 period, whereas in rural counties there has been a decline between 1996 and 2004.

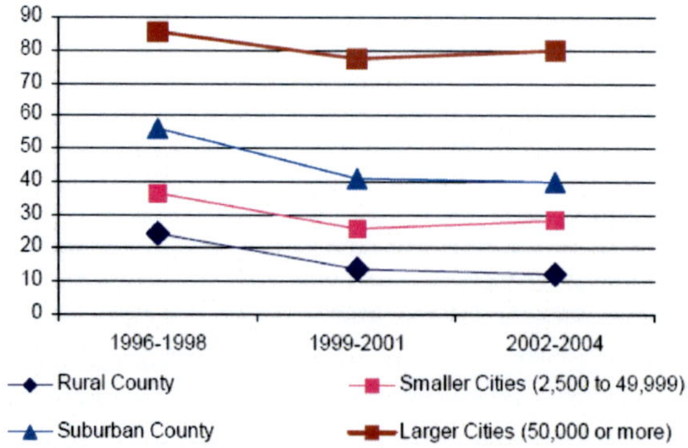

Source: NYGC Survey, 1997-2004.

Figure 1. Respondents Reporting Youth Gang Problemsby Size of Jurisdiction, 1996-2004 (in averaged percentages).

Of the 2,554 survey recipients, 2,296, or 90%, responded to the 2004 survey.[15] The 2004 survey summary reported that youth gang problems were reported by *all* large-city[16] law enforcement agencies that responded to the survey for the years 19962004. The majority of larger cities[17] law enforcement agencies that responded to the NYGC survey (82%) also reported youth gang problems. Forty-two percent of responding agencies serving suburban counties, 27% of agencies serving smaller cities with populations below 50,000 reported youth gang problems, as did 14% of responding rural-county law enforcement agencies.

Table 2 provides national estimates of gangs, gang members, and jurisdictions reporting gang problems reported by the NYGC from the annual surveys of law enforcement agencies for 1995-2004. As table 2 indicates, the national estimates of the number of youth gangs have been declining since 1996, whereas the estimated number of gang members has fluctuated over the years and seems to be rising since 2001. The most notable trend has been the decline in the total number of surveyed jurisdictions reporting gangproblems, which decreased 52% between 1996 and 2004 (as shown in the table). The drop in respondents reporting such problems raises questions about how reliably the survey results indicate whether or not the gang problem is or is not growing.

Table 2. NYGC Estimated Youth Gang Problem in the United States, 1995-2004

	1995	1996	1997	1998	1999	2000	2001	2002	2004[a]
Gangs (000)	23	31	30.5	28.7	26	24.5	N/A	21.5	24
Gang members (000)	664.9	846	816	780	840.5	772.5	693.5	731.5	760.0
Jurisdictions reporting gang problems	N/A	4,824	4,712	4,464	3,911	3,330	3,000	2,850	2,296

Source: U.S. Department of Justice, OJJDP, Highlights of the 2004 National Youth Gang Survey, #01, April 2006; and Highlights of the National Youth Gang Survey, 1995-2002.

[a] The OJJDP Highlights of the 2002-2003 National Youth Gangs Surveys June 2005, did not include estimates of gangs, gang members or jurisdictions (described separately below).

N/A = Not available.

A recent detailed reanalysis of the NYGC survey data from 1996 to 2001 provides some clues as to what may underlie these disparate survey responses and declining respondent numbers. According to NYGC reanalysis respondents from *all* the largest cities (populations greater than 250,000) and the vast majority of large cities (populations greater than 100,0000) reported gang problems in *all* survey years. Law enforcement agencies in small cities (populations above 2,500 and below 50,000) reported 16% fewer gang problems over the 1996-2001 survey period. In addition, rural and suburban counties reported significantly fewer gang problems over the same period. In the first two survey years, nearly 60% of suburban counties reported gang problems; however, the number of respondents declined steadily, and by the 2001 survey, suburban county respondents had dropped to just over one-third. Similarly, one-fourth of rural counties reported gangproblems in the first two survey years; however, the response rate of these jurisdictions also declined, so that by 2001 the response rate of rural counties was just over 1 in 10.[18]

There are many possible explanations for the decline in survey responses among small town and rural jurisdictions that could affect the gang estimates. One possible explanation could be that gang activity varies and may be more entrenched and constant in some areas, whereas in other areas, particularly in areas of low population density, gang activity could be a more episodic, fluctuating problem. In other areas, gangs could be a relatively new problem that perhaps has not yet firmly established itself in a community or area. As a result, the reported experience of gang problems reflected in the NYGC survey for larger cities remained fairly constant over the survey period. In smaller cities and rural and suburban counties, the decline in reported gang problems could reflect the variability of gang problems in these jurisdictions while simultaneously and disproportionately driving down the number of jurisdictions responding to the NYGC survey. Another explanation might be connected to the fact that responding to the survey is voluntary and not linked to any programmatic requirement or receipt of federal funding, which could help explain why law enforcement agencies, particularly in low-population jurisdictions with limited staff, might not consider completion of the NYGC survey to be the most important expenditure of staff time. Finally, the decline in survey respondents and gangs or gang membership might not reflect the experiences of all jurisdictions for reasons related to methodological issuesinherent in surveys and population sampling, including sample size and weightingof responses, which are beyond the scope of this report.

Although the NYGC survey may indicate that the reported youth gang problem could be receding in some areas, respondents to the survey reported that gang-related violence has been increasing in larger cities and some rural areas. The 2004 NYGC survey indicated that among larger cities (population of 100,000 or more), 173 cities reported both a gang problem and gang homicide data in 2004 (homicides involving a gang member). Of the 171 larger cities, approximately one-fourth of all homicides were considered gang related. In the two remaining large cities, Chicago and Los Angeles, more than half of all homicides were considered gang related. The combined gang related homicides in Chicago and Los Angeles accounted for nearly half of the total number of homicides (nearly 1,000 homicides) reported in the NYGC 2004 survey.[19]

In addition to the survey responses on gang homicides, the NYGC survey reports responses regarding the respondent's perception of whether the gang problem in their jurisdiction was improving or worsening. Of respondents to the 2004 NYGC survey, 52% of law enforcement officers indicated that they thought their youth gang problem was "getting worse," while 48% reported that there was "a decrease or no significant change" in their gang problem. According to the NYGC survey, since 2001, law enforcement officers have been reporting that the gang problem in their area is worsening: 27% in 2001, rising to 42% in 2002, and to 52% in 2004 (see figure 2).

The 2002-2003 NYGC Survey

In June 2005, OJJDP issued a fact sheet, *Highlights of the 2002-2003 National Youth Gang Surveys*, reporting that law enforcement agencies serving cities with populations of 250,000 or more *all* continue to report youth gang problems (95.7% responding).[20] Law enforcement agencies in jurisdictions with the smallest populations continued to be the least likely to report gang problems, and this was especially the case in rural counties (31.7% responding). Of the larger cities, more than one-third of the agencies reported an annual maximum of 10 or more gang-related homicides, whereas relatively few agencies serving rural counties and the smallest cities reported gang-related homicides in the study period. The analysis of the surveys over both years provided evidence that gangs, gang members, and gang-related homicides are predominately concentrated in larger cities.

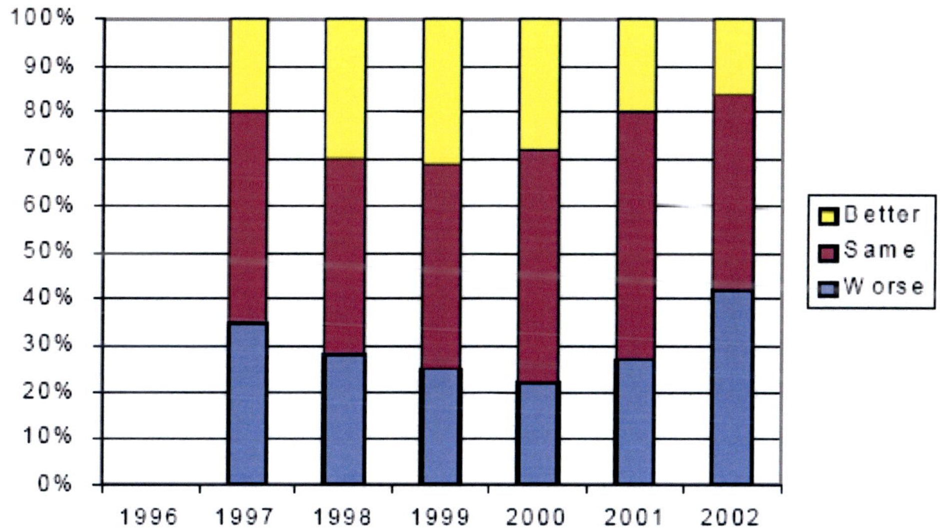

Source: NYGC 2002.

Figure 2. Status of Gang Problem in Jurisdiction of Survey Respondents, 1997-2002.

Although the fact sheet on the analysis of the 2002-2003 survey responses does not provide estimates of the number of gang members for those years, based on unpublished data for 2003, the NYGC survey estimated that the number of gang members was approximately 750,000 nationally.[21] According to the NYGC survey, the increasing number of gang members continues to be a serious policy issue. This trend indicates that there is still much to do at the federal level in the fight against the youth gang problem. Moreover, the migration of gangs into suburban and rural areas, beyond their traditional base of operation in the urban inner-cities, has also raised concerns about the possible spread of gang violence in areas of the country that have not been the types of communities usually besieged by gang activities and violence.

Crime Statistics

Crime statistics are often used as one measure of gauging the impact of gangs on communities. Much of the recent concern about gangs is attributed to the violent crimes that are often linked to gang activities. One would assume that if violent gang activity is increasing, this would result in a similar movement in violent crime statistics; however, as discussed below, this has not always been the case. Two crime data sources administered by the U.S. Department of Justice, the Uniform Crime Report (UCR) and the National Crime Victimization Survey (NCVS), are often used to frame a discussion of trends in gang criminal activity.

The FBI's UCR program compiles monthly crime reports from over 17,000 city, county, and state law enforcement agencies across the country. The UCR provides data on *violent crimes*, including homicide and nonnegligent manslaughter, forcible rape, robbery, and aggravated assault. *Property crimes* of burglary, larceny-theft, motor vehicle theft, and arson are also included in the UCR.

According to the most recent UCR, the number of violent crimes decreased 1.7% between 2003 and 2004.[22] The most significant decline was in cities with populations of one million and over, where the violent crime rate dropped an average of 5.4%. The declining trend in violent crime is not a new phenomenon. Since peaking in 1990 at a rate of 729.6 per 100,000 inhabitants, the crime rate dropped to a rate of 475 per 100,000 inhabitants in 2003, a decline of more than 34% over the period.[23] However, by 2004, the murder and nonnegligent manslaughter rates were beginning to inch upward.

Juvenile Gang Homicide

Much of the concern about the youth gang problem stems from the attendant violence associated with gangs and gang crime. Research indicates that the longer a gang member remains in a gang, the higher the risk they will become involved in crime, generally, and of particular concern, in violent crime. A CRS analysis of data from the FBI's Supplementary Homicide Reports (SHR), provided below, offers some insight into the commonly held view that gangs and youth gangs, particularly older juveniles, are more likely to be involved in violent crime. A similar analysis by the Justice Policy Institute of gang-related violent crime, as reported in the FBI's SHR from 1994 to 2003, concluded that over that period gang-related violent crime declined by 73%.[24]

Some critics have claimed that the FBI data on gangland and juvenile gang homicides may inadvertently give the impression that these homicides are primarily committed by juvenile offenders. Yet juveniles are responsible for a smaller proportion of all homicides included in this crime category than are young adults and adults who are included in the counts of these gang-related killings.[25] The SHR count of gang-related homicides includes offenders of all ages. According to the FBI data, a large majority of offenders of known age in gangland and juvenile gang killings are not juveniles.[26] The 2003 SHR includes records for 1,111 offenders in such killings; age data were reported for 52.8% (n=587) of the 1,111. Among offenders of known age, only 18.9% (n=111) were under 18 years of age, or juveniles (see figure 3).

Because no age data are reported for 47.2% (n=524) of offenders reportedly committing juvenile gang homicides, the exact proportion of all 1,111 offenders who are juveniles under 18 years of age is unknown. However, to hypothesize about the likelihood that those of unknown age are under or over 18 years of age, upper and lower bounds for those of unknown age can be established to determine the percentage of all 1,111 offenders who are juveniles. If the age-distribution of the offenders of unknown age were the same as that of offenders of known age, then 18.9% (n=210) of all offenders reported in 2003 would be under 18 because that is the proportion of offenders of known age reported in the SHR. Alternatively, if all offenders of unknown age were under 18, then 57.2% of all offenders would be under 18 (n = 111 + 524). Conversely, if all offenders of unknown age were 18 or older (n = 476 + 524), then 10.0% of all offenders would be under 18. Unless 85% or more of offenders of unknown age were under 18 (n = 445), a level that is 4.5 times this age group's share of offenders of *known* age, then it could be assumed that only a minority of the total number of offenders reported in the FBI's SHR as gangland and juvenile gang killings were in fact committed by juveniles. As a result, data on gang homicides must be considered with care if they are used in isolation as an indication of violent crime rates among juvenile gang members.

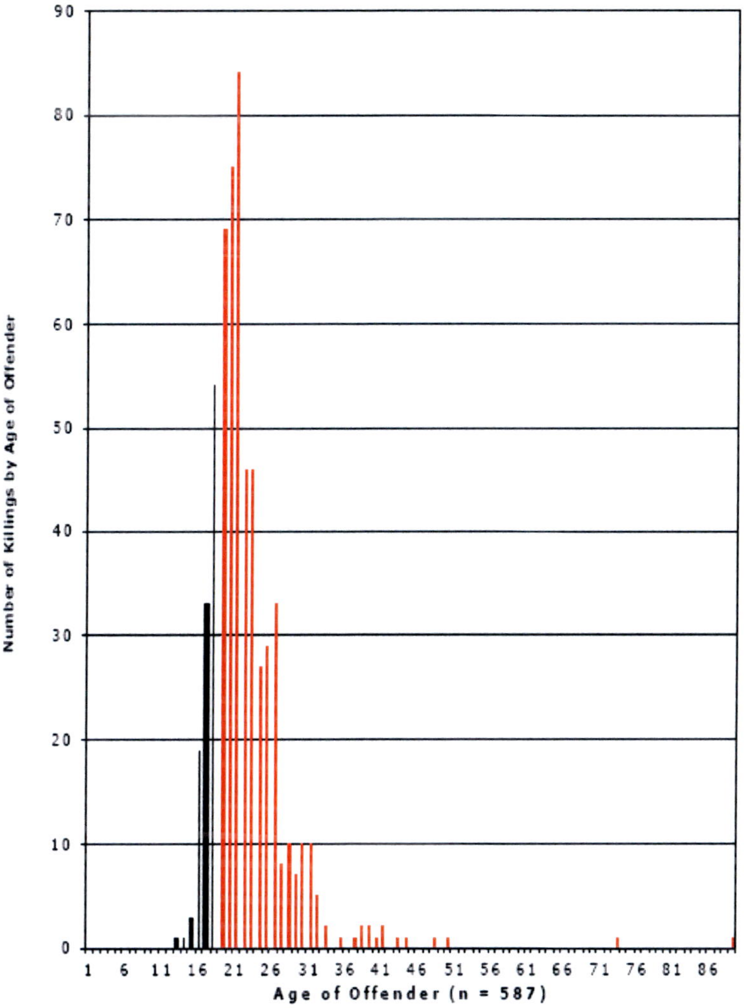

Source: CRS Analysis of FBI, Uniform Crime Reports, Supplementary Homicide Reports, 2003.

Figure 3. Gangland and Juvenile Gang Homicides by Age of Offender, 2003.

Despite the uncertainty about whether or not juvenile homicide rates reported in the SHR are actually perpetrated by juveniles or adults, most gang experts agree that gang members have higher offending patterns while they are actively participatingin a gang compared with before they join and after they leavethegang.[27] The historical trend in total juvenile gang murders provided by figure 4 indicates that juvenile gang homicides, as reported in the SHR, have decreased slightly since 2002. Overall, the rate of juvenile gang homicide in recent years continues to remain below peak levels last reached in 1995.

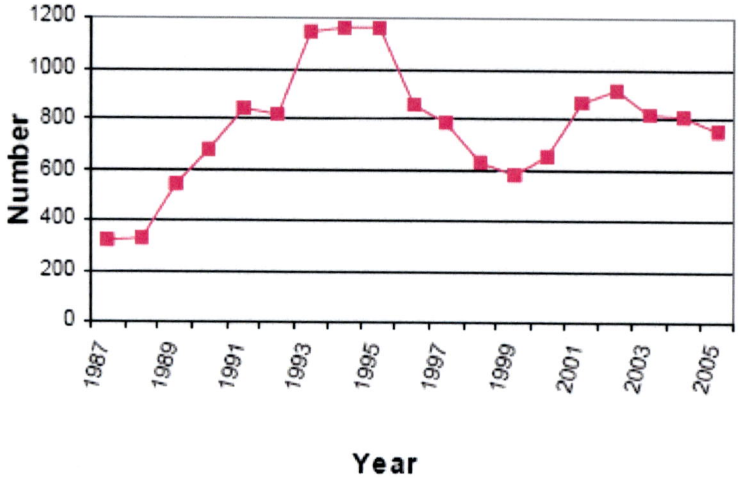

Source: FBI, Uniform Crime Reports, Supplementary Homicide Reports, 2005.

Figure 4. Juvenile Gang Homicides, 1987-2005.

National Crime Victimization Survey

The Bureau of Justice Statistics (BJS) administers the National Crime Victimization Survey (NCVS). Started in 1972, the NCVS is one of two DOJ measures of crime in the United States and is the primary source of information on criminal victimization. The NCVS data are obtained each year from a nationally representative sample of 42,000 households comprising nearly 76,000 persons that are surveyed on the frequency, characteristics, and consequences of criminal victimization. BJS statisticians then use the survey data to estimate the likelihood of victimization by various crimes, including rape, sexual assault, robbery, assault, and theft for the total population and for certain segments of the population such as women or the elderly. The NCVS provides the largest national forum for victims to describe the impact of crime and characteristics of violent offenders.

According to the survey, victims perceived perpetrators to be gang members in about 6% of violent victimizations between 1998 and 2003.[28] As a result, the NCVS estimates that gang members committed, on average for each year, approximately 5.7% (373,000) of the total 6.6 million violent victimizations over this period, including such nonfatal acts as rape/sexual assault, robbery, aggravated assault, and simple assault. In addition, the NCVS reports that, between 1994 and 2003, the rate of reported violent victimizations by perceived gang members declined by 73% over the period, from 5.2 per 1,000 to 1.4 per 1,000, after having peaked at 10% of all violent crime in 1996.[29]

Questions can be raised about the validity of the NCVS survey. Some have argued that the perceptions of crime victims are not anobjectivemeasure of anything more than an individual's recollection of a traumatic event, and that data collected through the survey cannot be deemed a reliable and objective source of criminal data. However, the NCVS has been systematically field tested and the methodology has been continually reviewed by an advisory panel of criminal justice policymakers, social scientists, victim advocates, and statisticians working in conjunction with a consortium of criminologists and social and survey scientists.[30]

National Gang Threat Assessment

The U.S. DOJ's Bureau of Justice Assistance (BJA), issued a report, *2005 National Gang Threat Assessment*,[31] that provides a national perspective on the threat posed by gangs. The report was produced in collaboration with members of the National Alliance of Gang Investigators Associations (NAGIA), including the FBI, the National Drug Intelligence Center (NDIC), and the Bureau of Alcohol, Tobacco, Firearms and Explosives (ATF). According to the report, gangs were pervasive throughout society and more sophisticated and flagrant in their use of violence and intimidation tactics. The report also found that when today's gangs migrate across the country, they bring drugs, weapons, and criminal activity with them. However, the report was not backed by hard data or crime statistics, and instead was based on a survey of law enforcement agencies and anecdotal accounts and experiences.

Law enforcement respondents to the 2005 assessment's questionnaire identified a number of trends across the country. Gangs were identified as the primary distributors of drugs throughout the U.S., sometimes associating with organized crime entities such as Mexican drug organizations and Russian organized crime groups, and engaged in low-level criminal activities such as protecting territories and facilitating drug-trafficking activities. Gang members were reportedly becoming more sophisticated in their use of computers and technologies for improved communications, facilitating criminal activity and avoiding detection by law enforcement.

Respondents identified the migration of California-style gang culture, along withgrowingHispanicgangmembership, as a particular threat as these gangs spread into new areas and promote the gang subculture. Although outside of the scope of this report, the expansion of outlaw motorcycle gangs into new territories and the formation of new gangs were also identified as a threat to communities asthesetypes of gangs battled over territories with increasing violence. In addition, 31% of survey respondents indicated that their communities refused to acknowledge the gang problem, and in some cases only began to address gang issues when a high-profile gang-related incident occurred.

The 2005 assessment identified a number of regional trends in gang activity affecting communities in the following areas:

Northeast Region

In the Northeast, neighborhood or homegrown gangs are increasingly visible and the growth of gangs within Hispanic immigrant communities has brought increased violence and crime to many communities. The region is identified as being particularly vulnerable to drug distribution by gangs because of the compact nature of the region and the well-developed transportation system throughout the region. Gangs are most frequently reported to be involved in crimes relating to vandalism and graffiti, firearms possession, assault, and homicide.

The South

In the South, the Mara Salvatrucha (MS-13), an Hispanic gang originally formed in Los Angeles, California, by immigrants from El Salvador, is reportedly one of the newest threats to the region, especially in Washington, DC, Virginia, and surrounding areas. Gangs in the South are reportedly most likely to be involved in the distribution and sale of marijuana and cocaine.

The Midwest

In the Midwest, gangactivity has increased around schools and college campuses, and gangs are concealing their affiliations and colors to hide from law enforcement. Gangs are increasingly cooperating with one another to facilitate crime and drug trafficking. Gang and drug activity in Indian Country has increased, and according to the assessment's respondents, Hispanic street gangs are using Native Americans to transport narcotics onto reservations.

The West

In the West, gangs are reportedly using increasingly sophisticated, well planned and executed criminal acts, especiallyagainst law enforcement officers. Street gangs are frequently involved in the distribution of both marijuana and methamphetamine, and the number of cases of identity and credit card theft by gang members has increased. In addition, respondents from the West reported that gang members were increasingly using firearms.

Characteristics of Gangs and Gang Members

Youth Gang Demographics

Historically, gangs have been most prevalent in the central cities of large urban areas and members were primarily young adult males from homogeneous low-income, inner-city, ghetto or barrio neighborhoods. Research indicates that most gang members join a gang as juveniles, some only participate sporadically, and a significant number leave, or 'age-out,' of gangs before they reach adulthood.[32] Typically, gangs have been racially/ethnically segregated and actively involved in a variety of criminal activities. However, there is evidence that some gangs have evolved into *hybrid gangs* that are mixed ethnically, racially, and by gender.

Based on data from an in-depth analysis of survey data from the 1996-2000 NYCG surveys published in 2002 (see discussion above), law enforcement agency respondents reported that 94% of gang members were male and 6% were female. The analysis also indicated that 39% of youth gangs had some female members. According to the analysis, gangs formed since 1985 were reportedly more likely to have proliferated into less traditional areas such as small cities, towns, suburbs, and rural communities.

Data on age and race/ethnicity were also collected from the NYGC surveys for the years 1996, 1998, and 1999. In 1996, respondents reported that half of gang members were juveniles below the age of 18 and half were adults 18 years of age and older. By 1999, the age balance had shifted toward older gang members and, according to survey respondents, 37% were under the age of 18. In 1999, respondents reported that 47% of gang members were Hispanic, 31% African American, 13% Caucasian/white, 7% Asian, and 2% other. During the three-year period, the reported distribution of race/ethnicity remained relatively constant (see table 3).

Table 3. Estimated Demographic Characteristics of Gangs (in percent)

	1996	1998	1999
Age			
Under 15	16	11	11
15-17	34	29	26
18-24	37	46	50
Over 24	13	14	13
Race/Ethnicity			
White	14	12	13
Black	35	34	31
Hispanic	44	46	47
Asian	5	6	7
Other	2	2	2

Source: NYGC (most recent detailed information available).

More recent demographic information on race and ethnicity from the 2001 NYGC survey show slight changes in gangcomposition (see figure 5).[33] As figure 5 indicates, the 2001 demographic data show increases among Hispanic (49%) and African American (34%) gang members, declines among Caucasian/white (10%), and Other (1%), and the percentage of Asian gangs remained the same (6%).

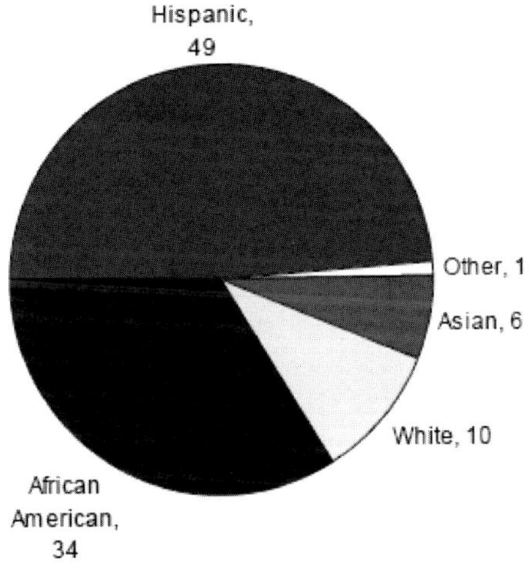

Source: CRS Presentation of NYGC data (most recent detailed information available).

Figure 5. Youth Gang Demographics (2001) (in percent).

Rural Gangs[34]

Small towns and rural areas across the country report gang problems. In small towns and rural areas the gang problem is not typically chronic and perpetual, but instead is episodic and not likely to persist as it is in larger urban areas where gang problems typically are chronic.[35] In part, this is due to the fact that these areas do not have the population base from which gangs can recruit new members. The small size of most rural or small town gangs makes them more vulnerable to disruptions such as arrest or members dropping out of the gang, and although all gangs are characterized by movement among members in and out of the gang over the course of a year, this dynamic has a more disruptive effect on the permanence of a rural, small-town gang.

A recent analysis of small town and rural county respondents to the NYGC's annual gang survey of state and local law enforcement agencies looked at responses from agencies representing populations between 2,500 and 25,000.[36] NYGC's analysis revealed that few of these agencies reported persistent gang problems. Of 27 rural counties responding to the survey, only 4% (1.08 counties) reported persistent gang problems. Similarly, of the 36 small town respondents, only 10% of small towns (3.6 small towns) reported persistent gang problems.[37]

The analysis of small town and rural county agencies found that agencies reporting persistent gang problems had a higher proportion of adult-aged gang members. In addition, jurisdictions reporting persistent gang problems were more likely to have also had gang-related homicides in their jurisdiction than jurisdictions reporting variable gang problems. Thus, the analysis found that the reporting of a sudden gang problem in a particular community might not always signal the beginning of a protracted or persistent gang problem or one which would be likely to develop into a serious problem like that seen in some larger cities.

NYGC's analysis identified population shifts and changing demographics in some small towns and rural areas as potential factors contributing to the emergence or escalation of gang problems. As in larger cities, language barriers and exclusion of newly immigrating youths were identified as factors which could contribute to the formation of groups that could coalesce into a gang. Examples of such possible situations included the rapid growth of Latinos in North Carolina and Salvadorans in northern Virginia, both situations which could potentially contribute to development of local gang problems for these areas. However, no data were presented indicating that these areas were experiencing such gang problems, and the analysis cautioned that the majority of youth gangs are "homegrown" with memberships composed of long-time residents in the particular area. Moreover, the analysis concluded that the formation of gangs was more likely to be the result of failed social institutions even in small towns and rural communities.[38] Broader applicability of the NYGC analysis to other similar areas across the country is, however, limited by the small sample size and small number of survey respondents, among other factors, which make it difficult to infer that the data are representative of all such jurisdictions across the nation.

Gang Presence in Schools

The threat of gang crime and violence exists in many schools across the nation. According to an OJJDP report, youth gangs are linked with serious crime problems in elementary and secondary schools in the United States.[39] The OJJDP study indicated that the incidence of several factors, including household income and drug availability, were positively related to the reported presence of gangs in schools.[40] The analysis also found a high correlation between gangs and the incidence of student victimization in schools. However, the authors concluded that although the presence of gangs in a school is correlated with criminal activity, it was not clear that gangs were a direct cause of criminal victimization at schools.[41]

The School Crime Supplement to the National Crime Victims Survey periodically surveys youth in school about the presence of gangs in their schools (see table 4). From the available data provided in table 4, survey respondents reported a gang presence in schools that increased dramatically between 1989 and 1995, an increase of 92%. As table 4 indicates, the percentage of students reporting a gang presence dropped precipitously between 1995 and 1999, a 41% decline; the percentage again rose and remained fairly constant at just over 20% in 2001 and 2003.

Table 4. Percentage of Students Reporting Gang Presence in Schools

Year	1989	1995	1999	2001	2003
	15.3	29.0	17.0	20.1	20.9

Source: U.S. DOJ, BJS, School Crime Supplement to the National Crime Victims Survey, for the most recent years available.

Of the students surveyed, students in urban schools were significantly more likely to report the presence of street gangs at their schools than were students in either suburban or non-metro schools (see table 5). In every residence category, whether student respondents lived in an urban, suburban, or non-metro area, the percentage of students reporting a gang presence increased significantly between 1989 and 1995. Although the percentage of students surveyed dropped between 1995 and 2003, the reported gang presence remained significantly higher in 2003 than it had been in 1989. The proportional increase between 1989 and 2003 was greatest in non-metro areas (57.7% increase).

Table 5. Percentage of Students Reporting Gang Presence By Residence

Year	Central City	Suburban	Non-Metro
1989	24.8	14.0	7.8
1995	40.7	26.3	19.9
2003	30.9	18.4	12.3

Source: School Crime Supplement to the National Crime Victims Survey, for the most recent years available.

Hispanic and black students were more likely than white students to report that there was a gang presence in their schools in 2003 (see table 6). Among students aged 12-18, Hispanic students in every residence category, except rural, reported the highest percentage of gang presence in their schools. Black students reported the highest percentage of gang presence in rural schools.

Table 6. Percentage of Students, Aged 12-18, Who Reported Gangs Were Present at School During the Previous Six Months, 2003

Race/Ethnicity	Total	Urban	Suburban	Rural
White	14	20	14	11
Black	29	33	28	22
Hispanic	37	43	35	13
Other	22	31	18	11

Source: School Crime and Safety: 2004, November 2004.

Students in public schools were more likely to report the presence of gangs than students in private schools; 35% of urban public schools surveyed reported the presence of gangs compared to only 6% in surveyed urban private schools. Similarly, in suburban public schools students reported 20%, whereas only 2% in suburban private schools reported a gang presence at school. In rural public schools the rate of reported gang presence was 12% compared to 4% in rural private schools.[42]

Gangs remain a serious concern for school safety and many advocate that particular attention should be given to signs of gang activity in schools. Gang-related fights and assaults are of a different nature and tend to escalate to other related, and occasionally larger, conflicts that can spill over into the neighborhood.[43] Some have argued that school-based, gang-related activity is often not reported, perhaps in part because of the negative attention that acknowledging a gang problem may bring to the school, parents, and surrounding community.[44]

Schools play a critical role in the socialization and development of children, and this is especially the case for at-risk children from strained families.[45] According to researchers, schools typically respond to gangproblems by suppression methods that include getting rid of the "problem" by separating gang members from the other students. Some researchers have concluded that this type of tactic can further marginalize at-risk youth, bond them more completely to gangs, and reinforce their loyalty to gangs.[46] These and other studies have led some researchers to conclude that a more balanced use of prevention, intervention, and suppression strategies starting in elementary school could help to reduce gang violence in schools.[47]

LATINO GANGS: MS-13, A CASE STUDY

In recent years, there has been growing attention in the press and among policy-makers on gang violence that is linked to gangs in Central America. Much of the concern about such gang members can be linked to the recent spread of certain Latino gangs from their origins in Los Angeles, California, into major urban and rural communities throughout the United States. Connections between gangs in the United States and gangs in other countries including Mexico, El Salvador, Guatemala, and Honduras have heightened concerns amongU.S. policymakers about the threat these gangs pose to domestic security.[48]

The Mara Salvatrucha (MS-13) gang was originally formed in Los Angeles, California, by refugees and immigrants from El Salvador who saw the formation of their own gangasa way to neutralize the gang threat to their community posed by the 18th Street Gang and others. MS-13 is reportedly one of the newest threats to the Washington, DC, metropolitan area, including the suburbs of Northern Virginia, Baltimore, MD, and other areas along the East Coast. According to testimony at a recent congressional hearing, the MS-13 gang is "estimated to have some 8,000 to 10,000 hardcore members [in the United States]."[49]

Although the estimated number of MS-13 gang members is a small fraction of the total number of U.S. gang members, they are reputed to be more violent. The MS-13 gang has followed the migratory pattern of Salvadoran immigrants, fanning out across the United States, and up and down the East Coast, in an effort to establish itself as a "national" gang organization. It is, by most estimates, the largest and most well organized of the Latino gangs, although other Latino gangs of concern across the country include the 18th Street Gang of West Los Angeles, the Latin Kings, and the Surenos 13. Many of these gangs that originated in California have also proliferated across the country, to some extent, but not to the extent of MS-13.

The FBI, other federal agencies, and local law enforcement agencies view the MS-13 gang as a national and international threat that must be addressed on several fronts. The Immigration and Customs Enforcement (ICE) bureau of the Department of Homeland Security (DHS) launched an operation focused on helping state and local law enforcement with the gang problem. ICE officials began an effort, *Operation Community Shield*, to use their immigration authority to detain and deport gang members of MS-13 from the United States.[50] The ICE effort focused on the cities of Los Angeles, Miami, Baltimore, Newark, and Washington, DC, and involved intelligence from state and local law enforcement, as well as the FBI, the Drug Enforcement Agency (DEA), the U.S. Marshals Service (USMS), and ATF.

On August 26, 2005, the ATF led a raid on MS-13 gang members in which 19 individuals were arrestedand charged with conspiracy to intimidate the communities of Silver Spring, Langley Park, and Hyattsville, MD, through murders, attempted murders, and kidnappings. These MS-13 suspects were named in a federal indictment alleging that the gang's activities violated federal criminal racketeering laws.[51] These Racketeering Influenced and Corrupt Organizations (RICO) statutes were originally designed to prosecute and convict organized crime groups like *La Cosa Nostra* under the premise that the violent operations of the Mafia were organized, structured, had leadership, and involved high-level, serious criminal activities. Hence, the organization and hierarchical structure of the MS-13 gang, rather than their violent criminal activities, will be what determines whether prosecution of MS-13 gang members under RICO statutes will be successful. Conviction under the federal RICO statutes carries a maximum sentence of life imprisonment without parole.

Gangs and the "Transnational Threat"

The prominence of gangs composed of recent immigrants from Central America, some of whose members are in the United States illegally, raises concerns about the ability of gang members to cross the southern border of the United States undetected. The porous southern U.S. border is often the method by which illegal goods and immigrants are smuggled into the country.[52] The continuing international connections between such Central American gangs raise the possibility that illegal entrants could pay gangs to smuggle them into the United States, and as such terrorists could also be illegally smuggled across the U.S. border by gangs.

The decision of DHS to crack down on MS-13 (discussed above) further indicates the significance of the transnational threat posed by gangs. The involvement of gangs in smuggling weapons, humans, and drugs has long been established. However, following the 9/11 terrorist attacks, there are heightened concerns that gang smuggling interests may be shared by terrorists groups interested in crossing the U.S. border illegally and undetected. Concern about the convergence of these smuggling interests may have been the impetus behind the sharpened focus of DHS on transnational gangs and their illegal activities, and particularly on Latino gangs, as a threat to domestic security.[53]

Despite the specter of transnational Latino gangs undermining domestic security, no evidence has been found linking U.S. gangs, regardless of their members' immigration status, with the smuggling of terrorists into the country. The *2005 National Gang Threat Assessment* concluded that despite their vigilance in looking for associations between gangs and international terrorist groups, few investigators identified any associations, and those who did described "the connections in terms of speculation [that was] supported by little evidence."[54] Furthermore, ICE recently reported that of the 1,057 gang members and associates arrested since February 2005 as a part of its recent crackdown on gang members crossing the southern U.S. border, none were found to have any terrorist ties.[55]

FEDERAL ANTI-GANG PROGRAMS AND INITIATIVES

For most of the history of gangs, the crimes they committed were generally the responsibility of state and local law enforcement. Gangs pose a significant threat to public safety, and as gangs have spread across the country the interest in finding adequate solutions to the problem has included all levels of government. In the mid-to late-1980s and early 1990s, Congress passed legislation federalizing certain gang-related crimes and providing additional penalties for individuals convicted under these laws. In addition, the federal government has taken an active role in helping state and local jurisdictions develop anti-gang responses through support for research on gangs, and through grant programs to help jurisdictions develop effective gang prevention and intervention strategies.

Developing an effective response to gangs, however, is complicated by the range of gang criminal activities (from juvenile delinquency to serious violent crimes by criminal organizations). Moreover, gang activities vary from community to community, making it difficult to establish national programs or provide uniform assistance. Strategies developed by the Congress to address the gang problem have included (1) *prevention*, aimed at preventing youths from joining gangs and engaging in gang behavior, by educating children and teens about the dangers of joining gangs;

(2) *intervention*, aimed at diverting at-risk youth from crime, by providing alternatives such as after-school programs, counseling, work-study, conflict-resolution, etc.; (3) *suppression*, law enforcement tactics that usually involve arrest, prosecution, and incarceration; or (4) a comprehensive approach which would combine some or all of the strategies to address the spectrum of the gang problem.

Selected Congressional Action

The federal focus on gangs began in the late 1980s when the OJJDP funded a research project dealing with drug use and delinquency among dropouts and gang members in New York City.[56] In 1987, OJJDP, in cooperation with the University of Chicago's School of Social Service Administration, initiated a major research and development program to address the gang problem. The project, the National Youth Gang Suppression and Intervention Program, was a four-stage process that included an assessment of the gang problem, the development of a model program for preventing youth gangs, a review of the literature on gangs, and a national survey of youth gang problems and programs.[57]

The federal response to youth gangs in the late 1980s was inextricably linked to drug trafficking and violence associated withwhatis often referred to as the "crack cocaine epidemic." The Anti-Drug Abuse Act of 1988 (P.L. 100-690) addressed the gang problem by establishing grant programs within OJP[58] and OJJDP designed to address a number of gang-related issues, including the prevention and treatment related to juvenile gangs, drug use, and drug trafficking. Further congressional action specifically on gangs did not occur until 1994, when legislation was enacted that took a more comprehensive approach to addressing crime and the youth gang problem.

The *Violent Crime Control and Law Enforcement Act of 1994* (P.L. 103-322) contained several anti-gang-related initiatives, including new or enhanced penalties for certain crimes that were often associated with gangs. The act provided new or enhanced penalties for gang-related crimes by (1) imposing an additional term of imprisonment of up to 10 years for involvement in a serious federal drug offense or federal violent felony affecting interstate or foreign commerce, (2) permitting the prosecution of youths 13 years of age and above if the juvenile possessed a firearm during a crime of violence, and (3) tripling the penalty for employing children to distribute drugs near schools and playgrounds. The law also authorized funding for a new grant program, the Gang Resistance Education and Training grants (G.R.E.A.T.) to state and local law enforcement and prevention organizations to be used for gang-prevention activities in schools. It also permitted existing grant programs, the Local Law Enforcement Block Grant and the Edward Byrne Memorial Grant programs,[59] to be used for various purposes, including multi-jurisdictional gang task forces. The act also directed the AG, in consultation with the Secretary of the Treasury, to develop a national strategy to coordinate gang-related investigations by federal law enforcement agencies.

In addition, P.L. 103-322 authorized the Community Oriented Policing Services (COPS) program, which was designed to put more police officers on the streets and make communities safer. The COPS program was generally designed to provide grants to state and local law enforcement agencies to fight crime at the local level through the strategy of having a larger police presence in high crime areas. Thus, COPS, by providing grants that could be used in preventing street crime, was indirectly providing assistance for fighting gangs and gang-related crime.

During the 107th Congress, anti-gang provisions were included in the *21st Century Department of Justice Appropriations Authorization Act* (P.L. 107-273). The law included a new Juvenile Accountability Block Grant (JABG) program that provides grants to states for strengthening the juvenile justice system. The grants can be used to fund projects designed to prevent and reduce the rate of participation of juveniles in gangs that commit crimes (particularly violent crimes), including the unlawful use of firearms and other weapons, or that unlawfully traffic in drugs. JABG funds can also be used to assist prosecutors to address drug, gang, and youth violence problems more effectively, and for acquiring technology, equipment, and training designed to help prosecutors with identifying and expeditiously prosecuting violent juvenile offenders.

More recently, the FY2005 Consolidated Appropriations Act (P.L. 108-447) earmarked $10 million to establish a National Gang Intelligence Center at the FBI. The center is to be a clearing house of information from the FBI, ATF, and other federal law enforcement agencies on gang intelligence on a national and international level. The act also appropriated funding for hiring additional FBI agents, analysts, and support staff to address the most violent gangs throughout the country.

Selected Proposals and Initiatives

Research on youth gangs indicates that each gang and each community is unique, so it is difficult to generalize and develop a "one-size-fits-all" strategy to address the issue. Over the last two decades, there have been many anti-gang projects and initiatives that have been developed and implemented in communities across the country. Federal, state, and local governments have actively developed approaches designed to prevent or stop gang involvement in violence, drug trafficking, firearms offenses, and other related activities of concern.

Research and experimentation on what might effectively end the gang problem has been a busy area of juvenile delinquency research. Currently, a mixture of approaches is being tried across the nation, but most programs attempt to integrate some component of prevention, intervention, and suppression strategies. Even municipalities have passed legislation and/or city ordinances targeting gangs. This section of the report will highlight a few of the most recent programs and strategies that have been and are being used to prevent youths from joining gangs and reduce gang membership and gang violence. The section will summarize some of the current federal programs and initiatives, followed by a generalized summary of state and local anti-gang initiatives.

Because gangs are involved in various types of criminal behavior, including juvenile delinquency, crimes of violence, property crime, firearms violations, and drug trafficking, various DOJ agencies are involved in fighting gang activities directly and indirectly. For example, through efforts to stop drug trafficking and crime, generally, the Drug Enforcement Agency (DEA) is working to address part of the gang problem to the extent that gangs are involved in drug trafficking. The U.S. Attorney's Office works to prosecute federal gang cases that are investigated by the FBI, or that involve the ATF, and as such are involved in battling gang criminal activity as it relates to, or involves, firearms violations and falls into their purview.

In addition, several federal agencies outside of DOJ administer programs that indirectly address some aspects of the gang problem. These efforts take varied approaches to countering gang activities. For example, the Department of Education administers grant programs designed to prevent juvenile delinquency and promote safe schools, which can have anti-gang components.

Compassion Capital Fund

In his January 2005 State of the Union address, President Bush proposed an initiative to provide $150 million over three years to community and faith-based groups to help troubled youth avoid gangs and prison. The initiative was proposed as a part of the Compassion Capital Fund (CCF) to help with building "service capacity and knowledge among faith- and community-based organizations and encourage replication of effective approaches to better meet the needs of low-income persons and families."[60]

FBI Efforts: The Safe Streets and Violent Crimes Initiative (SSVCI)

In January 1992, the FBI announced the SSVCI, an initiative designed to allow the Special Agent in Charge of each FBI field division to establish long-term, proactive task forces focused on reducing violent crime.[61] The task forces placed specific emphasis on the identification of major violent street gangs and/or drug enterprises of national scope by applying the same methods used to successfully wage war on traditional organized crime. According to FBI testimony before the Senate Judiciary Committee, one of the first gangs to be targeted by the gang task force was the MS13 gang. Moreover, the work of the task force enabled the U.S. Attorney for the Central District of California, Debra Yang, to successfully use statutes to prosecute the leaders of the 18th Street Gang and the Mexican Mafia, a prison gang.[62] The need for intelligence sharing forced uniformity and facilitated the FBI's development of an integrated information sharing systemfor trackingcriminalgang activit y through a national system capable of sharing information by computers in "real time."

According to the FBI, the task force concept increases the effectiveness and productivity of limited personnel and logistical resources, avoids duplication of investigations, and expands the cooperation and communication among law enforcement agencies. In response to the threat from gangs, the FBI established the Safe Streets Violent Gang Task Forces (SSVGTF) to coordinate the efforts of law enforcement at all levels of government and use the same statutes, intelligence, and investigative techniques against violent gangs that are used to fight organized crime. Between FY2001 and FY2006, the SSVGTF accomplished the following:

- 25,792 arrests
- 13,521 information/indictments
- 11,502 convictions
- 1,714 disruptions
- 301 dismantlements
- 344 RICO indictments
- 510 other racketeering statute indictments.[63]

For FY2006, Congress appropriated $5 million for SSVGTFs. The *Revised Continuing Appropriations Resolution, 2007* (P.L. 110-5) and the *Consolidated Appropriations Act, 2008* (P.L. 110-161) did not specify funding for SSVGTFs.

FBI National Gang Strategy (NGS)

The FBI's NGS is designed to incorporate the investigative and prosecutorial practices that had been successful in the Organized Crime/Drug Program National Strategy.[64] The NGS promotes the sharing of information among federal, state, and local law enforcement agencies, which in turn helps the FBI identify violent gangs with coordinated investigations that support prosecutions. The Strategy is a component of DOJ's overall Anti-Violence Crime Initiative, which is designed to promote the development of cooperative strategies among corrections, parole and probation, and law enforcement to work together and share information on gang-involved offenders.

FBI National Gang Intelligence Center (NGIC)

Pursuant to P.L. 108447, the FBI is in the process of establishing an NGIC. According to testimony at a congressional hearing, the NGIC "will enable the FBI and its local, state, and federal partners to centralize and coordinate the national collection of intelligence on gangs in the United States and then analyze, share, and disseminate" the information to the law enforcement community.[65] The NGIC, maintained and operated by the FBI, received appropriations of $4.7 million for FY2006. For FY2007, P.L. 110-5 did not specify funding for the NGIC. For FY2008, P.L. 110-161 similarly did not specify funding for the NGIC.

FBI's Criminal Investigations of Gangs

In September 2005, the DOJ Office of the Inspector General (OIG) released a report on how terrorism and the September 11, 2001, terrorist attacks transformed the FBI's investigative priorities.[66] Among the FBI's traditional criminal investigations, the OIG reported that the FBI did not reduce the number of agents involved in combating violent gangs between FY2000 and FY2004.[67] Despite the "reprioritization" of the FBI's operations to focus on stopping terrorist attacks, the number of FBI Field Agents used for investigating violent gangs increased from 266 in FY2000, to 315 in FY2004.[68] The number of violent gang cases opened by the FBI increased from 495 in FY2000, to 784 in FY2004, an increase of 58% during a period when the number of all other criminal enterprise cases declined.[69]

For most of the FBI's traditional criminal investigations in FY2004, fewer field agents were available as counterterrorism became the bureau's priority. In FY2004, there were 2,200 fewer field agents investigating criminal matters and the FBI opened 45% fewer criminal cases. However, the bureau's focus on fighting violent gang crime remained a priority.[70]

Organized Crime Drug Enforcement Task Force (OCDETF)

The OIG's report also included data on other criminal enterprise programs. OCDETF, a congressionally funded program administered by the Criminal Division of DOJ that focuses on the disruption and dismantling of major drug trafficking organizations, includes a gangs component. FBI agents participate in OCDETF efforts to combat drug traffickers and violent gangs. Although the number of agents utilized for all OCDETF matters dropped from 1,062 in FY2000 to 540 in FY2004 (49% decrease), the number of agents used on gang-related matters only dropped from 171 in FY2000 to 120 in FY2004 (30% decrease).[71] For FY2006, Congress appropriated $489.4 million for OCDETF. The *Revised Continuing Appropriations Resolution, 2007* (P.L. 110-5) specified FY2007 of $494.8 million for OCDETF activities. For FY2008, P.L. 110-161 included $497.9 million for the task force.

The Gang Resistance Education and Training (G.R.E.A.T.) Program

The G.R.E.A.T. program, administered by OJP, is designed to prevent children and young adolescents from joining gangs through a school-based curriculum presented by a law enforcement officer. The G.R.E.A.T program differs from other gang prevention programs because it is not directed at active gang members or at-risk youth, but instead is a broader program for all youths. The curriculum includes the following learning components: (1) crimes, their victims, and the impact of crime on the school and the neighborhood; (2) cultural sensitivity and prejudice and how these factors affect the school and neighborhood; (3) conflict resolution techniques to create an atmosphere of understanding that will help address interpersonal problems and solutions; (4) how to satisfy at-risk youth's basic social needs without joining a gang; (5) the diverse responsibilities of people in an at-risk youth's school and neighborhood; and (6) the need for personal goal setting and ways to establish short- and long-term goals.

The outcomes of the program are determined by followup surveys conducted between 12 and 18 months after completion of the program. The surveys indicate that students report lower levels of gang affiliation and delinquency, including drug use, minor offenses, property crimes, and crimes against other persons. When compared to the control group of students, those who had participated in the G.R.E.A.T. program reported fewer delinquent friends, more positive attitudes towards police, more negative attitudes about gangs, higher self-esteem, more commitment to success at school, higher levels of attachment to both mothers and fathers, and less likelihood of acting impulsively.

From October 1994 through December 2001, the National Institute of Justice (NIJ) funded a national evaluation of the G.R.E.A.T. program.[72] The evaluation had two purposes: (1) to find out if the program's components were being executed as designed, and (2) to observe the actual delivery of the program by law enforcement officers in the classrooms. The evaluation included both a cross-sectional and a longitudinal survey of middle school youths in selected locations.

The evaluation used a control group of students and a group of students that had participated in the G.R.E.A.T. program. The cross-sectional survey obtained information from 5,935 eighth graders in 315 classrooms at 42 different schools located within 11 diverse law enforcement jurisdictions across the country. The cross-sectional survey found that self-reported gang membership was significantly related to self-reported juvenile delinquency. The survey also revealed higher than expected levels of female and white youth gang members (38% female, 25% white).[73] The results of the cross-sectional survey supported the effectiveness of the program. These results were similar to previous evaluations of the program that had yielded modestly positive results.[74]

In addition to evaluating the G.R.E.A.T. program, a longitudinal study was conducted in six cities consisting of 3,500 students in 22 classrooms in 22 schools.[75] One year after participating in the G.R.E.A.T. program, the differences between the students who had participated in the program and those who had not were small. The longitudinal evaluation did not find significant differences in the groups of student participants until three or four years after program exposure.[76] Overall, the evaluation found that the program's outcomes measures were greater "than would be expected by chance."[77]

The evaluation of the G.R.E.A.T program concluded that significant reductions in gang membership or future reductions in delinquent behavior could not be credited to the program's nine-hour curriculum. However, the report credited the program with producing educational benefits and improved police relations with students and their communities. Advocates of the program maintain that G.R.E.A.T. can contribute to anti-gang goals as part of a broader program of prevention and intervention.

Under Title V - Incentive Grants of the Juvenile Justice Programs, Congress included appropriations of $25 million for FY2006 for the G.R.E.A.T. program (P.L. 109-108). The *Revised Continuing Appropriations Resolution* (P.L. 110-5) did not specify funding for the G.R.E.A.T. program. For FY2008, P.L. 110-161 provided $18.8 million for the program.

Project Safe Neighborhoods (PSN)

Project Safe Neighborhoods is an initiative designed to reduce gun violence. Although not specifically focused on youth gangs, the PSN program is an important part of reducing gun violence among the youth and reducing the use of guns in other criminal acts. The program includes five elements considered essential for a successful gun crime reduction strategy. The program is organized through the U.S. Attorney's Offices in 94 federal judicial districts across the county. The program has received funding of more than one million dollars since its inception in 2001. Funds can be used to hire new federal, state, and local prosecutors; provide training; hire research and community outreach support; and develop and promote effective prevention and deterrence efforts.

Under the PSN program, each U.S. Attorney develops a plan incorporating three national priorities: (1) increasedprosecution of violent organizations by aggressively using federal conspiracy, racketeering, narcotics, and all other available laws to attack and punish violent drug traffickers, violent street gangs, and violent robbery rings; (2) strictenforcement of all federal laws against illegal gun traffickers and their suppliers, with an emphasis on those gun traffickers who supply illegal firearms to violent organizations and to juveniles; and (3) aggressive enforcement of federal firearms laws against those persons prohibited from possessing firearms or who use firearms in furtherance of illegal activities, including those persons denied under the Brady Act.[78] The strategic plans are required to reflect the unique features and problems of the particular district, but with the goal of reducing the levels of gun crime.

Training is provided for participants inPSN through the collaborative efforts of several DOJ agencies, including ATF, who conduct the training of prosecutors, agents, and law enforcement officers involved in gun crime cases. U.S. Attorneys are encouraged to design and conduct their own training programs at the local level. Community outreach, public awareness campaigns, and public service announcements are all methods that can be used to convey the PSN message and get the support of the local community. U.S. Attorneys are encouraged to regularly assess the effectiveness of their plans, noting emerging trends, and they are required to report to DOJ on the status of their PSN strategy.

According to DOJ, the PSN program is responsible for a significant increase in the number of federal firearms prosecutions, which are up 76.2% since the initiative began. DOJ further notes that federal firearms defendants convicted of federal firearms offenses are being sentenced to significant jail time.[79] For FY2007, The *Revised Continuing Appropriations Resolution* (P.L. 110-5) did not specify funding for PSN. For FY2008, P.L. 110-161 did not include specific funding for the program.

OJJDP Gang Reduction Program

In FY2004, OJJDP initiated the Gang Reduction Program (GRP), a pilot program designed to reduce youth gangcrime and violence. GRP is underway in four pilot sites (East Los Angeles, CA; North Miami Beach, FL; Milwaukee, WI; and Richmond, VA) in targeted areas of approximately five square miles. The pilot sites were selected because these communities were characterized as already having significant existing anti-gang program investment, strong indications of citizen involvement in these anti-gang efforts, and high rates of crime and gang activity. The program is designed to integrate state, local, and federal resources to focus on prevention, intervention, and suppression with state-of-the-art, research-based practices. The program is designed to identify the needs at the individual, family, and community level and address those needs with a coordinated, comprehensive response. A three-year evaluation is being conducted by the Urban Institute to assess program implementation, examine outcomes related to reductions in crime and gang-activity, improvements in "prosocial" or positive activities for at-risk youth, and improved protective factors in the lives of high-risk youth.

Selected State and Local Programs and Strategies

States and cities have long been developing local approaches to the gang problem. Some of the areas that these initiatives and programs fall under are prevention, intervention, and suppression of youth gang activity. The following discussion is not intended to be a comprehensive review of the numerous anti-gang programs that have been initiated and developed by state and local governments, but a mere sampling of initiatives that are considered models for programs that may be generally applicable and replicable in other communities.[80]

Prevention programs developed by states and localities include those designed to improve the living conditions of at-risk youth and provide them with opportunities to replace gang activities with safer and more beneficial activities and services. Examples of these types of programs include providing alternative recreation opportunities where at-risk or high-risk youth and others involved in the juvenile justice system can be involved in safe alternatives to being out on the streets late at night. Prevention programs can also include early intervention programs for parents and infants or small children designed to provide parental training and childhood skills development, including preschool for early social and cognitive development. Preventive programs can also include school-based programs, to ensure in-school safety and control, in-school enrichment procedures, with formal links to community-based programs, as well as afterschool activities to keep youths safe and involved in recreational or educational activities such as mentoring programs.

Intervention programs seek to coax youth away from gangs and reduce the criminal activities of gangs, and can include such services as employment counseling, job placement assistance, advocacy assistance with the police and courts, and other social assistance such as health care and other services. Boys and Girls Clubs across the country provide gang intervention programs that provide life-skills development, education, and employment programs. Other programs are designed to provide alternatives to gang life through jobs in the community or through the enterprises developed by the project to provide employment opportunities for participants. One example of a California-based program funds a daycare center, a homeless shelter, an alternative school for gang members, and a tattoo-removal service. Another example of a gang intervention initiative developed by a faith-based organization provides jobs and refurbishes neighborhoods, including removing graffiti and providing landscaping.

Suppression programs are also designed to reduce gang crime by deterring such crimes through the arrest, prosecution, and incarceration of gang members. As early as 1979, Los Angeles, CA, created a prosecutorial gang suppression program through the city's District Attorney's office that targeted serious and violent juvenile gang-related crime. The formation of specialized "gang units" among local police departments improved intelligence gathering, investigation, and suppression of gangs through the use of gang sweeps, targeting gang gathering places or "hotspots," and intensified patrols in communities plagued by gang violence and drug trafficking to bring pressure to bear on gangs. In addition, there has been an emphasis on reducing handgun violence among gang members through various initiatives, often supported through grants from the federal COPS program (previously discussed).

Numerous communities across the country have used combinations of these examples and techniques to develop their anti-gang strategies. Community policing has been one strategy used to respond to gang activity, whereas other communities have approached the problem with strategies that combine local law enforcement with federal and state agencies. Many of these multiagency initiatives have been developed in Los Angeles, and other cities of southern California, where the gang problem is endemic. However, an influential multiagency project was developed in Boston, Massachusetts. Known as the *Boston Gun Project*, or *Operation Ceasefire*, the program is considered a "model" multiagency gang suppression initiative.[81] Under the program, gang violence is tracked to the neighborhoods where it occurs, there is an explicit communication campaign to let the community and gang members know that there will be zero tolerance of all gang violence, and that those offenders who violate these conditions will receive long prison sentences.

California's Street Terrorism Enforcement and Prevention Act

California has long had an endemic gang problem and, as a result, has been at the forefront of innovative approaches to respond to gang activity. The Street Terrorism Enforcement and Prevention(STEP) Act enacted on September 23, 1988,[82] combines prevention, intervention, and suppression approaches to the gang problem. The STEP defines what constitutes a "criminal street gang," what offenses are "gang offenses," and imposes penalty enhancements for gang-related crimes. Once an individual has been convicted under the STEP Act, the law requires the offender to register with the local law enforcement agency on release from prison, and failure to register is a misdemeanor offense, which if ignored can lead to further imprisonment.

Under the STEP Act, targeted gang members are notified that they can be prosecuted under this law and subjected to its penalties. The police and/or prosecutors then gather evidence on targeted gang members that fit the act's definition, and the information is presented to the court for a judicial order. Once a judicial order has been issued, convicted targeted gang members will have their imprisonment penalties enhanced.[83]

Several states have followed California's example and have enacted, or have considered enacting, gang-specific laws.[84] The California STEP Act has raised many constitutional questions involving freedom of association, vagueness, and overreaching, but has withstood the scrutiny of California's appellate court.

Gang Civil Injunctions

Gangs are often cited as major contributors to various types of crime, including violent crime. One response that is being taken by cities and jurisdictions across the country has been to use civil injunctions or nuisance ordinances to curtail the activities of gang members. Los Angeles, a city with one of the worst gang problems in the country, pioneered this response in 1987 in neighborhoods around the city particularly hard-hit by gang violence and crime.

Civil injunctions are legal actions that prohibit specifically named individuals from engaging in particular activities within a specified area. A *civil gang injunction* (CGI) can restrict or prohibit both legal and illegal gang activities.[85] For example, a CGI could be used to ban a gang from using public parks or wearing certain articles of clothing or publicly associating with known gang members. CGIs could also be used to make it a violation of the injunction to possess graffiti tools (spray paint) or to carry a pager or cell phone because these items could be used for illegal activities. CGIs have been applied to specifically named gang members who have been prohibited from engaging in certain activities within a specified area, in an attempt to create a "safety zone" within a high-crime neighborhood. If permitted by courts, CGIs have also included curfews, although generally these types of restrictions are typically only imposed on juvenile gang members named in an injunction. Violations of a CGI generally carry a fine or incarceration that varies depending on whether the case is brought in civil or criminal court. Typically, CGIs go into effect as soon the named gang members are served with a copy of the injunction order.[86]

Since Los Angeles first issued an injunction against a gang in 1987, the use of this type of local ordinance has spread throughout southern California communities and into other states. The rationale for CGIs is based on the finding that much of gang-related crime is perpetuated by a small proportion of gang members who are repeat offenders that can be identified and targeted. Proponents of CGIs report that a drop in crime in thetargetareasafter aCGI is imposed provides communities some "gang-free" time to organize and develop constructive ways of limiting a gang's effect on their community. If a CGI worked as intended, communities that impose such measures would expect gang-related crime rates to drop, and this experience has been reported by communities employing CGIs, at least in the short-run. However, CGI critics argue that the use of injunctions infringes on the rights of targeted gang members, violating their constitutional right to freely associate and assemble peacefully. Several of the CGIs have been litigated; however, generally the courts have upheld their use.

A recent studyof the use of CGIs in five neighborhoods in San Bernardino, CA, provides evidence supporting the use of CGIs as a strategic method of gang suppression.[87] The study found that CGIs were "relatively flexible tools" for fighting gang violence because they could be customized to address the particular needs of a community.[88] The studyfound that CGIs may also have an important psychological effect on gang members deterring them from criminal activities simply because of their concern about added police scrutiny resulting from a CGI.[89]

Surveys of residents in the CGI-covered communities found that the injunctions had an immediate impact on the visibility of gang members, and that theCGI,in turn, actually lowered the fear of gang members among residents.[90] Over time, the study found that the CGIs did have a positive effect on residents' perception of the gang threat even if the effect was temporary. The study concluded that even temporary reductions in gang activity and violence through CGIs have the potential to help communities reduce persistence of gang activity.

LEGISLATIVE PROPOSALS IN THE 110TH CONGRESS

In the 110th Congress, several bills have been introduced to address various aspects of the gang problem. These proposals comprise some comprehensive bills that include both enhanced criminal penalties for violent gang crime and authorize gang prosecution and prevention grants, while other bills would address the gang problem with more targeted prevention or intervention efforts. The following section briefly discusses some of the major anti-gang provisions under consideration by Congress.[91]

Criminal Street Gang and Associated Crimes and Penalties

Several anti-gang bills have been introduced, and one bill (S. 456) has been passed by the Senate, that would amend Title 18 of the U.S. Code to expand the definition of a criminal street gang and specify additional penalty enhancements for certain violent offenses committed by criminal street gang members. H.R. 880, H.R. 1582, H.R. 3156, H.R. 3547, S. 456, S. 990, and S. 2237 would specify federal gang-related crimes and increase the penalties related to violent criminal street gang activity.

H.R. 880 would provide *mandatory minimum* sentences for certain violent gang-related crimes, and would permit the imposition of a death sentence in cases where the violent crime resulted in the victim's death. H.R. 1582, H.R. 1692, H.R. 3156, H.R. 3547, H.R. 3922, S. 456, S. 990, S. 1860, and S. 2237 would provide *mandatory minimum* sentences of no less than 15 years and up to life in prison in cases where the gang offender had three prior convictions for violent or drug-trafficking felonies, the last of which had been committed within 10 years of the current offense. S. 990 and H.R. 1692 would make it unlawful to participate or cause another to participate in specified violent gang criminal activities, and would provide criminal penalties of up to 30 years. Under all of these bills, conviction for certain violent gang-related offenses could carry penalties of up to life imprisonment.

Among other provisions, H.R. 1582, H.R. 1692, H.R. 3547, H.R. 3922, S. 456, S. 990, and S. 2237 would also make it unlawful to knowingly recruit, employ, solicit, induce, or otherwise cause a person to remain as a criminal street gang member, or attempt or conspire to do so, with the intent that the person would participate in a gang crime.

Amendments to the Racketeer Influenced and Corrupt Organizations Statute

H.R. 880, H.R. 1582, H.R. 3150, H.R. 3156, H.R. 3547, S. 456, S. 990, and S. 2237 would increase the penalties for violent crimes committed in aid of racketeering. These bills would also increase the criminal penalties for certain violent offenses committed in the course of interstate and foreign travel or transportation in aid of racketeering.

Transfer of Juveniles for Adult Prosecution

H.R. 880, H.R. 3156, and S. 1860 would amend current law to permit the Attorney General (AG) to transfer juveniles for federal prosecution as adults if the alleged violent felony occurred after the juvenile's 16th birthday. Under these bills, the AG's decision to prosecute a juvenile as an adult would not be subject to judicial review in any court. H.R. 1692 and S. 990 would require a study to determine the costs and benefits of expandingfederal authority to prosecute offenders under the age of 18.

Gang Task Forces and Prosecutorial Assistance

Several bills would address the gang problem with targeted approaches such as establishing gang task forces designed to coordinate the investigation and prosecution of gang-related crime. For example, H.R. 638, H.R. 880, H.R. 1582, H.R. 1692, H.R. 3156, H.R. 3547, H.R. 3922, S. 144, S. 456, S. 990, S. 1296, S. 1860, and S. 2237 would designate High-Intensity Interstate Gang Activity Areas (HIIGAAs) where teams of federal, state, and local law enforcement authorities would coordinate the investigation and prosecution of criminal street gangs. Federal assistance would be provided by various federal agencies, and all necessary funding for the operation of the HIIGAAs would be federally authorized. In addition, these bills would authorize the AG to hire 94 additional Assistant U.S. Attorneys for assignment to the HIIGAAs and would authorize appropriations to fund the HIGAAs. H.R. 638 would authorize appropriations for grants to assist state and local prosecutors to fund technology, equipment, and training for prosecutors and law enforcement to help them identify and prosecute gang members and violent offenders, among other purposes, and it would authorize appropriations for the hiring 94 additional prosecutors to fight violent gang crime through the HIIGAAs.

Similarly, H.R. 1069 and S. 144 would establish comprehensive gang prevention and relief areas, as well as task forces to coordinate federal assistance to provide a comprehensive response to gang problems by focusing on early childhood intervention programs, at-risk youth intervention, literacy, employment, community policing, and comprehensive community anti-gang programs. In addition, the task forces would prioritize the federal funding needs of the areas under a number of federal programs. Among other provisions, H.R. 2466 includes a provision which would authorize the establishment of multi-jurisdictional anti-gang task forces. H.R. 3152 would also authorize multi-jurisdictional anti-gang task forces.

In addition, some bills would establish grant programs designed to assist state and local prosecutors in combating violent crime. H.R. 880, H.R. 1582, H.R. 3156, H.R. 3568, H.R. 3922, S. 1860, and S. 2237 would provide grants to prosecutors and law enforcement to combat violent crime, generally, and to fund technology, equipment, and training in order to increase the accurate identification of gang members and maintain databases of this information to facilitatecoordination among law enforcement and prosecutors.

H.R. 3150, H.R. 3474, H.R. 3922, and S. 2237 would expand the FBI's Safe Streets Program to establish a National Gang Activity Database for use in supporting criminal street gang enforcement teams. The bill would require the AG to establish a DOJ-administered database designed to collect and disseminate gang information to law enforcement agencies at all levelsof government, as well as provide aggregate statistical information on gangs, subject to appropriate controls. H.R. 3384 would authorize additional appropriations for the PSN program to improvethe enforcement of criminal laws against violent gangs.

H.R. 367 would require the Attorney General (AG) to develop and report to Congress on a national strategy to eliminate the illegal operations of the top three international drug gangs whose illegal activities include drug-related offenses with any international terrorist organization or state. S. 456, H.R. 1582, and H.R. 3922 would authorize appropriations to provide the FBI with more resources for the investigation and prosecution of violent criminal street gangs.

Gang Prevention Grants

H.R. 1070 would fund gang prevention programs from the proceeds of the sale of certain specially issued postage stamps. H.R. 1184 would permit the Secretary of Education to make grants to state educational agencies to award sub-grants to alternative schools or programs serving at-risk youth that agree to develop and implement a 100-hour community service requirement for students per school year. In addition, the bill would also require that students receive training and attend conflict resolution classes as a prerequisite to performing community service. H.R. 3168 would establish a grant program designed to help communities provide training, mentoring, and education programs designed to deter and prevent gang and youth violence by helping high-risk young adults become employable.

H.R. 1582, H.R. 3150, H.R. 3384, H.R. 3922, S. 456, and S. 2237 would expand the Project Safe Neighborhoods program, an initiative designed to reduce gun violence, to require each U.S. Attorney to identify, investigate, and prosecute significant criminal street gangs operating within their district. In addition, U.S. Attorneys would be required to coordinate these activities among federal, state, and local law enforcement agencies. The bills would authorize the AG to hire additional staff for carrying out the program.

H.R. 3846 would establish a series of new grants and would provide funding for coordinating entities charged with overseeing the implementation of the grants and creating an infrastructure between local units of government, state and local law enforcement agencies, and the federal government. Under H.R. 3846, evidence-based measures of local and tribal juvenile delinquency and criminal street gang activity prevention and intervention efforts would be used to identify promising prevention and intervention programs.

Other prevention initiatives would be supported by grant programs that would permit the development of a wide range of community-based programs for prevention and intervention alternatives for high-risk youth. H.R. 1582, H.R. 1692, H.R. 3922, and S. 456, S. 990, and S. 2237 would authorize grants for community programs designed to prevent young people from joining gangs. Generally, the grants could be used for a variety of gang prevention activities, including community and school-based projects designed to eliminate gang related crime through employment of security personnel; physical improvementsdesigned to enhance security; measures designed to reduce gang activity in and around public and low-income housing; mentoring, counseling, and other activities to improve educational attainment and employability; as well as intervention initiatives designed to enhance reintegration strategies for offender reentry. Among other provisions, H.R. 1806 would similarly authorize school and community based gang prevention grants.

Selected Issues Raised by Legislative Proposals

Most of the comprehensive anti-gang bills introduced in the 110th Congress focus on making changes to federal criminal law that would provide longer prison sentences for gang members convicted of certain violent felonies. These provisions would amend the current law definition of what constitutes a "criminal street gang" by lowering the number of affiliated persons required to trigger additional criminal penalties for serious violent offenses. Some of the bills address the gang problem through other indirect punitive measures, such as increasing the penalties for specified violent crimes, including the use of *mandatory minimum* sentences. Similarly, a few of the bills would permit the AG to determine whether a juvenile offender should be transferred for prosecution as an adult.

Proponents of these gang-related sentencing enhancements argue that these enhanced federal penalties are needed to address the rising gang crime in many communities. They argue that longer sentences could deter violent gang-related crime. In addition, the threat of a longer time in prison could encourage greater cooperation of gang members with prosecutors, which could lead to the identification, arrest, and prosecution of other gang members in exchange for a shorter sentence. Proponents of the anti-gang legislation argue that such measures are supported by law enforcement officials who contend that they need these tougher sentences to stop gang violence.[92] Similarly, proponents of *mandatory minimum* sentences argue that this type of sentencing offers greater incentives for criminals to cooperate with law enforcement, providing evidence in exchange for prosecution for a different or lesser charge that does not carry a *mandatory minimum* or carries a lesser sentence. Proponents of new additional federal criminal penalties for gang crimes argue that tougher penalties and federal *mandatory minimum* sentences for gang crimes are an essential deterrent to gang crime, particularly violent crimes.

Critics of *mandatory minimum* sentences argue on several levels against these proposals. On the broadest level, there are critics opposed to the further federalization of laws that have traditionally been under the sole jurisdiction of states and localities. They cite the growing number of new federal crimes, recently estimated at almost 4,000 crimes,[93] and that a federal approach is less desirable and unnecessary when there are already adequate *federal*, state, and local laws to address gang-related crime. It is also argued that, not only are federal resources strained as they cope with investigating and prosecuting national threats, but it is the state and local law enforcement officers that have the necessary experience and local intelligence sources to investigate and prosecute gangcrimes which mayvarygreatly by state, region, or locality. Opponents of *mandatory minimum* sentences for gang-related crime also point to the greater expense of imprisonment versus the costs of prevention and rehabilitation efforts. Moreover, it has also been argued that in certain situations, many individuals will break the law *nothwithstanding* severe criminal penalties,[94] questioning the crime deterrence effect of harsher penalties.

The issue of prosecuting juveniles as adults is a highly contentious issue discussed voluminously in the literature on juvenile delinquency, and is beyond the scope of this report.[95] However, provisions such as the one proposed in H.R. 880 that would permit federal prosecution of juveniles who commit gang-related crimes after their 16th birthday could have significant implications. For example, under provisions of this bill, juveniles prosecuted and convicted as adults for serious gang-related violent offenses could be subject to *mandatory minimum* sentences. Under provisions such as the enhanced criminal penalties for gang-related crimes found in H.R. 880, juvenile gang members transferred for federal prosecution as adults could be eligible to receive a sentence of death for certain violent crimes. Opponents of prosecuting juveniles as adults point to research that shows juveniles who are tried as adults and imprisoned in adult facilities have higher recidivism rates and higher rearrest rates compared to those of juveniles sentenced in juvenile court. Others argue that these measures could disproportionately affect racial and ethnic minority juveniles. In addition, they point to data from the FBI Uniform Crime Reports and the National Crime Victimization Survey (NCVS) reports (discussed above — Crime Statistics section) that indicate that juvenile gang crime has been declining.

Most of the comprehensive bills would amend the federal organized crime and racketeering statutes (RICO) to include provisions to make racketeering a gang predicate offense and increase penalties the penalties for such crimes. Proponents of such federal RICO amendments argue that these amendments are necessary to prosecute cases where drug trafficking activity has been conducted by gangs onto federal land and Indian reservations to avoid detection and state prosecution. Proponents argue that additional federal gang-specific RICO laws, as provided by some of these bills, would provide an important addition to the federal arsenal for investigating and prosecuting gang-related crime. Opponents argue that the existing federal RICO laws are sufficiently broad to provide for successful prosecution of gang-related crime. RICO prosecutions can present a number of obstacles to prosecuting gang violence and murder using these statutes. For example, one significant obstacle in a gang-related RICO prosecution can be the statutes requirement that a gang being prosecuted must be shown to have a defined structure and hierarchical organization, and that the crimes were committed, or that there was a conspiracy to commit crimes in furtherance of the gang.[96] Despite these and other evidentiary obstacles under existing federal RICO statues, there have been a number of successful RICO prosecutions for gang-related crimes.[97]

A more general criticism of many anti-gang legislation that has been introduced in previous Congresses has been that many of the bills were not sufficiently focused on gang prevention assistance and that there was a lack of innovation or expansion of prevention strategies. Similarly, some have criticized the lack of focus on intervention efforts designed to help keep ex-offender gang members from falling back into the gang life after imprisonment.

Supporters of gang prevention and intervention programs have long argued that these types programs have been subjected to funding cuts in recent years despite research indicating that gang prevention can be an important and effective way of stopping gang growth. Moreover, there are few specifically targeted OJP or OJJDP anti-gang prevention programs and no gang-specific intervention programs. Most of the remaining OJP and OJJDP programs are broad grant programs with numerous programmatic purposes among which anti-gang initiatives are one among many. Opponents of prevention programs raise concerns about the costs of such programs and their effectiveness. They argue that rigorous evaluations are needed to substantiate the cost and the outcomes of initiatives. Critics also argue that grant programs may not sufficiently reduce the gang problems facing communities across the nation. Given that, as some observers conclude, the root causes of gang formation and gang violence stem from poverty, a lack of employment opportunities, and alienation from the larger society, much more than grant programs may be needed to fully address the country's gang problem.

SELECTED OPTIONS FOR CONGRESS

The proliferation of youth gang problems has heightened interest in what can be done about gangs. Gang research indicates that youth gangs vary greatly, within and among communities, as well as across the nation. Gang members also vary by a number of factors including age, race or ethnicity, gender, and educational attainment, among many others. Research also indicates that there is much about youth gangs that authorities do not know, and may never fully understand because of the inherent complexity of the communities that give rise to gangs. As one researcher put it, "gangs emerge, grow, dissolve, and disappear for reasons that are poorly understood."[98] It is also important to note that gangs are dynamic entities that evolve over time further defying easy or static responses.

Evaluations of youth gang initiatives are complicated by the numerous levels that must be assessed. Often anti-gang strategies must encompass broad contributing factors such as the formation and dissolution of gangs, the diversion of youth from gangs, delinquency, and crime prevention and/or reduction. Anti-gang strategies also involve gang members, their parents, educators, community leaders, community organizations, providers, law enforcement, the police, prison systems, parole and probation officers, and judges. Once again, the lack of a commonly accepted definition of "youth gang" perhaps most fundamentally hampers evaluation measures.

Despite this array of obstacles, numerous evaluations of federal, state, and local anti-gang initiatives have been conducted and model programs have been identified by gang researchers as promising responses to the gang problem. Careful consideration of the outcomes of anti-gangprogram evaluations could also contribute to the development of federal programs and policies. The following are a small sample of the numerous anti-gang options that could be implemented or expanded at the federal level to address the problem of youth gangs in the United States.

Prevention Programs

- Congress could consider legislation to expand the G.R.E.A.T. program and require that it be provided (1) in all schools for all grades; or (2) in high-risk schools, in every grade; or (3) in all high-risk schools in each grade of middle school and high school.
- Congress could consider legislation to increase funding for grants to help fund after-school programs at schools with students at high-risk for gang participation. Research indicates that a disproportionate amount of juvenile crime occurs between 3-6 PM.

Gang Data Improvements

- Congress could consider legislation that would require the expansion of the National Youth GangSurveyto provide a larger sample of law enforcement agencies so that more data on state and regional gang activity could be available for policy development on gangs.
- Congress could consider legislation that would require greater standardization of crime statistics reporting at all levels of government with an emphasis on reporting gang-related crime. This could result in consistent crime statistics reportingand provide better informed policy development and strategically targeted anti-gang programs.
- Congress could consider enacting an anti-gang task force required to work with all interested parties (researchers, law enforcement, judiciary, policy makers) to reach a consensus on the definition of the term "youth gang" in order to assure a better measurement and response to the gang problem.

Comprehensive Approaches

- Congress could consider enacting a comprehensive, community-wide anti-gang program that would include prevention, intervention, and suppression elements, similar to the on developed by Spergel, et al,[99] for OJJDP as a model program that would include five core strategies: (1) community mobilization; (2) provision of academic, economic, and social opportunities; (3) social intervention; (4) gang suppression; and (5) organizational change and development.[100]
- Congress could consider enacting legislation to fund a program designed to target older gang members (age 17-24), designed to provide services to individuals rather than to the gangs as groups through two coordinated strategies: (1) control of violent or potentially violent youth gang offenders through increased supervision and suppression by probation and police officers, and (2) the provision of a wide range of social services and opportunities that would encourage and provide support to ex-offenders during their transition to legitimate behavior through education, employment, job training, family support, and brief periods of counseling.

Suppression Strategies

- Congress could consider enacting legislation to support the development of programs similar to the Comprehensive Strategy for Serious, Violent, and Chronic Juvenile Offenders, an OJJDP project first implemented in Rochester, NY, which provides for strategic community planning and program development targeting serious violent and chronic juvenile offenders through a framework of prevention, early intervention, and graduated sanctions.
- Congress could consider enacting legislation to support anti-gang programs that would consist of multi-agency initiatives, like the Boston Gun Project, for other cities. The Boston Gun Project is a model suppression program that targeted youth

and adult gang members who are repeat offenders in high-crime areas. The community is involved along with the police and probation officers to communicate and enforce a "zero tolerance approach" to gang violence.

- Congress could consider legislation to enact a grant program to assist communities with implementing anti-gang-related city ordinances and civil injunctions. As the experience of localities in California have shown, this type of strategy alone could not solve a community's gang problem, but coupled with some other strategies, it could provide communities with a pause in gang crime that is long enough to put in place more long-term anti-gang programs or initiatives designed to stop gang criminal activity.
- Congress could introduce legislation to provide for foreign policy initiatives to assist Latin American countries in addressing their serious and mounting gang problems like those of El Salvador and Guatemala.

No single program or initiative will work in every community facing a gang problem. Thus, program evaluations and other outcome measures would help to inform the development and evolution of programs and initiatives. Programmatic flexibility permitting adaptive changes to suit local needs also would bean important element of future federal efforts to address the gang problem at a national level.

CONCLUSION

The gang problem in the United States is complex and requires multiple strategies to fully address the problem. The history of gang problems indicates that total elimination of gangs or the social problems that foster their formation and development may always persist as a national concern. The range of gang problems, which span juvenile delinquency to drug trafficking and the serious violent offenses, indicates the complexity of addressing the problem and the need for multiple strategies targeted at different populations. Efforts to address the problem could be significantly improved by greater attention to data collection efforts on gang prevalence, characteristics, and criminal activities, as well as careful program evaluation measures to ensure that efforts to address the problem are functioning at optimal levels.

Law enforcement approaches at all levels of government could benefit from more coordinated efforts to assure that resources are being used in the most effective manner. Information and intelligence sharing between law enforcement at all levels of government could also enhance the development and execution of anti-gang strategies and could foster greater cooperation to address the gang problem.

Gang researchers have long advocated that a balance of strategies in the areas of prevention, intervention, and suppression may begin to effectively address the gang problem. Prevention strategies targeted on keeping juveniles from ever joining gangs, such as the G.R.E.A.T. program or Boys and Girls Clubs, offer some possible prevention approaches. Intervention strategies, such as training and employment assistance, to provide alternatives to the gang life for active members, is also suggested as a mechanism for providing economic alternatives to criminal gang activity. Imprisonment and other punitive measures such as forfeiture and fines are appropriate for serious violent gangperpetrators; however, such measures *alone* have not proven to be sufficient to stem the growth of gangs.

REFERENCES

[1] The terms "youth gang,""street gang," and "gang" are often used interchangeably in much of the literature on youth gangs, and generally, these terms are used to refer to individuals ranging in age between 12 and 25 years. In contrast, the term "juvenile" generally refers to individuals who are under 18 years of age. When the term "youth gang" is used, as it is in most of the literature on gangs, it is possible for some to assume incorrectly that a gang member is typically a juvenile although gang memberships also include adults. See Irving A. Spergel and G. David Curry, "Strategies and Perceived Agency Effectiveness in Dealing with the Youth Gang Problem," *Gangs in America*, 1990, p. 289.

[2] Both acts provided mandatory minimum sentences for drug traffickers who were found to be in possession of certain types of illicit drugs. The illicit drug trade is often associated with more highly organized criminal gangs.

[3] See the *Violent Crime Control and Law Enforcement Act of 1994* (P.L. 103-322).

[4] Luc Sante, *Low Life: Lures and Snares of Old New York*, 1991, pp. 198-199. In the late 1780s, there were at least five known gangs in New York City: the Smith's Vly gang, the Bowery Boys, and the Broadway Boys, who were white, and the Fly Boys and the Long Bridge Boys, who were black. Historically, most gangs have been locally based groups that often took names that indicated the neighborhoods where they lived and carried on their activities. For example, the Fly Boys were from the area around Fly Market, and like the Smith's Vly gang, their name was derived from the Dutch word *vly*, meaning valley.

[5] James C. Howell, "Youth Gangs: An Overview," *American Youth Gangs at the Millennium*, by Finn-Aage, p. 17.

[6] Kenneth J. Peak and Timothy Griffin, "Gangs: Origin, Status, Community Responses, and Policy Implications," in *Visions for Change Crime and Justice in the Twenty-First Century*, Roslyn Muraskin and Albert R. Roberts, eds. (2005), p. 44.

[7] Frederic M. Thrasher, *The Gang: A Study of 1,313 Gangs in Chicago* (1927), pp. 26-32.

[8] U.S. Department of Justice, Office of Juvenile Justice and Delinquency Prevention, *The Growth of Youth Gang Problems in the United States 1970-1998* (April 2001).

[9] U.S. Department of Justice, Office of Justice Programs, OJJDP, *Youth Gang Programs and Strategies* (August 2000), p. 27.

[10] 18 U.S.C. 521.

[11] This definition was added to current law in 1994 by Title XV §150001 of the *Violent Crime Control and Law Enforcement Act of 1994* (P.L. 103-322).

[12] The definition of a *criminal street gang* in federal statute is used for the purposes of federal prosecutions as sentencing enhancements, but is not a definition that has been used by the larger community of gang experts and researchers.

[13] It is important to note that in much of the literature on gangs, connections exist between street gangs and prison gangs, particularly among certain Latino gangs.

[14] U.S. Department of Justice, Office of Justice Programs, OJJDP Fact Sheet, *Highlights of the 2004 National Youth Gang Survey*, no. 1, April 2006.

[15] For the 2004 NYGC survey, local agencies in the nationally representative sample included all police departments servingcities with a population of 50,000 or more (n = 625); all suburban county police and sheriff's departments (n = 741); a randomly selected sample of police departments serving cities with a population between 2,500 and 49,999 (n= 696); and a randomly selected sample of rural county police and sheriffs departments (n = 492).

[16] Cities with a population of 250,000 or more.

[17] Cities with a population of 50,000 or more.

[18] Finn-Aage Esbensen, Stephen G. Tibbetts, and Larry Gaines, *American Youth Gangs at the Millennium*, "Recent Patterns of Gang Problems in the United States," by Arlen Egley, Jr., James C. Howell, and Aline K. Major, p. 96.

[19] According to the NYGC, Chicago and Los Angeles have historically had the highest rates of gang-related homicides of all U.S. cities.

[20] U.S. Department of Justice, Office of Justice Programs, OJJDP, *Highlights of the 2002-2003 National Youth Gang Surveys*, OJJDP Fact Sheet #01, June 2005.

[21] Personal communication with Arlen Egley, Jr. Ph.D., Senior Research Associate with NYGC, operated for OJJDP by the Institute for Intergovernmental Research, September 7, 2005.

[22] U.S. Federal Bureau of Investigation, *Uniform Crime Report* (2004).

[23] CRS Report RL32824, *Federal Crime Control: Background, Legislation, and Issues*, by Lisa Seghetti, Coordinator.

[24] Justice Policy Institute, "Gang Violence Declined 73% from 1994-2003," July 15, 2005, available online at [http://66.241.216.26/releases/press050715gang-crime.dwt], accessed on October 2, 2007.

[25] Tom Hayden, *Street Wars: Gangs and the Future of Violence* (New York: The New Press, 2005), pp. 7-8.

[26] Justice Policy Institute, *Ganging Up on Communities?: Putting Gang Crime in Context* (Washington, July 15, 2005).

[27] Cheryl L. Maxson, "Gang Homicide A Review and Extension of the Literature," *American Youth Gangs at the Millennium*, 2004, p. 275.

[28] U.S. Department of Justice, Office of Justice Programs, Bureau of Justice Statistics, Crime Data Brief, *Violence by Gang Members, 1993-2003*, NCJ 208875, June 2005.

[29] Ibid.

[30] Information on the NCVS is available at [http://www.ojp.usdoj.gov/bjs/cvict.htm], accessed on May 20, 2007.

[31] U.S. Department of Justice, Bureau of Justice Assistance, *2005 National Gang Threat Assessment*, National Alliance of Gang Investigators Associations, available at [http://www.nagia.org/PDFs/2005_national_gang_threat_assessment.pdf], accessed on May 18, 2007.

[32] T.P. Thornberry, D. Huizinga, and R. Loeber, "The Causes and Correlates Studies: Findings and Policy Implications," *Juvenile Justice*, vol. 10, no. 1, pp. 3-19, at [http://www.ncjrs.org/pdffiles1/ojjdp/203555.pdf], accessed on October 2, 2007.

[33] National Youth Gang Center, forthcoming, Frequently Asked Questions: *What is the racial and ethnic composition of youth gangs?*, at [http://www.iir.com/nygc/faq.htm], accessed on October 2, 2007.

[34] The NYGC analysis of small town and rural gangs is based on responses to the annual survey described at the beginning of this report from which national estimates of gangs and gang activities are derived. However, this analysis is a separate and special analysis based on data that are not reported in the annual summary of the NYGC survey.

[35] James C. Howell and Arlen Egley, Jr., "Gangs in Small Towns and Rural Counties," *NYGC Bulletin*, DOJ, OJJDP, no. 1 (June 2005), p. 1.

[36] NYGC's analysis is based on data collected between 1996-2001. In 2002, the survey began using a new sample of smaller city and rural counties.

[37] Ibid., p. 2.

[38] Ibid., p. 3.

[39] U.S. Department of Justice, Office of Justice Programs, OJJDP, *Juvenile Justice Bulletin*,"Youth Gangs in Schools," James C. Howell and James P. Lynch (August 2000).

[40] Ibid., pp. 5-6.

[41] Ibid., p. 7.

[42] U.S. DOJ, BJS, School Crime and Safety: 2004, p. 47.

[43] Kenneth S. Trump, "Gangs, Violence, and Safe Schools," *Gangs in America III*, 3rd Edition, ed. C. Ronald Huff (2002), pp. 121-122.

[44] Ibid., p. 124.

[45] James Diego Vigil, "Streets and Schools: How Educators Can Help Chicano Marginalized Gang Youth," *Harvard Educational Review*, vol. 69, no. 3 (Fall 1999), p. 272.

[46] Ibid., p. 278.

[47] K. Trump, "Gangs, Violence, and Safe Schools," pp. 126-128.

[48] For more information on Latin American gangs, see CRS Report RS22141, *Gangs in Central America*, by Clare Ribando.

[49] Testimony of FBI Assistant Director-Criminal Investigative Division Chris Swecker, in U.S. Congress, House of Representatives International Relations Subcommittee on the Western Hemisphere, *Gangs and Crime in Latin America*, hearings April 20, 2005.

[50] U.S. DHS, ICE, "ICE Launches Operation Community Shield, Arrest 103 MS-13 Gang Members in 6 Major U.S. Cities," *News Release*, March 14, 2005, available at [http://www.ice.gov/pi/investigations/comshield/index.htm], accessed on October 2, 2007.

[51] For more information on RICO statutes see, CRS Report 96-950, *RICO: A Brief Sketch*, by Charles Doyle.

[52] For more information on smuggling and related issues on the southwest border, see CRS Report RL33106, *Border Security and the Southwest Border: Background, Legislation, and Issues*, by Lisa Seghetti, coordinator.

[53] Testimony of FBI Assistant Director-Criminal Investigative Division Chris Swecker, in U.S. Congress, House of Representatives International Relations Subcommittee on the Western Hemisphere, *Gangs and Crime in Latin America*, hearings April 20, 2005.

[54] U.S. DOJ Bureau of Justice Assistance, *2005 National Gang Threat Assessment*, (February 2005).

[55] Congressional Quarterly, Homeland Security, *ICE Sweep Nets Nearly 600 Gangsters — but No Terrorists So Far*, by Eileen Sullivan, CQ Staff, (August 1, 2005).

[56] Jeffrey Fagan, *Drug Use and Delinquency Among Dropouts and Gang Members*, DOJ OJJDP, Grant #87JNCX0012, 1987.

[57] Irving Spergel and Ronald L. Chance, *National Youth Gang Suppression and Intervention Program*, National Institute of Justice Research in Action, June 1991, pp. 21-22.

[58] The lawcreated the Edward Byrne Memorial Grants, which were recently replaced by the Edward Byrne Memorial Justice Assistance Grant (JAG) program (P.L. 108-447) and provide grants to state and local and tribal law enforcement agencies for a number of purposes that can include anti-gang initiatives.

[59] Funding formerly provided through the Edward Byrne Memorial Formula Block Grant program is now funded through the Edward Byrne Memorial Justice Assistant Grant (JAG) program (P.L. 108-447). For additional information, see CRS Report RS22416, *Edward Byrne Memorial Justice Assistance Grant Program: Legislative and Funding History,* by Nathan James.

[60] For additional information on the CCF, see CRS Report RS21844, *The Compassion Capital Fund: Brief Facts and Current Developments*, by Joe Richardson.

[61] Testimony of FBISpecial Agent Grant Ashley, Assistant Director, Criminal Investigative Division, in U.S. Congress, Senate Committee on Judiciary, *Combating Gang Violence in America: Examining Effective Federal, State, and Local Law Enforcement Strategies*, (September 17, 2003).

[62] Ibid.

[63] FBI, *About Us - Our Post 9/11 Transformation - Fighting Gang Violence*, available at [http://www.fbi.gov/aboutus/transformation/gangs.htm], accessed on October 2, 2007.

[64] *In the Spotlight - Gangs*, U.S. Department of Justice, Office of Justice Programs, National Criminal Justice Reference Service, available at [http://www.ncjrs. gov/spotlight/gangs/summary.html], accessed on May 20, 2007. For more detailed information, see [http://www.fbi.gov/publications/strategicplan/strategic planfull. pdf],accessed on October 2, 2007.

[65] Testimony of FBI Assistant Director-Criminal Investigative Division Chris Swecker, in U.S. Congress, House of Representatives International Relations Subcommittee on the Western Hemisphere, *Gangs and Crime in Latin America*, hearings April 20, 2005.

[66] U.S. Department of Justice Office of Inspector General, *The External Effects of the Federal Bureau of Investigation's Reprioritization Efforts*, Audit Report 05-37, September 2005.

[67] Ibid., p. 68.

[68] Ibid., p. 56.

[69] Ibid., p. 57.

[70] Ibid.

[71] Ibid., p. 68.

[72] Finn-Aage Esbensen, Adrienne Freng, Terrance J. Taylor, Dana Peterson, D. Wayne Osgood, "Final Evaluation of the Gang Resistance Education and Training (G.R.E.A.T.) Program," *Responding to Gangs*, Winifred L. Reed, Scott H. Decker, eds., DOJ, OJP, NIJ, NCJ 190351, July 2002, pp. 139-167.

[73] Curry, G. David, Decker, Scott H., *Confronting Gangs: Crime and Community* (2003), p. 58.

[74] Ibid., p. 369.

[75] The cities participating in the program were: Philadelphia, PA, Portland, OR, Phoenix, AZ, Omaha, NE, Lincoln, NE (non-gang city), and Las Cruces, NM (small border town).

[76] Esbensen, Finn-Aage, Osgood, D. Wayne, Taylor, Terrance J.K., Peterson, Dana, Frang, Adrienne, "How Great is G.R.E.A.T.? Results from a Longitudinal Quasi-Experimental Design," *Criminology and Public Policy*, vol. 1, no. 1 (November 2001), pp. 108-109.

[77] *American Youth Gangs at the Millennium*, "Gang Prevention A Case Study of a Primary Prevention Program," by Finn-Aage Esbensen, Dana Peterson, Terrance J. Taylor, Adrienne Freng, and D. Wayne Osgood (2004), p. 363.

[78] The Brady Act (Brady Handgun Control Act), an amendment to the 1993 amendments ofthe *Gun Control Act of 1968* (P.L. 103-159), requires a waiting period of up to five days forhandgun purchases and requires purchasers to undergo a background check (18 U.S.C.922(s)(1)(C), (D)).

[79] Project Safe Neighborhoods, Executive Summary and other information on the program is available at the PSN website at [http://www.psn.gov/], accessed on May 18, 2007.

[80] For more detailed information on programs and initiatives designed for addressing the gang problem, see U.S. DOJ, OJP, NIJ, *Responding to Gangs: Evaluation and Research*, July 2002, pp. 329, available at [http://www.ncjrs.gov/pdffiles1/nij/190351.pdf], accessed on October 2, 2007.

[81] Ibid., pp. 265-288.

[82] "Selected 1988 California Legislation," *Pacific Law Journal*, Vol. 20 No. 2, 1998. (Cal. Penal Code §§ 186.20-186.33.)

[83] Some law enforcement sources think that these provisions may be responsible for the recent trend among gang members of trying to conceal their membership status.

[84] Arizona, Arkansas, Florida, Georgia, Illinois, Indiana, Iowa, Louisiana, Minnesota, Mississippi, Montana, Nevada, North Dakota, Rhode Island, and South Dakota have enacted STEP laws.

[85] Jeffrey Grogger, "The Effects of Civil Gang Injunctions on Reported Violent Crime: Evidence from Los Angeles," *Journal of Law and Economics*, vol. XLV, April 2002, pp. 69-90.

[86] Ibid., p. 86.

[87] CherylL. Maxson, Karen M. Hennigan, David C. Sloane, "'It's Getting CrazyOut There': Can A Civil Gang Injunction Change A Community?," *Journal of Criminology and Public Policy*, August 2005, vol. 4, no. 3., pp. 577-606.

[88] Ibid., p. 579.

[89] Ibid., p. 582.

[90] Ibid., p. 591, 596.

[91] This section does not discuss certain issues that are beyond the scope of a discussion of anti-gang legislation. For example, S. 456, H.R. 3547, H.R. 3922, and S. 2237 include provisions pertaining to short-term witness protection that are discussed in CRS Report RL33473, *Judicial Security: Comparison of Legislation in the 110th Congress*, by Nathan James. H.R. 3547 also includes a provision that would authorize the Attorney

General to deny the sale, delivery, or transfer of a firearm or the issuance of such a license or permit to a terrorist, which is discussed in detail in CRS Report RL33011, *Terrorist Screening and Brady Background Checks For Firearms*, by William J. Krouse.

[92] Supported by the Fraternal Order of Police, the National Sheriffs' Association, and the National Association of Police Officers, statement by Rep. John Gingery, Congressional Record, May 11, 2005, p. H3120.

[93] Paul Rosenzweig, "The Gang Act Needs Modification," Heritage Foundation, WebMemo, May3, 2004, available at [http://www.heritage.org/Research/Crime/wm494.cfm], accessed on October 2, 2007.

[94] Dan M. Kahan, Yale Law School, John M. Olin Center for Studies in Law, Economics, and Public Policy Working Paper Series, *The Logic of Reciprocity: Trust, Collective Action, and Law*, Paper 281, 2002, p. 23.

[95] For more information on juvenile justice, see CRS Report RL33947, *Juvenile Justice: Legislative History and Current Legislative Issues*, by Blas Nuñez-Neto.

[96] BNA Criminal Law Reporter, *Murdering Members of Rival Street Gang is Not Economic Activity for RICO Purposes*, September 22, 2204, Vol. 75, No. 23.

[97] For a recent example of successful prosecution and conviction under existing federal RICO statutes see, "3 MS-13 Leaders Convicted of Killings," by Ruben Castaneda, *Washington Post*, Saturday, April 28, 2007, p. B02, available at [http://www.washingtonpost.com/wp-dyn/content/article/2007/04/27/AR2007 042702108.html], accessed on May 18, 2007.

[98] Howell, James C., *Youth Gang Programs and Strategies*, National Youth Gang Center Institute for Intergovernmental Research, August 2000, p. 1.

[99] Spergel, I.A., Chance, R., Ehrensaft, K., Regulus, T., Kane, C., Laseter, R., Alexander, A., and Oh, S., *Gang Suppression and Intervention: Community Models*, U.S. Department of Justice Office of Justice Programs, OJJDP, 1994. (Also known as the NYGC Comprehensive Gang Model.)

[100] Howell, James C., *Youth Gang Programs and Strategies*, U.S. Department of Justice Office of Justice Programs, OJJDP, August 2000, pp. 34-35.

In: Youth Gangs: Causes, Violence and Interventions ISBN: 978-1-60692-547-8
Editor: John G. Cooper

Chapter 2

MAKING COMMUNITIES SAFER: YOUTH VIOLENCE AND GANG INTERVENTIONS THAT WORK

United States Government Printing Office

Hearing
Before the Subcommittee on Crime, Terrorism, and Homeland Security
of the Committee on the Judiciary House of Representatives

ONE HUNDRED TENTH CONGRESS FIRST SESSION
FEBRUARY 15, 2007
Serial No. 110–14
Printed for the use of the Committee on the Judiciary

THURSDAY, FEBRUARY 15, 2007
HOUSE OF REPRESENTATIVES, SUBCOMMITTEE ON CRIME, TERRORISM, AND HOMELAND SECURITY COMMITTEE
PUBLISHED BY NOVA SCIENCE PUBLISHERS, INC. ✝ *NEW YORK*
ON THE JUDICIARY, *WASHINGTON, DC.*

The Subcommittee met, pursuant to notice, at 10:06 a.m., in Room 2141, Rayburn House Office Building, the Honorabble Robert C. Scott (Chairman of the Subcommittee) presiding. Mr. SCOTT. Good morning. The Subcommittee will now come to order.

And I am pleased to welcome you today to this hearing before the Subcommittee on Crime, Terrorism, and Homeland Security on ''Making Communities Safer: Youth Violence and Gang Interventions that Work.''

Recent news reports cite increases in crime in several major cities, particularly violent crime. Much of the rise in violent crimes reported is attributable to youth, including youth associated with gangs. Even before the recent report suggesting increases in violence committed by youth, we have seen reports of increasing gang violence and other criminal activities on a local as well as international scale.

A few years ago, the Washington, D.C., area saw reports of gang violence attributed to gangs such as MS-13. There are also reports of gang rivalries resulting in murders of several youth in the District and the Maryland suburbs.

Congress thought to respond to these reports as we usually do with legislation calling for more death penalties, more mandatory minimum sentences and treating more juveniles as adults. We faced a similar situation in the mid-1990's with legislation such as the Violent Youth Predator Act. You can tell from the title what the bill called for, and it did, treating more juveniles as adults, mandatory minimums, death penalties and so forth.

We debated this type of legislation over several Congresses until then-Subcommittee Chairman Bill McCollum of Florida and I put together a hearing similar to this one and decided to propose bipartisan legislation based on recommendations from the researchers, practitioners and other experts we called as witnesses.

That legislation was the ''Consequences for Juvenile Offenders Act.'' It called for a system of early interventions with graduated sanctions of services as the individual case required to divert juveniles from further crime and violence. The legislation was supported by all Members of the Subcommittee and most of the Members of the full Committee, including the Chairman and Ranking Member. It was also supported by a broad spectrum of those working with juveniles, including advocates, researchers, juvenile judges, juvenile administrators, law enforcement, local and State, and others.

In addition, in the wake of the Columbine school shootings, then-Speaker Hastert and then-Minority Leader Gephardt appointed a bipartisan task force of Members who did the same thing as Bill McCollum and I did, called in some law enforcement officials and other experts and issued a report reflecting their recommendations, which were similar to those received at the Crimes Subcommittee hearing.

The legislation, based on recommendations of the experts, passed the House with a near unanimous vote and was eventually passed into law. Of course, the legislation took nothing away from the already existing tough laws and law enforcement approaches available to deal with juveniles and others committing crimes. Juveniles were already being routinely transferred to adult court for the very serious offenses and nothing in the legislation stopped that.

The U.S. already locks up more people per capita than any other country on Earth, by far. The average lock-up rate around the world is about 100 per 100,000. For example, Australia's rate is 126 per 100,000; Canada, 107; England, 148; France, 85; China, 118; Japan, 62; India, 30 per 100,000. The second highest rate is 611 in Russia. The United States' rate is 733. And rates of 1,000, 2,000 and 3,000 in inner-cities is not unheard of. One hundred per 100,000 international average.

Rather than simply adding to the world's worst incarceration rate, the legislation that we hope to enact will be aimed at cutting off the pipeline for the next group of offenders. It will be designed to add something else to the balance, what researchers and experts say is needed, and that is crime prevention.

Unfortunately, the funding that we authorized to implement the legislation was never provided. We ended up with 20 percent of the authorized level, and the level has gone down ever since. So we are once again considering what to do about the reports of juvenile crime without having done what we were told to do to begin with.

A lot has happened in the interim. We have learned more about effective approaches to addressing youth violence and youth crime. We have an impressive panel of experts here today to tell us about that research, the evidence and the experience, and hopefully they will give advice to Congress on how we can do the right thing.

I look forward to their testimony and working with Ranking Member Forbes in incorporating the testimony into legislative efforts and addressing youth and gang violence.

It is now my privilege to recognize our Ranking Member, the gentleman from Virginia, Congressman Randy Forbes, for his opening statement.

Mr. FORBES. Thank you, Mr. Chairman.

And let me also thank all of the witnesses for being here today.

Mr. Chairman, thank you for holding this hearing today.

One of the things that I think has become clear to us, although it wasn't clear to all of the Members of the Judiciary Committee last year when we tried to begin to put forward legislation dealing with gangs, is that we do have a gang problem in the United States and we had several of our Members who asked the question last year when we had this, ''Do we have a problem? Where is the problem? I don't see the problem.''

Well, I think everybody across the country now understands the significance of the gang problem.

As you and I are sitting here today, we have approximately 850,000 criminal gang members in the United States. And if you put a touchstone that gives us a little better measuring device on that, we would have approximately the sixth-largest army in the world, that is within our borders right now.

The whole scope of gangs has changed enormously. Although many of you have dealt with this problem longer than I have, I have dealt with it now about 16 years, and I remember when we started dealing with it back in the late 1980's and the early 1990's, as we would go to groups and talk to them about what causes you to get into gangs, it would be the same things that we would hear over and over again: sense of belonging, wanting to have a family connection, ''The gangs were like our families.''

As we have looked, since the year 2000, that has metamorphasized quite a bit and it has changed dramatically now. And more and more now we are hearing people tell us, ''We need to be in gangs for protection, because we are afraid that if we are not in a gang, there is no way that we can be safe out on the streets.''

One of the things that we all feel that we see in our offices is I have my door opened all the time to people coming in to chat with me who want funding, and in almost every situation, I can tell you, it doesn't matter, whether they are renovating an old school or whether they have a martial arts program, one of the things that they always tell us, as soon as they are in there and they have told us their funding needs, the next two things is, they tell us this has something to do with homeland security or juvenile crime prevention. And we are looking in there, shaking our heads, saying, ''How does renovating this old school do anything to protect us from terrorism? How does your program over here do anything to help us deal with juvenile crime prevention?''

Just two last points, and I will put my full remarks in the record, but the Chairman mentioned the fact that we need to cut off the pipeline, and the greatest pipeline that we have out there today are these gang networks.

Sometimes we think that the gang leadership are 15-or 16-yearolds, running around. Many of the gang leaders that we see in our country today are actually moving on up in age.

Some of them are in their thirties, some forties. In fact, it is funny because we see some of the old gang leadership now going around in wheelchairs and, you know, we jokingly say they are going to be coming in here asking us for retirement benefits later on down the road.

But we have, if you are looking at the pipeline and you are looking at how do we really cut that pipeline off, what can we do for gang prevention, one of the things we have to keep on the table is reaching up and pulling those gang networks down and the leadership down that is continuing to try to franchise their efforts and what they are doing, because the gangs we have today that really frighten us the most are no longer just local gangs. They are international gangs and national gangs, and they have networks of communication and travel like we have seldom seen before.

And the last thing, Mr. Chairman, we have an unusual panel, not just in your talent and your ability, but it is almost impossible, when you have logistically staged the way we have and you have eight members sitting out there to testify, that we will be able to ask you all of the questions we want to ask you, but we are going to try, and if we can't get them in today, we will try to supplement that with maybe some written questions to you down the road.

So thank you for being here. We look forward to being able to ask you some questions and hearing your testimony as we move forward with the hearing.

Mr. SCOTT. Thank you very much.

We are joined by the gentleman from North Carolina, Mr. Coble, and the gentleman from Ohio, Mr. Chabot.

Without objection, all Members may include opening statements in the record at this point.

In response to the ability to question witnesses, we would expect more than one round if necessary so that we can get in as many questions as we can.

We have a distinguished panel of witnesses here with us today to help us consider the important issues that are before us.

Our first witness will be Professor Del Elliott, who is the director of the Center for the Study and Prevention of Violence at the University of Colorado, where he is also a distinguished professor emeritus for the Department of Sociology.

Prior to holding his current office, he served as the director for the University of Colorado's program on problem behavior as well as for the behavioral research institute in Boulder. In recognition for his efforts, he has received numerous national awards, including the Public Health Service Medallion for Distinguished Service from the U.S. Surgeon General and an outstanding achievement award from the U.S. Department of Justice.

He received his Bachelor's degree from Pomona College and his Master's degree and Ph.D. from the University of Washington in Seattle.

Our next witness, Dr. Jeffrey Butts, is a research fellow with the Chapin Hall Center for Children at the University of Chicago, where he also teaches in the School of Social Service Administration.

He began his juvenile justice career as a drug and alcohol counselor with the Juvenile Court in Eugene, Oregon and has since served as a senior researcher at the National Center for Juvenile Justice and as the former director of the program for youth justice at the Urban Institute.

Dr. Butts has a Bachelor's degree from the University of Oregon, a Master's degree in social work from Portland State University and a Ph.D. from the University of Michigan.

Next is professor Lawrence Sherman, director of the Jerry Lee Center in Criminology at the University of Pennsylvania, where he is also a professor in the departments of Sociology and Criminology.

Prior to his current post, he was the chair of Criminology and Criminal Justice at the University of Maryland at College Park and also taught at Yale, the State University of New York at Albany, Rutgers University and Australian National University.

He holds a Bachelor's degree from Dennison University and Master's degrees from University of Chicago and Yale University as well as a diploma in criminology from Cambridge University.

Next we will hear from David Kennedy. Mr. David Kennedy is director of the Center for Crime Prevention and Control at the John Jay College of Criminal Justice in New York City, where he is also a professor in anthropology. Prior to his position at John Jay College, Mr. Kennedy was a senior researcher and adjunct professor at the program in Criminal Justice Policy and Management for the Kennedy School of Government at Harvard University.

He received his Bachelor's degree with high honors in philosophy and history from Swarthmore College in Pennsylvania.

Then we will hear from Chief James Corwin, chief of police of Kansas City, Missouri, Police Department. He served with Kansas City, Missouri, Police Department since his appointment as a police officer in 1979. He also serves on numerous boards in the community, including the Missouri Emergency Response Committee and the Kansas City, Missouri, Crime Commission.

He holds a Bachelor's degree from Central Missouri State and a Master's degree from Webster University. He is also a graduate of Kansas City, Missouri Regional Police Academy, the Missouri State Highway Patrol Academy and the 192nd Session of the FBI National Academy.

We will hear from Mai Fernandez, the legal and strategy director for the Latin America Youth Center in Washington, D.C., where she has also served as a special assistant to the assistant attorney general in the Office of Justice Programs.

Prior to her current post, Ms. Fernandez also served as an assistant district attorney in Manhattan and also as an aide to Congressmen Mickey Leland and Jim Florio. She is a graduate of Dickinson College, received her Master's degree in public administration from Harvard University and a Law degree from American University.

Next is Paul Logli, chairman of the board of the National District Attorneys Association. Mr. Logli is currently serving as an elected States attorney in Winnebago County, Illinois, where he has also served as vice president of the County Bar Association.

Prior to his current position, he served as an associate judge for the 17th Judicial Circuit in Illinois and also as a member of the Governor's Commission on Gangs in Illinois.

He is a graduate of Loras College and the University of Illinois College of Law.

Our final witness will be Mr. Teny Gross, executive director of the Institute for the Study and Practice of Nonviolence in Providence, Rhode Island. Prior to holding his current position, he served as program coordinator for the Youth Focused Community Initiative in Dorchester, Massachusetts and a senior street worker for the City of Boston and also first sergeant in the Israeli Army Reserves.

He received his Master of Theology Studies degree from Harvard University, Bachelor of Fine Arts degrees from Tufts University and the School of Museum of Fine Arts in Boston.

Each of the witnesses has a written statement which will be made as part of the record in its entirety.

I would ask each witness to summarize his or her testimony in 5 minutes or less. And to help stay within that time period, you have a little light gizmo which will start off green and go to amber when it is time to start wrapping up. Then it will go to red. Nothing draconian will happen when it turns to red, but we would appreciate it if you would wrap up at that time.

We will begin with Professor Elliott.

TESTIMONY OF DELBERT ELLIOTT, DIRECTOR, CENTER FOR THE STUDY AND PREVENTION OF VIOLENCE, UNIVERSITY OF COLORADO

Mr. ELLIOTT. Chairman Scott and other distinguished Members of the Committee, it is a pleasure to be here and to talk with you.

I am the director of the Center for the Study and Prevention of Violence at the University of Colorado and the editor of the ''Blueprints for Violence Prevention Series,'' which is a series of model violence prevention programs that meet a very high scientific standard, good enough that we could implement those programs on a national level.

We have looked at over 600 violence prevention programs, and out of those 600 programs, 75 to 80 percent of those programs have no credible evaluation. Of the others that do have a credible evaluation, a majority of those don't work. That is, the evidence that we have suggests that they are not effective.

Fortunately, we have also a number of programs—not enough— but we have a number of programs that are very effective and have very good effect sizes. That is, they can really have a significant effect upon violence and drug use and delinquency.

Unfortunately, I have to tell you we also find a few programs that are actually harmful, that are doing more harm than good.

So the first recommendation that I would like to make to the Committee is that we deal with this huge expenditure of money invested in programs in which we have no idea whether they work or not. That means we either need to mandate the use of effective programs, research-effective programs, or we need to invest in evaluations of those programs.

To continue to fund programs that we have no knowledge about whether they work or not is not a good idea, particularly when we know in some cases, although well-intended, they actually do harm. The ethics of delivering programs requires that we know whether those programs are effective or not.

Secondly, I would like to recommend that we stop funding the programs that we know don't work. That is, of those programs that we have looked at where the evidence is compelling that they don't work, we need to stop funding those programs. And there are a number of those programs, unfortunately, which we are continuing to fund. The traditional DARE program, shock probation programs, waivers out of the juvenile system and into the adult criminal system all have either no effect or negative effects and we need to stop investing our dollars in those kinds of programs.

Third recommendation I would like to make is that whenever it is possible, we should mandate that Federal funds be used for effective programs or invested in the evaluation of promising programs, to bring them up to the level that they can be implemented on a wide scale with certainty.

This will not require any major increase in funding. It involves first of all a reallocation of the dollars which we are currently spending, the vast majority of which right now are going into programs that aren't effective. If we reallocate those dollars, that is the first way that we can implement good programs without increasing the necessary funding.

Secondly, if we are funding evidence-based programs that meet a high standard, they do not need to have outcome evaluations, and we save money with respect to evaluation dollars. Those programs have been demonstrated effective at a level and there are continuing evaluations of them, so local agencies do not need to engage in evaluation if they are using evidence-based programs.

Third, these programs are so cost-effective that they will be paying for themselves in a very short period of time. The State of Washington has done an analysis in which they looked at a very modest portfolio of these evidence-based programs and have demonstrated that within 4 years those programs are paying for themselves. They estimate it would cost $60 million to implement that portfolio statewide and in 4 years the taxpayer benefits in savings would equal $60 million. At 10 years, the taxpayer savings from reduction in crime costs would be $180 million and 20 years later the savings would be $480 million for a $60 million investment in evidence-based programs.

These programs are also very cost-effective. If we look at a model program like Life Skills Training, which can reduce the onset of illicit substance use by 50 to 70 percent, that program, if we were to put that program in every middle school in this country, it would cost somewhere in the neighborhood of $550 million. That program could cut the onset of illicit drug use 50 to 70 percent. That $550 million represents 1.5 percent of our current spending on drug control.

And, finally, I would simply like to recommend that we establish a Federal standard for what it means to be certified as an evidence-based program. A lot of confusion right now because the standard dues on all of these lists which are available is very, very different.

There is a Federal working group on the Federal collaboration of what works which has proposed a standard, and I recommend that you look at that standard carefully. It is an excellent standard and it would resolve all of this confusion about what it means to be an effective program.

Thank you.

[The prepared statement of Mr. Elliott follows:]

PREPARED STATEMENT OF DELBERT S. ELLIOTT

Background

The demand for effective violence, drug, and crime prevention programs continues to grow. It is now common for Federal and State Agencies, private foundations and other funders to require or at least encourage the use of "evidenced based" programs. While this is an important new direction for current policy, the great majority of programs implemented in our schools and communities still have no credible research evidence for their effectiveness.

In their national review of delinquency, drug and violence prevention/intervention programs, the Center for the Study and Prevention of Violence has identified over 600 programs that claim to prevent or deter violence, drug use or delinquent behavior and less than 20% have any rigorous evaluation. There are several reasons for this. First, the new evidence-based policy is typically only a guideline and is not mandated or enforced. The process for selecting programs remains largely informal, relying on local expertise and "old boy/girl networks," and in many instances does not include scientific evidence of effectiveness as an important selection criterion. There is still a relatively strong aversion to "canned" programs developed outside the local area. Second, many of the lists of approved programs provided by funding agencies either have no scientific standard for selection or a very low standard. The scientific evidence for effectiveness is highly questionable for a significant number of lists. Third, few programs on these lists have the capacity to be delivered with fidelity on a wide scale. According to a recent national survey of school-based prevention programs, most programs being implemented were not evidence-based and even when they were, they were often being delivered with such poor fidelity that there is no reason to believe they could be effective in preventing violence, drug use or delinquency.[1] *The fact remains that most of the resources currently committed to the prevention and control of youth violence, drug use and delinquency, at both national and local levels, has been invested in unproven programs based on questionable assumptions and delivered with little consistency or quality control.*

Moreover, the vast majority of these untested programs continue to be implemented with no plans for evaluation. This means we will never know which (if any) of them have had some significant deterrent effect; we will learn nothing from our investment in these programs to improve our understanding of the causes of violence or to guide our future efforts to deter violence; and there is no meaningful accountability of the expenditures of scarce community resources. Worse yet, some of the most popular programs have actually been demonstrated in careful scientific studies to be *ineffective or even harmful,[2]* and yet we continue to invest huge sums of money in them for largely political reasons.

What accounts for this limited investment in the evaluation of our prevention programs? First, there is little political or program support for evaluation. Federal and state violence prevention initiatives often fail to provide any realistic funding for evaluation of the programs being implemented. Moreover, program directors argue that in the face of limited funding, every dollar available should go to the delivery of program services, i.e., to helping youth avoid involvement in violent or criminal behavior. The cost of conducting a rigorous outcome evaluation is prohibitive for most local programs, exceeding their entire annual operational budget in many cases. Without independent funding, they can not undertake a meaningful evaluation. Finally, many program developers believe they know *intuitively* that their programs work, and thus they do not think a rigorous evaluation is required to demonstrate this.

Unfortunately, this view is very shortsighted. When rigorous evaluations have been conducted, they often reveal that such programs are ineffective and can even be harmful.[3] Indeed, many programs fail to address any of the known risk factors or underlying causes of violence. Rather, they involve simplistic "silver bullet" assumptions and allocate investments of time and resources that are far too small to counter the years of exposure to negative influences of the family, neighborhood, peer group, and the media. Violence, substance abuse and delinquency involve complex behavior patterns that involve both individual dispositions and social contexts in which these behaviors may be normative and rewarded. There is a tendency for programs to focus only on individual dispositions, with little or no attention to the reinforcements for criminal behavior in the social contexts where youth live. As a result, any positive changes in the individual's behavior achieved in the treatment setting are quickly lost when the youth returns home to his or her family, neighborhood, and old friends. This failure to attend to the social context also accounts for the "deviance training" effect often resulting from putting at-risk youth into correctional settings or other "group" treatment settings which rely on individual treatment models and fail to properly consider the likelihood of emerging delinquent group norms and positive reinforcements for delinquent behavior. On the positive side, we have a number of very effective violence prevention andintervention programs. We have a universal drug prevention program (Life Skills Training) that can reduce the onset of illicit drugs by 50–70 percent and alcohol and tobacco use by as much as 50 percent; an intervention program for adjudicated youth (Multisystemic Therapy) that reduces the probability of recidivism by as much as 75 percent; an early childhood program (Nurse Family Partnership) that reduces arrests by 59 percent. See table A for a list of Blueprint Model Programs. We have the means to significantly reduce current levels of violence and substance abuse, but we are not implementing effective programs on a level that can have any significant effect on overall rates of violence and substance abuse in our communities

Specific Recommendations

1. The funding of unproven programs must include an evaluation.

Progress in our ability to effectively prevent and control crime requires evaluation to identify effective programs and a commitment to implement these programs with fidelity. Only those programs with demonstrated effectiveness and the capacity to be delivered with fidelity should be implemented on a wide scale. We have a long history of pushing untested programs for political reasons only to discover later that they did not work (e.g., D.A.R.E., boot camps, shock probation, juvenile court transfers/waivers). A responsible accounting to the taxpayers, private foundations, or businesses funding these programs requires that we justify these expenditures with tangible results. No respectable business would invest millions of dollars in an enterprise without assessing its profit potential. No reputable physician would subject a patient to a medical treatment for which there was no evidence of its effectiveness (i.e., no clinical trials to establish its potential positive and negative effects). No program designer shouldbe willing to deliver a program with no effort to determine if it is effective. Our continued failure to provide this type of evidence for prevention programs will seriously undermine public confidence in crime prevention efforts generally. It is at least partly responsible for the current public support for building more prisons and incapacitating youth—the public knows they are receiving some protection for this expenditure, even if it is temporary.

The costs of a randomized control trial is quite high, well beyond the capacity of most programs. Federal funding for promising prevention/intervention programs is critical to advancing both the number of programs that can be certified as effective and the diversity of populations and conditions under which theseprograms work

2. Stop funding programs that don't work.

The available evidence indicates that a number of very popular crime prevention programs don't work and a few appear to be harmful.[4] Some of the better known programs and strategies that appear not to work include: shock probation (e.g., Scared Straight), waivers of juveniles into the adult criminal court, traditional DARE, gun buyback programs, vocational programs, juvenile intensive parole supervision, reduced probation/parole caseloads, and STARS. Whether the accumulated evidence for these programs is conclusive depends on the standard we use to certify programs as effective or not effective, but there is clearly reason to be very cautious about continuing these programs until some positive evaluation outcomes are obtained.

3. Clarify what is meant by ''evidence-based'' and establish a national standard for certifying programs as ''model'' programs

There is a lot of confusion about what constitutes an evidence-based program. There are those who think that positive testimonials by clients is sufficient evidence to claim their program is evidence-based; to be certified as a model program in the Blueprints for Violence Prevention series, the program has to have two random control trials or very rigorous quasi-experimental trials that show positive effects plus evidence that the effect is sustained for at least one year after leaving the program. Most of the ''lists'' of Federal agencies require at least one RCT or quasi-experimental study. This is not a very demanding standard—one study, typically by the designer of the program in a specific location under ideal conditions. The standard for certifying a program as a model program, that is, a program that qualifies to be implemented on a statewide or national level, must have a very high probability of success. Should they fail, we will quickly lose build public support for funding them, not only for the program that failed, but for other programs that might be truly effective. Unfortunately, our record for the success of programs that have been widely implemented (e.g., DARE) has not been very good and that is because we have not required a high scientific standard for programs being implemented on this scale.

There is a proposed standard that should be carefully considered. The Working Group of the Federal Collaboration on What Works was established in 2003 to explore how Federal agencies could advance evidence-based crime and substance abuse policy. The Working Group included officials from Department of Justice, Department of Health and Human Services, Department of Education and representatives from the Coalition for Evidence-Based Policy and the National Governor's Association. The Working Group has recommended an excellent standard and classification system for certifying a program's level of demonstrated effectiveness. If this standard was formally adopted, it would both clarify what ''evidence-based'' means and set a required scientific standard for programs that are considered ready for widespread dissemination.

4. We should promote widespread implementation of cost effective evidence-based programs.

The implementation of evidence-based prevention and intervention programs will result in saved lives, more productive citizens, and significant reductions in crime and violence. The estimated cost for putting Life Skills Training, in every middle school in America has been estimated to be $550M per year. This represents less than 2 percent of national spending on drug control ($40B). The benefits of this program extended beyond the actual participants in the program to their associates and to a shrinking of the drug market allowing for more targeted and effective law enforcement. In this analysis, the effects of law enforcement and prevention/intervention were about the same. Clearly we need both. The Washington State Institute for Public Policy estimates that it would cost about $60M a year to implement a portfolio of evidence-based crime and violence prevention/intervention programs. After four years, the savings associated with reductions in crime would equal the cost of the portfolio; in 10 years, the cost benefit would be $180M; and in 20 years, the cost benefit would be close to $400M for the $60M investment in the evidence-based program portfolio.

Conclusion

Nationally, we are investing far more resources in building and maintaining prisons than in primary prevention or intervention programs.[5] We have put more emphasis on reacting to criminal offenders after the fact and investing in prisons to remove these young people from our communities, than on preventing our children from becoming delinquent and violent offenders in the first place and retaining them in our communities as responsible, productive citizens. Of course, if we had no effective prevention strategies or programs, there is no choice. But we do have effective programs and investing in these programs and the development of additional effective programs is effective, both in terms of human resources and taxpayer savings. Prevention and intervention must be part of a balanced approach to crime reduction.

TESTIMONY OF JEFFREY A. BUTTS, SENIOR RESEARCHER, CHAPIN HALL CENTER FOR CHILDREN, UNIVERSITY OF CHICAGO

Mr. BUTTS. Good morning, Mr. Chairman, Members of the Subcommittee, thank you for the opportunity to speak with you today and to be a part of this panel.

I also apologize. I had a cold last week and my voice is still not what it was.

As part of my testimony, I provided the Subcommittee with a Chapin Hall issue brief that I wrote 3 months ago with my friend and colleague Howard Snyder of the National Center for Juvenile Justice. In that report, titled ''Too Soon To Tell: Deciphering Recent Trends In Youth Violence,'' we reviewed the past 30 years of data about youth crime, including national arrest estimates based on the FBI's juvenile arrest data for 2005, which is still the most recent year for which national data are available.

[The report referred to is located in the Appendix.]

When we looked at trends through 2005, we found that it is too soon to predict a national increase in violent crime. Overall, crime remains at a 30-year low. According to the crime victimization surveys conducted by the U.S. Department of Justice, an American's chances of being a victim of a violent crime are still lower than in any point since the 1970's.

Table A. Blueprint Programs

PROJECT	TARGET POPULATION	PERCENT REDUCTION (EFFECT SIZE)[1]	REPLICATION	BENEFIT PER DOLLAR OF COST[2]	SUSTAINED EFFECT	TYPE OF PROGRAM
Nurse Home Visitation (Dr. David Olds)	Pregnant women at risk of preterm delivery and low birth weight infant	Arrests = -.53	Yes	$2.88	Through age 15	Prenatal and postpartum nurse home visitation
Bullying Prevention Program (Dr. Dan Olweus)	Elementary and middle/junior school (universal intervention)	Delinquency = -. 34	Yes		2 years post-grant-supported treatment-Canada; Most evaluations have long-term data	School anti-bullying program to reduce victim/bully problems
Promoting Alternative Thinking Strategies (M. Greenberg/C. Kusche)	K-5 school children (universal intervention)	Externalizing = -.07 Conduct Prob. = -.12	Yes		2 years post-treatment	School-based program designed to promote social and emotional competence
Big Brothers Big Sisters of America	Youth 6 to 18 years of age from single-parent homes	Drug Use = -. 50	Multisite Single Design, 8 sites	$1.01	18 month post-test	Mentoring program
Towards No Drug Abuse (TND) (Dr. Steve Sussman)	Alternative & public high school youth	Drug Use = -.55 Victimization = -.14	Yes		Two years post-treatment	Drug use prevention and Intervention
Multisystemic Therapy (Dr. Scott Henggeler)	Serious, violent, or substance abusing juvenile offenders & their families	Delinquency = -.66 Drug Use = -.75 Arrests = -.70	Yes	$2.64	4 years post-treatment	Family ecological systems approach
Functional Family Therapy (Dr. Jim Alexander)	At-risk, disadvantaged, Adjudicated youth	Arrests = -.78	Yes	$13.25	30 months post-treatment	Behavioral systems family therapy
Midwestern Prevention Project (Dr. Mary Ann Pentz)	Junior/middle school	Drug Use = -.37	Yes		Through high school (some results through age 23)	Drug use prevention curriculum with sequential components that involve parents, media, and community
Life Skills Training (Dr. Gilbert Botvin)	Junior/middle school	Drug Use = -.44	Yes	$25.61	Through high school	Drug use prevention (social skills and general life skills curriculum)
Multidimensional Treatment Foster Care (Dr. Patricia Chamberlain)	Adjudicated serious and chronic delinquents	Delinquency = -.56 Arrests = -.85	Yes	$10.88	1-year post treatment	Temporary structured foster care with treatment

[1] Source: Huizinga and Mihalic, 2003. Effect sizes are taken from only one evaluation per program, thus across multiple program evaluations effect sizes could be higher or lower.
[2] Source: Washington State Institute for Public Policy, 2004

Violent youth crime has increased at the national level, but only slightly. Between 2004 and 2005, the violent crime arrest rate for youth under age 18 grew by just 1 percent. The total increase amounted to 12 new violent arrests for every 100,000 juveniles in the population. This is about one-twentieth of what it would take for violent crime to return to the level of 1994, the most recent peak in violent crime.

In other words, we would have to see the same increase for 19 more years before we would return to the scale of violence seen just a little more than 10 years ago.

Obviously, we should not wait 19 years to respond to rising crime rates, but it is too soon to characterize the recent data as a national trend. What the data do suggest is that we have a number of cities, and probably neighborhoods within cities, that are starting to experience rising serious violence. The question for policy-makers is, how should we respond to these increases?

At some point in every conversation about violent youth crime, someone will make the observation that to truly ensure public safety we have to intervene earlier with youthful offenders. We cannot wait until a young person is already involved in serious violent crime and then try to stop it. Waiting is not only ineffective it is expensive. I have heard this throughout my 25-year career in juvenile justice and I am sure everyone here has heard it. Many of you have probably said it at one time or another.

Why don't we ever seem to make good on this promise? Why are we still unable to intervene effectively with young people as soon as they become involved in crime? I don't believe it is a matter of resources, that we can't afford to do it. We have decades of research showing us that high-quality early intervention actually saves money.

I think we fail to intervene early and effectively with youthful offenders because we continue to base our policies and programs on the wrong theories. For some reason, we seem to believe the best way to change the behavior of a 14-year-old is to use fear and domination. We use the threat of punishment to instill fear and then a series of increasing restrictions to establish dominance over youth.

Certainly there are some young offenders for whom this is the only feasible approach. But fortunately that number is very small. For the vast majority of young people involved in crime, this is simply the wrong approach.

We also apparently believe that young people who commit crimes are defective and that they need to be fixed by professional therapists, social workers and psychiatrists. Much of what passes for intervention in the juvenile justice system today is based on a deficit model of adolescent behavior. Whether it is family therapy, drug treatment and anger management training, our first response to young offenders seems to be fix their pathology.

Again, for some youth, therapy may be exactly what they need. But for many juveniles, and I would argue most in the juvenile justice system, this is just bad theory. Criminologists will tell you that all people are capable of committing crime given the right circumstances. The impulse to take advantage of other people is nearly universal.

The critical question is not why are some people criminals. The critical question is why are most young people not criminals. Researchers have started to answer this question by identifying the protective factors and social assets that reduce the young person's chances of getting caught up in crime. We are learning that youth with positive and supportive relationships are less likely to engage in crime, violence and substance abuse. We are also finding that being rewarded for learning and trying out new skills helps to keep young people attached to conventional institutions, such as family, school and work.

And we are discovering that just like everyone else, young people value their communities when their communities value them. In other words, youth are less likely to get involved in crime when they participate in community affairs and when they have a voice in public dialogue.

All of these lessons are now known as positive youth development or the youth development approach. Using the youth development approach with young offenders makes obvious common sense. It is essentially an effort to import the benefits of a middle-class upbringing into high-risk and distressed neighborhoods.

The youth development approach suggests that even poor and disadvantaged youth should experience the social bonding that comes from having an adult mentor, from knowing success in school and from being involved in civic activities, sports, music and the arts. If we had a juvenile justice system that brought these assets into the lives of more young people, we might be able to head off the next wave of rising youth violence and make our communities safer.

Certainly we will always need a justice system that deals aggressively with dangerous youth, but we should also want a system that responds effectively to young offenders before they are violent. Developing this sort of juvenile justice system is hard work, but thankfully research shows that it will be cost-effective. Early intervention does pay.

One strategy that we know does not pay, in fact, the most expensive form of juvenile justice is delay and punish, where we put off doing anything serious and meaningful with a young offender until he or she does something truly horrible. Yet that is still the most common form of juvenile justice system that we have today.

Thank you for your time, and I look forward to the discussion.

[The prepared statement of Mr. Butts follows:]

PREPARED STATEMENT OF JEFFREY A. BUTTS

Good morning Mr. Chairman and members of the subcommittee. Thank you for the opportunity to speak with you today and to be a part of this panel.

As part of my testimony, I provided the subcommittee with a Chapin Hall Issue Brief that I wrote three months ago with my friend and colleague, Dr. Howard Snyder of the National Center for Juvenile Justice.

In that report, titled ''Too Soon to Tell: Deciphering Recent Trends in Youth Violence,'' we reviewed the past 30 years of data about youth crime, including national arrest estimates based on the FBI's juvenile arrest data for 2005, which is still the most recent year for which national data are available.

When we looked at trends through 2005, we found that it is too soon to predict a national increase in violent crime.

Overall, violent crime remains at a 30-year low.

According to the crime victimization surveys conducted by the U.S. Department of Justice, an American's chances of being the victim of a violent crime are still lower than at any point since the 1970s.

Violent youth crime has increased at the national level, but only slightly.

Between 2004 and 2005, the violent crime arrest rate for youth under age 18 grew by just one percent.

The total increase amounted to 12 new violent arrests for every 100,000 juveniles in the population.

This is about one-twentieth of what it would take for violent crime to return to the level of 1994, the most recent peak in violent crime.

In other words, we would have to see the same increase for 19 more years before we would return the scale of violence seen just a little more than 10 years ago.

Obviously, we shouldn't wait 19 years to respond to rising crime rates, but it is too soon to characterize the recent data as a national trend.

What the data do suggest is that we have a number of cities, and neighborhoods within cities that are starting to experience rising violence.

The question for policymakers is, "how should we respond to these increases?"

At some point in every conversation about violent youth crime, someone makes the observation that to truly ensure public safety we have to intervene earlier with youthful offenders.

We cannot wait until a young person is already involved in serious and violent crime and then try to stop it.

Waiting is not only ineffective; it is expensive.

I have heard this throughout my 25-year career in juvenile justice. I am sure everyone here has heard it. Many of you have probably said it at one time or another.

Why don't we ever seem to make good on this promise?

Why are we still unable to intervene effectively with young people as soon they become involved in crime?

I don't believe it is a matter of resources—that we can't afford to do it.

We have decades of research showing us that high-quality, early intervention actually saves money.

I think we fail to intervene early and effectively with youthful offenders because we continue to base our policies and programs on the wrong theories.

For some reason, we seem to believe the best way to change the behavior of a 14-year-old is to use fear and domination.

We use the threat of punishment to instill fear and then a series of increasing restrictions to establish dominance over youth.

Certainly, there are some young offenders for whom this is the only feasible approach, but fortunately that number is very small. For the vast majority of young people involved in crime, this is simply the wrong approach.

We also apparently believe that young people who commit crimes are defective, and that they need to be fixed by professional therapists, social workers, and psychiatrists.

Much of what passes for intervention in the juvenile justice system today is basedon a deficit model of adolescent behavior.

Whether it is family therapy, drug treatment, or anger management training, our first response to young offenders seems to involve fixing their pathologies.

Again, for some youth, therapy may be exactly what they need, but for many juveniles (I would argue most), this is just bad theory.

Criminologists will tell you that all people are capable of committing crime, giventhe right circumstances.

The impulse to take advantage of other people, even to hurt other people, is nearly universal.

The critical question is not, ''why are some young people criminals?''

The critical question is, ''why are most young people not criminals?''

Researchers have started to answer this question by identifying the ''protectivefactors'' and ''social assets'' that reduce a young person's chances of getting caught up in crime.

We are leaning that youth with positive and supportive relationships are less likely to engage in crime, violence, and substance abuse.

We are also finding that being rewarded for learning and for trying out new skills helps to keep young people attached to conventional social institutions, such as family, school, and work.

And, we are discovering that, just like anyone else, young people value their communities when their communities value them.

In other words, youth are less likely to get involved in crime when they participate in community affairs, and when they have a voice in public dialogue.

All of these lessons are now known as ''positive youth development'' or the ''youthdevelopment approach.''

Using the youth development approach with young offenders makes obvious, common sense. It is essentially an effort to import the benefits of a middle-class upbringing into high-risk and distressed neighborhoods.

The youth development approach suggests that even poor and disadvantaged youth should experience the social bonding that comes from having an adult mentor,from knowing success in school, and from being involved in civic activity, sports, and music.

If we had a juvenile justice system that brought these assets into the lives of more young people, we might be able to head off the next wave of rising youth violence and make our communities safer.

Certainly, we will always need a justice system that deals aggressively with trulydangerous youth, but we should also want a system that responds effectively to young offenders even before they are violent.

Developing this sort of juvenile justice system is hard work, but thankfully, research shows that it is also cost-effective. Early intervention pays.

One strategy that we know does not pay off—in fact, the most expensive form of juvenile justice—is ''delay and punish''—where we put off doing anything seriousand meaningful with a young offender until he or she does something truly horrible.

Yet, that is still the most common form of juvenile justice system today.

Thank you for your time and I look forward to our discussion. The views expressed in this testimony are the author's alone and do not necessarily reflect the views of the employees, administrators, or board members of the University of Chicago or Chapin Hall Center for Children.

TESTIMONY OF LAWRENCE SHERMAN, DIRECTOR, JERRY LEE CENTER OF CRIMINOLOGY, UNIVERSITY OF PENNSYLVANIA

Mr. SHERMAN. My name is Lawrence Sherman and I am grateful for the opportunity to discuss the 100,000 murders of Americans on the streets of our cities since 9/11/2001, a problem that I am delighted this Committee is addressing, especially with its focus on youth and gang violence.

What I would like to focus on is what we have found in Philadelphia and appears to be true in many other cities, which is that homicide is heavily concentrated among people who are already under court supervision. Much of my data pertains just to the Adult Probation and Parole Department, but if we add pretrial supervision, youth probation, State parole boards, we estimate that as many as three out of four murders in the City of Philadelphia may be committed by people who are under court supervision.

And what I would like to propose is that this Committee offer legislation that would create a Federal grants and aide program to support probation, parole and pretrial services agencies that would undertake an evidence-based approach to the prediction and prevention of homicide within people on their caseload.

This problem includes both victims. If I can get the number, I think we will see that 16 percent of the murder victims in Philadelphia last year were on adult probation at the time; 22 percent of the murder arrests in Philadelphia were of people who were on adult probation at the time. This doesn't include State parole or juvenile probation.

And what we may find is that if we look for the needles in the haystack among the 52,000 cases under adult probation, to look for the 108 victims and offenders identified in 2006, we will see that most of them were predictable, and predictable by a realization of the fact that 3 percent of that group is eventually going to be charged with murder or attempted murder, and that with new advanced data mining techniques and supercomputers coming down in price, it is now possible for every community supervision agency in the country to do what Professor Richard Burke has done, and we have recruited him to Philadelphia from UCLA precisely to help us work on this problem, which I think we can illustrate best with the key predictors, which start with something which has already been mentioned, and that is age at first arrest, arrest that is prosecuted as an adult by direct file to adult courts, along with current age.

Those seem to be the two biggest factors in predicting who is likely to be charged with murder or attempted murder while on probation or parole with the county adult system in Philadelphia.

And if I could just focus the Committee's attention on the age at first adult prosecution, whether or not the offender is convicted, the younger that age, the more likely it is that this person, when they go on adult probation, will be charged with murder or attempted murder within a several-year time frame.

So starting with age 14, which is absolutely the highest murder, controlling for other factors that we have in this model, we see a rapid falling off with people being charged at the older age, but it is precisely, as Mr. Butts has said, it is precisely at those early ages that what we do is delay and we try to come to some other accomodation or even fail to get a conviction or an adjudication because the witnesses won't come.

If we could say that what this graph tells us is that 70 percent of all murders or attempted murders were committed by people who were charged as adults before the age of 21 and 40 percent of them were committed by people who, in their previous lives were charged as adults before the age of 18.

Another way of looking at this is the falling likelihood of being charged with homicide based on age. So the Committee's focus on youth is absolutely right. And the problem is that the juvenile justice system cuts it off at age 18, whereas the risk is really heavily concentrated under 21 to 25. The youth violence reduction partnerships in Philadelphia have set, actually, a 25 year definition of youth, which is consistent with that graph, showing us that offenders committing a murder on probation over age 45 in a very large sample is zero. But of those who are under 20, 15 percent were going to go on to be charged with murder or attempted murder.

And so what I would like to do is to agree with Dr. Butts' assertion that most people in the juvenile justice system do not need the kind of intensive therapy that we have found that the people who are most likely to kill or be killed need because they are suffering from undiagnosed and untreated post-traumatic stress disorder, they have chronic depression, they have anxiety disorder, they have things that are well known to be treatable within clinical psychology, but they are not getting that kind of treatment.

And what Philadelphia has done is to create both a special unit to provide those kinds of services and a randomized, controlled trial to find out whether that approach is effective in not only reducing homicides and other serious crime, but also reducing the incarceration rate, which is very costly to the State and, of course, a waste of human potential.

If we had a Federal grants program that would reward through a peer-review process, no earmarks, those proposals that develop an effective statistical prediction model and offer a randomized trial to evaluate the effects of their program, we would not be guaranteed to lower the homicide rate, but we would be guaranteed to develop a robust body of evidence on what works and what doesn't work to try to prevent homicide by young people.

Thank you for this opportunity.

[The prepared statement of Mr. Sherman follows:]

PREPARED STATEMENT OF LAWRENCE W. SHERMAN

Penn
UNIVERSITY of PENNSYLVANIA

Jerry Lee Center of Criminology
3718 Locust Walk, Suite 483
Philadelphia PA 19104
215-898-9216
lws@sas.upenn.edu

Lawrence W. Sherman
Albert M. Greenfield Professor and Director

REDUCING HOMICIDE BY ENHANCING HIGH-RISK PROBATION AND PAROLE: A Peer-Reviewed Grants Program

Summary. The growth of homicide in American cities is highly concentrated among young people on probation and parole. In Philadelphia in 2006, for example, over 22% of the murder arrests, and 16% of the murder victims, were clients of the Adult Probation and Parole Department (APPD) of the First Judicial District of Pennsylvania. Virtually all were under 25 years of age. But they were needles in the haystack of the 52,000 people assigned to the 285 APPD officers. New statistical techniques can identify the highest-risk offenders under community supervision. A national program of competitive grants to apply those techniques in ways that can prevent homicide among high-risk likely killers (or victims) could be the most direct route to lowering homicide through federal policy.

Crime in Philadelphia and the APPD

Homicide in Philadelphia has risen by over 25% in the past three years, to a total of 406 murders last year. Many if not most of these murders were committed by or against people who were under court supervision at the time as probationers, parolees or pre-trial releasees—possibly as many as 75% of the murders. For just the local adult probation and parole department (APPD) cases, two numbers stand out:

> 55 = the number of APPD cases who were murdered by gun in 2006
> 53 = the number of APPD cases who were arrested in 2006 for murder by gun

To convert these numbers to appropriate percentages, two separate denominators are required: the number of murders by gun, and the number of arrests for murders by gun. The Philadelphia Inquirer total of 344 gun murders in 2006 (http://inquirer.philly.com/graphics/murders_map/) provides the first denominator, which is 85% of all murders reported in Philadelphia in 2006. The APPD Gun Court records of 235 arrests for homicide by firearm in 2006 (regardless of the year in which the homicide was committed) provides the second denominator. Using these denominators produces the following findings:

- APPD cases were killed in 55 of all 344 gun homicides in 2006, or 16%
- APPD cases were arrested in 53 of the 235 murder arrests for 2006, or 22%

Because the majority of homicides do not lead to an arrest, it seems likely that even more of the offenders in these cases are APPD cases. A rough estimate based on a 50% clearance rate would be that APPD cases would have committed 22% of all 2006 murders, or almost 100—in addition to the 55 APPD cases who were killed. This would mean that almost 4 out of ten murders involved an APPD case as victim or offender.

In 2006 the City of Philadelphia's 406 homicides yielded a rate of 270 homicides per million people. If we calculate the homicide victimization rate for the APPD, based on a caseload of 52,000 people, the comparable number would be 1,000 per million. If people among APPD's 52,000 cases *committed* the estimated (solved and unsolved) 100 murders, the roughly comparable number for the homicide commission rate (assuming one offender per homicide) would be 1,920 per million people.

This means that

- The homicide victimization rate for APPD cases is four times the city-wide rate
- The homicide offending rate for APPD cases is seven times the city-wide rate

None of this should be surprising, since recently convicted offenders are well-known to be more likely to commit murder than other people. Nor does it mean that this murder rate is caused by any aspect of APPD's operation within the standard US interpretation of the probation mission. Its significance, rather, comes from the fact that APPD cases provide a prime focus for homicide prevention. In contrast to programs that spread a wide net over low-risk and high-risk people alike, APPD is a program that is far more tightly focused on the higher risk Philadelphians who disproportionately suffer, and commit, the city's homicides.

The APPD is not the only agency with a high-risk caseload. As a community supervision agency, it shares this challenge with the Pennsylvania Board of Probation and Parole, as well as with two other First Judicial District agencies: Juvenile Probation and Pre-Trial Services Division. Collectively, these agencies supervise almost 1 out of every 15 of the 1.5 estimated Philadelphia residents. Their respective caseloads are as follows

Agency	Persons Supervised	Percent of Total Supervised
APPD	52,000	54%
Pre-Trial Division	30,000	31%
Juvenile	5,000	5%
State Parole	9,000	9%
Total	**96,000**	**100%** (with rounding)

This analysis of crime, and especially homicide, in Philadelphia suggests that the caseloads of these other agencies are also at high risk of committing murder or being murdered. If the risks are equal across offenders in the caseloads of all agencies, barring some adjustments for overlapping caseloads, the analysis suggests that offenders under supervision could jointly account for 44% of murder offenders and 32% of murder victims. Adding these two statistics could mean that ***as many as 76% of all murders in Philadelphia involve convicted or charged offenders under supervision of community supervision agencies.***

If three out of four of all murders occur in a population required by law to be in constant communication with court-appointed supervisors, it seems important to ask whether our City is making the most of the opportunity such supervision provides to prevent those murders. This question can be broken down into several specific questions:

- Are some supervised offenders more at risk than others?
- Are there ways to re-allocate a constant budget based on risk?
- Would more probation officers for high-risk cases reduce murder?

The answer to all three questions is "yes." The following sections document the basis for that answer, in the context of describing options for a re-engineering of APPD. A similar approach, of course, could also be taken with other offender supervision agencies, including—with a broader definition—the Philadelphia Police Department.

Risk Analysis: Old and New

"Are some supervised offenders more at risk than others?" That is the old way to ask the question. The term "risk," when defined, usually meant at risk of repeat offending, repeat arrest, or repeat conviction for a new offense. Any new offense. Regardless of the level of harm a new crime caused, or how many years in prison it would require to punish it, or whether a child was harmed, or any other criteria of seriousness, the standard risk assessment tools in probation give the same answer. Both shoplifting and homicide receive the same weight. So, too, do auto theft and kidnapping children for sexual assaults. The "old," and still dominant, approach to risk analysis in probation and parole across the US does not distinguish different levels of risk by different levels of seriousness.

What the old approach does do is to distinguish levels of probability. Risk assessment tools focused on recidivism are able to classify offenders based on high, medium or low risks of repeat offending of any sort. This process certainly addresses a key question, but without the component of seriousness. In the following diagram, it is apparent that for someone to be at "high risk" to the community, at least in colloquial discussion, they must be both highly likely to commit an offense, and the offense they commit must be highly harmful. Rather than lumping together categories 3 and 4, as mapped by the diagram, what the community may prefer is that their tax dollars be heavily invested in category 4—with commensurate reduction of investment in the other three categories.

Priorities for Offender Risk Assessment

Likelihood of New Crime	Harmfulness of New Crime	Harmfulness of New Crime
	Low	High
Low	1	2
High	3	4

A new approach to risk assessment, in contrast, focuses solely on category 4 above. Using advanced data mining tools made possible by the advent of inexpensive supercomputers, the University of Pennsylvania has provided APPD with a new means of identifying offenders under its supervision who are most likely to be charged with murder or attempted murder. Based initially on all 519,168 cases assigned to APPD on electronic record for 1969-2005, the data on which these analyses are based are currently drawn entirely from more recent (21st Century) data.

These new risk assessments, developed under grants from the University of Pennsylvania, the Jerry Lee Foundation, and the Pennsylvania Commission on Crime and Delinquency, are the first of their kind ever offered to a probation agency. Their development has been led by Philadelphia's own Richard Berk, a Professor of Criminology and Statistics recently recruited by Penn from UCLA. Working in collaboration with the research staff of the APPD and other criminologists at Penn's Jerry Lee Center of Criminology Professor Berk has focused on ways to distinguish probationers most likely to be charged with murder (or attempted murder) from those who are not. His analysis can identify APPD cases who are up to 42 times more likely to be charged with such offenses than other probationers, on average. By using a range of information already found in the offenders' criminal histories, these tools forecast homicide risks among individual probationers and parolees using statistical methods similar to those employed in hurricane forecasting: identifying rare events, like needles in a haystack.

These statistical assessments yield an equation that identifies, in each case, a likelihood assessment based on each of the risk factors examined. It then takes all of the risk factors into account in a kind of statistical "parliament" adding up the yeas and nays on all the factors, with a summary score that identifies the estimated risk level for each case. The equation is derived from one large sample, and then use to predict the results for another large sample with a high degree of accuracy. By testing the model with actual cases of homicide and attempted homicide (as well as APPD cases not leading to such charges), the equation offers great confidence in forecasting homicide charges in the future.

The relative predictive power of each of the risk factors in one of the earlier versions of the analysis is depicted in the following graph presented by Richard A. Berk at the American Society of Criminology last November. Each dot reflects the degree of error that deleting the risk factor would add to the overall model—a reverse statement of how important the factor is to making the model accurate.

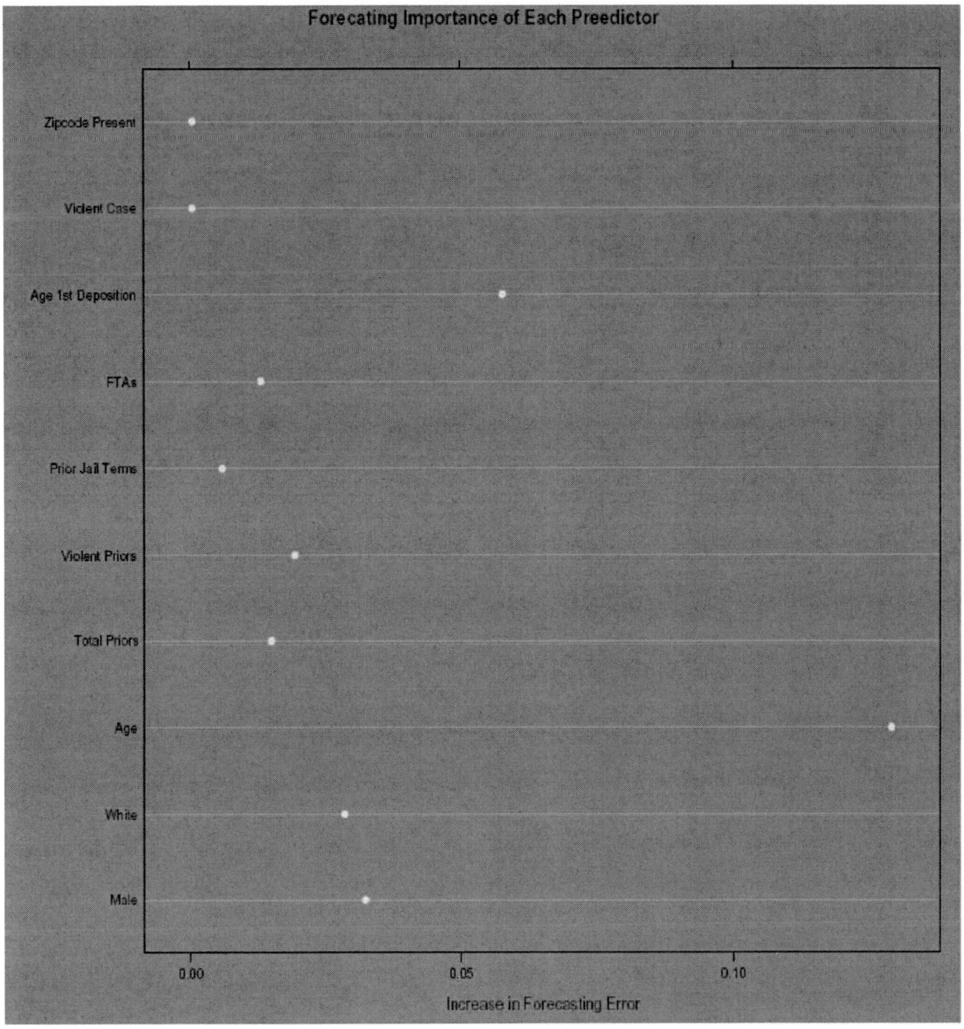

The analysis shows, for example, the substantial importance of age at first adult prosecution (labeled in the above graph as "first deposition") or "disposition," regardless of whether a conviction resulted. The younger someone is when they are direct-filed on adult charges, the more likely that makes them to be charged with homicide or attempted homicide after being assigned as an APPD case. The following graph prepared by Dr. Berk for the 2006 ASC Meetings in Los Angeles depicts this relationship.

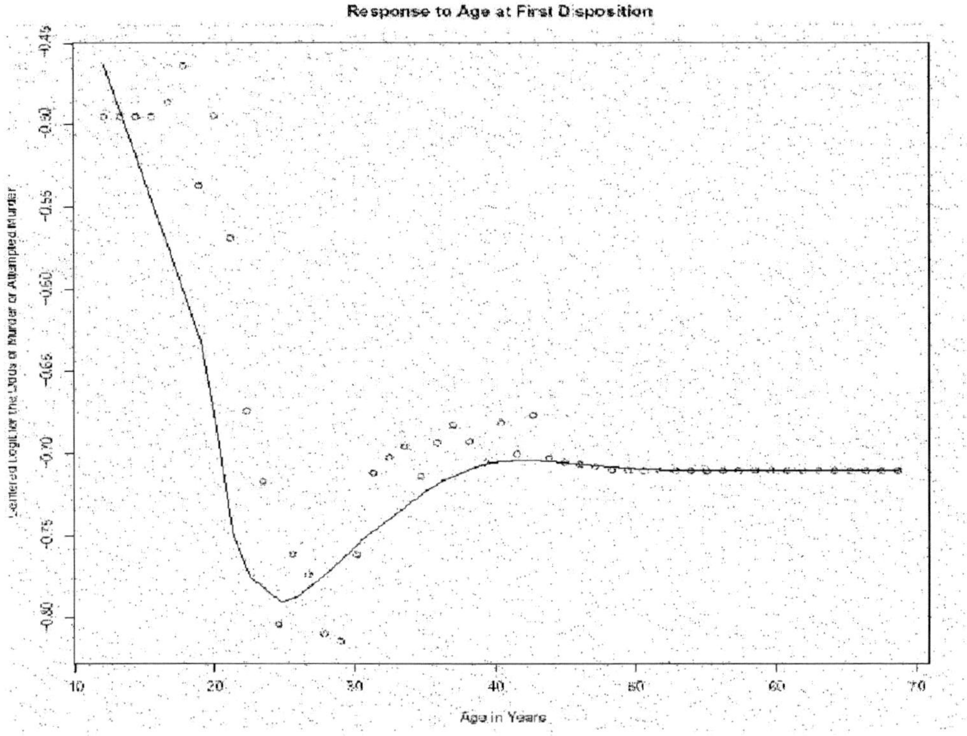

From these and many other analyses of APPD data, some APPD cases are clearly far more at risk of causing serious harm to the community than others. When that harm is defined as homicide, the probability that some will—and others won't—becomes so great that the APPD cases provide an extreme version of the city at large. In the Philadelphia population, APPD cases (and community supervision cases generally) pose much greater risk to the community than others. Within APPD cases, the difference is even more extreme.

By focusing on the cases most likely to commit the most serious offense—homicide—the APPD now has access to what may be the most advanced risk assessment tool in the country. Not even New York has yet moved beyond the analysis of recidivism for any offense type, despite its many advances in risk analysis. What New York does have, however, is a model for how to use risk analysis to restructure operations in order to invest more resources in its highest-risk cases.

The New York Experience

Since the mid-1990s, the New York City Probation Department has divided its cases into two categories based on probability of recidivism. The low probability cases include about 75% of the caseload, according to NYC Probation Commissioner Martin Horn. Both Commissioner Horn and some 30 of his highest-level officials came to Philadelphia last September to demonstrate their management system in the Ceremonial Courtroom ay City Hall. These low probability cases are assigned to probation officers with a caseload of 500 offenders per officer. The reason such a high caseload is feasible is that the probationers perform their regular visits with computers rather than the officer.

On each visit, a low-risk probationer logs on to a computer screen by placing his or her palm flat upon the screen. This biometric identification triggers a response in the probationer's language (English or four others), either in words on the screen or—if the offender is coded as illiterate—in audio. The computer then asks the probationer the same questions that a human probation officer would usually ask: a checklist of items updating the probationer's home address, employment, compliance with probation conditions, and other matters. If the probationer has failed a drug test or been arrested since the last visit, the act of placing the palm on the screen triggers a notice to a security officer to come into the room where the probationer is standing to take the probationer into custody. In such cases, the probation officer managing the probationer will take appropriate action.

Because such actions are required so rarely, it is possible for one officer to supervise 500 low-risk probationers. And because this caseload allows many other officers to manage caseloads of 50 or less, the offenders at higher risk of recidivism get more attention. The time for this attention allows more intensive planning and action about how to turn the probationer's life around, from education to job training to job placement and mental health or drug treatment services.

The ten years of experience with this approach in New York has been enhanced by the growth of data-driven management systems, focused on a monthly meeting reviewing performance trends in each component unit managing the caseload. These management systems track the use of resources, the meeting of operational goals (such as completion of pre-sentence reports on time), and the failure rates of probationers—including the rate at which they are arrested for murder.

These systems are impressive and promising in their potential application to Philadelphia. The recent implementation of CPCMS in the First Judicial District makes the adaptation of such a COMP-STAT-like system even more feasible for Philadelphia. What New York can offer as a model is impressive. But so is what Philadelphia has recently initiated.

Recent Philadelphia Initiatives in Adult Probation and Parole

In April of 2005, the APPD co-chiefs initiated the planning process for a partnership with the University of Pennsylvania's Jerry Lee Center of Criminology. This process led to a data sharing agreement in November of 2005, and the approval of the Penn Violence Reduction Partnership (PVRP) by the FJD's Administrative Governing Board in early 2006. In August of 2006, the FJD announced the PVRP's homicide prevention initiative under a special appropriation from the Philadelphia City Council, sponsored by former City Councilman Michael Nutter. In addition, Governor Rendell signed the state budget directing the Pennsylvania Commission on Crime and Delinquency to fund a research grant in support of the APPD initiative. In combination with $500,000 from the Jerry Lee Foundation, the $500,000 in city and state funding brought the APPD homicide prevention initiative to $1,000,000 in first-year funding.

These funds have been spent to refine the forecasting model for murder and attempted murder, especially by employing the revised data from the CPCMS system. More important, they have been used to launch the 5-officer Strategic Anti-Violence Unit (SAV-U). In weekly meetings held since January 2006, Penn criminologists and APPD officials have met at the Jerry Lee Center of Criminology to develop and plan the SAV-U protocol implemented January 1, 2007. Since then, the APPD's SAV-U has developed and tested its protocol for supervising a randomly selected sample of the highest-risk people in the APPD caseload. The elements of this protocol include the following:

- Low Caseloads—from 3 to 15 cases per officer
- Psychiatric assessments for each case by a Penn psychiatric social worker
- Cognitive Behavioral Therapy provided by Penn for indicated cases
- Educational and literacy support as needed
- Targeted patrols by two plainclothes PPD officers and one probation officer to each case each week, on both scheduled and unscheduled occasions.
- Weekly and up to daily contacts between the probation officer and the case
- Preparation and support for re-entry if the case client is incarcerated
- Assistance in locating housing, drug treatment or other services

Cases selected for the SAV-U caseload are ineligible if they are already designated for YVRP, wanted on a warrant for failure to appear, or sentenced to a long-term incarceration for a new offense. All other high-risk cases are eligible, including those who are in Philadelphia Prisons at the time of the transfer of the case to SAV-U.

By the end of 2007, it is possible that the SAV-U caseload will rise to 75 cases, each of which will remain assigned to SAV-U for up to five years. The potential number of eligible high-risk murder cases, however, will be over 1,000. Using less serious crimes, such as rape, robbery and aggravated assault, the number of higher-risk offenders would rise to 15,000 or more. If each of those cases were assigned to probation officers with SAV-U caseloads of 15, there would need to be 1,000 probation officers just for those cases. These calculations raise questions about staffing levels, training, and standards, starting with the key question that can be addressed by federal grants-in-aid to jurisdictions that would use such money effectively to drive down the local—and hence national—homicide rate:.

Do Big Cities Have enough Probation and Parole Officers?

Judging by the Philadelphia staffing levels, there may be a critical shortage of community supervision staff capable of working with high-risk offenders. The question of how many offenders should be assigned to each probation officer is impossible to answer in the abstract. As an "issue paper" posted on the American Probation and Parole Association's website indicates (at http://www.appa-net.org/about%20appa/caseload.htm),

> **"The search for the single "magic number" for the optimal caseload size is futile, and counterproductive. It runs contrary to the current knowledge and practice in the field, and sets forth an unrealistic expectation that such a standard can be set, be achieved, and produce desirable results."**

While the national workload for Probation Officers in Sweden, for example, is only 15 cases per officer for all kinds of cases, it is not clear that a single caseload is used for all offense types. Hence the APPA issue paper illustrates the diversity of caseloads that might be possible by distinguishing workload and caseload. In the case of priority levels—whatever the basis for the priority—the workload could be officers with different caseloads. This result is computed by applying a dif of hours to cases of different priority levels, as follows:

(Begin Quotation from http://www.appa-net.org/about%20appa/caseload.htm)

Case Priority	Hours Per Month	Total Caseload
High	4 hours	30 cases
Medium	2 hours	60
Low	1 hour	120

*One caseload officer = 120 hours per month

If the maximum number of hours available to the caseload officer is 120 per month, the caseload can be made up of 30 high priority cases, 60 medium priority cases, or 120 low priority cases. In all three instances, the officer would have a full workload, i.e., one where the number of hours needed to fulfill the minimum requirements on all the cases (demand) is equal to the amount of hours available to the officer (supply).

As the table illustrates, there are three caseloads where the total **number** of cases is very different, but the total **workload** is equal. When there is a mixture of all three priority level cases in one caseload, there are almost endless possibilities (between 30 and 120 in the example) as to the total number of cases in a given caseload that would equate to a full workload." (end quotation).

Even using such a formula, the caseloads across jurisdictions would vary widely. Philadelphia's APPD caseload is far more likely to commit murder than the caseload of other probation and parole agencies across the state, judging from the statistics reviewed above, the high percent of all homicides statewide in Philadelphia (380 out of 749 in 2005, or 51%), and the fact that Philadelphia's APPD has only 24% of the adult offender probation and parole caseload of the entire Commonwealth (214,400 as of 2005; see http://www.pbpp.state.pa.us/pbpp/lib/pbppinfo/stats/CAPP_Report_2005.pdf) and 280 of the 1,340 county probation officers in the state. Put another way, Philadelphia has

- 50% of the murders in Pennsylvania
- 24% of the county-level adult probation & parole caseload
- 21% of the county probation officers

While Philadelphia may not have more *cases* per officer to supervise, it certainly has more potential for *crimes* per offender, and per probation officer caseload, than any other county in the state. It is the problem of risk, rather than caseload, that makes national standards problematic for Philadelphia. Whatever is true for murder is also true for other serious crimes, for which Philadelphia in 2005 had

- 1,024 of 3,400 rapes statewide—30%
- 10,069 of 19,000 robberies statewide—53%
- 10,139 of 28,000 aggravated assaults—36%

Based on the statewide percentage of murders, Philadelphia would need to have the same ratio of adult probation officers per murder as the rest of the state did in 2005. This formula equals

State PO total = 1340, minus 285 for Philadelphia = 1055
State murder total = 749 – 380 in Philadelphia = 369
Non-Philadelphia Probation Officers per murder 2005 = 1055/369 = 2.86
2.86 POs per murder statewide outside of Philadelphia
Philadelphia murders 2006 (406) X 2.86 POs per murder =
1,161 APPD officers

A risk-based standard of workload, in contrast to a case-based standard, yields a substantially higher optimal complement of adult probation officers than Philadelphia has at present. This calculation is based solely on the risk-based standards for the rest of the rest of the state as of 2005. It is not suggested that this is the best or most appropriate standard. Rather, it simply illustrates the far higher risk level associated with the APPD caseload—and that of other FJD agencies—than is found, case per case, in other Pennsylvania counties.

Risk-Based Probation and Parole

Whether a community corrections agency has 1,000 officers, 500 or even 400, their best use for ***homicide prevention*** would be guided by a risk-based classification of probationers. This classification would not be based on the seriousness of the offense for which they have been assigned to community supervision. It would not be based on the seriousness of their prior convictions. Nor would it be based on the simple likelihood of recidivism in any offense category. If a probation, parole or pre-trial supervision agency were staffed in accordance with its caseload's risk of homicide, it would be best advised to allocate caseloads according to risk of committing or attempting murder. A closely related option would be based on a probationer's risk of committing murder, rape, robbery, aggravated assault or a sex offense against a child.

Whatever the exact definition of the serious offense profile to be used as the basis for risk analysis, Philadelphia's APPD now has the capacity to forecast who is most likely to be charged with those offenses, based on their past behavior. This forecast can divide all APPD cases into three groups, like an emergency room "triage" process:

High-risk violent offenders
Medium-risk violent offenders
Low violence-risk offenders

The third group may consist of cases with a high risk of property offending, but with a low risk of committing the serious violent offenses that the other two groups are likely to commit. The Medium-risk violent offenders would be people who pose a substantial threat, but for whom current resources do not allow the same intensity of supervision and support as those provided by the SAV-Unit. The high-risk violent offenders would be limited to the most highly ranked group of offenders identified by the advanced risk analysis model, with the cutoff mandated by the number of officers available to provide the SAV-U protocol.

Under this model, the APPD would be re-structured as a pyramid of caseloads and serious violence risk levels. At the top of the pyramid would be the smallest caseload with the highest risk. Just below would be a larger caseload with somewhat lesser risk. At the bottom would be the largest caseload with the lowest risk. An illustration is presented below:

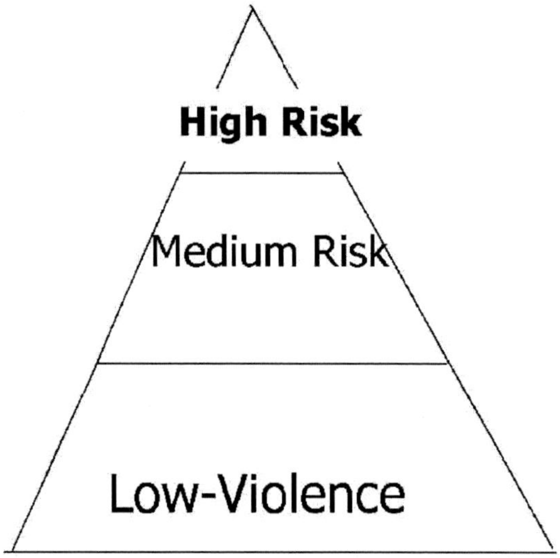

Re-Structuring Current Operations

Re-engineering caseloads based on offender risk level could be done with or without adding more probation officers. Three main steps would be required: testing and implementing automated supervision for low violence-risk cases, expanding the application of the SAV-U protocol to high-risk cases, and reducing the caseloads for the probation officers supervising the offenders in medium-risk group.

Depending on where the statistical threshold is set for membership in each group, the 285 APPD officers could be assigned in something like the following structure

Risk Level	Caseload	(%)	Cases Per Officer	Total Officers
High	750	(1.4)	15	50
Medium	12, 250	(23.6)	55	222
Low	39,000	(75)	500	78
Total	52,000	(100)	149	285

This is not a model that could be implemented overnight. Each of the three steps could be taken simultaneously, but in a deliberate and careful fashion.

Automated Case Supervision could be tested on a pilot basis with a sample of 2,000 cases randomly assigned to either of two groups:

- 1,000 to the current system of face-to-face supervision with a high-caseload probation officer with 175 cases
- automated supervision by computers monitored by an automated case officer with 500 cases

After a six month period, the two groups could be compared for their rates of serious violent crime, as well as their rates of absconding, failure of drug tests, re-arrest for any offense, and reconviction (direct violation). If there is no difference between the two groups, or if the automated supervision group does better than the standard treatment group, then the APPD could proceed to implement the automated case supervision model with the entire caseload meeting the statistical standard of low risk. That standard would be set by the Chief of APPD, in ongoing consultation with the Jerry Lee Center of Criminology at the University of Pennsylvania.

Reducing Caseloads with Medium Risk Offenders. As the number of cases under automated supervision grows, the number of cases per probation officer can be reduced for supervising medium risk offenders. From a starting point in regional units of about 175 per officer at present, the caseload could move to the pyramid model of about 50 cases per officer. This figure, however, may still be far to high for effective prevention of serious crime, or for effective provision of support and surveillance. Lowering it still further would depend on increasing the complement of probation officers.

Expanding the SAV-U Protocol. This step can move forward independently of the automated case supervision process as the SAV-U protocol itself develops. Also required is the increasing availability of qualified, trained staff through recruitment and training. This step can be taken even without increasing the total APPD complement, but it would move much faster if that complement were to be increased.

Adding Officers for High-Risk Supervision

Federal recognition of the very high rates of homicide among community corrections caseloads may contribute to a dialogue about the ideal investment in adult probation and parole. Evidence on the effectiveness of low caseloads for high-risk offenders is also needed. The Philadelphia APPD is currently assessing the impact of the SAV-U protocol on the rates of serious crime committed by APPD cases. A randomized, controlled comparison between standard supervision and the 15-case maximum SAV-U protocol will be completed by early-to-mid 2008. Further conclusions can be drawn at that time, even while the question of how best to support high-risk people is being developed by trial-and-error.

Offenders identified by the forecasting model are typically people who have suffered enormous problems in life. They have often been abused as very young children. They have seen brothers and sisters shot or beaten. They have been arrested for dealing drugs as accomplices of their parents. They may have chronic depression, post-traumatic stress disorder, anxiety disorder or chronic substance abuse. They may also be psychotic or suffer from bipolar disorder.

Given the complexity and needs of each offender, there is almost no limit to how much a probation officer can do to help bring order and hope to a (usually) young person's life. The only limitations are time, money, and imagination. Of the three, imagination may be the most important. The frustrations of working with such difficult cases are great. Such work is not for everyone. It is a far cry from spending the day asking questions and recording the answers. The SAV-U protocol requires a very different set of tasks and skills from the standard model of probation. It also requires a mutually supportive work culture, in which small teams of probation officers can support each other, sharing challenges, ideas, and commitment.

For these and other reasons, it may be best to grow the use of the SAV-U protocol through new recruitment, as well as by careful selection and training of experienced officers. That is exactly how the first 5 SAV-U officers were chosen, with 3 experienced APPD officers and 2 (plus one analyst) recent Master's degree in criminology graduates. The team is well-blended with different strengths and skills. Following that model might be accomplished most easily with a national recruitment and local retention program (see section 13 below).

Police Partnerships

One of the many questions about how best to supervise the most dangerous offenders is the role of the police in making sure offenders do not possess or carry guns. If greater investment in field contacts is shown to be an effective way to reduce murder, there will be a need for substantial increases in police officers dedicated to offender supervision. Two officers are needed for each probation officer during field visits. If a PO performs field visits 16 hours weekly, that would require 32 hours of police time. With preparation and intelligence work on each household to be visited, this would mean about one police officer for every probation officer working under the SAV-U protocol.

The number of police officers needed will therefore depend on the level of the city's investment in high-risk supervision. Assuming 50 high-risk probation officers with no increase in APPD staffing, there would need to be a minimum of 50 police officers assigned fulltime to SAV-U visits. If the City were to add 50 new APPD officers solely for the purpose of high-risk supervision, then the police complement required would be 100. If the City added 150 to high-risk supervision, the police complement needed would be 200.

Each of these police officers would be dedicated to a highly specific crime prevention mission. Consistent with the recent National Academy of Sciences review of the effectiveness of police strategies (http://books.nap.edu/openbook.php?record_id=10419&page=R1), the use of police for such highly specific purposes is likely to be more effective than increasing the capacity to respond to 911 calls. Thus any program of adding police officers to the PPD, as many have recently proposed, could be accomplished by increasing the capacity of APPD to prevent homicide.

A Federal Grant Program

Since 9-11-2001, over 100,000 Americans have been murdered on the streets of our cities. The cost of preventing even a portion of these murders could be minimal in relation to what has been spent since that date on defense and homeland security. The federal government could invest in a high-yield program to gain knowledge about what works, at the same time that it could reduce homicide, by creating a program that would fund state and local probation, parole, pre-trial supervision, and juvenile probation and aftercare agencies to use their court-ordered conditions of community supervision in the following way:

1. Conduct a homicide-focused risk analysis of the factors best predicting homicide in the agency's caseload over at least 10,000 cases over at least two years.
2. Identify current cases with the high-risk factors identified by the risk analysis.
3. Assign a randomly selected sample of the high-risk cases to a low-caseload community supervision unit.
4. Focus the unit on working with offenders to prevent violence, by any appropriate, evidence-based and legal means indicated in a diagnosis of the offender's life history and mental health needs. This could include clinical treatments for such chronic disorders as PTSD, drug abuse, or depression.
5. Focus the unit on insuring that the offender does not carry or gain access to any guns.
6. Collect and record data among all high-risk offenders, both those randomly assigned to low caseload supervision and those in the "control" group, compiled in regular reports for federal publication of the comparative rates of homicide victimizations, arrests on charges of murder or attempted murder, and other crimes.

The grants would pay for university-agency partnerships, supporting the costs of both data analysis and community corrections staff. Minimum grants of $500,000 per year would be needed to create the scale necessary for successful projects, which could be limited to agencies in jurisdictions with at least 50 murders per year. Such a program would be rational, risk-based, and evidence driven to learn whether or not it works, city by city, using randomized controlled experiments that would allow comparisons of effective and ineffective programs in terms of how they differed in their content. The result may or may not be a reduction in homicide in the short run. But in the long run the best way to combat murder is with scientific knowledge. That is something that the proposed program, if administered based on peer-reviewed decisions rather than earmarks, would be guaranteed to deliver.

TESTIMONY OF DAVID M. KENNEDY, DIRECTOR, CENTER FOR CRIME PREVENTION AND CONTROL, JOHN JAY COLLEGE OF CRIMINAL JUSTICE, NEW YORK, NY

Mr. KENNEDY. I would like to begin by offering my sincere thanks to Chairman Scott and to the Committee as a whole for holding this hearing and allowing me to be a part of it.

Individual lives, the trajectory of families and communities and in a very real way the success of the American experiment are at stake here for this issue is infused with race, however much we might wish it were not.

Getting this right means a new way of thinking and acting. I am now persuaded that we could put 100 times more gang members in prison or fund 100 times the number of prevention programs and that would not work either.

My simplest and most profound message is that we know today how to address this problem in a way that saves lives, reduces incarceration, strengthens communities, bridges racial divides and improves the lives of offenders and ex-offenders.

In 1996, the famous Boston Miracle cut youth homicide by two-thirds and homicide city-wide by half. What Boston did was both simple and profound. Boston assembled law enforcement, social service providers and community actors, including my old friend Teny, into a new partnership that created sustained relationships with Boston's gangs.

The partners stood together and spoke with one voice face-to-face with gang members. The violence was wrong and had to stop, that the community needed them alive and out of prison and with their loved ones, that help was available to all who would take it and that violence would be met with clear, predictable and certain consequences.

The new approach worked with an existing law using existing resources. The results were shockingly different. The first face-to-face meeting with gang members took place in May 1996. By the fall, the streets were almost quiet. The city averaged around 100 homicides a year through mid-1996. In 1999, it had 31.

The approach has worked just as well in jurisdictions all over the country. The nature of these interventions does not allow the strongest random assigment evaluation design, but in Chicago a sophisticated quasi-experimental evaluation by University of Chicago and Columbia researchers of a Justice Department project showed homicide reductions in violent neighborhoods of 37 percent.

When Richmond, in Chairman Scott's district, had its first offender call in, former Virginia U.S. Attorney Paul McNulty, now deputy attorney general, traveled back to Richmond to address the gang members personally. Last year at this time there had been 15 homicides in Richmond. This year, there have been four.

I am working with a team in Cincinnati in Congressman Chabot's district and with the U.S. attorney in Milwaukee in Congressman Sensenbrenner's district, and I will say to them what I have said to their constituents: We are now essentially certain from years of experience that if the work is done seriously, the results will follow.

Not all jurisdictions have implemented the strategies properly. Many that have, including Boston, the first and still best known site of when effective interventions fail, this has highlighted the need for attention to institutionalization and sustainability. Frameworks for adapting the strategy to the most demanding jurisdictions, such as Los Angeles, need to be developed, but the record is increasingly compelling.

In the most recent strand of this work, begun in High Point, North Carolina, in Congressman Coble's district, we for the first time faced squarely the toxic racial tension that saturates these issues. In High Point, law enforcement spoke honestly to communities that enforcement was not succeeding, that they knew that, that they had never meant to do harm through relentless enforcement, but they had come to realize that they had.

Communities looked inward and realized that in their anger over historic and present ills, they had not made it clear to their own young people that gang and drug activity was wrong and deeply damaging to the community. Both law enforcement and community came to understand that what they were dealing with was not so much depraved individuals as it was out of control peer group and street dynamics.

So when the partnership met with High Point's drug deals, the community voice was clear and amazingly powerful. Scores of community members, including many immediate family, told the dealers that they were loved, needed, vital to the future of the community and would be helped, but were doing wrong, hurting themselves, hurting others and had to stop. Overwhelmingly, they have stopped.

This is transformational. Gang violence and drug crime is an obscenity, but so is mass incarceration. It is important that at-risk youth get help, but it is equally important that seasoned offenders get help. It is important to have firm law enforcement, but it is even more important to have firm community standards. It is important that law enforcement take action when the dangerous will not stop and that the community supports them when they do.

We now know that all of that can be brought to pass with in existing law, within existing resources and remarkably quickly.

The demand for these interventions nationally is enormous. These demands cannot be met. All of us involved in this work are swamped with pleas for help that we cannot answer. There is no larger framework in place to go to scale to help localities understand how to implement these approaches, learn from the constant refinements and innovations that occur at the local level, address key issues, such as sustainability and enhance the state of the art.

The Federal Government should make creating and supporting that framework a priority. We have learned profound lessons about how to address gangs, gang violence, the drug-driven crime that invariably travels alongside and, blessedly, how to begin to address the racial divides that undergird and perpetuate all of it and make us all less than we should be. We can do better.

[The prepared statement of Mr. Kennedy follows:]

Prepared Statement of David M. Kennedy

I would like to begin by offering my sincere thanks to Chairman Scott, and to the committee as a whole, for holding this hearing and allowing me to be a part of it. Our topic today is profoundly important. Individual lives, the trajectory of families and communities, and in a very real way the success of the American experiment are at stake. Both the problem and our response to the problem have grave implications. The life of an individual and a city can be destroyed by gang violence. But those lives can also be destroyed by the demonization of offenders and well-intentioned but profligate law enforcement: by the demonization of law enforcement and what follows in its wake, such as the toxic ''stop snitching'' thug culture; and by the well-intentioned failures of powerless prevention and intervention programs. Getting this right is crucial.

Getting it right means a new way of thinking and acting. I am now persuaded that no amount of ordinary law enforcement, no amount of ordinary intervention, and no amount of ordinary prevention will get us what we want and need. I do my work amongst extraordinary people: police officers and prosecutors, gang outreach workers, social service providers, parents, ex-offenders. They work with profound seriousness and commitment. But it does not solve the problem, and I think it neverwill. We could put 100 times more gang members in prison, or fund 100 times the number of prevention programs, and that would not work either. Our traditional framework for addressing this issue is simply unsuccessful.

There is now more than ample evidence that there is a different and far better framework: one that is successful. My simplest and most profound message today is that we know, today, how to address this problem: in a way that saves lives, reduces incarceration, strengthens communities, bridges racial divides, and improves the lives of offenders and ex-offenders. The evidence has been accumulating for over a decade and is now extremely persuasive. In 1996, the famous ''Boston Miracle'' cut youth homicide by two-thirds and homicide city-wide by half.[6] The Boston work was fundamentally simple and unexpectedly profound. Violence and drug activity in troubled neighborhoods is caused predominantly by a remarkably small and activenumber of people locked in group dynamics on the street. Boston assembled law enforcement, social service providers, and community actors—parents, ministers, gang outreach workers, neighborhood associations, ex-offenders, and others—into a new partnership that created sustained relationships with violent groups. The partners stood together and spoke with one voice face-to-face with gang members: that the violence was wrong and had to stop; that the community needed them alive and outof prison and with their loved ones; that help was available to all who needed it; and that violence would be met with clear, predictable, and certain consequences.

There are many myths about Boston. It was not draconian; there were very few arrests, and most enforcement used ordinary state law and probation supervision. It did not wrap every at-risk youth with services and support; we did not have the resources or capacity to do that. It did not rely primarily on law enforcement, orservices, or the community; until the full partnership and strategy was created, no single group was very effective. But with the new approach, within existing law, using existing resources, everything changed. The first face-to-face meeting with gang members took place in May of 1996. By the fall, the streets were almost quiet. At its worst, in 1990, the city had 152 homicides. In 1999, it had 31.

The approach worked just as well elsewhere. Minneapolis was next—in the summer of 1996, there were 32 homicides; Minneapolis began its work over the winter, and in the summer of 1997, there were eight. The Indianapolis Violence Reduction Partnership, launched in 1998, cut homicide city-wide by 40%, and robberies and gun assaults in one of its most dangerous neighborhoods by 49%.[7][2] In Stockton, California Operation Peacekeeper, implemented in late 1997, cut homicide among Hispanic gangs by about three-quarters.[8] In Rochester, New York, gang violence fell by two-thirds between 2004 and 2005. In Chicago, a Project Safe Neighborhoods initiative evaluated by the University of Chicago and Columbia University cut homicide among violent parolees by nearly 75%; they became nearly as safe as residents of the safest neighborhoods in the city.[9] In Lowell, Massachusetts a strategy adapted to Asian gangs shut down shooting almost entirely.[10] In Nassau County, Long Island, the strategy has been effective against a gang problem that includes the notorious MS-13 network. In High Point, North Carolina, in Congressman Cobles's district, a parallel approach aimed at drug markets has virtually eliminated overt drug activity, violent crime is down over 20%, and a rich community partnership is working— often successfully—to help former drug dealers regain their lives.[11] Inspired by High Point, Winston-Salem, Greensboro, and Raleigh have all followed suit, as have Newburgh, New York and Providence, Rhode Island, with others on the way. In Richmond, in Chairman Scott's district, a city partnership began meeting with gangs city-wide in October of last year. I spoke with police department officials last week,before being invited to this hearing, and they are getting the same wonderful results we have come to expect. Last year at this time there had been fifteen homicides in Richmond. This year, there have been four. I am working with a team in Cincinnati, in Congressman Chabot's district, and with US Attorney William Lipscomb in Milwaukee, in Congressman Sensenbrenner's district, and I will say to them what I have said to their constituents: we are now essentially certain, from years of experience, that if the work is done seriously, the results will follow.

This is not an unalloyed success story. Not all jurisdictions have implemented the strategies properly. Some who have (including Boston, the first and still best-known site) have let effective interventions fall apart, highlighting the need for attention to institutionalization and sustainability (notably, Boston has recently expressed its commitment to reinstating Ceasefire in the face of a spiraling homicide rate).Frameworks for adapting the strategy to the most demanding jurisdictions, such as Los Angeles, need to be tested and refined. And the theory of the gang strategy— that cities have basic gang dynamics that need to be addressed as a whole—has made it impossible to set aside offenders, gangs, or neighborhoods as ''controls'', thus foreclosing the strongest random-assignment social science evaluations.

The evidence, however, is now quite clear. City after city has gotten the samekind of results. The strongest evaluation, the sophisticated quasiexperimental design used by the Chicago and Columbia researchers, shows the same impact as the original city-wide studies. The approach has been endorsed by both the Clinton Administration, through its Strategic Approach to Community Safety Initiative, and the Bush Administration, through its flagship Project Safe Neighborhoods initiative [12] and the Executive Office for United States Attorneys (EOUSA). When Richmond had its first offender call-in early last year, former Virginia US Attorney Paul McNulty, now deputy attorney general, traveled back to Richmond to address the gang members personally. It has been endorsed by groups as diverse as Fight Crime Invest in Kids, in a report presented by law enforcement legend William Bratton; [13] by the Children's Defense Fund; [14] and by the National Urban League.

The story thus far is only a beginning. The Boston work is now over ten years old, and much has been learned during that time. The basic approach has always consisted of three essential elements: law enforcement, social service providers, and communities, all directly engaged with offenders. The most recent work, developed in High Point, has begun to show us how extraordinarily important the community component is, particularly what I have come to think of as ''the moral voice of the community''. In the High Point work, we for the first time faced squarely the heavily and toxically racialized narratives that lie at, or barely below, these issues. When law enforcement feels that communities have completely lost their moral compass, they will not think to work with or influence communities. When communities feel that law enforcement is part of a conspiracy to destroy the community, they will not think to work with or influence law enforcement. When networks of offenders tell each other that they are not afraid of prison, not afraid to die, and have to shoot those who disrespect them, then they will do so.

But if I have learned anything during my career, it is that law enforcement desperately wishes to help, that communities desperately want to be safe and productive, and that nobody wants to go to prison or die. This is the transformative lesson of the High Point work: that none of us likes what is going on. Law enforcement does not want to endlessly arrest and imprison, without making any impact. Communities do not want to live with violence and fear. Even gang members and drug dealers love their families and want to be safe and successful. Everybody wants those who will take help to have it. Everybody wants the truly dangerous to be controlled. We do not think we are of one mind, but in the most important ways, we are.

In High Point, law enforcement spoke honestly to communities: that they were not succeeding, and they knew it; that they had never meant to do harm to communities through enforcement action, but had come to realize that they had; that they wouldlike to act differently. Communities looked inward and realized that in their anger over historic and present ills, they had not made it clear to their own young people that gang and drug activity was wrong and deeply damaging to the community. Both law enforcement and community came to understand that what they were dealing with was not so much individuals making bad decisions as peer, group, and street dynamics. So when the partnership met with High Point's drug dealers, thecommunity voice was powerful, clear, and amazingly powerful. Scores of community members, including many immediate family, told the dealers that they were loved, needed, vital to the future of the community, would be helped: but were doing wrong, hurting themselves and others, and had to stop. Overwhelmingly, they heard, and they did. Very, very few had to be arrested subsequently, and many are now living very different lives. And offenders, communities, and law enforcementsee each other in very different ways than they did only a short time ago.

This is transformational. Gang violence and drug crime is vicious, but so is mass incarceration. It is important that "at risk youth" get prevention, but it is equally important that seasoned offenders get it. It is important to have firm law enforcement, but it is even more important to have firm community standards. It is important that law enforcement take action when all else has failed, and that the community support them when they do. We now know that all of that can be brought to pass: within existing law, within existing resources, and remarkably quickly. This work is not just about crime prevention; it is about redemption and reconciliation. And it is real.

I want to say again that I cannot imagine any scale of investments in traditional activities, or even the starkest increase in legal sanctions, producing these results.We can do this today, immediately. If, ten years ago, the medical community had discovered a way to reduce breast cancer deaths among middle-class white women by 70%, every hospital in the country would now be using that approach. We have learned something that profound about this kind of crime problem. We should act like it.

The demand for these interventions is tremendous. Currently there is a small (butgrowing) number of researchers and practitioners who understand the underlying principles, have successfully implemented the strategies, and who continue to refine the basic approach. The logic of the approach is now quite well developed, as is its application in meaningfully different circumstances (west coast gangs vs. loose drug crews, for example); key analytic and organizational steps necessary for implementation; supporting aspects such as data and administrative systems; places in theprocess where errors are likely to be made; and the like. This is not a "cookbook" process, but the basic path and how to manage it is quite well understood. At the same time, the demand vastly outstrips current capacity to address it. New interventions are primarily driven by isolated researchers operating in "Johnny Appleseed" mode, working with individual jurisdictions to address their local problems. These researchers cannot begin to respond to even the requests that come to them directly. There is also increasing attention to these approaches from national groups such as the Urban League and the Children's Defense Fund. These demands cannot be met. When EOUSA held a two-day conference at the National Advocacy Center in Columbia, South Carolina in January of this year, some 200 people came from all over the country; many left committed to doing the work and are calling for help, but we have no way to give it to them.

There is no larger framework in place to ''go to scale:'' to help implement the approaches where they are needed, learn from the constant refinements and innovations that occur at the local level, address key issues such as sustainability, and enhance the state of the art. The Justice Department's Project Safe Neighborhoods, which strongly endorses these strategies, has gone some distance in supporting these needs, but additional focused and very practical help to jurisdictions nationally is badly needed.

A national effort to go to scale is entirely possible. It would have something like the following elements:

- A national set of ''primary'' jurisdictions, distributed regionally and chosen to incorporate the range of gang issues (i.e., west coast gangs, Chicago gangs, MS-13, drug crews);
- Close, continuing support from the current pool of experienced researchers and practitioners to work with researchers and practitioners in these jurisdictions to help them implement the strategies locally;
- Regular convening of teams from the primary jurisdictions, teams from a larger set of ''secondary'' jurisdictions, the core pool of researchers and practitioners, and a larger pool of ''secondary'' researchers and practitioners. In these sessions, the basic strategies would be explained, implementation andimplementation issues addressed; core technical assistance provided; on-theground experience from the primary sites shared and analyzed; innovations identified and shared; and key issues needing more detailed attention identified.
- Key documents such as implementation guides, research and assessment templates, process histories, case studies, evaluations, ''lessons learned'', and the like developed and distributed. These could be bolstered with more or less real-time websites supporting implementation, answering common questions, presenting site findings and progress, noting local innovations, etc.
- As the ''primary'' sites solidified, the focus could shift to the ''secondary'' sites, which would now be well prepared to undertake their own initiatives. Horizontal exchanges between sites by a now considerably larger pool of experienced researchers, law enforcement, service providers, and community actors would now be possible. Continued convenings, or perhaps a series of regionalconvenings, would support the work in the new sites, address issues arising in the original sites, and allow the national community working on these issues to learn from local experience. This ''seeding'' process could continue as long as necessary to ''tip'' national practice to regarding these strategies as the norm. The large number of actors participating in the effort would add to this through their natural participation in local and national discussions,writing and publishing, professional activities, and the like.
- In this setting, a core research agenda, addressing for example new substantive crime problems and institutionalization and accountability issues, could be framed and pursued. Findings could be translated quite directly intoaction on a national scale.

Funding for this effort would be necessary for the technical assistance, convening,documentation/dissemination, and site exchange components. While additional funding for operational elements would of course be welcome, experience shows that re-directing existing resources in alignment with the basic strategy can produce dramatically enhanced results.

We now know how to address gang issues of great significance to troubled communities and to the nation. Despite this fact, understanding and implementation is proceeding slowly and is not likely to govern national policy and practice without a deliberate strategic effort. The federal government should take the lead in ensuring that this happens.

TESTIMONY OF JAMES CORWIN, CHIEF OF POLICE, KANSAS CITY, MO

Chief CORWIN. Thank you.

Mr. Chairman, Members of the Subcommittee on Crime, Terrorism, and Homeland Security, thank you for the opportunity to present this testimony.

My name is James Corwin and I have been a member of the Kansas City, Missouri, Police Department since 1979 and the chief of the department since 2004.

As a law enforcement leader, I have been committed to community-oriented policing approaches and problem solving in Kansas City. This approach has served our city well, especially the year before last when we faced a spike in homicide, going from 91 in 2004 to 127 in 2005. The homicide rate went back down in 2006.

Groups of individuals, typically neighborhood-based groups, rather than traditional gangs like Crips, Bloods and MS-13, were involved in many of those homicides. That is why I am grateful for this opportunity to share information with you about what works to reduce youth and gang violence.

I am also a member of the Fight Crime: Invest in Kids, an organization of more than 3,000 police chiefs, sheriffs and prosecutors and victims of violence who have come together to take a hard-nosed look at the research on what keeps kids from becoming criminals. As a police chief, I know there is no substitute for tough law enforcement, yet law enforcement leaders like myself know better than anyone that we cannot arrest and imprison our way out of this crime problem.

Fortunately, research and our experience has shown that targeted investments that help kids get a good start in life and that intervene effectively to redirect juveniles onto different paths and prevent crime and make our communities safer.

To reduce crime in our communities, we should begin at the beginning. Beginning at the beginning means offering services to new moms, such as voluntary in-home parent coaching and ensuring that kids have access to quality early education and childcare. After school programs during the hours of 3 p.m. to 6 p.m., primetime for juvenile crime, on school days can also help in preventing crime.

Law enforcement is doing the best job we can do to deal with juvenile crime when it happens and to make sure dangerous juveniles are taken off the street. Most juveniles arrested are not likely to become serious offenders. Nationally, 6 in 10 juveniles brought before a juvenile court for the first time will not return to court on another charge. In recent years, there have been approximately 100,000 juveniles in custody nationwide. The vast majority of these troubled youth will be released back into the community with their expected prime crime years ahead of them and facing a re-arrest rate up to 75 percent. But it doesn't have to be that way.

A significant amount of the research has identified several effective approaches to help young offenders avoid committing further crimes, thereby enhancing public safety. For the most dangerous young offenders, especially those who are involved in a violent gang, the combination of intensive police supervision, expedited sanctions for repeat violence and expedited access to jobs, drug treatment and other services, a carrot-and-stick approach has shown in a number of cities that it can cut homicides among violent offenders in high-crime neighborhoods.

In Chicago, for example, when the carrot-and-stick approach area, there was a 37 percent drop in quarterly homicide rates when the project was implemented, while the decline in homicide in another similar neighborhood during the same period was 18 percent.

Simply warehousing high-risk offenders during their time in custody is not adequate. They need to be required to do the hard work of confronting and changing their antisocial beliefs and behaviors. Aggression replacement therapy, ART, can teach teens to stop and consider the consequences of their actions, to think of other ways of responding to interpersonal problems and to consider how their actions will affect others.

Young people in Brooklyn gangs without ART services had four times the number of arrests of similar young gang members receiving ART.

For offenders who do not need high-security lock up, individual placement in multidimensional treatment foster care, or MTFC, home can be used. Foster care may sound like a pass for juveniles who should be paying a more severe price for the crime they have committed, but for teens who are often used to running the streets and see a month in custody as just another chance to socialize with delinquent friends or learn new criminal behaviors, this is a more controlled experience and a tough intervention.

The MTFC approach cuts the average number of repeat offense for serious delinquent juveniles in half. MTFC saves the public an average of over $77,000 for every juvenile treated.

Similar cost-effective models that can be implemented in communities are functional family therapy programs and multisystemic therapy. Approximately 500,000 juveniles a year could benefit from evidence-based like FFT, MST, MTFC, yet only 34,000 are currently being served.

Here are the steps that Congress can take to implement those proven, effective crime-prevention therapies: implement effective, research-proven strategies, such as voluntary in-home parenting coaching, quality early childhood care and education and bullying prevention programs; ensure that any legislation to address gang violence provides funding for communities to implement comprehensive, coordinated carrot-and-stick response; enact and fund legislation such as the Second Chance Act to enable juvenile ex-offenders to successfully reenter their communities; reauthorize, strengthen and increase funding for Federal juvenile justice and delinquency prevention programs.

Being tough on violent crime is critical. However, once a crime has been committed, neither police nor prisons can undo the agony of the crime victim and repair the victim's shattered life. Thus prevention and intervention programs that use research-based techniques to prevent further crime and critical tools for making our neighborhoods safe.

I and my colleagues at Fight Crime: Invest in Kids, who are leaders of American law enforcement, are grateful that the Subcommittee is holding today's hearing and we look forward to working with you in implementing these recommendations.

Thank you.

[The prepared statement of Chief Corwin follows:]

PREPARED STATEMENT OF JAMES CORWIN

FIGHT CRIME: Invest in Kids

3,000 Police Chiefs, Sheriffs, Prosecutors, other Law Enforcement Leaders, and Violence Survivors Preventing Crime and Violence

United States House of Representatives
Committee on the Judiciary
Subcommittee on Crime, Terrorism, and Homeland Security

February 15, 2007
Hearing

Making Communities Safer:
Youth Violence & Gang Interventions that Work

Testimony by:
Chief James Corwin

Chief of Police,
Kansas City, MO

On Behalf of
Fight Crime: Invest in Kids

1212 New York Ave. NW, Ste 300 • Washington, DC 20005 • (202) 776-0027 • Fax (202) 776-0110 • www.fightcrime.org

Mr. Chairman and Members of the Subcommittee on Crime, Terrorism and Homeland Security:

Thank you for the opportunity to present this testimony. My name is James Corwin and I have been a member of the Kansas City Police Department since 1979 and Chief of the Department since 2004. During my thirty-year tenure in law enforcement, I have held numerous patrol, investigative, and administrative assignments. As a law enforcement leader, I've been committed to community-oriented policing approaches in Kansas City, and have applied that more holistic approach, working in coordination with the five sectors of our community: education, businesses, non-profits, faith-based entities, and neighborhood organizations. This approach has served our city well, especially the year before last, when we were faced with a spike in homicides—going from 91 in 2004 to 127 in 2005. (The homicide rate went back down in 2006.) Groups of individuals (typically neighborhood-based groups, rather than traditional gangs like Crips, Bloods, and MS-13) were involved in many of those homicides. That's why I'm grateful for this opportunity to share information with you about what works to reduce youth and gang violence.

I am also a member of FIGHT CRIME: INVEST IN KIDS, an organization of more than 3,000 police chiefs, sheriffs, prosecutors, and victims of violence, who have come together to take a hard-nosed look at the research on what keeps kids from becoming criminals.

As a police chief, I know there is no substitute for tough law enforcement. Yet law enforcement leaders like myself know better than anyone that we cannot arrest and imprison our way out of the crime problem. Fortunately, research—and our experiences—show that targeted investments that help kids get a good start in life and that intervene effectively to redirect offending juveniles onto a different path can prevent crime, and can make our communities safer.

To reduce crime in our communities, we should begin at the beginning. When children are having children, and there's no support structure in place for that family, we can't be surprised when some of those kids don't grow up to become successful adults. Beginning at the beginning means offering services to new moms, even before their kids are born, and preventing child abuse and neglect – that's one of our strongest weapons in the fight against crime. Child abuse and neglect increases the likelihood by 29 percent that an at-risk child will commit a violent crime when he or she grows up. Fortunately, quality, voluntary in-home parent coaching can help stop this cycle of violence. Voluntary, in-home parent coaching (or "home visiting") programs help new parents get the information, skills and support they need to be better parents and promote healthy child development. One program, the Nurse Family Partnership (NFP), has been shown to cut child abuse and neglect of at-risk children in half and reduce kids' and moms' later arrests by about 60% - saving an average of $27,000 (net) for each family in the program. Unfortunately, most at-risk families do not have access to these vital services.

Head Start and other quality early education is another proven approach for preparing kids for school and keeping them away from crime. At-risk kids who were left out of Chicago's Child-Parent Centers, a pre-k program similar to Head Start, were 70% more likely to have been arrested for a violent crime by age 18 than similar kids who participated. Head Start research confirms these findings.. When you can offer kids a chance to be ready for school, they'll do better, be less likely to drop out, and be more likely to become productive citizens. And it makes sense that you'll save money – you've even got Federal Reserve Bank officials, like Art Rolnick, and Nobel Prize-winning economists, like James Heckman, touting the 16% return on investment from quality early education, a return that far exceeds the return on most public projects that are considered economic development. However, due to lack of state and federal financial resources, there remains significant unmet need with only about half of eligible poor kids nationally served by Head Start and less than 5% of eligible infants and toddlers in Early Head Start.

For school-aged kids, after-school programs that connect children to caring adults and provide constructive activities during the hours of 3:00pm to 6:00pm—the "prime time for juvenile crime" on school days—can also help in preventing crime. For example, a study compared five housing projects without Boys & Girls Clubs to five receiving new clubs. At the beginning, drug activity and vandalism were the same. But by the time the study ended, the projects without the programs had 50 percent more vandalism and scored 37 percent worse on drug activity. Regrettably, more than 14 million children nationwide still lack adult supervision after school.

The widespread problem of bullying affects one out of every three American children in sixth through tenth grade and can lead to more serious consequences, including violent crime and death. The most serious bullies are seven times more likely than other kids to carry a weapon to school, and one study demonstrated that four out of every ten boys who bullied others as kids had three or more convictions by the time they turned 24. Fortunately, there are cost-effective, evidence-based programs that can prevent bullying and reduce later crime and violence. The Olweus Bullying Prevention Program, for example, produced a 50 percent reduction of bullying in Norway and a 20 percent reduction when it was replicated in South Carolina. Moreover, for each high-risk juvenile prevented from adopting a life of crime, the country could save between $1.7 million and $2.3 million. Currently, not enough is being done to address the problem of bullying in our schools. Further action needs to be taken to implement evidence-based bullying prevention program components in every school district across the nation.

Law enforcement is doing the best job we can to deal with juvenile crime when it happens, and to make sure dangerous juveniles are taken off the streets. Most juveniles arrested are not likely to become serious offenders. Nationally, six in 10 juveniles brought before a juvenile court for the first time will not return to court on another charge. Research shows that the best results in reducing crime are achieved by targeting the worst offenders. The reason why is straightforward: one cannot prevent most low-risk juveniles from committing more crimes because they were not going to do more crimes anyway. But high-risk offenders are very likely to commit more crimes, and often. So any progress achieved with higher-risk juveniles results in very meaningful reductions in future crime. Effective screening tools exist to distinguish chronic and violent offenders from less serious offenders.

More serious juvenile offenders end up in custody. In recent years, there have been approximately 100,000 juveniles in custody nationwide. The vast majority of these troubled youths will be released back into the community, with their expected "prime crime years" ahead of them and facing recidivism rates of up to 75%. But it doesn't have to be that way. A significant amount of research has identified several effective approaches to help young offenders avoid committing further crimes, thereby enhancing public safety.

For the most dangerous young offenders, especially those who are involved in violent gangs, a combination of intensive police supervision, expedited sanctions for repeated violence, and expedited access to jobs, drug treatment or other services—a carrot-and-stick approach—has shown in a number of cities that it can cut homicides among violent offenders in high-crime neighborhoods. The carrot-and-stick approach has been successful in cities throughout the nation, including Chicago, Boston, and Philadelphia. In Chicago, for example, this comprehensive, community-wide approach was tried in a group of west side Chicago neighborhoods with a long history of high levels of homicide, with another set of dangerous neighborhoods on the south side of serving as the control group. In the carrot-and-stick approach area there was a 37 percent drop in quarterly homicide rates when the project was implemented, while the decline in homicides in the other neighborhood during the same period was 18 percent. David Kennedy's the expert on this approach, so you'll hear more from him about it.

The "Carrot and Stick" Approach Cuts Homicides

Project Safe Neighborhood included increased federal prosecution for gun crimes and used offender notification meetings and increased services—a "carrot and stick" approach—that sharply brought down homicides in the west side Chicago neighborhood where it was tested. Homicides also dropped, but not as fast in a similar south side control neighborhood and city-wide.

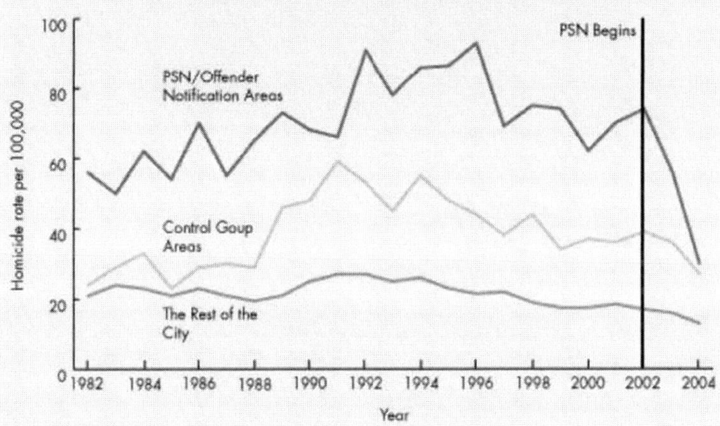

Simply warehousing high-risk offenders during their time in custody is not adequate. They need to be required to do the hard work of constantly confronting and changing their anti-social beliefs and behaviors. Cognitive Behavioral Therapy (CBT) uses tested, concrete methods, such as Aggression Replacement Therapy (ART), to teach teens to stop and consider the consequences of their actions, to conceptualize other ways of responding to interpersonal problems and to consider how their actions will affect others. By learning what triggers their negative behaviors and by identifying and practicing more pro-social and effective ways to respond, CBT consistently reduced repeat crimes among juveniles. Young people in Brooklyn gangs without ART services had four times the number of arrests of similar young gang members receiving ART.

For offenders who do not need high-security lock-up, individual placement in a Multidimensional Treatment Foster Care (MTFC) home can be used as an alternative to lock-up. Foster care may sound like a pass for juveniles who should be paying a more severe price for the crime they committed. But for teens who are often used to running the streets, and who see a month in custody as just another chance to socialize with delinquent friends or learn new criminal behaviors, this is a more controlled experience and a tough intervention. MTFC provides specially trained foster parents and ongoing supervision by a program case manager, as well as frequent contact and coordination of services with a youth's parole or probation officer, teachers, work supervisors and other involved adults during and after a youth's out of home placement. This approach incorporates effective reentry practices. Compared to similar juveniles placed in non-secure group facilities, the MTFC approach cuts the average number of repeat arrests for seriously delinquent juveniles in half, and six times as many of the boys in MTFC as boys in a group home successfully avoided any new arrest. MTFC is also cost-effective. MTFC saves the public an average of over $77,000 for every juvenile treated.

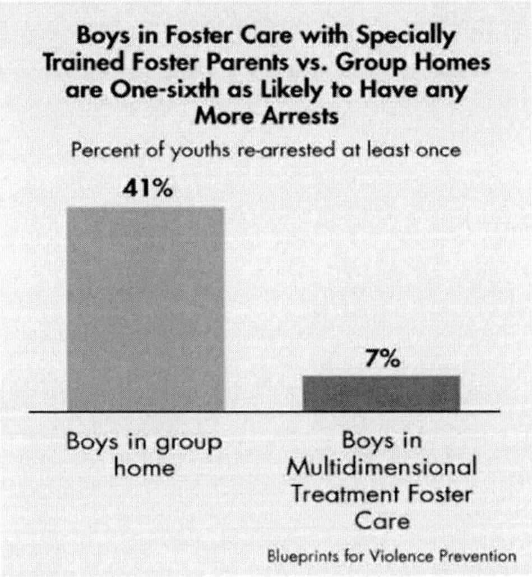

Effective interventions that incorporate community sanctions have also been shown to reliably cut crime. One such program is the Functional Family Therapy (FFT) program. FFT works to engage and motivate youth and their families to change behaviors that often result in criminal activity. In one evaluation from Salt Lake City, families with troubled youths were randomly assigned to either a group that received FFT or one that did not. The youths who families received FFT were half as likely to be re-arrested as the youth whose families did not receive the family therapy. By reducing recidivism among juvenile offenders, FFT saves the public an average of $32,000 per youth treated.

Similarly, the Multi-Systemic Therapy (MST) program targets kids who are serious juvenile offenders by addressing the multiple factors – in peer, school, neighborhood and family environments – known to be related to delinquency. One MST study followed juvenile offenders until they were, on average, 29-years-old. Individuals who had *not* received MST were 62 percent more likely to have been arrested for an offense, and more than twice as likely to be arrested for a violent offense. It is also less expensive than other mental health and juvenile justice services like residential treatment and incarceration, saving the public $4.27 for every dollar invested. While there are times when the nature of the crime or crimes committed simple demand that a juvenile be sentenced to custody, there are other situations that court ordered alternative sanctions and interventions that do not include custody may actually work better to reduce future crime.

What reduces crime saves money[103]	Savings or costs per participant				
	Costs avoided by crime victims[104]	Savings to taxpayers from crime reduction only[105]	Program Costs	Net savings to taxpayers	Net savings to taxpayers and victims
Functional Family Therapy for youth on probation (FFT)	$19,529	$14,617	$2,325	$12,292	$31,821
Multi-Systemic Therapy (MST)	$12,855	$9,622	$4,264	$5,358	$18,213
Multidimensional Treatment Foster Care (v. regular group care) (MTFC)[106]	$51,828	$32,915	$6,945	$25,970	$77,798
Aggression Replacement Training (ART)	$8,897	$6,659	$897	$5,762	$14,660

Washington State Institute for Public Policy 10/06

Law enforcement agencies made an estimated 2.2 million arrests of youth in 2003. Approximately 500,000 juveniles a year could benefit from evidence-based programs like FFT, MST and MTFC, yet only 34,000 are currently being served—only about 1 in 14. The remaining chronic, serious or violent juvenile offenders are often placed in less effective, and, therefore, ultimately more costly alternative programs, or no programs at all.

Approaches with proven results like those outlined above should be more widely implemented across the nation. Fortunately, some states have begun to integrate these types of interventions into their juvenile justice systems. Missouri, with a strong track record of reducing repeat crimes by changing juveniles' antisocial behavior, serves as a model for restructuring juvenile facilities. By moving teens needing confinement from large impersonal institutions to smaller facilities where they may receive the individual training they need to control their anti-social behaviors, Missouri has cut re-committal to its state juvenile facilities within three years of release to 15 percent. Troubled teens in these smaller, more effective facilities are not just doing their time, they are learning to change their lives.

Although certain states have begun to implement these proven approaches, it frequently takes federal leadership to encourage communities to experience the value of certain programs.

Here are steps that Congress can take to implement these proven, effective crime prevention strategies:

- Expand efforts to prevent child abuse and neglect by enacting and funding legislation to expand and improve evidence-based in-home parent coaching programs for at-risk families ("the Education Begins at Home Act");
- Expand and improve quality early childhood care and education by reauthorizing and fully funding Head Start and Early Head Start;
- Reauthorize and increase funding for 21st Century Community Learning Centers in order to improve quality and expand access to the program, particularly among at-risk middle and high school students who now experience the greatest unmet need;
- Enact legislation to help schools implement evidence-based solutions like the Olweus bullying prevention program;
- Ensure that any legislation to address gang violence provides funding for communities to implement comprehensive, coordinated "carrot and stick" responses;
- Enact and fund legislation to help states and localities to develop and implement strategic juvenile offender reentry plans, similar to the 109th Congress' Second Chance Act, to enable juvenile ex-offenders to successfully reenter their communities;
- Reauthorize, strengthen, and increase funding for federal juvenile justice and delinquency prevention programs.

Being tough on violent crime is critical. However, once a crime has been committed, neither police nor prisons can undo the agony of a crime victim and repair that victim's shattered life. Thus, prevention and intervention programs that use research-based techniques to prevent future crime are critical tools for making our neighborhoods safer.

I and my colleagues with FIGHT CRIME: INVEST IN KIDS who are leaders of American law enforcement, are grateful that this Subcommittee is holding today's hearing and we look forward to working with you to implement these recommendations.

Thank you, and I would be happy to answer any questions that you may have.

7

Mr. SCOTT. We have been joined by the gentleman from California, Mr. Lundgren. Thank you.

Ms. Fernandez?

TESTIMONY OF MAI FERNANDEZ, LEGAL AND STRATEGY DIRECTOR, LATIN AMERICAN YOUTH CENTER, WASHINGTON, DC

Ms. FERNANDEZ. Good morning, Mr. Chairman and Members of the Committee. I want to thank you all for having me here today.

And I would also like to invite you all to the Latin American Youth Center, which is about a 20-minute cab ride here from Congress. So if you want to see a program that works, get in a cab, go 20 minutes north and you will be there.

I would like to tell you a little bit about the Latin American Youth Center where I work. We have been in D.C. for over 30 years and a little over a year ago we opened three sites in Maryland. We are a community-based, multicultural, multilingual youth and family development center. We provide educational programs and tutoring to enable youth who are in school to stay in school and go on to college. For young people who have dropped out, we provide GED preparation and workforce training. We offer alternatives to incarceration programs for youth inside the juvenile justice system and reentry programs for youth exiting it.

Additionally, we provide counseling and substance abuse assistance, foster care and residential placement for youth in need of such services.

Through our different programs, we serve about 3,000 youth annually. I think it is safe to say that many of our youth and young people are gang involved or have been gang involved at some point in their life. However, only a small number of our young people are involved in criminal activity. Let me explain.

Many of our parents of our youth emigrated to the United States to find safety and a better way of life for their children. On arriving in the United States, many of these parents find themselves needing to work two and three jobs just to make ends meet. Keeping the family clothed, fed and housed becomes the priority. Unfortunately, this means that children are not provided the proper supervision, and schools are not prepared to meet this need.

The lack of supervision often leads to boredom and a sense of insecurity, which causes the children to join gangs. Joining a gang gives youth a group of friends to hang out with and a sense of security which they cannot get elsewhere in their lives. These kids are not super-predators. They are young people looking for a sense of belonging. Most youth who are in gangs are not criminals.

Having said this, I am a former prosecutor from Manhattan and do believe that when a gang member gets involved in criminal activity, there needs to be decisive law enforcement response. Three and a half years ago, our neighborhood, Columbia Heights, D.C., where the youth center is located, was plagued with a spree of Latino gang-related murders. Law enforcement acted swiftly in their investigation of these cases and apprehended the perpetrators.

Several of these young people are now serving life sentences. The law enforcement response sent a clear message to other gang-involved youth: You commit crimes, you will be punished.

During this gang crisis, both the community and the police realized they should not only respond to gang-related criminal activity, but should also work together to prevent it. As a result, the Gang Intervention Partnership, the GIP, was created. The GIP brings together police, probation officers, prosecutors, community-based and social service providers and develops intervention strategies for youth who are at high risk for committing crimes.

GIP has focused not just on reducing violent behavior but on addressing the myriad of social and economic issues, such as family situations, employment status, school attendance, peer relationships and limited recreational opportunities which can create environments that lead to violence amongst young people. GIP's holistic approach marries prevention and intervention initiatives with intelligence gathering and law enforcement efforts, providing a new model for reducing gang violence.

As a GIP community partner, the Latin American Youth Center has focused its efforts on outreach to gang-related youth, working closely with gang-involved young people to offer them educational, art, recreational and leadership programs as well as other opportunities to help them live healthy lives and connecting with caring adults.

From its inception, GIP has concentrated on a set of core strategies, conducting intensive targeted police work and building on strong police community partnerships, providing targeted outreach to gang-related youth and their families, educating parents and community members and improving and expanding access to service to critical families and strengthening and diversion.

What often occurs is that a community member will find out that a youth is in some kind of trouble. The members of the GIP come together to ensure that the youth is supervised, that he or she is involved in structured activities. In instances where the youth has faced real security problems, arrangements have been made to place a youth in witness protection programs.

This last fall, the GIP program was independently evaluated by the Center for Youth Policy Research. The evaluations found that the GIP's comprehensive approach dramatically reduced Latino gang-related violence in D.C. Their findings cited that there has not been a Latino gang-related homicide in the District of Columbia since October 9, 2003. Our results are significant.

In a 4-year period prior to forming the GIP, there were 40 shootings and stabbings. Twenty of those victims died. In the 3 years since the GIP has been developed, there have been five shootings and stabbings. Only one has led to a homicide.

In addition to reducing violence, the evaluation found that GIP achieves each of its other four goals: decreasing gang membership, reducing the number of gang-related suspensions in targeted schools, increasing the involvement of at-risk youth in recreational and productive activities and building community capacity and consciousness about gangs.

Thank you very much.

[The prepared statement of Ms. Fernandez follows:]

PREPARED STATEMENT OF MAI FERNANDEZ

Good afternoon, Chairman Scott and members of the Subcommittee. It is a pleasure to be before you today to speak on issues related to youth violence and gang interventions that work.

Before I go into the substance of my testimony, I would like to tell you a bit aboutthe Latin American Youth Center (LAYC) where I work. We have been in DC for more than years and a little over a year ago we opened 3 offices in Maryland. We are a community-based, multi-cultural and multi-lingual youth and family development center. We provide educational programs and tutoring to enable youth who are in school to stay in school and go on to college. For young people who have dropped out of school, we provide GED preparation and work-force training. We offer an alternative to incarceration program for youth inside the juvenile justice system and re-entry programs for youth exiting it. Additionally, we provide counseling, substance abuse assistance, foster care and residential placement for youth in need of such services.

Through our different programs, we serve about 3,000 youth annually. I think that it is safe to say that many of them are gang involved or have been gang involved at some point in their life. However, only a small number of our kids are involved in criminal activity.

Let me explain. Many of the parents of our youth immigrated to the United States to find safety and a better way of life for their children. Upon arriving in the U.S., many of these adults find themselves needing to work 2 to 3 jobs just to make ends meet. Keeping the family clothed, fed and housed becomes the priority. Unfortunately, this means that children are not provided the supervision that they need.

The lack of supervision often leads to boredom and a sense of insecurity which cause the children to join gangs. Joining a gang gives a youth a group of friends to hang out with, and a sense of security which they cannot get elsewhere in their lives. These kids are not super-predators—they are kids looking for a sense of belonging. Most youth who are in gangs are not criminals.

Having said this, I am a former prosecutor from Manhattan, and do believe that when gang members get involved in criminal activity there needs to be a decisive law enforcement response. Three and half years ago, Columbia Heights, D.C., where the Youth Center is located, was plagued with a spree of Latino gang-related murders. Law enforcement acted swiftly in their investigation of the cases and apprehended the perpetrators. Several of these young people are now serving life sentences. The law enforcement response sent a clear message to other gang-involved youth—if you commit crimes you will be punished.

During this gang crisis, both the community and the police realized that they should not only respond to gang related criminal activity, but should also work together to prevent it. As a result the Gang Intervention Partnership—the GIP—was created. The GIP brings together police, probation officers, prosecutors and community-based social service providers to develop intervention strategies for youth who are at high risk of committing crimes.

GIP has focused not just on reducing violent behavior, but on addressing the myriad social and economic issues, such as family situation, employment status, school attendance, peer relationships, and limited recreational opportunities, which can create environments that lead to violence among young people.

GIP's holistic approach marries prevention and intervention initiatives with intelligence gathering and enforcement efforts, providing a new model for reducing gang violence.

As a GIP community partner, the Latin American Youth Center has focused its efforts on outreach to gang-related youth, working closely with gang-involved young people to offer them arts, recreational and leadership programs as well as other opportunities to help them live healthy lives and connect them to caring adults.

From its inception, GIP has concentrated on a set of core strategies: 1) Conducting intensive and targeted police work and building strong police/community partnerships; 2) Providing targeted outreach to gang-related youth and their families; 3) Educating parents and community members and; 4) Improving and expanding access to services critical to family strengthening and diversion.

What often occurs is that a community member will find out that a youth is in some kind of trouble. The members of the GIP come together to ensure that the youth is supervised and that he/she is involved in structured activities. In instances where the youth has faced real security problems, arrangements have been made to place the youth in witness protection programs.

This last fall, the GIP program was independently evaluated by the Center for Youth Policy Research. The evaluators found that the GIP's comprehensive approach dramatically reduced Latino gang-related violence in DC. There finding's sited that there has not been a Latino gang-related homicide in the District of Columbia since October 9, 2003.

The numbers of youths shot or stabbed in the Columbia Heights/Shaw neighborhoods dropped from 40 in the four-year period before GIP (summer 1999-summer 2003) to five in the three years since GIP was created (August 2003-August 2006). In the four years preceding GIP, 21 young people died as a result of the 40 violent attacks. Since GIP was introduced, just one of the five shootings/stabbings resulted in loss of life and each of the shooting cases has been closed by MPD within 48 hours.

In addition to reducing violence, the evaluation found that GIP achieved each of its other four major goals—decreasing gang membership; reducing the number of gang-related suspensions in targeted schools; increasing the involvement of at-risk youth in recreational and other productive activities; and building community capacity and consciousness about gangs.

The evaluation demonstrates clearly that when there is close coordination and collaboration between law enforcement, government officials, the schools and community partners, there can be great strides in battling youth violence.

Importantly, the evaluation shows that a youth who has been involved in gang-related criminal activity can turn around his/her life.

GIP's success results from not focusing on one piece of the gang equation, but instead dealing comprehensively with the education, prevention and enforcement pieces and then coordinating these activities in a very disciplined manner.

For other jurisdictions working to reduce gang-related violence, the Gang Intervention Partnership offers three years of experience, providing a guide to some of challenges and obstacles that may arise when a community puts together a holistic, multi-agency and highly effective response.

In the past three years, we've learned a lot through the GIP—about the importance of communication, coordination and collaboration. About the need for multiple sectors to work together. About the need to respond quickly and aggressively to even small incidents—so that they're dealt with before they flare up into violence or additional violence. We've also learned how important it is to be in the schools—to be getting information to the schools as well as back from the schools.

Our community has been able to tailor an effective and appropriate response to gang-related crime in our area. I want to emphasize, however, that different gangs have different ways of operating and, therefore, community leaders need flexibility to respond to the unique gang problems in their area.

Even within a small geographic area such as DC, the types of interventions that will work in Columbia Heights may, for example, differ from the precise intervention needed in Southeast.

The Federal Government should facilitate the process of developing community responses to gang prevention and intervention by providing resources and technical assistance. Congress should not pass legislation that applies a universal solution to all jurisdictions.

Thank you for your time. I am available to answer questions at this time.

Mr. SCOTT. Thank you.

Mr. Logli?

TESTIMONY OF PAUL LOGLI, CHAIRMAN OF THE BOARD, NATIONAL DISTRICT ATTORNEYS ASSOCIATION, WINNEBAGO COUNTY, IL

Mr. LOGLI. Thank you. And I want to thank you, Chairman Scott, on behalf of the National District Attorneys Association for this opportunity to present our concerns about gang violence and to share some thoughts on what we as America's prosecutors and you, the Congress, can do to counter this growing threat to public safety.

The views that I express today represent the views of our association and the beliefs of thousands of local and State prosecutors who have primary jurisdiction in the matter of violent crime and specifically in the area of youth and gang crime.

I was privileged to testify before this very same Committee 2 years ago and I am going to use some of that testimony as a basis for my testimony today.

After hearing many of the members of this distinguished panel, there is not a whole lot new that we can add. There are some very fine programs out there that I think America's prosecutors are embracing. Many of those programs wouldn't work except for the involvement of local prosecutors. And so I want to disabuse anyone of the idea that I or any of the other local prosecutors are only concerned with trying and imprisoning gang members.

To counter the gang problem, we need effective community partnerships, to deter our children from becoming enamored with the gang life. While we need strong and effective criminal prosecution, we also need those diversion programs to prevent young people from making bad decisions, getting into trouble, bringing back those that have already started to make bad decisions and gotten into trouble. And, lastly, we need to develop meaningful reentry programs so that those persons who have already been convicted and sent to prison can somehow be reintegrated back into our societies with a chance to succeed.

When I testified 2 years ago, based on recent Federal reports we estimated there were 731,000 gang members. Two years later, in the same report, and that was the report for 2004, it appears that there are now 760,000 gang members, and I heard a figure this morning from the Chairman that it is estimated that today, 2007, there are about 850,000 gang members. So the problem continues to grow as we discuss this problem and try to define strategies.

But numbers don't tell the full story. If you talk to any local prosecutor, you will find out that more and more of the gang members are increasingly young, 12 or 13 years old. We have an increasing problem with witness intimidation. People who do step forward to testify against gang crime many times pay the price with their very lives. We see that gang members are now using technology more and more. They have their own Web sites. Major gangs have their own Web sites. Google up the gang names.

We have disputes that have begun in our community, my jurisdiction of Rockford, Illinois, where we think we have got the situation kind of calmed down, well, then the gang members use their pages on MySpace to further disrespect other gang members, competing gang members, and the fight begins again. What starts on MySpace erupts into violence in the community.

We see gangs out of Chicago moving into central Wisconsin with the Native Americans and developing new drug markets by introducing cheap drugs and then eventually raising the prices when they get the young members of the tribes in Central Wisconsin addicted to drugs. Very effective marketing strategies. These are sophisticated organizations.

We need the combined efforts of State, local and Federal law enforcement, but local prosecutors can lead community involvement. We are connected to the community. We can bring those resources together and combine effective prosecution for those gang members who have already stepped over the line, but also mobilizing the community to prevent it in the first place.

We welcomed Mr. Kennedy to our jurisdiction just recently and we are laying the groundwork for a program that he described this morning within my jurisdiction.

We, in our team effort, welcome the assistance from Federal law enforcement, the ATF, ICE, Secret Service, FBI, the local U.S. Attorneys Office. And, in fact, the local U.S. Attorney is working with us on Mr. Kennedy's program and helped to bring several of our local people down to the National Advocacy Center in Columbia, South Carolina for training just in that program.

We could also use Federal assistance in the area of preventing witness intimidation. We support, in principle, I believe we support specifically H.R. 933, introduced by Mr. Cummings, that would provide Federal support for local efforts to protect witnesses to violent crime.

We need to be proactive in our communities, to identify gang threats early and to respond decisively. As we testified, the gang problem is growing.

On behalf of America's prosecutors, I and the National District Attorneys Association urge you to take steps to provide Federal assistance to State efforts to fight our gang problems, to provide us with the resources to effectively prosecute and to protect victims and the witnesses to violent crime.

Thank you, Mr. Chairman.

[The prepared statement of Mr. Logli follows:]

Prepared Statement of Paul Logli

My name is Paul Logli and I am the elected State's Attorney in Winnebago County, Illinois. I am now the Chairman of the Board of the National District AttorneysAssociation.

I want to thank Chairman Scott, on behalf of the National District Attorneys Association, for the opportunity to present our concerns about gang violence and share some thoughts on what as America's prosecutors, and you the Congress, can do to counter this threat to public safety. The views that I express today represent the views of our Association and the beliefs of thousands of local prosecutors across this country.

I was privileged to testify before you in April 2005 and would like to begin with that testimony as the juncture for where we go today. I would also like to commend to you the testimony by the Honorable Robert P. McCulloch, Prosecuting Attorney of St. Louis County, Missouri, when he was NDAA president, before a hearing of the Senate Committee on the Judiciary on September 17, 2003

LOCAL GANG PROBLEMS

When I testified before you previously I cited the 2002 National Youth Gang Survey, published by the Office of Juvenile Justice and Delinquency Prevention of the Department of Justice which then estimated that there were approximately 731,500 gang members and 21,500 gangs were active in the United States in 2002.

That same report for 2004 (published in 2006) indicates that the number of gang members had grown to 760,000 and there were 24,000 gangs; increases of 4% and 12% respectively in a 2 year period. Please remember that this report is three years old and we can only expect that the next will show a comparable or even greater increase.

Two years ago in April 2005, I testified before this very same Committee and described the gang situation in my jurisdiction of Winnebago County, Illinois, population 290,000. Let me remind you, my jurisdiction is located in the top tier of counties in the State of Illinois. We are an easy 1 1/2 hour drive from Chicago and, to our north, Milwaukee, Wisconsin. Both cities have experienced significant gang activity and that gang activity has certainly had an effect on my jurisdiction. Two years ago I mentioned that Hispanic or Latino gangs had become major players in criminal activity in Winnebago County. Inter-gang warfare between several of those gangs had resulted in fire-bombings and murders. Recently the Rockford Police Department, which is the largest law enforcement agency in my jurisdiction, prepared a report detailing gang-related activity from August through December 2006. Inthose 5 months we had identified 101 major felony arrests tied into various street gangs. Thirty-seven firearms were recovered in the investigations surrounding those incidents.

In that 5 month window we have identified nearly a dozen street gangs, but the criminal activity is definitely dominated by the Latino gangs namely, the Latin Kings and the Surreno 13. The gangs do not appear to be highly structured or organized. They are, however, comprised of individuals who once having identified an enemy and starting a dispute will keep that dispute alive until it erupts into violent activity in the streets of our city. Many of the gang members now use their pages on MySpace to disrespect opposing gang members. It seems that just when a dispute might settle down it is quickly re-energized through the trading of on-line insults and other methods of disrespect. Quickly the dispute once again escalates intoviolence on our streets. Investigation into these incidents is obviously hampered by language difficulties and a lack of cooperation among many of the young people of the Latino community. A distrust of the police and authorities in their native countries has been transferred to this country.

NUMBERS DON'T TELL THE FULL STORY

As with all things, pure numbers don't portray an accurate picture of what law enforcement is seeing in the way of several disturbing trends

Younger Gang Members and Victims

Perhaps most troubling is that we are seeing even younger children recruited into the gangs, providing support for the activity of gangs or being caught up in gangviolence. Couple this with parents or adult mentors who entrench the gangster mentality in these children and the availability of illegal guns and drugs and you have the making of our current predicament.

In Sacramento a 15 year old boy was shot in the head as he was walking with students leaving his high school at 2:30 in the afternoon. The drive by shooting was witnessed by police officers and a vehicle was stopped. The first person out of thevan was a six year old holding his birthday balloon. A mother and her three children were accompanying her boyfriend and his gangster friends on a drive-by shooting. It was the six-year-olds birthday.

In San Mateo, California, it is not unusual to find ''third strikers'' who are not even 21 but facing life in prison.

Last week there was the story from New Orleans of the mother who gave her sona gun after he lost a fight. His mother sent him back out with a gun clear and instructions to get revenge. He did as his mother instructed and killed the 17 year old boy who had beaten him up. At home ''mother'' had a picture of her son holding the murder weapon and a wad of money.

In Queens, New York, an undercover drug operation in public housing last year led to the arrest of defendants who ranged in age from 15 to 62. They included fivealleged Bloods gang members and nine GIB (acronym for ''Get It In Bricks'') gang members who were charged with selling crack and powdered cocaine, heroin, oxycontin and marijuana to undercover police officers on more than 140 separate occasions

Albuquerque tells us that a very violent gang there is currently moving large amounts of meth out of Mexico, hiring Mexican nationals to run the drugs for them,and then selling it on the street with the use of younger, minor gang members. The increasing use of 16- and 17-year-olds involved in violent crimes, usually with an older gang member who has the juvenile ''do the dirty work'' is based on the belief that the juvenile will not get any time. In some cases this is true.

Wichita, Kansas tells a similar story. In 2005, 141 juveniles between the ages of 13 and 17 joined gangs and 147 juveniles between the ages of 13 and 17 became ''associate gang members.'' The youngest child claiming to be a gang member was 7 years old!

Columbia, South Carolina is also facing an increase of younger gang members. An 11 year old claimed to be the ''baby set'' king for Folk Nation; 20 kids wore home made t-shirts to schools on the same day that read ''Stop Snitching'' to scare a fellow class mate who was helping the police investigate a series of car break-ins; and school official estimate that a quarter of the fights that break out in Middle School and High School usually involve someone ''disrespecting'' someone else's gang by using the words ''Donut'' (insults a Folk), ''Crab'' (insults a Crypt) and ''Slob'' (Insults a Blood). Most schools have cracked down on kids wearing certain colors so the kids have begun to change the color of their shoe laces, wear band-aids in certain locations, or wear name brand name university logos that have gang meanings (e.g. UNC for Crypts).

Gang ''wanna be's'' also contribute to the increased participation of juveniles in gang activities. In Kalispell, MT, the ''406 Crips'' appeared and ultimately turned out to be a half dozen local boys aged 14–16 that formed that ''gang.'' New initiates had to get jumped by their crew to be initiated. In addition to the ''406 Crips'' there are also the ''F 13's'' and the ''440 GGG's.'' The latter is a new group to law enforcement but they believe that its members range from 13–16 years of age and are a mix of males and females. They do know that several purported members have had previous contact with the Youth Court.

Even when they don't actively join a gang, the violence associated with gang life impacts our children. Hmong gangsters in Sacramento spotted rivals in the middle of a crowded intersection at 1:00 on a Sunday afternoon. Two of them got out of their vehicle and fired fourteen shots into their enemy's car. They did this while standing next to a church bus filled with children on a field trip. The shooters walked back to their car but the light was red and they were stuck in Sunday afternoon traffic. Twenty five children witnessed a gang execution, along with countless citizens stuck at a major intersection of south Sacramento

Witness Intimidation

In my previous testimony I alluded to ''Attacks on Our Criminal Justice System'' and the problems we were encountering in protecting witnesses to gang criminal enterprise. This has almost become epidemic in proportion.

Let me have the words of a veteran prosecutor from Queens, New York, portray what they face:

> ''There are issues that are inherent to these (gang) cases and experienced by gang prosecutors throughout the country. The most vital issue is the issue of witness cooperation. Victims of gang violence and eyewitnesses are loathe to report or cooperate with the police and the Prosecutor's office. The universal reason is fear. They fear retaliation. Unlike perpetrators of other types of crime, gang members who are arrested, leave behind armies of loyal members who are free to intimidate and threaten witnesses. Many of the crimes occur either at or near the victim/witness' home or school. These are areas that the victim or witness must return to on a daily basis. These types of crimes cannot be prosecuted without civilian witnesses. In order to win the battle against these violent gangs we must be armed with more resources to ensure the safety of witnesses. Witness protection funds are generally scarce and precious. Due to the limited nature of such funds, the guidelines for moving someone out of a public housing project usually require an actual threat. We cannot cultivate a witness' trust and confidence in the Criminal Justice System if we are saying to them ''we cannot help you until the gang has made its move.'' Increased funding will allow us to take preemptive steps such as relocation, assignment of detectives, or even a simple cell phone to facilitate contact with the police.''

Across the county, in San Bernardino, California, two recent cases aptly make the New York prosecutor's point. In the first, a gang member, paroled from prison after serving time for a carjacking, forced his way into the house of a witness who had testified against him. He shot and killed the witness and has father and wounded the witnesses' infant son who was sitting on his lap. In the second case, a witness, who had testified against 2 gang members in a murder trial, was dragged from his apartment, after being beaten and when his body is found later it had 25 bullet holes in the head and chest. According to media reports the witness had known that the gang was after him, and "lived a 'life on the run'—even sleeping while wearing his shoes and using drugs to stay awake as much as possible."

A young girl paid with her life in Houston, Texas, for taking a stand against a gang. One gang member got into an altercation with another drug dealer from New Orleans over whose turn it was to sell drugs to a crackhead. After the fight was over, the defendant told the other drug dealer that he was going to come back and kill him, and that is exactly what he did. A fifteen year old girl was the only witness and she was brave enough to come forward and tell the police. A cousin to the first defendant found out she was talking to the police and he and the defendant threatened to kill her if she continued to cooperate with the law. Because she continued to cooperate, the defendant was arrested and when the cousin found out, he assaulted the girl. The cousin was charged with retaliation. Then the fifteen year old girl turned up missing. She was finally identified as a homicide victim just a few days after the retaliation warrant was executed. She was found with multiple gunshot wounds to the head and body in the parking lot of an apartment complex some distance from her home.

Use of Technology

Gangs are also becoming more sophisticated in the use of technology to bolster their efforts. Social networking sites on the web are replacing graffiti on walls as places for gangs to boast of their exploits and recruit members. Perhaps most chilling are reports from Mexico where gangs have adopted the media techniques of Middle Eastern terrorists and show scenes of torture and murder on these sites to scare off competitors and boast of their both prowess.

Nationally gangs such as 'The Latin Kings,' 'Bloods,' and 'Crips,' have websites on the Internet. They are savvy at protecting the contents of the sites from nonmembers by creating viruses that attack a nonmember's computer of they get onto the sites. This allows Sets from all over the country to communicate with each other. The "My Space.Com" is highly popular with Gangs, promoting gang culture to other teens and posting photos of young members holding weapons and other criminal proceeds.

Most drug gangs have began to use anonymous, throwaway phones and switching out chips in phones to avoid wire taps. Law enforcement in Staten Island had information that one of these gangs had gotten their wire tap information from watching "The Wire."

The District Attorney in Albuquerque tells us that after a recent homicide of a 17-year-old gang member, a social website showed his picture with an X across it and 187. The numbers "187" refer to a part of the California penal code on murder, thus making it made clear this was retribution for a previous shooting.

An interesting article last Sunday, from Newhouse News Service, articulated how thug life has realized the value of the internet. The article stated that:

> "But in a few clicks of a computer mouse, online viewers can see all sorts of videos, music and other Web postings with clear depictions of young men who authorities say are known members of Trenton's Sex Money Murder Bloods.
>
> In about 15 videos posted on YouTube.com and at least two My Space.com pages, young men who identify themselves as members of the gang have posted rap music

> videos and other footage and pictures of them hanging out on Trenton streets and partying together, clad in red and flashing what authorities say are gang signs.
>
> In several of the YouTube videos, city housing projects are clearly visible as young men brag using their street names. And in one, a man is filmed arriving at his sentencing at the Mercer County Courthouse in Trenton, bidding his friends farewell as they sip from a bottle of Remy Martin cognac.''

Providence, Rhode Island has seen this use of social web sites to glorify gang life. Recently there was a felony assault on a Crip by a Blood using a baseball bat. The victim barely survived and had no idea who attacked him. Members of the Providence Police Gang Squad started to monitor web sites. They found a site created by one of the Blood members. That member had included on his site a hard-core rap song that he sang bragging about the specific details of the crime.

One prosecutor from the Washington suburbs painted this use if technology in perhaps a much more personal vein.

> ''Less than two years ago, my daughter was in 6th grade in a public school. One day I was talking with my wife about gang activity. My daughter chimed in with some disturbing statements: that their are mostly CRIPS in her school, that CRIPS aren't that bad, that lots of kids wear colors, that a CRIP had been knifed (in New Jersey). She also asked whether all CRIPS were bad people and similar suggestive questions. As it turns out, in addition to the stories and glorification of gangs being spread by other kids in school, she had also been online chatting (AIM) with a proclaimed CRIP in New Jersey who passed on the knifing story. My daughter was also going through a phase that included rap/ hip hop style music which led her to innocently mimicking some gang hand signs when having her picture taken. Needless to say, the AIM program was deleted and other precautions have been taken.''

To see how gangs use the web visit *http://www.clantone.net/ ; www.chicagomobs.org ; www.chicagogangs.org*

New Markets and Threats

The ''business plan'' of some of the gangs could be used as a text book study in any MBA program. A rural county in Wisconsin is home to a rather significant population of Native American members of the Ho Chunk Nation. Over the past few of years a group of members of Gangster Disciple gangs in Chicago have traveled to this rural area for the purpose of expanding their crack cocaine distribution network. Crack cocaine has obviously been a problem for some time but in this case the method of distribution was new. Gang members began going there 2 years ago and setting up drug houses where cocaine was given away or sold at fire sale prices for the purpose of growing the market base and creating new addicts. The dealers would rotate; some would travel for re-supply while others sold. As the market expanded these dealers targeted the Native American population and began appearing en masse on ''Per capita payment day,'' a quarterly event where members of the Ho Chunk Nation received their portion of the tribes gaming proceeds. Reminiscent of the traders on the frontier the gang members would sell crack cocaine to all of the newly grown addicts at full price.

The adaptability of gangs is something we all need to take into consideration when we explore the means and methods to counter or end their influence. Nothing is more illustrative then their increasing forays into the sale and distribution of meth. With the passage of the Combat Meth Act the Congress gave the states a powerful tool by which they apparently have been able to drastically reduce the number of meth labs. While the Combat Meth Act helped the environment and has provided added protections for our children who were exposed to the harmful by-products of meth production there is still a demand for meth. Gangs have been able to swiftly and effectively exploit that need for meth and fill that void.

Gangs are also starting to go into mortgage fraud; an easy way to launder their money and look legitimate in the process. Cook County (Chicago) just charged a Gangster Disciple with mortgage fraud. He would buy a property at foreclosure, get a phony appraisal, get an unsuspecting buyer, phony up their income, then make a profit at closing. The Black Disciples have also engaged in mortgage fraud and even also bought a radio station and used it to warn their dealers on the street when the police would be coming.

Gangs are expanding beyond their ‘‘historical’’ turf in new and alarming ways. Houston has experienced what may be a new trend in violent gang crime, where gangs have been sending for a member from another state or country to do a hit. They then send the hit man back home and there is little, if any trail, of the hit man.

And perhaps most disturbing is the recent report from Los Angeles where ethic ‘‘cleansing’’ has become a goal of gang life. This is a concept alien to the American culture but it appears that Hispanic gangs have set out to kill members of the African-American community because they live in a largely Hispanic community.

Popular Misconceptions

First I want to disabuse the members of this Subcommittee, and any who read my testimony, from thinking that I, or any other prosecutor, is only concerned with trying gang members. To counter this gang problem we need effective community partnerships to deter our children from becoming enamored with the ‘‘thug life.’’ While we need strong and effective criminal prosecutions we also need diversion programs to lure back those that have crossed the line. Lastly we need to develop meaningful re-entry programs to give those who have known little else but gang life a chance to succeed after they serve time.

No one facet of this will accomplish what we need to do. If we don’t deter our youth from the gangs then we will have a never ending prosecution and imprisonment process we have to remove those who serve as evil influences—either by incarceration or by changing their desire to be a gang banger by giving them a chance to a meaningful existence.

Secondly I want to emphasize that gang members are not dumb—their use of technology, and what can almost be described as ‘‘business plans’’ and their adaptability aptly illustrate their ‘‘smarts.’’ Unhampered by the need for legislative action or procurement rules they can be much more responsive to changing circumstances than law enforcement—unless we work smarter.

EFFECTIVE STRATEGIES

Community Teamwork

Many of our communities have developed what appear to be effective strategies to counter the gangs, and gang ''wanna be's'' that threaten their safety and security.

The combined efforts of state, local and federal law enforcement are key elements but they cannot succeed without enlisting the will of the community. To this end we need to make sure that we use our all too scarce resources effectively and efficiently. As I stated when I testified before you in 2003

> ''Local prosecutors are successful in prosecuting crime because they have the expertise, experience and connection to the community that is needed to combat the types of crimes that most affect the American people, and, under consideration here, in combating gang violence.''

I think the key words here are ''connection to the community.'' We have the abilityto be able to mobilize all the resources of our towns and counties to end gang violence. This is the ultimate in the idea of ''community prosecution''—that is getting out into our communities to work with our citizens and to mobilize their efforts and talents.

As part of our responsibilities we need to lead efforts for gang deterrence programs and be instrumental in the re-entry effort. In the summer of 2005 the Boardof Directors of NDAA adopted a formal resolution that states

> ''(T)he National District Attorneys Association believes that prisoner reentryhas become a crucial criminal justice issue. While the NDAA recognizes that the role of prosecutors in the arena of prisoner re-entry will vary according to individual state law, America's prosecutors should, where practicable, be participants in addressing this issue in an effort to reduce recidivism and ensure the safety of victims and the community.''

A copy of that complete policy can be found the NDAA our website at *http://www.ndaa.org/pdf/policy—position—prisoner—reentry—july—17—05.pdf*

In this team effort we do need assistance from Federal law enforcement. The ATF, ICE , the Secret Service and all the other federal agencies have played key roles in those communities that have shown the most success in combating gangs. These agencies have the resources and technical capabilities many local agencies do not have or need only on rare occasions. As the gangs become more dependant on technology the federal capability to conduct electronic surveillance, for instance, is crucial.

I repeat what I said the last time I was here because it is crucial to what we need to do.

> ''It is the ability to bring the respective talents and resources of the local and federal authorities together at the appropriate times that result in the successes we are all looking for in the fight against gangs. I would urge that this become the hallmark of your efforts in ending gang violence.''

As a cautionary note, however, I would like to emphasize that the federal tendency to make ''one size fit all'' works counter to the strength of utilizing community efforts. Our communities differ, our gang problems differ and accordingly our responses must differ. What Congress can bring to this is the flexibility and adaptability to meet the will of our communities.

Witness Intimidation

Prosecutors across the county believe that the issue of witness intimidation is the single biggest hurdle facing any successful gang prosecution. As you've seen from the trends we're facing, the problem of witness intimidation and retaliation is increasing drastically. Various jurisdictions have tried to establish some type of witness protection program but lack of resources and fearful witnesses are difficult obstacles to overcome.

While NDAA had not taken a formal position on H.R.933, introduced by Mr. Cummings, we have supported this effort in the past and I would see no reason why we won't be supportive in this Congress. It would establish within the United States Marshals Service a short term State witness protection program to provide assistance to State and local district attorneys to protect their witnesses in cases involving homicide, serious violent felonies, and serious drug offenses, and to provide Federal grants for such protection.

In addition I would urge that you consider providing funding to study what works for witness protection programs at the state and local level, provide ''seed'' money to begin programs and then help the states find sources of revenues to continue to fund these programs.

Funding for Local Prosecution Efforts

We need to be proactive in our communities to identify gang threats early and respond decisively. Two years ago I testified that our resources were stretched thin—since then the resources of all local prosecutors in the United States have been cut even more.

DeKalb County, Georgia is a prime example of the problem that faces local law enforcement. The County has a population of 700,000 with over 2500 documented gang members representing over 140 gangs. The local police department has only 1000 officers; meaning they have anywhere from 2.5 to 5 gang members for every police officer on the street. Only 4 officers are designated as Gang Detectives and 1 ICE agent is assigned to this area. There are approximately 107,000 students in local schools and only 2 School Resource Officers are dedicated to gang intelligence. The County does not have the ''luxury'' of dedicating even one prosecutor full time for gangs; they hope one will be funded out of their next budget

Clearly, additional resources in this area are a critical need and if used wisely they will make a positive difference.

On behalf of America's prosecutors I, and the National District Attorneys Association, urge you to take steps to provide federal assistance to state efforts to fight our gang problems and to provide us with the resources to effectively protect those brave enough to confront the gang bangers. We look forward to continuing to work with you on addressing this growing problem.

TESTIMONY OF TENY GROSS. EXECUTIVE DIRECTOR, INSTITUTE FOR THE STUDY AND PRACTICE OF NONVIOLENCE, PROVIDENCE, RI

Mr. GROSS. My name is Teny Gross. It is a true honor to be here.

I wish my parents were alive. My dad, after World War II—my first bar of chocolate was from an American G.I., and my older sister used to take me to the American Embassy for the library every Tuesday to borrow books, and I ended up marrying an American girl and ended up working in Boston for 10 years and now 5 years in Providence, Rhode Island.

What happens in this civilization matters a lot. This is the longest running democracy on the planet, in history, in fact. The Athenian democracy lived a lot shorter and it does concern a lot of us; the levels of violence are absolutely astounding. It is actually safer to be an Israeli soldier in uniform in Lebanon than it is to be an African-American man in Washington, D.C., between the age of 17 to 40. That is a staggering, staggering statistic.

We have lost in the last 25 years about 580,000 people to homicide; 10 Vietnam Wars. Those are things that we live in. I dream of speaking to our elites at 3 in the morning at the emergency room when we are picking up the pieces.

Before I move on, I just want to introduce three of our street workers that we brought over from Providence who work at the Institute. Senior street worker A.J. Benson, street worker David Cartagena and street worker Sal Monteiro, who have seen the streets, have been involved with gangs, have been involved with violence and are now legends and constantly called upon by educators, by social workers, by doctors, by police officers, to mediate conflicts in the city.

I have studied in some very, very fine schools in this country and I love philosophy, but what I will speak about today is from pure experience of 15 years in the trenches.

In two cities now, particularly in Boston and in Providence, where I have worked, I have seen that a smart group, a partnership by a very motivated and concentrated group of people, like prevention, like a few academics, gang unit officers, clergy and youth workers can make a huge amount of difference. When you bring these five groups together, you basically have the intelligence on the whole city, who is committing the violence.

One of the efforts that David led in Boston was, initially the problem was 60,000 children. We narrowed it down to 1,200 gang members, 300 are hard core. You see how it becomes a more rationale problem to tackle?

And then, really, we are the linebacker. We are really the ones who are everyday trying to hit those conflicts, work on them, mediate them. Violence is very, very rarely random. It is between known people.

So Philadelphia recently, by November 15, I think I read in the Enquirer, picked up 5,000 guns and still homicide peaked over 400. We cannot just go after the guns. Someone is using it against someone they know.

What we do in Providence now, we have perfected the Boston model. It is a more sophisticated one. Any time there is a conflict in school, little things, we are already jumping on it. We have meetings like police com stat, where we look at the current conflicts, we assign them to street workers. Street workers know different gangs, they come from different gangs, they come from different sides of town.

So we always, as opposed to the social worker model, where you know a client and you try to serve them, we actually know your enemy. The fact that Teny now wants to go to college after he has inflicted pain on his city meant nothing if my enemy doesn't let me do that. You need someone on the other side, and that is what we do.

When I went out, recently, about a year ago, a major shooter of an Asian gang said to me, away from his crew, in the park, he said, ''Teny, I am exhausted. I wish I could live in the suburbs.''

Well, David has worked with him in that year, and he has been taken away to Job Corps in another State, removed from that environment, which is what he wanted. You keep him in that environment, he is going to continue to be a shooter. He has too many conflicts.

So there is no cookie cutter solution, but we do know the solutions now. It is going to take having practitioners. One of the things that I am dazzled with, when I come at 3 in the morning, back from an emergency room and I have to wind down, I look on the Internet. We spend a lot of money on research, we spend a lot of money on pilot programs. We have no stamina. I wish we picked up a little bit from the Japanese and looked a little bit at longer-term solutions.

It is almost like sending the Army to Iraq just for having researchers at the Pentagon. You need people in the trenches. And most of us work in programs. I have the greatest support of the mayor. The chief is on our board. The U.S. Attorney has helped fund us. And it is still a massive struggle to fund 13 street workers.

So there are good programs, and I am here on the panel with people I admire and there are everywhere around the country great people, and we are all burning out. There is nothing to sustain us. And so using Congress actually—I was listening to talks related to the funding community and foundations, none of them really fund practitioners. They have moved now to change policy. They have moved now to pilot programs.

We need to change the model of funding. There are people who need to be in this field and you cannot keep them. It is an anomaly to have someone like me, with a Master's from Harvard, staying in this field at 41 with no retirement. It is an anomaly. It shouldn't be.

We need to rebuild—if I would suggest research as well, to have a practical research that, what will it take to build an infrastructure of youth workers around the country. What are the expenses? We will have a library on the second floor. There will be a jazz orchestra where the kids learn. There will be a theatre program.

We need to bring civilization back to the neighborhoods where violence happens. I was stunned in Providence that only one full-time person is in a rec center and the only training they had in the last 20 years is CPR. And those are the people we want to turn the attitudes of our kids? We are absolutely shooting ourselves in the leg.

I have to stop here. Thank you.

[The reference material of Mr. Gross follows:]

REFERENCE MATERIAL OF TENY GROSS

Teny Gross

From: Teny Gross [teny@nonviolenceinstitute.org]
Sent: Sunday, July 09, 2006 12:44 PM
To: 'teny@nonviolenceinstitute.org'
Subject: Edwatch by Julia Steiny: A plea to turn mean streets into a 'beloved community' (Providence Journal)

projo.com
The Providence Journal

Edwatch by Julia Steiny: A plea to turn mean streets into a 'beloved community'

Sunday, July 9, 2006

According to Teny Gross, "Boston has 11,000 summer jobs for kids. D.C. has 11,000. Providence has maybe 400, and 37 of them are ours."

By "ours," Gross means jobs offered by the agency he directs, the Institute for the Study & Practice of Nonviolence. The institute focuses much of its effort on urban youth, and summer is a volatile time for high-energy teens. Gross, the institute's executive director, all but gloats over a report by the Justice Policy Institute that found a direct correlation between unemployment rates and incidents of violent crime and juvenile justice referrals. In short, summer jobs reduce street crime.

Gross says, "During the summer, city kids learn how to be in a gang, how to drink, take drugs. Their parents are working and can't be home to watch them. But the kids are still learning. The human mind is always learning, but we leave thousands of kids to learn what they can from the streets in the summer. We've forgotten what childhood is. It's the boot camp of adulthood. And what is boot camp but the place that teaches you the culture of the organization. This is how we do business here. So the summer is absolutely critical."

On Wednesday, Gross stood with Providence's Mayor David Cicilline and Police Chief Dean Esserman at a news conference, urging the business community to either hire kids directly or to create 20-hour-a-week work opportunities that the institute can combine with training in nonviolence, for the "Beloved Community" summer program.

Nonviolence-education programs are the institute's stock in trade. The programs run in the public schools, the Police Academy, the Training School and the Adult Correctional Institutions. For a taste of their message, here's what Gross said recently to a group of fathers in maximum security at the ACI, "We got to stop this pit bull society. You train your boys, your sons, to look hard on the street. I want you to show your boys how to be soft -- crying, laughing. Looking hard doesn't look so tough in the funeral home. Teach them to be soft so they can stay alive. Teach them that learning is what's hard."

As an Israeli, Gross grew up in the midst of war and was himself a soldier, so he added, "Being an Israeli helps on the streets. People know I don't come from soft." (The institute's Web site has more on his personal story – www.nonviolenceinstitute.org)

But you can't teach peace only by talking about it. Peace in American cities also requires getting out onto the streets themselves and befriending kids. Sadly, the principal education of many young people in urban poverty is on the streets. Poor males may not have money or opportunity, but they have their dignity, which for many is hard won in literal battles – fistfights, gang warfare and other proving grounds. The currency most valued is a reputation for being tough and hard.

Gross is hell-bent on reshaping that culture by getting as many nonviolence-trained adults as possible out there. He's a nut about how badly all kids need close adult relationships. Only when they have personal relationships with peaceful adults will there ever be any hope of turning them away from the real-life violence so irresponsibly glamorized by the entertainment industry.

Gross illustrates the kinds of toxic adult relationships all too available to urban teens by relating what a drug dealer, Sal, told him years ago. "Sal says, 'I'm here in the morning when Johnny goes to school. I'm here when he goes home. His mom gives him a buck to get milk; I give him another for orange juice. I'm here all the time. You're not. I win.' "

So the institute hires streetworkers -- there are 10 now -- to provide alternatives to the Sals of this world. The streetworkers make themselves available to anyone trying to settle a beef; they mentor kids and hang out wherever folks gather in order to learn about potentially explosive parties, feuds, tempers, the flow of drugs and so forth. The institute would dearly love to have 15, but money is a persistent and burdensome problem.

The streetworkers are men and women who themselves grew up steeped in street culture, experts, as it were, on the harsh, macho rules of engagement that quickly escalate to violence if left unchecked. Some have been to jail; some have not. But neighborhoods trust these people. Perpetrators of gun battles and fights have been known to protect streetworkers from harm. Gross believes that the 'hood would never trust people from the outside with the kind of information that helps the workers disarm or stop fights.

Not surprisingly, the streetworkers and the police have rubbed each other wrong, on occasion, but in general, the institute has an excellent working relationship with the police. Gross admires Chief Esserman and appreciates his department's partnership. Gross notes that "even the cops say we can't arrest our way out of this problem. But this country always chooses law enforcement solutions."

Gross would invest in relationships. "The trend in America has been: Let's fund the research and evaluation. So we're funding the thinking class, the chattering classes. But what you need is boots on the ground. And those boots need to be hired from the neighborhoods.

"We need to get off our high horses and get with the kids. When kids drop out, we, the adults, failed them."

No kidding. And in the summer, when most schools are taking a break, business, government and after-school programs need to pick up the slack. Perhaps it's time to invent a youth WPA summer project -- fix up a school, plant a park -- something in which the kids can take ownership, learn useful skills, interact with community adults and be proudly productive. Hopefully, more and more people, businesses and agencies will help Gross and the institute do the job this culture shirks.

Gross can't believe what a low priority kids are in America.

Neither can I.

THE RELUCTANT

WARRIOR

As the intrepid director of the Institute for the Study and Practice of Nonviolence, **TENY GROSS** survives on caffeine and willpower. But the prophet of Providence would love to put himself out of a job.

by DENISE DOWLING photography by JARED LEEDS

It's Halloween night, near the witching hour.

Boys lurk behind bushes, eggs cradled in their palms, ready to strip the paint job from another car. Teny Gross, executive director of the Providence-based Institute for the Study and Practice of Nonviolence, steers his Ford Contour with such ease that a passenger feels safe even on shooting gallery streets. In the Smith Hill section of Providence, Gross spies a boy called Trouble and brakes to say hello. Trouble is what most people smell when he approaches. They avert their eyes, willing themselves invisible and refusing to *truly see* Trouble. The sixteen-year-old agrees to visit the Institute for job corps training the next day. He had promised to go that afternoon, so his words may echo tomorrow, but the hello from Teny could sway Trouble. "Jobs are part of the solution, but they're a vehicle," Gross says. "Kids want that relationship with adults."

Gross has just left Rhode Island Hospital, where he watched a twenty-year-old stabbing victim being wheeled into the operating room. As the man flutters between life and death, retaliation is a threat. Gross learned the color of the victim's bandana, so he knows which crews to check on. At one stop, baby-faced boys play Dominoes at a card table in an apartment complex driveway. A cooler of Poland Spring and Heinekens ice at their feet, but most tug at the water. They belong to one of the city's most prominent Cambodian gangs. The eldest plans to move to Texas and get lost in the biggest state in the union because there's no shelter in the smallest. "To really retire from a gang, you have to move out of state," Gross says, "especially in the Cambodian community, where friends and enemies are tightly knit." The boys are on the cusp of adulthood. The American Dream is on their horizon, but they suffer from what writer Katherine Boo terms a "poverty of the imagination — the inability to envision a future truly different from the present."

The forty-year-old Gross is accompanied by Senator Juan Pichardo, the Democratic representative for district two, which spans the West End, Reservoir district and Elmwood, where Gross resides. "The eldest is lucky to be alive," Gross says as they climb back in the Contour. "A good chunk of his brain was blown away." Another boy, soft-spoken and sixteen, just dropped out of school. He grew up with six brothers but only three remain: one died in Thailand and two more were shot in Providence.

Gross wanted Pichardo to hear the boys' foggy dreams — to graduate high school, get a driver's license and a job — before judging them for their alleged crimes. Some of these sober, polite boys await trial; they are charged with being the trigger fingers in a few homicides. "Gang members are not freaks," Gross says. "These are not sophisticated Mafioso organizations — it's a bunch of kids fighting other kids." If the eldest chooses to exit the gang, the Institute street workers can negotiate that he be courted or walked out (allowed to leave without consequence), instead of being jumped out (beaten up by the group). In one such case, they could only help to minimize a boy's beating. This is the currency of nonviolence work: bartering for one less broken rib, for bruises instead of blood.

Between mediating at the police station and the hospital, Gross is out until 3 a.m. He will wake four hours later for a meeting at the police department. Gross doesn't take vacations, sick days or weekends off; he remembers to eat lunch if he has a lunch meeting. His cell phone is an alarm clock bleating in the dark to summon him to another drive-by or another stabbing. As he glides to the emergency room, Gross may be listening to Miles Davis, but his own sound loop nags: *Why? Why did this happen? What could I have done to prevent it?* He is deeply forgiving of others but merciless on himself.

Gross had an ulcer by age nineteen. He was a soldier in the Israeli Army when the burning began, a soldier who became sergeant during three years of duty. Bombs and bullets rained like fireworks in his homeland, but Gross says there is more danger to dodge on Providence streets than in his native Israel. This city of 178,000 people suffered twenty-two homicides in 2005; six of those victims were eighteen years old or younger. During a fifty-four-hour span this past New Year's weekend, at least four people were stabbed and two were shot dead. "Ask any minority kid in Providence if they know someone who died, and they will say yes," Gross notes. "As a soldier and someone who grew up under constant war, I didn't know people who died. I should not be in the richest country in the world doing a job that is riskier than growing up in Israel. We blame the families and the victims and their behavior, but violence is a manmade crisis. It's the result of choices made by the state and by all of us. I understand there are people who made it out of the ghetto and became successful, but it's not a good

Teny Gross and Providence police officers at Kennedy Plaza. Below: Gross points out gang graffiti on Bucklin Street in Providence's Elmwood neighborhood.

yardstick. People made it out of Auschwitz, too." The ulcer is gone, but Gross still burns.

Gross was hired in 2001, a year after the nonprofit was founded by the team ministry of St. Michael's Rectory in South Providence. Institute tentacles stretch from the halls of justice to halls of lockers. A power blazer hangs from a nail on his office wall at St. Michael's, but Gross favors T-shirts and jeans. Standing six-feet one-inch with a crown of salt and pepper curls, he is a striking presence whose speeches are poetry. Institute endeavors are too myriad to detail, but include finding jobs and Graduate Equivalency Degree classes for dropouts and placing students in after-school programs so their hands won't be idle and their minds will be opened. It also facilitates safety transfers, escorting students who avoid school because they are easy targets en route. Nonviolence is about teaching communication skills that prevent violence, Gross says. His staff educates the public and police about juvenile crime,

advocates for children in court, mediates family and gang feuds and trains students in conflict resolution by having them act out different scenarios.

If MS-13, a gang rumored to use knives or machetes instead of guns — supposedly to avoid federal time and because they like to see their victims up close and personal — has a beef with the Original Crib Gang, the Institute is on call. When Club Diesel shuts its doors at 2 a.m., youth workers idle outside, ready to defuse a Molotov cocktail of booze, brawn and bullets.

"The lack of empathy from these kids can be stunning, but if you breed ignorance, if you show people you don't care about them and you mix guns with that indifference, you will get brutal results."

One of Gross's youth workers was shot at and a few others witnessed a murder. Risking their lives to prevent death is beyond reproach, but the Institute has its critics. For starters, Gross is a maverick who doesn't mince words. "I can be a bit brash," says the Israeli who had the chutzpah to meet with members of Hamas, the militant Palestinian party. If he was willing to risk his life going into Lebanon and Palestinian refugee camps as a soldier, Gross reasoned, he should be prepared to gamble it for peace. When a seventeen-year-old couldn't participate in job corps because he'd be a ghost if enemies knew his routine, Gross paid the boy to read books. "Teny is fearless and tenacious," says Jed Hresko, who supervised Gross's street work in Boston. "He stands up to people when no one else will, and he gets away with it because he deals straight with adults just like he does with kids."

Police Captain Anthony Sauro, who supervises districts one through five in Providence, credits the Institute for changing district four (the West End and Federal Hill). "It was the most violent district, but a year and a half after the Institute's presence, violent crime was down 50 percent," Sauro notes. "Last fall we had a riot at Kennedy Plaza. The street workers weren't there, and police were trying to control about 400 kids. We made eight arrests that afternoon. It was East Side versus South Side kids, throwing bottles and bricks at each other, breaking car windows. All of a sudden George Lindsey [co-coordinator of the street worker program] drives up to the South Providence guys and says, 'What are you doing? Let's get out of here.' And they just turned around and followed him."

"There's no question that the Institute deserves credit for helping to reduce the violence in this city," says Providence Police Chief Dean Esserman. "I respond to every shooting and go to every hospital bed. I have never been there without running into Teny or one of his street workers." The partnership between the police department and the street workers is unusual, he says, so there have been "growing pains." Although they won't be quoted, some cops resent the Institute "getting in the way" at crime scenes or refusing to share confidences that would help to solve a crime (but jeopardize the Institute's credibility). Gross didn't hire social workers to reach kids — his five full-time and five part-time street workers are mostly ex-offenders and former gang members or leaders. "Not long ago, the police were arresting these guys," Gross says. "Now they're called the peacekeepers. The cops are like, 'yeah, right.' But street workers are a daily reminder to all those in power that people who have done wrong in the past can be among the most useful members of our society.

"What we do has a different resonance than an outside advocacy group," he adds. "It allows the community to work on its own problems with its own people." The street worker approach is known as Yale and Jail. "It's important to have people who've been there, meaning in jail and in gangs," says Hresko, thirty-eight. "But it's also important to have intellectuals who can tie theory to practice. Teny is a white intellectual; he can't go into these neighborhoods like he's their buddy. His only choice is to tell these kids the truth. People are testing you because there's a long line of do-gooders who made promises they didn't deliver on."

Make an appointment with Gross or ask for his help, and his stock reply is

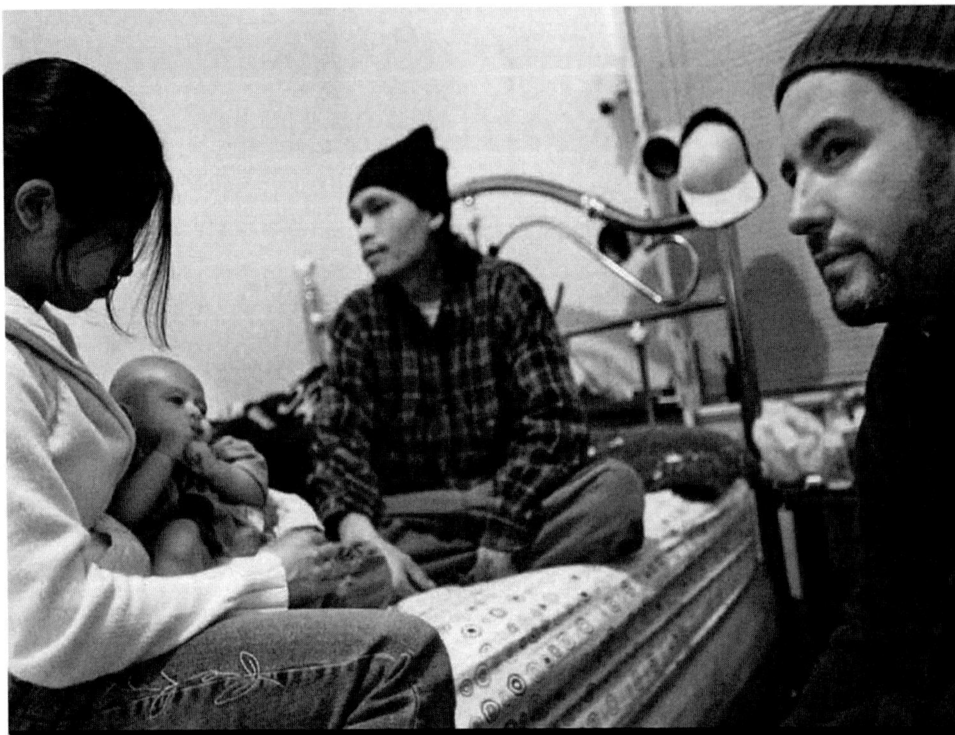

Teny Gross visits Dyna Kun, his wife Betty, and their baby, Tommac. Facing page: Gross at the Institute office; street worker Brother Ray Smith in background.

"yougotit." He uses the phrase so often, he slurs it, punctuated by a thumbs-up or a wink. "I was skeptical of Teny at first," says Pichardo, thirty-nine. "Every year, officials and community leaders would hold vigils but then not take action. The Teny wannabes gain people's trust and move on when their research is done. Teny has an open dialogue that allows him to build bridges, and his staff has gone through the struggles of the inner city. If you hire social workers, gangs are something they have read about in books."

Gross wants to be a safety net before kids seek support from a gang, which means reaching them before puberty since most are recruited by age twelve or thirteen. Providence is home to at least fifteen gangs. Most use acronyms, and some of the names — the Oriental Rascals, Providence Street Boyz, Tiny Rascal Gang — make them sound like loveable scamps. Gangs offer protection and a surrogate family for adolescents who are torn between American culture and that of their immigrant parents. The parents are in crisis as well. As Gross told the Providence *Phoenix*, "After escaping genocide and refugee camps, Southeast Asian parents thought they were coming to the Promised Land, and now their kids are being killed on the streets."

On Halloween evening, Gross cruises a block near Providence College where toga-costumed students spill onto the streets. "These college kids live next to hard-core gang members, but there's been only one fight between them," he says. Gangs don't kill someone white — there's immunity. Black kids know they can kill black kids and Asian kids know they can kill Asian kids. There are a lot of subtle and unsubtle messages in our society about whose life is worth something and whose isn't.

"The lack of empathy from these kids can be stunning," Gross continues, "but if you breed ignorance, if you constantly show people you don't care about them and you mix guns with that indifference, you will get brutal results. I see gang members as *our* kids. If someone is really doing bad things, I might see that person as ignorant and misguided. I have to recognize that I'm successful today because people had the heart and the means to inspire and challenge me. Our president struggled for a long time, and with Daddy's money he succeeded. What would have happened to George W. without that? What would have happened to me if I grew up on the South side of Providence?"

"As a kid," says Sister Ann Keefe, one of the Institute founders, "Teny was no angel." His family called him the black sheep; his older sister was the golden girl, a commander in the Israeli Air Force.

"My parents worried about what would happen to me," Gross says. "I was a very lazy and argumentative teenager. I always had a righteous streak and a temper — once I slapped the Bible teacher in the face because he told me not to touch my lunch. Now my anger is channeled. People can grow and change — it's about finding your niche in life."

Like Holden Caulfield, the narrator of J.D. Salinger's *The Catcher in the Rye*, Gross is the guardian who wants to catch the children playing on a cliff and save them from plummeting into the abyss. "We feel that every time a kid is killed, we failed them," says Sister Ann. "There is a personal feeling of failure on Teny's part when that happens." Gross rarely gets enough sleep to dream, but when he does, he dreams of one he couldn't catch. One who almost made it to the other side.

Gross moved to the States to study photography at Tufts University Museum School of Fine Arts. He pointed his lens at Boston's Ten Point Coalition, a group of ministers who instituted a tough love approach in directing kids to jobs, counseling and education. Reverend Eugene Rivers, the most charismatic of the original Ten Point ministers, introduced him to Sal Brown. Brown was a drug dealer with an AK-47 and a database of customers. He wanted out of the business, but not into a McJob. Brown educated Rivers about reaching the drug dealers, and the Reverend struck a deal with the F.B.I.: Brown would be sent to a southern college instead of prison. "He really struggled with his conscience, with his loneliness in being a fish out of water," Gross says of Brown's collect calls in the belly of night. "The rewards are different in school; it's not about fear and power and an AK-47. It's about knowledge and things that look weak. I saw Sal as a tragic figure from classic literature. He felt a bit like Moses in that he could not cross to the Promised Land. I think Sal felt that even if he finished college, what was out there for him?"

Brown returned to Dorchester for summer break. He had stopped dealing but not consuming drugs. On a Thursday evening, he told Gross and Reverend Rivers that it was too late for him, they needed to save the children. The next night, Brown overdosed while speed-balling heroin and cocaine. "His death was an accident," Gross says. "Where the accident began is a matter of opinion. After Sal died," says Gross, casting his gaze to the window, "I felt I couldn't leave street work. I'd be a wimp if I did."

Gross photographs in black and white and struggles with accepting shades of gray. "Teny is extremely bright," says Sister Ann, fifty-three. "His conversations take grassroots street experience and translate that to democracy, yet he has this wide-eyed innocence about how political pressures affect policy change." Boston colleagues called him Don Quixote. Gross has always pushed at windmills, imagining them to be giants. But even he is not immune to the burnout that is an occupational hazard. In the late nineties, when his compassion ebbed and Gross began seeing teens as *them* instead of *our kids*, he took a sabbatical to study ethics at Harvard Divinity School.

Philosophers have said that a bystander's silence is more damaging than an aggressor's cruelty. "Not being a bystander will resolve a lot of conflicts," Gross agrees. He is haunted by the Holocaust. Partisans killed his grandfather, a Christian Serb and city mayor, as World War II ended. "One of the war photos that filled me with so much outrage was the naked mother in front of the ditch, being separated from her baby," Gross murmurs. "I ask myself, 'How can such a civilized society, one that produced such artistic beauty, murder so brutally?' It's a lesson that we have to be vigilante about preserving democracy…and that we are all potentially murderous. I believe that if you neglect something, it's gonna come back to haunt you.

"Sometimes I feel I'm speaking like a prophet because so many people don't see [the violence] as a fatal illness," he adds. "But like they say, you're never a prophet in your own city." Gross calls himself a realist whose advocacy is rooted in economics, not charity. To lock a juvenile up in the Training School costs taxpayers an average of $98,000 per year. To house an inmate at the Adult Correctional Institutions is $41,000 annually. And don't get Gross started on how many prisoners are repeat guests. "With that money," he says, "I could take a kid, pay his tuition at Harvard, buy him a Lexus and a laptop, and give him a good amount of drinking money for four years of the best education." Gross is flummoxed: "How can the richest nation in the world have a homicide rate of 16,000 victims a year, a statistic second to Northern Ireland, where civil war rages?"

His wife, Julia Clinker, a documentary photographer and daughter of the Warwick-based activist minister Duane Clinker, calls her husband "the reluctant warrior." "People think I love the intensity of this job, but really I'm a secluded, very peaceful person," Gross insists. "I'm forced to be intense because I cannot be innocent about what I see and what I know." As committed as he is to social justice, Gross yearns to live in a monastery and bury himself in the classics. "And I'd love to study art history in Rome. You can have those two conflicting desires."

Parenting the streets means time away from his own kids, John, four, and Julian, eighteen months. "The cost is family," Gross says. "I try to come to dinner and bedtimes, but I often have to think, 'Do I put my kids to bed or do I do that extra thing?' I do that extra thing because I think it's necessary." On Christmas night and into the next morning — his birthday — Gross was on the streets until 2 a.m. after shots were fired by revelers.

"I don't know if Teny could ever stop doing this work," says Clinker, thirty-seven. "It's who he is, not a profession he chose. He talks about studying art in Italy, but I think that even in Rome, Teny would gravitate to the 'hood. This is Teny's calling. His mission is to the world, not just to the three people around him. If a family on Prairie Avenue needs his help, it's as important to be there for them as it is to be here for dinner. As difficult as his absences can be on the family, his work is something I can respect, and we're all very proud of it. Our children now have a broader scope of the world. Our four-year-old ponders who Martin Luther King was and thinks it's his dad's job to teach people that guns are not OK, that they have to use their words."

Gross is an artist who sees his subject's future while most of us see only a shadow, the silhouette of a killer, rapist, felon, junkie, robber, ex-con, gangster. He views the world through their lens. The gangster was a child with a heroin-addicted mother and a mercurial father. In one frame, a teenager tries to do the right thing. With the shutter's next wink, he does wrong. Last summer, Jamont Richardson, a fourteen-year-old Smith Hill resident, was shot dead after his friend failed to pay for a $10 hair-braiding session. The hairdresser had asked her cousins to fetch her money, and a fight ensued. The day before, the fourteen-year-old who allegedly shot Richardson had visited the Institute. He asked to be part of its summer job program, but there were no more jobs. There was no money to hire additional kids.

Gross is always hustling for dollars and can't understand why youth — our future — is such a low priority. According to the 2004 census data, Providence ties with New Orleans as the third-poorest city in the nation for children. Gross promised to do whatever he could for the boy. Their encounter was a page from one of his lectures: instead of focusing on violence, Gross says, we need to focus on opportunities for kids. If he can't bring gang members jobs and keep them in schools, there will be violence. "I saw the X-ray of Jamont's head," Gross says. "I saw the bullet lodged in his brain. That's something you don't forget."

A photographer floats the negative into a chemical sea. The first bath is developer, then stop, then fixer. But a potential picture is just that. If the darkroom door opens and light floods an image before it's fixed, the promise of beauty is destroyed. ■

APRIL 2006 Rhode Island Monthly 7

Mr. SCOTT. I want to thank all of our witnesses for their tremendous testimony.

I recognize myself for the first round of questioning.

Mr. Elliott, you mentioned the need for research. Where is the research done? Mr. Gross mentioned where some of it could be done. Would it be colleges, the National Institutes for Science? Where should we be looking for research?

Mr. ELLIOTT. In the area of violence reduction, of course, I think that research ought to be in the Justice Department and the Department of Education is doing some of that. But I think the primary location would be in the Department of Justice. And, you know, a lot of the work currently going on is in the Department of Justice.

The National Science Foundation, I think, could also be funding general youth development kind of programs, like Dr. Butts talked about, but when we are talking about violence and crime reduction, I think that research ought to be in the Justice Department.

Mr. SCOTT. And you mentioned several things that didn't work. Your testimony specifically mentions waivers to adult court. What is the research on that?

Mr. ELLIOTT. The research on that suggest that the waivers to the adult court increase the risk of victimization for those adolescents who have been put into the adult criminal system as compared to the juvenile system.

There is a greater risk of reoffending when they get out and there is also some evidence for discriminatory processing with respect to which kids get waived and transferred and which kids don't, when that is left up to the prosecuting attorneys.

Mr. SCOTT. Is that statement based on control groups? Because you would expect the more serious offenders to be waived to adult court, so you might be talking about apples and oranges. Or are you talking about the modest-risk people, if they are treated in adult court, they are more likely to offend?

Mr. ELLIOTT. The studies have, in fact, controls for that issue. They are not randomized control trials, which would be the best evidence, but they are quasi-experimental trials in which they have matched the control group with the experimental group with respect to the seriousness of the offense.

Mr. SCOTT. Thank you.

Dr. Butts, you indicated that you need to—let me ask it another way. In terms of what you do to the juveniles that are here today, whatever you do to them, what does that do for the next cohort of juveniles in terms of what they may be doing or what trajectory they are on.

Mr. BUTTS. I think you heard some of the other speakers refer to the changing of culture at the neighborhood level, certainly at the family level. Everyone you are exposed to as you are coming up as a young person influences you, and to the extent we can surround young people with positive pro-social adults who see a role for families who have jobs, who have faith in their own futures, youth will pick up on that attitude and start to adopt it themselves.

So stopping, you know, you have referred to the phrase before as closing down the pipeline, reducing the number of people that a young person is exposed to who advocate and enjoy a criminal life style is critical for making those cultural changes.

Mr. SCOTT. And if you don't change the trajectory, does it matter for the next cohort what you have done to the last cohort?

Mr. BUTTS. The trajectory of an individual?

Mr. SCOTT. If young people are headed toward prison rather than college, if you don't do anything about that trajectory, what can we reasonably expect the next cohort to end up?

Mr. BUTTS. Well, some people refer to the ''little brother effect'' to explain the declining crime during the late 1990's. And that, simply put, is when you are 12 years old and you see your 18-yearold brother shot and killed, go off to prison, and a lot of your brother's friends are doing the same thing, it changes you as a 12-yearold. And some people theorize that and the many other factors, including the decline in crack use, contributed to the overall decline.

So the whole pipeline effect, you know, stopping things early and reaching kids when they are young is of the utmost importance.

Mr. SCOTT. And what kinds of things actually make a difference in that trajectory?

Mr. BUTTS. What I was suggesting in my statement was that we pay attention to common sense. None of us here are threatening each other with bodily harm right now. And that is not because we were surrounded by a team of psychiatrists when we were 13 years old. It is because we learned to play by the rules, we learned to enjoy the benefits of living in society and to respect one another.

Those are pretty simple lessons and you don't need skilled therapeutic professionals to do that. We rely upon skilled therapeutic professionals because that is our funding mechanism and that is how we can create systems of intervention.

It is much harder to create neighborhood-based, volunteer-based pro-social activities and groups for young people. But if we were going to focus on common sense and create service networks that make sense, I think that is what we would do. It takes a long time and you need good community-based workers, like some of the young men sitting behind us.

Mr. SCOTT. Thank you.

Mr. Sherman, you indicated your entire research identified a group at high risk of offending. With those in supervision, are there things we could do while they are on supervision to reduce the risk that they will offend?

Mr. SHERMAN. Mr. Chairman, there is a wide range of things we can do. What we haven't done is to test the matching of certain response to people with certain kinds of diagnoses.

We do have some ideas, like across the board provide frequent checks to make sure that these people at very high risk, and I should say with the new models we can identify that people who are 42 times more likely to be accurately forecast to commit a murder or attempt a murder than the average person on probation.

So by focusing on a very tiny portion of that group, we could then say even within that portion does everybody need to be monitored, whether they are carrying guns, and that is currently one of the strategies that is being used but hasn't been evaluated carefully. For those who have post-traumatic stress disorder because they have seen their brother shot or they have seen their parents fighting in very violent ways.

Does treatment of post-traumatic stress disorder reduce their likelihood of killing somebody? For people who are chronically depressed, does treatment for depression reduce their post-traumatic stress disorder?

Again, these are not things that you I think should be doing across the board in either the juvenile or the adult system, but where for the tiny fraction who based on their prior record or at very high risk, we could be said to be under serving them in terms of their mental health needs.

And not every city has a gang problem. Philadelphia really doesn't have the evidence of the kind of thing that we are hearing about in Providence or Boston. So, indeed, we may be able to help these folks get their lives together, get into the high school completion. Some are in community college right now. Give them some parent training. You know, there are fathers out there, as well as mothers, who are raising kids, and we have got some of them in this program.

And if in every way, the probation officer, possibly even on a one-on-one basis, can help to turn their lives around, that could save an enormous amount of money if not in terms of gunshot wounds at over $100,000 per injury, then in terms of $35,000 a year in prison for possibly 40 years.

We don't know exactly what to do, but I think the progress we have made now that would support creation of Federal grant program is that we have a much better idea where to focus these efforts.

Mr. FORBES. Thank you, Mr. Chairman.

First of all, again, I want to thank all of you for being here and thank you for what you are doing, and with the possible caveat that Mr. Elliott may tell us that one of your programs is harmful, we just appreciate all of them that you are doing.

I want to just say a couple of things at the beginning, because we hear a lot of buzz phrases and buzz words, and let us just make clear for the record that nobody here thinks you can arrest or incarcerate your way out of the gang problem. I have heard that language. Nobody seriously believes that. Nobody thinks that abusive or illegal law enforcement activities work well. None of us think that.

Nobody thinks we should not have a comprehensive program to address the gang problem, which includes law enforcement tools and prevention programs. Nobody thinks the Federal Government can pass a single act that will deal with all the components of gang crime, nor should we. That is not what we are about.

Our goal is trying to strike a balance between what the Federal Government can and should do, what the State government can and should do, what communities can and should do and what the private sector can and should do.

Just to give you a couple of examples, one of the most popular gang leaders that I read about in the 1970's was a guy named Nicky Cruz, who was a gang leader at 19. Teen Challenge converted him to a faith program. Nicky has spoken now to 40 million people about self-improvement around the world. I mean, that was a winner. The Federal Government, Mr. Chairman would say, we shouldn't get involved in helping those kinds of programs.

Just this past week, I was at a community center that combined a library-rec center to help prevent gangs and juvenile crime. Wonderful program.

So we think those programs are great. What we are trying to do is say what should the Federal Government be doing and how should we be doing it.

Now, Mr. Elliott, I looked at your testimony and one of the things that I looked at was the bio that you gave to us, and one of the things the Chairman and the Chairman of the Committee has encouraged us to do is oversight. And as I was looking at the studies and the grants that you just listed down here, and I am sure there are a lot more, that you were the principal investigator of, they totaled over $38,526,000 in grant programs just to programs that you listed that you were principal investigator. That is a lot of money to research and evaluate programs.

And after doing that, the conclusion that I read in your written testimony, I just want to read it back to you, that you identified over 600 programs that claim to prevent or deter violence, drug use or delinquent behavior and less than 20 have any rigorous evaluation.

Was that your statement?

Mr. ELLIOTT. Twenty percent.

Mr. FORBES. I am sorry, 20 percent.

The other testimony that you had in your written statement was the fact remains that most of the resources currently committed to the prevention and control of youth violence, drug use and delinquency at both national and local levels has been invested in unproven programs based on questionable assumptions and delivered with little consistency or quality control.

Fair statement?

Mr. ELLIOTT. Correct.

Mr. FORBES. And then the other thing that you indicated was that this was a complex behavior problem, when we are looking at gangs, that includes these things: family, neighborhood, peer group and the media is what you listed.

Were they accurate components, according to your testimony?

Mr. ELLIOTT. yes.

Mr. FORBES. And then you also said any positive changes in the individual's behavior achieved in the treatment setting are quickly lost when the youth returns home to his/her family, neighborhood and old friends.

So basically we are looking at a situation where all of those components are influential in what happens with any particular program that we have, how strong the family unit is, what the neighborhood looks like, what the peer groups are, how the media responds.

Fair statement?

Mr. ELLIOTT. Each of those contexts does contribute to the incident or the likelihood of violence.

Mr. FORBES. But we have to look at each of those components when we are trying to measure gang activity, correct?

Mr. ELLIOTT. Correct.

Mr. FORBES. The other thing is, we have had testimony before our Committee, and forgive me for being quick, I only have 5 minutes. We have had testimony before our Committee that the number-one gang problem in the United States today, according to the Attorney General, was MS-13. That is his testimony, whether we agree with it or disagree with it.

And then we have had further testimony that between 60 and 85 percent of the members of many of the MS-13 groups are here illegally.

Can you tell me, from that $38 million of evaluation on the programs that you have had in your examination of these prevention programs, what prevention programs have you found that effectively works to stop gang activity from those individuals who are here illegally on the worst gang that we have in the country today?

Mr. ELLIOTT. I am not sure I can address that specific gang and those specific situations, but we have two programs, for example, that we know are very effective in working with deep-end offenders, and that is multisystemic family therapy and——

Mr. FORBES. Are they for illegal——

Mr. ELLIOTT. They would work for illegals.

There are a number of programs which have been validated to work with various ethnic populations. Some programs, unfortunately, have been validated only with respect to the majority population, so you have to be careful when you look at the program to see, but those are two programs, for example, that have demonstrated the effectiveness of working with different racial and ethnic groups and have been effective in working with kids like the kids that are in gangs in general. I can't speak specifically to the MS-13 group.

Mr. FORBES. My time is up, but that is one of the dilemmas with have with having so many people on the panel, we can't get to everybody to ask all the questions we want to ask. Hopefully we will have several rounds to do so.

The only thing I would follow up with you, if you can submit to us at some point in time, in writing, from your evaluations, specifically the programs that you have found to be effective in working with the illegal group of people that are here, on groups like MS13 and some of the other groups that seem to be so prevalent.

Mr. SCOTT. Thank you.

We have been joined by the gentlelady from California, Ms. Waters.

Do you have questions?

Ms. WATERS. Thank you very much, Mr. Chairman. I apologize. I am in Financial Services and I was not able to be here earlier.

I must also admit I have not had an opportunity to read all of the testimony that has been presented here this morning, but I wanted to come over for several reasons.

One is, as you know, I urged and encouraged that we focus some attention on the gang problem in America and shared with you the seriousness of the gang problem in the Greater Los Angeles area. I have not read all of the testimony. I do know about one of the programs that simply talks about law enforcement, community leaders, et cetera, coming together and addressing gang members and somehow either convincing them or threatening them, maybe both, and it having some great impact.

I have a lot of experience working with gangs. I started many years ago in some of the largest public housing projects in the Greater Los Angeles area: the Nickerson Gardens Housing Projects and the Imperial Courts, Jordan Downs, the Pueblos, Gonzales Housing Projects. These are areas where we had Crips and Bloods, Grape Street, all of the notorious gangs of the South Central Los Angeles area.

And I think I have learned a few things. I have learned that you cannot simply deal with the problems of gangs with police enforcement and just simply getting tough and locking up people. It does not work. It creates a lot more resentment because oftentimes the police don’t know a gang member from Ms. Johnson’s son, who is not a gang member, who is in school every day, and happens to be at the laundromat and ill-informed and ill-trained police officers just see all Black youth in the same light and they not only apprehend and arrest but create a lot of confrontation and friction and other kinds of things.

Now our communities have marched, they have prayed, they have got ministries involved, but I have found, through a program that I started with discretionary money that came from the Federal Government to the State when I was in the State legislature, I created a program for public housing projects.

It was a program that I simply sat at my kitchen table and wrote. And we took this discretionary money, went into the public housing projects and we put flyers out, we walked the neighborhoods, and we convinced the public housing authority to give us space where we opened offices and we used their gymnasiums for the programs that I ran for almost 10 years.

We took this money, we took this free space, we walked the neighborhood and we convinced city government, who was running the Private Industry Councils at that time, if any of you remember, the so-called job training programs, the Private Industry Councils, that did not touch inside these public housing projects. Many cities do not afford the services to some of the poorest areas and certainly to public housing projects that they should be affording. They act as if they are not in their city.

And so the job training programs never reached, and so I started these programs because young people, mostly young Black males at that time, were just hanging every day in public housing projects. They didn’t really live there—they did live there. They were not on the rolls because of the policies of Federal Government. They lived with girlfriends and grandmothers and wherever they could because they didn’t have jobs and they didn’t have homes.

And so the Government, we all pretend that they don't live there. We recruited them in the gymnasiums, and I had a program where, the way I structured it, we met about 4 days, and in those 4 days I insisted on using some of the money to pay a stipend for those who attended the programs. I had food. I had food when they came in in the morning and I had something for lunch. And we had very simple programs where we started out by talking about do you really want to work? What do you want to do with your life?

We found out a lot about folks. We found out that, surprisingly, most of the people in the program those days had graduated from high school in that area. We also found out that most of them were involved in drugs in some way.

I started right at the height of the crack cocaine explosion in South Central Los Angeles, where everybody was trying to make a buck with small amounts of crack cocaine, et cetera. I discovered that the 1st day that I had this program, we had standing room only. It dispelled the notion that these poor people, these gang members, did not want jobs. They did not want to work. We also did all of the regular stuff of 4 days of learning how to fill out a job application, role playing.

But the most important thing was the talking and getting to know people and people getting to trust you and beginning to share with you. People would come up to me afterwards and say, "Ms. Waters, I want to but I can't read." I mean, that is not something that they were able to really talk about. Some had dropped out of school or had been just pushed on through despite the fact they couldn't read. And for all intents and purposes, their lives were kind of over.

Others were the children of crack-addicted mothers and there was no safety net. Others had fathers and mothers who were in prison. Others had simply no connections and they were living in vacant buildings at times with gangs. So out of all of that, what we did was we said to the City of Los Angeles and the Private Industry Council, you have got to get your people here. We have got to have the job developers. They have got to get not only into real training programs once they come out of what I am doing, but we have got to have job developers who really develop jobs.

And everybody who came into the public housing projects after that, whether it was the Housing Authority itself attempting to do rehabilitation or the telephone companies laying cable, we made them employ the people who lived in those public housing projects or they couldn't work there. They just couldn't do it. We were sick and tired of people coming in, earning the money, taking it and going on across town somewhere into another county while people standing there unemployed had nothing to do.

Jobs will do a hell of a lot to reduce crime and violence. Out of those years, we have homeowners, we have people that got connected because we created the Maxine Waters Employment Preparation Center under the unified school district to make sure there were alternatives.

And so I just came here to say this, and I know you want me to wrap up, Mr. Chairman. I have a real appreciation for academicians and the research you may have done and what you understand about gangs. But I want you to know, until you have been on the ground with Crips and Bloods, Rolling 40's, 50's and 60's, and gotten to know these kids and these young people and the anger and the disappointment and the lack of trust that they have basically in our society and in adults who have let them down time and time again, the only power they have is the power of the gun and the power to threaten and the power to control some territory that you may not think is worth anything, but to them that is their power, to say that you can't come here, you can't do this.

This is a complicated problem that requires money, it requires sustained training and development. There should be no poor communities in housing projects that do not have social services, do not have job training programs. There should be no programs that do not have stipends. Don't ask poor people and gang members to sit in training programs every day hungry. I made sure they had money for food, to get their clothes clean, to get grandmamma to watch the baby, whatever, so that they could listen and try to be a part of it.

I have found most people, whether they are gang members or just dropouts or poor people, really aspire to everything else all Americans aspire to. Everything that we see on that television. They want homes, they want cars, they want to be able to go to concerts. They want that. So I don't talk to people about just being good, just saying no. I try to empower people with real assets, with real stuff to be able to live with.

If you do that, and people see that they can get some money and they can pay the rent, they can buy some houses, we can go a long way toward breaking up gangs, breaking up concentrations of gangs in communities.

I just had to have my say and I thank you for the time, Mr. Chairman. And I will spend a little time before I go back to financial services, because I want a rebuttal.

Mr. SCOTT. Thank you, Ms. Waters.

We will ask the witnesses to respond as part of your other responses, but thank you. You went a little over.

The gentleman from Ohio?

Mr. CHABOT. Thank the gentleman, and I want to thank him for holding this hearing. I think it is a very important and timely hearing.

Before I get into my questions, I wanted to mention our colleague, Mr. Coble, who was here earlier, had to leave because he went to Georgia for the funeral service of one of our colleagues, Charlie Norwood, who passed away, and that may be why there aren't more Members here today.

He also wanted to let you know, Mr. Kennedy, that his assistant chief of police back in High Point, North Carolina, sent his thank you for the work that you have been doing in their community. And I also want to thank you for agreeing to work with the city of Cincinnati in its efforts to decrease youth violence. I was honored to serve on the Cincinnati City Council for 5 years, this is quite a few years ago, and live in the city and as a citizen have a lot of concerns about the level of violence in our community.

Last year, we, for example, suffered the highest homicide rate that we have had in our city's history, which is obviously most unfortunate, and many of those were related to gangs and to violence relative to drug transactions and most of them were in the city. So we appreciate your input and hope that you are successful.

We had a chance to talk shortly before this hearing and I was encouraged to hear how certain you were that you will be successful here, assuming that you get the cooperation of the community and their involvement.

And I would start out by mentioning, you had an article that appeared by the National Institute of Justice, titled "Pulling Levers," and you advocated the strategy. Could you describe what that strategy is, what it encompasses, and how that would apply in Cincinnati?

Mr. KENNEDY. Thanks. Sure. I had to make it really complicated to get it into NIJ. It is actually pretty simple.

And to not rebut but endorse what Congresswoman Waters said, you are exactly right, and this is what Teny has been saying, it is what Mai has been saying. It is what the chief and the D.A., we are all saying the same thing here.

I learned what I know about this from Teny, from gang officers, from community people. The literature helps, but that is where I have gotten everything most important in my career.

The version that NIJ wouldn't publish is the version that, my mother goes to cocktail parties and says that I learned all of this from here, and she is fundamentally correct. We bureaucratize this, we abstract it, we put it in fancy language, but any good parent sticks with their kid, establishes rules, helps them learn, punishes them appropriately when they need punishment, but doesn't go away at that point. They don't turn them over to somebody else.

If we did families the way we do crime, we would have one parent responsible for love and support, one for rules and discipline. We would have to find a third parent for spiritual guidance. And the parents would be forbidden by statute from speaking to each other. This is ridiculous.

So all "pulling levers" is, and I don't even like that term anymore, but all it is is a way of engaging consistently with the groups of the kind of really extreme offenders that Larry has been describing, and he is absolutely right about what is going on out there, and saying to them consistently over time there are things that we won't put up with. Here is exactly what is going to happen if you do these things. People you respect want you to stop this and want to help you if you will let them help you.

And the piece that we don't think about very much, the, say, you know, moral voice, this is wrong and you know it is wrong, and it turns out that even the most hardened offenders, or most of them, really care a lot when their grandmother looks at them and says, "You are really disappointing me."

I am a deterrence theorist, and deterrence theory tells me that if I am more afraid of my grandmother than I am of the police, let us organize the grandmothers. And that is in fact what is going on out there. It is really very simple.

Mr. CHABOT. Thank you very much.

Mr. Sherman and Mr. Logli, if I could ask you the question, for those that have shown by their behavior to be particularly violent and some that are predators on the community, could you talk about the important aspects of law enforcement in dealing with those individuals and what we ought to do as a society and as a Government?

Mr. SHERMAN. I would start with making sure that they are not in possession of or carrying guns. That nexus is very clear. There is a lot of controversy about how to deal with that problem at large in the community. I believe once people have been convicted and put under conditions of community supervision, the opportunity exists for a judge to reinforce the existing law that says as convicted felons they—or even as adjudicated delinquents—that they would not have any right to legal possession of guns.

The problem is doing that in a way that is respectful, that doesn't provoke the resentment and further anger that Congresswoman Waters has quite rightly drawn our attention to, and one of the things we are working on right now in the probation-police partnership in Philadelphia is trying to make the home visits, both scheduled and unscheduled, as dignified and supportive of an experience for the offender on community supervision, as possible.

So that even though there are two plainclothes officers in an unmarked car who drive the probation officer to the house, what the probation officer does primarily while looking around the house, in addition to other things, is to talk with the family, to talk with grandmother or to talk with whoever is there, about the hopes and aspirations, the education plans, the occupational goals that the probationer has, so that the attempt to monitor and regulate the critical issue of gun possession is tied to an expression of concern for and respect for the young offender and his home and the people in the home—and by young, again, I mean under age 25—so that we don't make the anger at police from a disrespecting kind of contact in order to preserve their non-gun carrying part of a larger set of causes of what makes them violent.

I think we can do that, and I think that if we are able to pursue not only the gun issue but also issues of compliance with programs that—because Philadelphia probation officers have 180 cases per officer, so if an offender doesn't show up for drug treatment or doesn't go to alcohol treatment or even therapy programs or education programs as required or as agreed to, nothing happens. There is no consequence.

So to lower that caseload, especially with these high-risk people, and the astonishing fact that in Philadelphia we have only one-fourth as many probation officers per murder as in the rest of Pennsylvania. We would need four times as many probation officers just to come up to that ratio in the rest of the State. Which is why, you know, in the short run, something like a Federal grants program to support this sort of high-risk community supervision would be extremely helpful and have, I think, an immediate possibility of reducing the homicide rate in the nation.

Mr. LOGLI. Thank you.

If I understand the question, Congressman, it is what do we do with those people that have already started to offend. And, of course, as a local district attorney, many times our first contact with somebody is they show up on our arrest sheet.

District attorneys have been described as holding a quasi-judicial office, and I take that terminology seriously. Every morning in my office we go through a veritable triage of screening cases and making charging decisions, and somehow we have to make wise choices. We have got to at some point look at an individual and say this person is still worth working with. This person can still, with the proper support, turn his or her life around.

Then we get to the other extreme. This person, but virtue of what we have seen and their actions in the community, this person is beyond that point, and our job now is to simply prosecute that person effectively and put that person away as long as we can.

There are hundreds of gradations in between those two extremes. What helps us make those decisions is if we have available to us programs, many of which have been described this morning, that give us alternatives, that shows us that if this person can be put into that anti-truancy program, if we can work with that family to get that person to go to school and to learn how to read and write and how to develop job skills so that they can get a job, the most important thing for many of these people is to have a job, so they can support a family and make their mortgage payments.

But if we don't have programs that bring them there, then my job is tougher. I don't need any more laws. I have got all the criminal laws I need in the State of Illinois. I don't need any more sanctions. The sentences are plenty tough. I have got all the discretion I need.

What I need is what Teny talked about, and that is programs on the street that have staying power and that have credibility and that will work with people, that I can refer people to. Because what I do have is the hammer. I have the coercion that might just make that person stick to a program, whether you call it pulling levers or anything else. We make that decision, whether they are worth working with or it is just time to warehouse them. And that is a real loss to society.

Mr. SCOTT. Thank you.

The gentleman from California?

Mr. LUNGREN. Thank you very much, Mr. Chairman.

This is a difficult hearing, because we have eight or nine witnesses and all of them have excellent qualifications and all of them have something to say.

Mr. SCOTT. Will the gentleman yield?

Mr. LUNGREN. Yes.

Mr. SCOTT. We expect to have more rounds of questions——

Mr. LUNGREN. I understand that, but it makes it difficult for those of us who are in several Committees to come here and at least ask questions.

Just a suggestion, it is just, they all have excellent ideas and perspectives and it would be good if we would have a chance to concentrate on several of them rather than all of them.

I am not into rebuttals, but I am a little concerned that the only reference made to the Los Angeles Police Department was a negative one, about officers exacerbating the situations.

Maybe I take it personally because my brother used to be an L.A. police officer and I recall him responding to a call for drug dealers in Nickerson Gardens, and I recall that it was a drug dealer who had vowed to kill a cop. And I recall that he had my brother directly in his sights and my brother would have been a victim had not another officer come upon the scene and caused the person to leave.

I think we have to understand that while there are bad cops in bad situations, my judgment is most of them want to help the people and the communities that they serve.

When I was attorney general of California, I changed the name of the program we had from the Crime Prevention Center to the Violence and Crime Prevention Center, because oftentimes if you wait until it is a crime, it is too late. And I really wanted to treat violence as well, because we needed to have programs of education before you got to intervention, and then intervention and deterrence and punishment. I mean, it is a continuum, it seems to me. I hope that no one disagrees with that.

One of the toughest things I had when I put together a juvenile violence task force is to get everybody to talk together. I had a group that was about four times this size representing all the disciplines, and the first time they came in the room it was kind of interesting. It was kind of like dogs circling one another and not sure what they ought to do because everyone thought if that person gets money, we are not going to get money. And yet at the end of about a year process, they found common ground, as I think we have here.

I will never forget going to a program and one of the high schools in Los Angeles had been the site of a shooting and talking about the Safe Schools Program that we had developed and urged onto other schools, and after it was all over a young girl, about 14 or 15, came up to me. She happened to be African-American. She said, ''Why did it take the death of one of my classmates for you adults to take this seriously?'' And her emphasis was, why don't you do that which is necessary to provide a safe school environment for me?

And so that is why I take the comments of the representative of the prosecutors here very seriously. We all, I think, want to do things that are in that continuum, but that doesn't mean that we don't understand that you have to have a sense of order backed up by a sense of enforcement backed up by a prospect of punishment if all else doesn't work.

I rarely found a victim in a crime say to the responding officer or paramedic, ''What was the socioeconomic background of the person who just beat me up?'' Basically, ''Please take care of my wounds. Please catch that person and make sure he or she doesn't do it to somebody else.''

So I guess my question to the representative of the district attorneys is this: There has been at least some reference of a critical nature to trying juveniles as adults. I view that as an unfortunate but necessary part of the overall system. And I wonder if you could give us the thoughts from your perspective on how you make that decision, what it gives you in the way of alternatives, and whether or not you believe it is effective in certain circumstances.

Mr. LOGLI. I do believe it is one of the more difficult decisions I have to make. And although I have 47 assistant States attorneys, any decision to transfer a young person into the adult system is made only with my knowledge and ascent. That is how serious I believe it is.

Some of that discretion has been taken away from us with recent legislative changes in my State and many other States, and that is if you charge somebody who happens to be 14 or 15 years old with murder, that is an automatic transfer. If you charge somebody with a sexual assault, a violent sexual assault at a certain age, that is an automatic transfer. There may be no discretion there.

There are still some discretionary transfers. Now I can still short circuit that State law because I can charge something less than murder. I can charge a lower-level sexual assault, perhaps. You know, I am not in the business of writing fiction. You have got to charge what the conduct really is.

But in those cases where we have the discretion, yes, it is based on prior record, it is based on threat to the community. Many times, it is based on the fact that there are no programs in the juvenile system that is really going to have a credible impact on that young person, and we really have no choice when we are looking at preventing future victimization. And if we don't have anything in the community that can really address that young person's problems and specifically, I am talking about sometimes the 15-or 16year-old sexual assault of them. Now I know we are here talking about gangs, but I mean, that is one of the situations where there are very few alternatives to just try to protect the community.

When it comes to gang involvement, I think we have a few more alternatives. But, again, I mean, I don't go out of my way to transfer aggravated batteries or the lower-level felonies into adult court. I think that we can deal with that in juvenile court. When it comes to gang affiliation and gang-related criminal activity, there having effective programs that can deal with that would certainly prevent some of that transferring. But in certain cases where there is murder, there is a serious sexual assault that may be somehow gang related, you know, I think it is probably in many of those cases a tough decision whether we have to move them up.

Mr. SCOTT. Thank you.

We are going to have another round of questions.

I will now defer to the gentlelady from California.

Ms. WATERS. Thank you very much.

I just want to take the first minute to say to my colleague from California that we are all sensible adults, elected by the people because we have demonstrated some quality that our people support. Nobody suggests that all cops, all police are bad police. I qualified my remarks somewhat about ill-trained, insensitive, and there are those too.

So we understand that there are good cops and there are bad cops. And I have to put that on the record because oftentimes these statements are made in ways that would have listeners believe that somehow there are only a few people who care about the good cops and others who do not.

I do know over my years of experience, and if you read the papers and you know anything about Los Angeles, we have a history of the tension between the police and the community, and that is not fictional. That is real, whatever the reasons are for that.

I understand there was some discussion about the truce work. I know that we have programs in Los Angeles and we have some people who have been involved for quite sometime in doing truce work, and a lot of our young ex-gang members, the O.G.s, are advocates for funding for truce work.

I am not so sure that there is any permanency to it, that sometimes you can put out a potential confrontation, but there appears to linger the possibilities of confrontation because when there are, you know, various gangs in these communities, you have friends, relatives who have been killed, and the revenge motive does not go away easily.

Who can tell me about your successful truce work that is sustainable that has made a difference?

Mr. GROSS. I think that you are very right. When there is a homicide, it is a lot harder to come back than a simple shooting, all right, and anger resides for a long time.

I think first, before you bring sides together, you just try to get a ceasefire, all right. Can we just calm down? Can we work?

We support the victims' families. Mothers are a great asset, a moral voice. I will never forget, in 2001, I was stunned. I run a nonviolence institute. A mother who lost her son, about 20 minutes later on TV says absolutely no revenge in my name. We are still working together. Obviously a moral voice has a lot of clout. Her side has not retaliated. It is now 2007.

We take very seriously funerals. We go to funerals. We just had the funeral of Young Blood. Everyone was in red. We support them. We help them get some funds. We help with the family. We got them a refund from the funeral home. We coddle them, yes, we do, so there is sympathy and help.

We help one of the O.G.s say on the side to one of our Cambodian street workers, ''Can you get me some mental health?'' He wouldn't say it in front of his crew.

So there is a surge there and there is an understanding and you reason that, do we need another life lost. We use the parent. Look what they are going through. Does the other side, who is also Cambodian, need to go through that?

Ms. WATERS. Okay.

Mr. GROSS. Another thing, real quick, if I can say it?

Ms. WATERS. Yes.

Mr. GROSS. Following Monday, we went to see one of the main shooters of this gang, twice convicted of gun charges, in jail. Had a conversation then. He reached out to that. He is seeing now differently.

So you pull any lever you have. We don't mind walking on the carpet on our knees as long as we can create the conditions to calm this thing down.

Ms. WATERS. Does anyone else have a model for truce work that is sustainable, that works, that has caused the cessation of warfare over any sustained period of time?

Yes, Mr. Kennedy?

Mr. KENNEDY. There are examples of truces like that, so here in the District the Alliance of Concerned Men has truces that I think are over 10 years old now, and they work as Teny works.

There is no model for that. There are examples, but there are no examples of ways to consistently do that when one or both parties aren't willing, and I think that is the state of the art.

Ms. WATERS. May I ask also if any of you, with the connections or the work that you do, calls a meeting of shot callers from gangs, would the police allow you all to meet?

Let me hear from Mai Fernandez.

Ms. FERNANDEZ. Yes, we work in very close collaboration with the police department here in Washington, DC, and now that we are in Maryland, we have also worked very closely with them. They know the gang members. They know that they come to our youth center. They talk with them regularly. They talk to their parents regularly.

Ms. WATERS. So you don't have gang injunctions, where either one of several situations exists: a condition of parole is they cannot be in the company of other gang members, or injunctions such as the one in the Greater Los Angeles area, they can't be in certain places, they can't languish, they can't linger, they can't associate, and a meeting would be considered a violation of that. You don't have that situation?

Ms. FERNANDEZ. There may be individual cases where that exists, but that is not something that we have used nor I have known in my experience.

I also think that even if that injunction existed and that meeting was called by both community and law enforcement officials, that it probably wouldn't be a violation.

Ms. WATERS. Not law enforcement. Community leaders, program operators who really want to talk without intimidation, without fear, without the thought that the police is listening. If you called that kind of meeting, would you have any kind of interference, surveillance or intimidation?

Ms. FERNANDEZ. No. I mean, I think because we have worked so closely with the police department and the public officials in D.C., we wouldn't. There is a trust that is developed between us and them. That didn't always exist. It has existed, probably, we have developed it over the last 10 years.

Ms. WATERS. Thank you.

Mr. FORBES. Thank you, Mr. Chairman.

Mr. Butts, you have been the lost man for a few minutes there, so I want to come back to you with just some of your testimony that you mentioned earlier.

I think I heard you right, but did you say 1994 was the last year we really had, like, a spike in violence? Or did I misinterpret that?

Mr. BUTTS. If you plotted out the incidence rate of serious violent crime, you would see it climbing throughout the late 1980's, peeking about 1994, 1995, and then falling dramatically.

Mr. FORBES. So if I had a graph and I could draw it, I would draw it up like this, from the 1980's to 1994, and then from 1994 to today it is——

Mr. BUTTS. Till about 2004.

Mr. FORBES [continuing]. It has been on a decline?

Mr. BUTTS. Right. And then it starts to pick up again.

Mr. FORBES. Good.

So the periods of time in which the Chairman was referencing all of the bills the Judiciary Committee and all has worked on, during that period of time there has been a decline by that graph in violent crime in the United States.

The other question I have, Mr. Sherman, I just wanted to make sure I heard you correctly or read your testimony correctly.

You said as many as 76 percent of all murders in Philadelphia involve convicted or charged offenders under supervision of community supervision agencies?

Mr. SHERMAN. As either victims or suspects, recognizing the fact that over half of the murders go unsolved. So we can measure 100 percent of the victims, but we are taking educated guests based on the arrests that have been made, as to how many of those in which no arrest is made were also committed by people who were either under supervision of the court because they were awaiting trial but in the community, and that is 30,000 people in Philadelphia; on probation or parole at the county level, that is 52,000; on State parole, that is 9,000; or in juvenile probation, which is 6,000.

It adds up to one out of every 15 people in Philadelphia is in the community at large under court supervision, but only a tiny fraction of them are highly likely to kill somebody.

And what we are doing is trying to reinvent probation and parole, at least at the adult level, to focus on the very dangerous people and to use New York's model, using a simple computer with palm print identification, to have the monthly visit with all the low-risk probationers.

Mr. FORBES. Mr. Kennedy, one of the statements that you made was about organizing the grandmothers to do that, but one of the things that was shocking to me, I was speaking in Arkansas at a gang summit that they had out there, and Luis Cardona, who Mr. Sherman is probably familiar with from Maryland and you might be familiar with, Ms. Fernandez, too, who is one of their key people, is a former gang member, works for the State of Maryland now in gang prevention.

But he told me something that just shocked me. He said the number-one group that works against his efforts, he said, in Maryland, he said, "You will be shocked at who this group is." And I said, "Who?" And he said, "It is the mothers." He said, "The mothers scream at me and curse at me because they want their kid involved in these gangs because of the economic benefits they are getting from them."

And, Mr. Logli, I am looking here at your testimony that you had earlier about this story of the mother in New Orleans, that was in your written testimony.

Mr. LOGLI. Yes, sir.

Mr. FORBES. Who, as I understand it, actually took the gun and put it in her son's hand and told him to go out and kill the person he was in a fight with, and had a picture of it on her wall. Is that——

Mr. LOGLI. She had a picture from a previous time of the young man holding a weapon, and when that young man was beaten up by a rival and came home, she said, "Well, go out there and make your revenge."

And he went out, within I think it was 20 or 30 minutes had killed the other young man.

Ms. WATERS. Will the gentleman yield for a moment?

Mr. FORBES. Pardon me?

Ms. WATERS. Is that an aberration or something that——

Mr. FORBES. Well, I don't know. Mr. Cardona, from Maryland, is the one who told me. We can bring him in to testify.

Mr. KENNEDY. Can I respond to that?

Mr. FORBES. Sure.

Mr. KENNEDY. I want to be careful here because I don't know him and I don't know what he said——

Mr. FORBES. And I had never met him before, but——

Mr. KENNEDY. In 25 years of doing this, I have never, ever seen any organized group in a community, mothers or anybody else, oppose efforts to get their kids out of trouble or oppose efforts to help them——

Mr. FORBES. And I think that is what we would normally——

Mr. KENNEDY [continuing]. Or to organize in——

Mr. FORBES [continuing]. Assume, but——

Mr. KENNEDY. That is unheard of.

Mr. FORBES. But we are hearing testimony of that. There was a case on TV not too long ago where a lady actually drove her son to a home to send him in to rob someone at gunpoint. He was a member of a gang. He was shot, came back out and they had to call 911 to pick him up because she was arrested.

But whatever the case, that makes it very difficult sometime on prevention programs, if we do have that.

Mr. Logli, I wanted to ask you a question also. You tell us that, you know, there has been this huge shift in gangs that we have seen in more of the international gangs that are coming into the country now. As I mentioned in our testimony earlier, we have high percentages of gang members who are here illegally now. And also the whole meth trade has shifted in just the last few years. It used to be kind of the homegrown variety. Now we have these Wal-Mart, if you would, kinds of meth cartels that are being put in Mexico with the gang networks coming into the United States.

Your written testimony talked about those and the increasing use of 16-and 17-year-olds to do their activity because of ''the belief that juveniles will not get any time.''

And my question to you is this: We have heard testimony in here that if we simply arrest the 16-or 17-year-old, 20 more will pop up in their place because these gangs will continue to recruit and put them in there. With the laws that you currently have as a State prosecutor, how are you going after those national gangs that may be located in other States with their headquarters in other places out there?

Mr. LOGLI. Well, I really, as a local prosecutor, am not in too much of a shape to go after the organization as an organization. We deal with the individuals.

We have unique challenges with those gangs. In my community, I have bilingual police officers and bilingual prosecutors, but probably not enough. And so there is a communication problem. Not that we get tremendous cooperation from all gang members, but we get less cooperation from the Latino or Hispanic community, especially recent arrivals, simply because they came out of countries where the police were very corrupt and the government was very corrupt. And they carry that distrust with them into our nation.

And so we have a real problem getting cooperation in terms of witnesses. We find that a lot of those gangs, because of that, will simply seek out their own revenge.

Mr. FORBES. And I understand that and don't disagree with you at all on that, but what I am trying to get at specifically is, how do you as a local prosecutor go after the gang networks on these national and international gangs?

Mr. LOGLI. That is, as we used to say in the service, that is above my pay grade.

Mr. FORBES. So you really can't?

Mr. LOGLI. We really can't, and there is where we rely, probably, on cooperation with the U.S. Attorneys Office. They have got the resources. They have got the network of officers in other States, prosecutors in other States. They can really go after more the organization. Our efforts are directed at the individual.

Mr. FORBES. And would you agree with me that it is important to go after the networks and try to pull the networks down?

Mr. LOGLI. If we can, certainly. I mean, if you can go to the head of the organization and decapitate the head, you will reduce their effectiveness.

But I have got to tell you, Congressman, I do not believe that the Latino gangs that we are seeing are terribly organized. I don't believe they are highly organized. I think there is a lot of loose associations. They are not as organized as the Bloods, the Crips, the Gangster Disciples, the Vice Lords. They have got almost a business organization. We haven't quite seen that yet with the Hispanic or Latino gangs.

Mr. FORBES. And last two questions, and I know my time is expired too, but Mr. Kennedy, again, I would love to sit down sometime and talk with all of you at length because you have all got some great ideas, but one of the things that you did emphasize in terms of the balance of your testimony, I think, before, is you stated at one time before that the use of Federal sanctions was very important in ceasefire and knocking the homicide rate way down. And you specifically talked about the effectiveness of the Federal prosecutions, if they were used properly and their judicious use.

And then, Ms. Fernandez, when you talked about the homicides in Washington, D.C., I believe it was five or eight, but those homicides were prosecuted and the people incarcerated, wasn't that correct?

Ms. FERNANDEZ. Yes.

Mr. FORBES. And after that, there were no additional homicides that you could report today, of that group?

Ms. FERNANDEZ. Correct. We put the program in place while the homicides were taking place, and I think that it was both, again, the——

Mr. FORBES. A combination of the two.

Ms. FERNANDEZ. Correct.

Mr. FORBES. Thank you, Mr. Chairman.

Mr. SCOTT. Thank you.

Chief Corwin, your written testimony mentions a Nurse-Family Partnership. Can you describe the effect of that program?

Chief CORWIN. The Nurse-Family Partnership? I am not real familiar with that particular program. It is the Kids Network that are really familiar with that, but we can provide additional information for you if you would like.

Mr. SCOTT. In your written testimony, you indicate that it has shown a reduction in crime, significant reduction in crime, for those that have had that resource. Can you tell us the multidimensional foster care program?

Chief CORWIN. I can give you the other information. I will provide that research to you.

Mr. SCOTT. Okay. And bully prevention?

Chief CORWIN. I believe there is actually people here on the panel who can probably speak specifically to those particular programs.

Mr. ELLIOTT. Mr. Chairman?

Mr. SCOTT. Mr. Elliott?

Mr. ELLIOTT. Those are blueprint programs and I can describe them for you.

The Nurse-Family Partnership is a program that initiates with single at-risk mothers, first pregnancy. It involves a nurse visitation program when she registers for prenatal care and continues with nurse visits to the home until the child is 2 years old. So it is about a 2.5-year intervention.

That intervention has proved very, very effective. It reduces the incidence of child abuse by almost 80 percent. It reduces the unemployment rate on the part of the mothers, the drug involvement on the part of the mothers, and 15 years later, when those kids are adolescents, it reduces the risk for arrest by 60 percent and conviction by almost 90 percent for those kids.

MST is multisystemic family therapy. I mentioned that earlier. It is a program which is a clinical intervention, 6 months. It is a family-based intervention which has proved to be very effective. It can reduce the risk of recidivism by as much as 75 percent.

The multisystemic treatment foster care program is one of the most cost-effective programs we have. It returns about $13 for every dollar we invest in it. It is also for deep end, what we call deep-end kids, but it is a foster care program. And it is one of the programs which we recommend as going to scale with across the country. All three of those programs are programs we could put in across the country.

Mr. SCOTT. And the importance of bully prevention?

Chief CORWIN. The bully prevention program, it is a blueprint program, it is the one developed by Dan Olweus in Norway. That program reduces the incidences of bullying on our elementary and middle school campuses by 50 percent and has a dramatic effect about the social climate of the school and actually increase school performance as well.

Mr. SCOTT. And, Mr. Kennedy, your program has shown success in getting truces. Have you seen any successes in reducing gang membership to begin with?

Mr. KENNEDY. Well, what we produce aren't truces because we don't ask. Truces are voluntary. This is not voluntary. Offering health and bringing in the community is not the same as saying if you don't go along with this, we are going to let you do that. There is an ''or else'' here that is very important.

But, yes, the fact is, and I am now convinced that the absolute most important preventive action we can take is to dethrone the very hard core that is controlling the streets, modeling behavior for younger kids and making the community and all the rest of us look like idiots. And if they lose their standing on the street, then that no longer becomes an attractive track for younger kids and the danger and the fear that drives them into banding together for self-protection is greatly eased.

And if I can refer back to Mr. Forbes' question, we are seeing this basic framework work equally effectively with MS-13, with the Sureno West Coast gangs. We don't see, and nobody that I know that is engaged with MS-13 at the local level, sees the kind of organized, purposeful structure that we are being told MS-13 has. And I think the stories that are being told about MS-13, particularly by the FBI, are profoundly misleading. And I don't know any gang researchers or any people in local law enforcement that agree with those pictures.

Mr. SCOTT. Mr. Logli, you mentioned witness intimidation as a problem. What can we do to address that problem?

Mr. LOGLI. The biggest problem we have at the State level is resources, and——

Mr. SCOTT. What would you do with additional resource?

Mr. LOGLI. We don't have to move people great distances. We can move them from one side of town to another side of town. We can move them temporarily into a motel. We can give them a cell phone so they can call the police if there is a problem. We don't need new identities and move them off into some community in Arizona.

But our resources are really tight on that, and if the Federal Government could provide some money to get these programs going, and then through matching grants and that type of thing encourage States to start their own funding stream, that would be a huge step in a very constructive direction.

Mr. SCOTT. And, finally, Ms. Fernandez, does your GIP program reduce gang membership?

Ms. FERNANDEZ. Yes, it does.

Mr. SCOTT. How does it do that?

Ms. FERNANDEZ. Well, if you come down and talk to any of our kids, a lot of times you find out that the reason that they are in a gang is because they are bored, they didn't have anything to do after school. We get them involved in other stuff.

We have art programs, we have dance programs, we have leadership programs. You name it, we have got an alternative for it, and it is that which the kids are looking for.

You know, in the cases that they have dropped out of school, they need jobs, and so we help them get into those. So it is really creating alternatives that is the key.

Mr. SCOTT. Thank you.

If there are no other questions——

Mr. FORBES. Mr. Chairman, I have a follow-up question for Mr. Kennedy.

Mr. Kennedy, you talked about the fact that these gangs aren't organized. You are aware that the Attorney General and Salvadorian president have just entered arrangements and agreements between the two countries because they felt that they were highly organized and coming back and forth.

So you think that they were both wrong in that recognition?

Mr. KENNEDY. What we see where MS-13 and other Hispanic gangs, which is mostly what we are talking about, with ties, generally it is three-way ties. It is local in the U.S., there is a California connection and then there is a Latin American connection.

What we see going on at the local level is very high levels of crime, including some extremely serious violence. So this is not to say it is not important. It is important. It is very real and it is very dangerous.

But what we see driving that is the same kind of local nonsense that we see with other gang structures. The shots are not being called either from California or from San Salvador. So that is all I can speak to, is what the local presentation is.

Mr. FORBES. In Boston, where you had such good success and all in your process there, now that they have had this up tick, I think, have they asked you to come back there and reinstitute your program there?

Mr. KENNEDY. We have been discussing that, yes.

Mr. FORBES. Have you——

Mr. KENNEDY. They don't need me, all right. There are people in Boston who know this inside out. And the commitment—the public—this is a nasty story, but Boston has now said in plain language, we kicked this thing to the curb, we made a mistake and we need to put it back together.

Ms. WATERS. Mr. Chairman, if I may?

First, I would like to ask you, are there any former gang members in the audience that I could hear from with just their thoughts or their advice about what they think we could be doing?

I don't know. It is up to the Chairman. May I hear from one?

And while they are coming——

Mr. SCOTT. Did you have a question?

Ms. WATERS. I do. Well, that is my question. If I could hear from a gang member their thoughts about what they have heard, any advice that they may have. And before he starts to say to Mr. Kennedy he missed one connection with the so-called Mexican gangs, and that is the prison where the shot callers are. All right. If it is all right with the chair——

Mr. SCOTT [continuing]. Objection to——

Mr. FORBES. Mr. Chairman, the only thing, I would love to hear from them, if we could schedule a time, but we have got several of our Members left. They don't get to ask any questions and all at this particular point in time, so why don't we schedule——

Ms. WATERS. I would ask unanimous consent of my colleagues to allow that to happen.

Mr. SCOTT. Is there objection?

Mr. FORBES. Mr. Chairman, I would just say this. I would think we ought to have an opportunity to have every member be here, just to hear what they say. We want to hear from them. And schedule an opportunity that they can come back and testify. We would love to have them. I would love to hear them and bring in Mr. Cardona and several other people, if you would like to do that.

Ms. WATERS. If I may, Mr. Chairman, I, too, would agree that we should have additional hearings to further explore this——

Mr. SCOTT. There will be additional hearings on this issue, hopefully even field hearings, so we can have additional hearings out in the field, where these situations are.

Ms. WATERS. I would appreciate that. And I would also, if I may, and I don't like pushing this hard, but one of the things that I have discovered working with young people is, they don't think they get their chance at the table. And they don't think we listen and they don't think we care. So if I could indulge my colleagues, I would like to hear from——

Mr. SCOTT. If we can hear briefly, we have to be out of the room by 12:30, okay.

Was there objection?

If you could identify yourself and make a brief statement.

Mr. CARTAGENA. My name is David Cartagena. I would like to thank you for giving me the privilege and opportunity to speak to the Committee.

Thank you, Mr. Chairman.

Thank you, Ms. Waters.

One of the things that I can say real briefly is, growing up with gang affiliation, growing up in a housing project, growing up as an inner-city minority, although I don't have the appearance, what I found is that in my upbringing there was a lot of negative influences. There wasn't no Big Brother program for me. Although it existed, it wasn't in my neighborhood. There wasn't no lawyers, clergy or any positive, basically, male role models, positive influences.

So what I have done in my occupation as a Provident street worker is to become that for youth and kids that have gang involvement, is become somebody, become somebody whose been there, done that and who also now is aspiring to live positively and to try to get them to aspire to want to achieve bigger and better things versus living negative, being reactionary rather than proactive.

So not only am I a nonviolence street worker, I am also a youth advocate. I do job advocacy. I do court advocacy. I got to court and advocate when I can. I am a mentor. I am a mediator. You know, I am a licensed mediator, facilitator. And I am also, more importantly, I am a positive role model, somebody whose been there, whose made the mistakes, who has overcome obstacles and is now willing to give back to the community and help young kids not make the mistakes I have made.

And what I have come to find is that is the thing that strikes a chord with them the most. What they need is people that have lived there, people that are just like them, but that live a whole different frame of mind now, that are trying to steer them away from making it versus in their neighborhoods they have drug dealers, low-level to mid-level. They have people that are emersed in gang activity. And those are their role models. Those are their peers. Those are the people they look up to. Those are the people they look to for input, for information, for guidance.

So I come and I try to intercede and I try to give them better information. I try to give them real street knowledge about, you know, the dangers of being involved in that kind of behavior and stuff.

Thank you.

Mr. FORBES. Can I ask David a question?

David, what gang were you in? I am sorry, you said it was David. Did I misunderstand? I thought you said your name was David, wasn't it?

Mr. CARTAGENA. Yes, that is correct.

Mr. FORBES. David, what gang were you in, if you don't mind telling us.

Mr. CARTAGENA. Almighty Latin King Nation.

Mr. FORBES. And, David, how are you dealing with the young people that you have to deal with in terms of their fear, you know, their desire for protection from other gangs? Is that a very big element out there among them? How do you help them with that?

You know, it is one thing if you have got the guy on the street that is trying to get them involved in buying or selling drugs for monetary reasons, but we are hearing a lot from gang members who say that they were just afraid if they didn't join one gang that they would be intimidated and threatened by another.

Are you experiencing that? And how do you try to protect them from that?

Mr. CARTAGENA. One of the ways that I am able to protect them is that I have no bones or problems with speaking to the opposition, speaking to the other gangs. I am out at 2 p.m. or 2 a.m. It doesn't matter. Anyway I can to try and better the life of a young individual, it is what I am going to do.

So if they feel, if they say, ''Look, you know, I want to come out, but the only thing is, I have a problem because, you know, my manito over there, or my senior, he ain't really going to be looking too favorably at that.''

I will go talk to that individual and I will go speak to the gang itself and I let them know who I am, what I do. And basically, people for the most part, not just gang members, they know right from wrong, you know. They know right from wrong. So if they know I am actually caring and I am coming with compassion and love for that individual, more than likely they don't want any static or bad publicity or anything like that that can come upon them.

Most of the time, they leave the kid alone. Especially because I work with a lot of kids that are under the age of 17.

Mr. FORBES. Any threats upon you individually in doing this?

Mr. CARTAGENA. Not yet. Not yet.

Mr. MONTEIRO. Good afternoon. My name is Sal Monteiro. I represent the Institute for the Study and Practice of Nonviolence.

This is just to the question that you asked earlier, about if gangs get together in a city, do the police say anything or is it a violation of parole.

We work in Providence, and Providence is very small. You know, it is not real big. And we have gang members on all sides of town. And being as small as Providence is, they are going to meet. They are going to run into each other, you know, whether it is at the mall, whether it is at the store, whether it is at the corner or whether it is at the club.

So being as street workers, we are, like Mr. Kennedy said, most of these gangs, there is only two or three guys in there that are really running things and are really saying, you know, running and calling the shots.

So instead of waiting for them to meet each other on the street, whether it is a violation of their parole, we are going to go as street workers, we are going to go get those two or three individuals that are really calling all the shots, and we are going to sit them down and we are going to talk to them and we are going to try to mediate the situation to solve the problem, because most of the problems come from either ''he say,'' you know, ''he say'' information gathering, you know, ''this person said this about me, that person said this about me.''

And, you know, before it gets out of control, instead of letting them meet each other out in the streets, out in public, where, you know, gunshots and fighting and other individuals can get hurt, we bring them down, we are going to sit them down and we are going to talk to them. We are going to mediate the situation. We are going to come to them and find out what the problem is, why you are fighting, what is the problem, and we are going to settle it.

So whether it is a case of violating parole, I don't think we even take that into consideration. The fact is that we want the violence to stop. We don't want gang members.

And also, another thing that we tell the gangs, the young kinds, how we get across to them, that if me and, you know, this gentleman have a problem, he is in one gang, I am not in a gang but I have a problem with him, I go join another gang. Now all the problems—I had one problem with him, but now I got a problem with every person in his gang. I got a problem with all the people that he has a problem with in his gang.

So there is a lot of different ways that, when you come from the street, when you live out there in the 'hood, there is a lot of certain ways that we come across these kids that they see it, they don't see it anywhere else.

Mr. SCOTT. If there are no further questions, I would like to thank the witnesses for there testimony today.

Ms. JACKSON LEE. Mr. Chairman? Mr. Chairman? Might I, please?

Mr. SCOTT. The gentlelady from Texas?

As I had indicated, we need to be out of the room by 12:30.

Ms. JACKSON LEE. I thank the Chairman very much.

This is a issue that I would like to credit Chairman Scott for beginning even before 1995, my 1st year in the United States Congress and certainly the work of Congresswoman Waters and a lot of other Members. I remember flying around on field hearings, asking attorney generals and law enforcement officers in 1995 not to fall victim to the crime bill and believe that incarceration was the only answer.

And we have reaped what we have sowed. We literally ceded America to gangs and gang violence, primarily because we left no other alternatives and opportunities for young people.

This may be the most historic and real opportunity for us to get real and to be able to confront many of these issues.

I would just ask two straightforward questions, David, one, and then to the distinguished academicians. Who is first?

David, is there hope? Can intervention now really work? Can we explain or get the word by way of resources and prevention dollars to the folk on the street and folk like you who are working to make a real decided change?

Mr. CARTAGENA. I would just like to try to give you a brief example, all right?

I have a 16-year-old juvenile who is part of an African-American gang on the east side of Providence that I work with on a constant basis. I do follow up. I constantly outreach to him.

He called me about 3 weeks ago. He was at a basketball game, playing a rival team. There were 30 or 40 kids there from another rival faction that he has beef with that all wanted to get him. And because he was on the other side of town, he had no protection. He didn't have any of his companions with him, his colleagues or whatever, compadres, and he called me.

And he said, ''Look, David, I am at this basketball game. I don't know what I am going to do. These dudes really want to get at me. What am I going to do?'' I said, ''I will be right there.''

Ms. JACKSON LEE. SOS.

Mr. CARTAGENA. I shot right over there. I sat in the bleachers with him, because his game had already passed. I sat in the bleachers with him.

At the conclusion of the game, I actually had assistance from some of my colleagues and some of the faculty at the school to whisk him out of the back of the school and get him out of there.

Now, upon the conclusion of the game, police came to the area, responded, because they heard of a threat of gang violence potentially happening. They pulled over a car and arrested four juveniles who were his potential enemies and confiscated a firearm in the car.

So what I am saying is, does it work? Of course it does. He could have probably got killed. He could have got stomped to death that night, you know. But because he believed in a youth worker, he believed in an adult that could help him and assist him and get him out of that problem, he is been all right.

And since then, he hasn't even hung with his east side buddies. He hasn't been in any trouble. He has been working. He has been going to school, minding his business. He is still on the basketball team. He just steers clear from certain games. But that is my——

Ms. JACKSON LEE. And he is alive.

Mr. CARTAGENA. And he is alive. That is my testament to the fact that this does work——

Ms. JACKSON LEE. Can I just quickly, for Dr. Elliott, just very quickly.

They laughed at me——

Mr. SCOTT. Excuse me. I ask the gentlelady from Texas to suspend because, as I indicated, we have to be out——

Ms. JACKSON LEE. Is it 12:30 already? I can't see the——

Mr. SCOTT. It is after 12:30. And we can have written questions for our witnesses, which we will forward to you and ask that you answer as promptly as you can. They will be made part of the record.

And without objection, the hearing is adjourned.

[Whereupon, at 12:32 p.m., the Subcommittee was adjourned.]

APPENDIX
MATERIAL SUBMITTED FOR THE HEARING RECORD

Prepared Statement of the Honorable Sheila Jackson Lee, a Representative in Congress from the State of Texas, and Member, Subcommittee on Crime, Terrorism, and Homeland Security

Mr. Chairman, I move to strike the last word.

Thank you, Mr. Chairman for holding this hearing. Let me congratulate you also on your election as Chairman of this very important subcommittee. Congratulations also to you Mr. Forbes, on assuming leadership of this panel for the minority. I am confident that working together, we can achieve great things for the American people. We have much work to do and I look forward to working with all members of the subcommittee to address the real challenges facing our country in the areas of youth violence, juvenile crime, and gang intervention.

Let me also welcome each of our witnesses:

1. Professor Delbert (Del) Elliott, Director of Center for the Study and Prevention of Violence University of Colorado;
2. Dr. Jeffrey Butts, Senior Researcher, Chapin Hall Center for Children University of Chicago;
3. Mr. David Kennedy, Director, Center for Crime Prevention and Control John Jay College of Criminal Justice;
4. Mr. Teny Gross, Executive Director, Institute for the Study and Practice of Nonviolence, Providence, RI;
5. Ms. Mai Fernandez, Legal and Strategy Director Latin American Youth Center, Washington, DC; and
6. Chief James Corwin, Chief of Police, Kansas City, MO;
7. Professor Lawrence W. Sherman, Director, Jerry Lee Center of Criminology University of Pennsylvania; and
8. Mr. Paul Logli, Chairman of the Board, National District Attorneys Association.

I look forward to their testimony.

The subject of today's hearing is ''Making Communities Safer: Youth Violence and Gang Interventions that Work.'' This hearing could not be more timely, Mr. Chairman.

Recent news reports cite an increase in crime in several major cities, particularly violent crimes. Much of the rise in violent crimes reported is attributed to youths, including youths associated with gangs. Even before the recent reports suggesting increases in violence committed by youths, we have seen reports of increasing gang violence and other criminal activities on a local as well as international scale.

Mr. Chairman, today, state juvenile justice systems are overburdened and underfunded. Ongoing budget reductions at both the federal and state levels have closed programs vital to impoverished communities and children. These programs keep children out of trouble and out of the juvenile justice system, providing mentoring, after-school opportunities, and other evidenced-based prevention services. By the same token, there is little, if any, funding available for proven intervention programs such as substance abuse prevention and treatment, mental health screening and treatment, gang prevention and intervention and more.

The result is a disturbing reality. The only thing our nation guarantees a child in need is a detention or prison cell after they get into trouble. Research shows that there are many prevention and early intervention programs that work, yet we seem fixated as a society on waiting for kids to get in trouble and commit crimes, including violent crimes, then by spending much, much more on increased incarceration, the most expensive and least effective option available to address the problems presented by at-risk youths.

Punitive incarceration approaches such as mandatory minimum sentences and prosecuting juveniles as adults to apply them are justified by, and geared to, the most violent youth offenders. Yet, the vast majority of youths caught up in the snare of these type punitive approaches do not commit violent offense. Only 25 percent of the youths incarcerated have committed a violent offense. A recent report showed that two-thirds of the detention facilities in 47 states hold youth who do not need to be in detention as they wait for mental health services. Over a six-month period in 2003, nearly 15,000 incarcerated youth, some as young as seven, were held in hundreds of juvenile facilities across the country because mental health services were not available in their communities.

While only a small percentage of children have committed violent offenses, we are incarcerating children because we literally do not have effective alternatives in place, hardly in keeping with the original intent of the juvenile justice system. According to a report from the American Bar Association: "[I]ncreasingly, it is not so much the criminality of the behavior but the lack of alternatives for children with severe emotional and behavior problems, children who have been expelled from school, and children whose families cannot provide adequate care that brings them into the juvenile justice system."

The lack of available services for poor children who need them creates an enormous disadvantage and makes it much more likely that they will be incarcerated than children from families with resources.

And there is another grave impact from the tendency of our nation to concentrate on costly, after-the-fact punitive approaches as opposed to effective prevention and early intervention strategies. Statistics demonstrate racially disparate application upon our youth of many of the most punitive laws, particularly drug laws. For those charged with drug offenses, Black youths are 48 times more likely to be incarcerated than White youths. For violent offenses, Black youths are nine times more likely to be incarcerated than are White youths for the same offenses. Among youth with no prior admissions, Latinos are 13 times more likely to be incarcerated than Whites for drug offenses. For violent offenses, Latinos are five times more likely to be incarcerated.

Children may receive a more punitive disposition than they might otherwise if their parents are not involved or are unable to leave work to accompany them to court, since there is no advocate to assure the court that they will monitor the child's progress and conditions of release. In addition, sentencing patterns have been shown to have a racially disparate impact due to many factors.

Studies show that, given the same behavioral symptoms, more Black youths than White youths are arrested, prosecuted, convicted and incarcerated, and more White youths than Black youths are placed in mental health institutions as opposed to penal institutions. As Ed Latessa, a criminologist at the University of Cincinnati notes, ''[I]f your family has money, you get psychiatric intervention . . . if they don't, you get the prison psychologist.''

Mr. Chairman, we know what works: prevention. Collaborative and comprehensive approaches to community violence that create working partnerships between law enforcement and prevention-intervention groups work. Prevention saves lives and money. It pulls poor and minority children out of the ''cradle to prison pipeline.'' It saves enormous amounts in the long run, yet can generate higher costs in the short run. Thus, garnering the political will among elected officials on two-, four, and six-year electoral cycles to invest in prevention for at-risk youths is an ongoing and difficult challenge.

Prevention and intervention programs keep children from getting into trouble and pull children out of trouble. These programs also save lives and taxpayer dollars. For every child diverted from a lifetime of crime, we save between $1.3 and $1.5 million, which is a conservative estimate since potential cost benefits such as better salaries and reduced public service costs outside the justice system are difficult to measure. To put these savings in perspective, a program that costs $10,000 per child, and has a success rate of only one in 100, still saves us more by serving 100 children and saving only one child than it would cost to lose that child to a lifetime of crime. Our public policies must be responsive to research and evaluation findings on the value of prevention and intervention.

Again, thank you Mr. Chairman for holding this hearing. I look forward to hearing from our distinguished panel of witnesses. I yield back my time.

Eastern District of New York

United States Attorney's Office

The United States Attorney's Office for the Eastern District of New York ("EDNY") headquartered in Brooklyn, New York, serves approximately 8 million people, who are geographically distributed throughout three of New York City's five urban boroughs (Brooklyn, Queens and Staten Island). The district also encompasses the largely suburban communities of Nassau and Suffolk Counties, Long Island, which nevertheless have quasi-urban centers with large low income residents and growing immigrant communities. The large size, dense population and the ethnic diversity within the District presents significant challenges to a unified law enforcement effort to combat gangs in the District.

The EDNY has been a leader in crafting innovative responses to the ever-growing violent-gang crisis, and was at the forefront in embracing a task force approach to combating violent gangs. In 1994, the EDNY established a section of experienced prosecutors devoted to the prosecution of violent gangs and other violent criminal enterprises. The EDNY's approach to combating gang violence has been widely used as a model for other U.S. Attorney's Offices. EDNY prosecutors have also been active in participating in and teaching at gang-related training sessions, including at the National Advocacy Center. Additionally, EDNY prosecutors have lectured in Jamaica (at the invitation of OPDAT) on investigative and prosecutive strategies in dismantling violent gangs, to the NYPD concerning gang issues, and at an FBI-sponsored Safe Streets training session in Denver, Colorado.

The success of the EDNY for more than a decade has hinged on the ability to combine local and federal law enforcement efforts at the investigative level. Unlike the classic task force model often used by the FBI or DEA, in which Special Agents are teamed with particular police detectives in standing task forces, the EDNY found it desirable for federal law enforcement to work with the New York Police Department ("NYPD") at the precinct level, teaming up on a neighborhood-by-neighborhood basis to attack the deep-rooted problem of neighborhood-based gangs. Because police precincts are the greatest source of knowledge about the violent crime problem in New York neighborhoods and have access to the detailed history of the worst gangs operating within each precinct, their inclusion on federal investigations has been crucial in identifying and prosecuting members of dozens of gangs throughout the years. This approach has been particularly useful in developing our successful Public Housing Initiative, aimed at entrenched gangs that control the area in and around dozens of large housing complexes. To address the challenges presented by gangs on Long Island, where chapters of La Mara Salvatrucha ("MS-13"), Bloods, Crips, Latin Kings, Salvadorans With Pride (SWP) and Nétas gangs maintain chapters, the EDNY spearheaded the formation of the Long Island Gang Task Force in 1999. Currently, the Task Force encompasses agents and officers of the FBI, Immigration and Customs Enforcement ("ICE"), the New York State Police, Nassau County Corrections and the Nassau County, Hempstead, Freeport and Port Washington Police Departments.

The Eastern District of New York has found that the arrest and ultimate conviction of an entire gang, together with the stiff federal sentences that are inevitably imposed, permanently disable the gang and allow the Office to focus our resources on the next problem area. The formula has been quite successful for many years. Indeed, according to data recently compiled by Executive Office of United States Attorneys for the period FY 2003 to the present, the EDNY leads the nation in the number of prosecutions of violent gang members through the use of racketeering statutes. Below is a representative sample of the tremendous success the EDNY has had in combating gangs.

EDNY Successful Prosecutions

1. Stapleton Crew

This Office used the federal racketeering statutes to dismantle the Stapleton Crew, a violent narcotics trafficking gang that operated in the Stapleton section of Staten Island from late 1999 until March 2003. The crew maintained an arsenal of illegal firearms, available to all members, which were used to protect its narcotics operation and to intimidate and eliminate its enemies through repeated acts of violence. In March 2003, one of the Crew's members, Ronnell Wilson, murdered two undercover New York City Police Department detectives who were attempting to purchase firearms from the Crew. The government charged six members of the enterprise, five of them with RICO, RICO conspiracy, murder in aid of racketeering, narcotics trafficking, robbery and other charges. Five defendants pled guilty, four of whom have been sentenced to terms of incarceration of ten, twelve, twenty-five and twenty-seven years, respectively. Another defendant is cooperating with the government. The final defendant, Ronnell Wilson, was found guilty after a jury trial in December 2006 of murdering the two dectectives. In January 2007, the same jury voted to impose the death penalty.

2. United States v. Kenneth McGriff ("Supreme Team")

This Office charged three defendants with racketeering crimes related to the efforts of legendary Queens, New York gang leader Kenneth "Supreme" McGriff and others to rebuild his violent narcotics organization after his release from federal prison in 1993. McGriff and a co-defendant were recently convicted and will receive life sentences. The remaining defendant pled guilty pursuant to a cooperation agreement

3. La Mara Salvatrucha ("MS-13") Street Gang

La Mara Salvatrucha ("MS-13") is a violent gang, composed primarily of immigrants from Central America with chapters throughout the United States, including Long Island and Queens, New York. The gang engages in murder, robbery, narcotics trafficking, gang assault, firearms trafficking, interstate transportation of stolen vehicles, sexual assault, witness tampering and obstruction of justice, among other crimes. As detailed below, this Office has indicted MS-13 gang members in both Long Island and Queens.

a. **Long Island MS-13 Prosecutions**

In a series of prosecutions charging violent crimes in aid of racketeering pursuant to Title 18, United States Code, Section 1959 ("VICAR") from 2003 through 2005, more than thirty members of MS-13 have been prosecuted for a series of violent crimes, including murders and assaults, as well as firearms offenses. To date, more than twenty MS-13 members have pled guilty to violent racketeering charges while four others were convicted on murder and assault counts in three trials. The victims of the charged murders and assaults included innocent bystanders, rival gang members and MS-13 members who were assisting law enforcement authorities. Some of the victims were as young as 15 years old.

b. **Queens MS-13 Prosecutions**

In 2006, several members of MS-13 chapters located in Queens, New York have been charged with violating RICO and VICAR to include charges of murder, attempted murder, assault and robbery. The defendants are awaiting trial and face sentences ranging from ten years' to life imprisonment.

4. **Woodbine Crew**

The Woodbine Crew was a violent gang based in the Bushwick neighborhood of Brooklyn, New York, that engaged in murder, heroin trafficking, violent robbery of rival narcotics traffickers, witness tampering and obstruction of justice. Members of the Woodbine Crew were charged in two separate indictments with RICO, RICO conspiracy and murder in aid of racketeering violations. After two trials in 2001 and 2004, the government convicted ten members of the Woodbine Crew, who were sentenced to lengthy terms of imprisonment, ranging from twenty-six years' imprisonment to life.

5. **United States v. Dwayne Stone et al., ("Folk Nation")**

Seven members and associates of the Folk Nation gang were charged in 2005 in a twenty-eight-count indictment with RICO and RICO conspiracy, which included six murders, five attempted murders, murder conspiracy, assault and related firearms counts. The charges relate to a number of gang-related murders and other acts of violence, including a drive-by shooting that resulted in the death of an innocent bystander and the attempted murder of several New York City Police Department officers. This case is awaiting trial.

6. **United States v. Damion Hardy, et al. (Cash Money Brothers)**

Seven members of a violent narcotics gang known as the "Cash Money Brothers" were charged in 2005 with RICO, RICO conspiracy, murder in aid of racketeering, kidnaping and robbery. Two defendants were convicted in October 2006 after trial of these charges. The other five defendants are facing racketeering and murder in aid of racketeering charges. Two other defendants have pled guilty to racketeering charges.

7. Patio Crew

This Office convicted six members of the "Patio Crew," an extraordinarily violent Jamaican narcotics gang that dominated the drug business in the Flatbush area of Brooklyn between 1989 and 2001. These defendants were convicted of a combination of narcotics, RICO, RICO conspiracy, firearms and murder charges. Two defendants, Emile Dixon and Humphrey Stewart, were convicted in separate trials in 2003 and 2004. In the Dixon trial, this Office sought the death penalty based on Dixon's participation in an obstruction of justice murder and a separate narcotics-related homicide. The jury convicted Dixon of all counts, including RICO, RICO conspiracy, murder-in-aid-of-racketeering, murder in furtherance of narcotics trafficking, narcotics conspiracy, robbery and firearms charges, but did not vote to impose the death penalty. Emile Dixon and Humphrey Stewart were each sentenced to life imprisonment while Jermaine Dixon received a sentence of thirty years' imprisonment.

8. United States v. Darryl Tyler, et al (D-Nice Enterprise)

This Office charged eight members and associates of the "D-Nice Enterprise," a violent narcotics gang that sold massive quantities of crack cocaine and cocaine in Brooklyn, New York and Baltimore, Maryland from the early 1980s until 2000. The defendants were charged with RICO, RICO conspiracy, murder, murder conspiracy and narcotics trafficking. None of the charged defendants were juveniles, but the enterprise frequently employed juveniles to work as low-level drug sellers. Five defendants were convicted in two separate trials in 2002 and 2004; one was sentence to life imprisonment; three defendants were sentenced to thirty years' imprisonment, and one defendant was sentenced to ten years' imprisonment. The other defendants pled guilty.

9. United States v. Tyrone Hunter, et al. ("The Enterprise")

Five members of a violent narcotics trafficking organization, charged in the indictments as the "Enterprise," were charged with RICO, RICO conspiracy, murder in aid of racketeering, narcotics trafficking and money laundering. The gang operated primarily in the East New York section of Brooklyn from approximately 1985 until 2003. Enterprise members and associates committed acts of violence and murder to protect their narcotics operation and the reputation of the Enterprise and routinely committed shootings and assaults for the purpose of collecting drug debts. The Enterprise members also made money by murdering and robbing other criminals of their drugs and cash. Three defendants have pled guilty pursuant to cooperation agreements. Two defendants were convicted last week on charges including RICO, RICO conspiracy, murder, obstruction of justice, robbery, and money laundering.

10. United States v. Curt Mathews, et al ("M&P Crew")

Three defendants were charged in 2004 with RICO, RICO conspiracy, murder in aid of racketeering, attempted murder in aid of racketeering, bank robbery conspiracy, kidnaping, and several other charges. Three other defendants pled guilty to other charges related to the crew's crimes. The charges stem from the defendants' participation in a violent Brooklyn-based crew that sold narcotics, robbed banks and other businesses and kidnaped rival drug dealers from 1998 through 2002.

11. Martin Family Crew

Eleven members of a violent narcotics trafficking gang, the "Martin Family Crew," that operated in Brooklyn and several other cities along the Eastern seaboard were charged in 2005 with racketeering-related charges, including RICO, RICO conspiracy and murder in aid of racketeering (nine other members of the gang were charged with non-racketeering charges). All defendants have pled guilty and are awaiting sentencing and most face potential life sentences.

12. United States v. Laval Farmer, et al. (Bloods)

In 2004, five members of the Bloods' "Velt Gangsta Lanes" ("VGL") set, located in Roosevelt, New York, were charged with various violent crimes in aid of racketeering pursuant to Title 18, United States Code, Section 1959 (VICAR), involving murder and a firebombing. The five VGL members were among over fifty Bloods members on Long Island who have been prosecuted by this Office. One of the leaders of the VGL set, Laval Farmer, was convicted after trial in 2006 on VICAR murder charges for the killing of a 14-year-old whom Farmer mistakenly believed to be a member of the Crips, and the shooting of a fellow Bloods member. This case effectively dismantled the VGL set on Long Island.

13. The Crime Family

Twelve members of a violent narcotics trafficking gang known as "The Crime Family" were charged in 2001 with RICO, RICO conspiracy, narcotics trafficking and murder in aid of racketeering. Another twenty defendants were prosecuted by the Brooklyn District Attorney's Office as part of a coordinated state-federal investigation. The Crime Family ran a retail crack cocaine distribution operation from a public housing development in the East New York section of Brooklyn between 1997 and 2001 and regularly engaged in violence to protects its drug proceeds and reputation. The Crime Family possessed an arsenal of illegal firearms which were used by Crime Family members in several shootings, including a murder committed on January 25, 2000. The leader of the organization was convicted after trial in 2003 and sentenced to life in prison. The co-leader of the gang pled guilty and was sentenced to thirty-three years' imprisonment. The other defendants also pled guilty.

14. Boston Crew

Four members and associates of a violent narcotics organization, identified in the indictments as the "Boston Crew," were charged with racketeering-related charges, including RICO, RICO conspiracy and murder in aid of racketeering, as well as narcotics charges. The organization operated in New York City, the Dominican Republic and Boston, Massachusetts. All of the defendants, including one who was extradited from the Netherlands to the United States, pled guilty.

15. FDP Crew

Thirteen members of a violent narcotics gang known as the "FDP Crew" were indicted in 2005 on RICO, RICO conspiracy and other offenses including narcotics trafficking, robbery, murder in aid of racketeering and firearms charges. Two members of the crew are charged with attempted murder for shooting at law enforcement officers on the crew's block. One defendant is charged with the murder of a rival gang member. Eight of the defendants have pled guilty or cooperated. The remaining five defendants are awaiting trial.

16. United States v. Carlos Gil, et al. (Latin Kings)

Two members of the Almighty Latin Kings Nation have been charged with murder in aid of racketeering for the 2001 murder of a rival gang member. Carlos Gil was charged with murder in aid of racketeering in December 2004 and is awaiting trial.

17. U.S. v. Amadeo Rodriguez, et al. (Nétas)

Seven members of the Nétas' Freeport, New York "chapter" were charged in 2004 in an indictment and an information with VICAR murder, conspiracy, and assault charges, as well as firearms offenses. The defendants included the Nétas' Vice President and the gang's "Leader of Discipline." Most of the charges relate to a street war between the MS-13 and the Nétas, which originated with the November 1999 murder of a pre-med student at Stonybrook University. The victim was with several of the Nétas defendants when he was repeatedly shot and killed after MS-13 members mistakenly believed him to be a Nétas member. During the war with MS-13, two Nétas members murdered an innocent victim whom they mistakenly believed to be one of the leaders of MS-13 on Long Island.

18. Pagans Outlaw Motorcycle Club

On February 22, 2002, dozens of heavily-armed members of the Pagans Outlaw Motorcycle Club descended upon the Vanderbilt Catering Hall in Plainview, New York to attack a public event hosted by the Hell's Angels. About a dozen people were shot, stabbed or beaten, and one Pagan was killed. Approximately sixty-five Pagans – including three members of the Pagans' "Mother Club" – pled guilty to VICAR racketeering charges stemming from the fight, and a holdout defendant was convicted of VICAR racketeering counts at trial. The defendants were sentenced to between two and seven years' imprisonment for their involvement in this brawl. This prosecution essentially eliminated the presence of the Pagans on Long Island.

19. Park Hill Bloods

This Office charged Constantine McLaughlin with conspiracy to commit murder and murder in aid of racketeering and related firearms charges stemming from his participation in a murder for the purpose of gaining entrance to the Park Hill Bloods, a violent street gang. McLaughlin, who was 29 at the time of the indictment, was convicted after trial in 2005 of murder conspiracy and was sentenced to the statutory maximum ten years in prison.

EDNY Gang Prevention Efforts

The District has leveraged resources and coordinated the juvenile gang prevention and early intervention activities of PSN, Weed and Seed and the Public Housing Safety Initiative. Weed and Seed's popular and successful DEFY Program operates in the same neighborhoods as the designated PSN enforcement Hot Spots. Through DEFY, at-risk young people from the Weed and Seed neighborhoods are offered intensive summer camp programs with follow-up mentoring activities during the school year. Through the Public Housing Safety Initiative funding, the Queens District Attorney's Office and the Center for Court Innovation are expanding the Youth Court program in one of the most gang-impacted neighborhoods in the City – also a Weed and Seed neighborhood. Related initiatives led by PSN partners include the Queens County DA's Star Track and Nassau County DA's Rising Star programs, which provide school-based mentoring by Assistant District Attorneys.

The District's Weed and Seed and Public Housing Safety Initiatives also support the Kings County DA's Offices reentry program for parolees. In this program, called ComALERT for Community and Law Enforcement Resources Together, counselors screen parolees ages 16-24 for substance abuse and refer eligible parolees for treatment and focused assistance for transition back to society. The participants attend weekly individual- and group-counseling sessions. Parolees participating in the ComALERT program also receive employment assistance, including referral to transitional employment or training. ComALERT clients also receive housing assistance as needed.

On November 16, 2006, the U.S. Attorney's Office for the Eastern District of New York took part in the Youth Violence & Gangs Conference sponsored by the Safe and Supportive Schools and Community Consortium and Hofstra University. The conference focused on community-based services for gang prevention. The U.S. Attorney's Office teamed with PSN partners, including the Nassau DA's Office and representatives of local school districts, to provide an overview of coordinated enforcement and prevention efforts. The workshop, "Project Safe Neighborhoods - A Strategic Approach to Combating Gang and Gun Violence," was well received by community and law enforcement participants and the office has been asked to replicate the presentation in other parts of Long Island.

On December 1, 2006, the U.S. Attorney's Office held a Gang Prevention Summit at the Federal Courthouse in Central Islip, NY. The Summit was attended by over 100 people, representing 6 Federal agencies, and 12 local law enforcement and district attorney's offices.

The day-long conference included a panel discussion entitled "Alternative Strategies: Prevention, Intervention & Deterrence."

The District's PSN School Violence Prevention Initiative (SVPI) is being implemented in partnership with the Nassau County DA's Office, The Urban Institute, and the School Districts of Uniondale, Hempstead, Roosevelt, Westbury, and Freeport. The first phase began a year ago and has shown promising results. The initiative incorporates the Second Step and Peacemakers programs and educates youth in anger management and conflict resolution at the middle school level. The participating schools held a joint ceremony on October 18, 2006, the Day of National Concern about Young People and Gun Violence. The program included awards for the youth anti-violence poster contest and Student Pledge against Gun Violence. The District has begun the second phase of this PSN violence prevention initiative in Suffolk County, building upon the demonstrated success of the first year.

Project Safe Neighborhoods and Anti-Gang Grants - FY 2006

Anti-Gang Initiative - $578,967. Project end date: 12/31/2008
The Fund for the City of New York's Center for Court Innovation will use $578,967 in FY2006 Anti-Gang grant funds to support anti-gang and firearm prosecutions in the five counties that comprise the Eastern District of New York: Kings, Nassau, Queens, Richmond and Suffolk. Funds will be used for precinct-level investigators and local prosecutors dedicated to gang and firearms cases. Funding will also be used to contract a community resource specialist through the Urban Institute to assess and advise on the initiative's impacts.

BJA FY 2006 Project Safe Neighborhoods - $276,099. Project end date: 05/31/2009
The Fund for the City of New York will use $276,099 in funding for the Eastern District of New York. Activities will be administered through the Center for Court Innovation with the following five contracts: 1) a part-time Assistant District Attorney in Kings County to focus on screening and referring cases for Federal prosecution as well as track gun cases in targeted hot spots; 2) a part-time Assistant District Attorney in Queens County to focus on interstate gun trafficking through the Narcotics Investigation Bureau; 3) a part-time Assistant District Attorney in Richmond County to focus on criminal enterprises centered in and around housing complexes on Staten Island; 4) a combination of law enforcement investigation, prosecution, and probation strategies will be staffed in Nassau County; and 5) the Urban Institute will conduct prevention and intervention programs in schools to deter youth from gangs, guns, and violence as well as provide on-going assessments of the PSN effort for the district.

Southern District of Texas

United States Attorney's Office (USAO)

The Southern District of Texas USAO promotes prevention initiatives by funding programs which include community education of federal and state gun laws and the distribution of consequence information for committing crimes with firearms especially, directed toward (1) re-entering offenders, (2) those currently on probation, and (3) juveniles.

The Texas Attorney General's Office, a grant recipient, created the "Consequences" curriculum for middle and junior high school students. The curriculum includes 10 chapters relating to gun crime, hate crime, violence and gangs. The program utilizes an interactive CD-Rom which includes interviews with Texas Youth Commission students who specifically address the consequences of gang involvement and firearms possession. Over 10,000 CD-Roms have been distributed across the state to nearly 550 agencies, schools and service providers. Fort Bend County Juvenile Probation Department's "Choices and Consequences" diversion program utilizes the "Consequences" curriculum as a means to prevent further juvenile criminal activities. Attendees are tracked for future interaction with the Fort Bend County juvenile justice system. From January 1, to June 30, 2006, Fort Bend County reported a recidivism rate of only 15% for youth that attended the program during the previous year.

The Texas Department of Criminal Justice (TDCJ) Parole Division has now completed production of a 17-minute "Drop the Gun" videotape, customized for Texas parolees. This video features three Texas U.S. Attorneys with opening comments from the Texas Department of Criminal Justice Executive Director. The video consists primarily of excepts from interviews with three convicted felons who had previously been paroled from state prison and subsequently were prosecuted by federal authorities and received federal prison time for firearms violations. Each of these convicted felons discuss their lack of knowledge of federal gun laws as they relate to convicted felons, as well as their shock that their federal sentences were not subject to parole, as is often the case in the state system. These interviews include powerful accounts of the impact the federal convictions had on them and their families, including the recognition that federal prisoners are often incarcerated away from their home states. The "Drop the Gun" video was distributed to approximately 100 TDCJ Institutional Division Units. It is shown as part of the Pre-Release Changing Habits and Achieving New Goals to Empower Success (CHANGES) curriculum. This video will be shown to approximately 25,000 offenders annually as well as paroled offenders during the "New Arrival" orientation classes. Pre and post-tests of content understanding are also administered to all offenders who view the video for subsequent evaluation by administrators. The video was reproduced and adapted for the state probation audience and is in the process of distribution to probation offices statewide.

One of the District's strongest non-law enforcement partners in Houston is the Mayor's Anti-Gang Office whose mission is intervention and prevention of gang involvement. The coordinators for the Weed and Seed sites in Houston are housed within this office. Mayor's Anti-Gang personnel work directly with gang involved youth to help them move away from the gang lifestyle and provide both youth and adult educational programs to increase awareness of the dangers of gang involvement.

The district has held the first of three gang summits. The first occurred in Houston and was attended by approximately 75 individuals from numerous law enforcement agencies and community organizations. Attendees included representatives from the U.S. Attorney's Office, Houston Independent School District, Harris County Sheriff's Office, HPD, Harris County Juvenile Probation Services, Harris County District Attorney's Office, ATF, FBI, DEA, ICE, Federal Detention Center, U.S. Marshal Service, U.S. Probation, Texas Youth Commission, Texas Department of Public Safety, TDCJ, TDCJ-Gang Division, Texas Attorney General's Office, and HIDTA. Through the summit, the District was able to (1) share what each agency is accomplishing regarding gang enforcement, prevention, intervention and education, (2) identify gaps in services, (3) identify strengths and weaknesses, and (4) discuss future strategies. Additional summits are planned for Victoria and Laredo.

Additional Grants focused on Gang Prevention

Gang Resistance Education and Training - $196, 510. Project end date: 06/30/2007
The Office of Harris County Constable Precinct 7 has adopted a multifaceted stance against gangs involving prevention, education, enforcement, community involvement, referral, and collaboration. With the G.R.E.A.T. program and curriculum as the key mechanisms in combating gang proliferation, the Precinct's strategy is to expand the G.R.E.A.T. program, to expand its reach in the community, and to continue to work with the community, interfaith programs, and other agencies to achieve this. The Precinct 7 G.R.E.A.T program is central to the Precinct's fight to deter youth from becoming involved in gangs and street crime. Funding from this grant will be used to expand the reach of Constable Precinct 7's G.R.E.A.T. program. This will include enhancement of the Summer Program, introduction of the Families Training Program, and the assignment of additional officers to help reach all eligible and at-risk schoolchildren in the Precinct.

Gang Resistance Education and Training - $50,000. Project end date: 06/30/2007
The Precinct 6 G.R.E.A.T. program strives to impact the lives of students participating in the program by providing gang-awareness education classes, enhancing self esteem, and providing alternatives, such as youth sports and activities. The program will reach about 4,800 high-risk students in both elementary and middle schools within the Precinct this year. The deputies assigned to the G.R.E.A.T. program seek to better educate children, parents and the general public about the negative effects of gang involvement and activities, while performing proactive community policing. To carry out the mission of G.R.E.A.T, Precinct 6 will continue to implement the program's four components; elementary, middle school, family training, and summer activities. It is the intent of Precinct 6 to reach the precinct's most vulnerable and susceptible children, as identified by the abovementioned methods. With these grant funds, Precinct 6 will increase the number of officers assigned full-time to the G.R.E.A.T. Program from two to four to meet the increasingly difficult challenge from the influence of gangs. Currently, Precinct 6 is participating in all four of the G.R.E.A.T. programs. The Deputies are devoted 100 percent of the time to implementing the G.R.E.A.T. program, frequently working overtime without compensation in order to see to the success of the program.

The Houston Mayor's Anti-gang Office operates a Gang Free Schools and Communities project originally funded by OJJDP in 2001 and continuing through 2007. This project targeting the

Eastern District of Virginia

United States Attorney's Office – Gang Prevention Summit

The United States Attorneys for the Eastern and Western Districts of Virginia, along with the Governor and Attorney General of Virginia, hosted a gang prevention summit on December 11, 2006, in Richmond. The summit focused on prevention, intervention, and suppression efforts, and the audience included police chiefs and sheriffs, Commonwealth's Attorneys, federal law enforcement managers, state probation officers, and social service organizations from throughout the state. The enforcement component included a presentation by Director General Rodrigo Avila Avilez of the El Salvadoran National Police (Policia Nacional Civil) and facilitated discussions amongst law enforcement leaders to share successful gang strategies from around the state.

Additional DOJ Grant-Funded Activities

The Richmond, Virginia Gang Reduction and Intervention Project is the local name for the Gang Reduction Program that is operated by the Attorney General's Office for the Commonwealth. This project is based on a collaboration of State, local, community- and faith-based organizations engaged in gang prevention, intervention, and enforcement. The program was originally funded in 2003 through a $2.5 million cooperative agreement that continues through 2007. The program target area is on the south side of Richmond in an area identified as the Broadrock corridor.

The Richmond Police Department received $60,000 in FY 2006 to facilitate the G.R.E.A.T. Program in each of the nine middle schools that have approximately 2,400 7th graders. A large concentration of effort and resources will be for two middle schools that serve the South Richmond target area. Those schools are Boushall and Elkhardt Middle Schools. Collectively those schools serve approximately 650 7th grade students. The program curriculum will be taught by G.R.E.A.T. certified officers.

The Newport News Police Department was awarded $122,974 under the G.R.E.A.T program. The Police Department in conjunction with the Boys & Girls Clubs of Virginia Peninsula, and the U. S. Army (Ft. Eustis) will use the grant funds to center efforts around a one-week summer camp for 12-17 year old children who are susceptible to gang influence and involvement. Specifically, the grant funds will be used to: 1. Hire one full-time officer to serve as the G.R.E.A.T. coordinator for the middle schools, to administer Police Academy for Youth, and to coordinate the summer camp program, as well as other youth-related prevention programs in the department. 2. Implement an experimental summer camp program for 2006 that will serve 120 students in the middle and high schools. 3. Implement the G.R.E.A.T. Family Component into the existing Citizens' Police Academy for Youth. 4. Improve the existing G.R.E.A.T. Program at Huntington Middle School by providing incentives to the participating students and expand the G.R.E.A.T. Program to the other seven middle schools.

The City of Norfolk will use JAG funds ($292,001) to: support police overtime for community policing activities; purchase computer hardware and software for advanced crime

Northern District of Georgia

The Northern District of Georgia's PSN Initiative has partnered with several community-based prevention programs to combat gang violence: the Boys and Girls Club on Singleton Road in Norcross, Georgia was funded to institute its national anti-gang program in an area that is a hotbed for Hispanic gang activity; Caminar Latino, a faith based, life-skills program that attacks gang influence by creating a strong home environment; the Latin American Association, perhaps the most vibrant Latino based organization in metro Atlanta; and the Pan-Asian Society, which specializes in after-school programs and anti-gang messages for Asian children.

In addition to partnering with local community organizations, in December 2006 the District hosted an Anti-Gang Summit that focused on prevention. Almost 200 people attended the full-day Summit. Attendees were drawn from school systems where gang violence is an unfortunate reality; Latino and Asian community outreach organizations; law enforcement; and District Attorneys' offices. Speakers included all of the USAO's anti-gang partners; an Atlanta-based investigative reporter who has repeatedly run stories on gang violence; a juvenile court judge; local district attorneys who have aggressively targeted gang violence; an update of federal prosecution; and the vice-chair of the American Bar Association's new programs targeting youth at risk. Additional guests were a group of "at risk" teens and pre-teens who were asked what they thought would best work to combat the influence of gangs. Attendees reinforced the idea that providing a safe place for these young adults to gather in the critical 3 p.m. to 8 p.m. time would do the most to thwart peer pressure for gang membership. To that end, the Northern District of Georgia supports Boys and Girls Club's anti-gang programs and a local boxing club that requires high school age students who train there to stay in school.

Southern District of New York

The Southern District of New York's Weed and Seed sites are creating and disseminating anti-gun crime messages and providing evidence-based programs within the safe havens and middle schools in the target sites to deter at-risk youth from committing violent crime. The Bronx DA's Office offers a multifaceted approach to battling narcotics and violence through a community outreach program for school children and their parents to inform them of the negative effects of gangs, gun crime, and drugs. The NYC Department of Probation is utilizing funding in part for intense supervision of probationers identified as most likely to recidivate.

The District's Anti-Gang strategy, based on a partnership with the Bronx, Westchester, Dutchess and Orange County district attorneys and federal and local law enforcement agencies, coordinates enforcement and prevention initiatives. Funds go to the Weed and Seed sites to support their anti-gang Task Forces, training programs and prevention programs for at risk youth. Asset maps are being created to leverage existing resources for gang prevention programs, and youth volunteers work with the police to remove graffiti.

The Southern District of New York's USAO (SDNY) held a Gang Summit in October 2006, which included a wide range of participants from law enforcement, prevention, intervention, education and community-based organizations providing comprehensive social services to at-risk youth. The Summit, through a combination of plenary speakers and workshops facilitated by content experts in enforcement and prevention, identified key problems, barriers and solutions to support SDNY's efforts to prevent gang violence.

FY 2006 Project Safe Neighborhoods and Anti-Gang Funding

BJA FY 2006 Anti-Gang Initiative - $388,217. Project end date: 6/30/2007
The Fund For the City of New York's Center for Court Innovation will use $388,217 in funding to support the anti-gang efforts of the Southern District of New York's Project Safe Neighborhoods Task Force. Funds will be directed to support the suppression, intervention and prevention of gang activity in the following five Weed and Seed sites located in the Southern District: Poughkeepsie - Main Street and North Side; Bronx - Mott Haven; Bronx - Bruckner; Yonkers - 3rd Precinct and Ashburton; and Newburgh. Also, the Center for Court Innovation will use 10 percent of these funds for administrative costs, and the Urban Institute will use $10,000 for a process evaluation of these anti-gang efforts.

BJA FY 2006 Project Safe Neighborhoods - $208,309. Project end date: 5/31/2009
The Fund For the City of New York's Center for Court Innovation will use $208,309 in funding to establish Weed and Seed sites (in conjunction with the FY 2006 anti-gang funding target areas), to debrief defendants in gun cases, improve collection and sharing of gun-related data, and expand Federal prosecutions for gun-related crime. Activities will also include prevention and intervention, establishing hotlines, and creating and disseminating anti-gun messages to at-risk youth.

Issue Brief

CHAPIN HALL
CENTER FOR CHILDREN
AT THE UNIVERSITY OF CHICAGO

NOVEMBER 2006

Too Soon to Tell: Deciphering Recent Trends in Youth Violence

By Jeffrey A. Butts and Howard N. Snyder

Mayors and police chiefs recently sounded an alarm about rising crime in the United States. Their apprehensions were sparked by predictions of law enforcement advocates who argue that new crime statistics indicate a "gathering storm" of violent crime (Police Executive Research Forum, 2006). In heeding these warnings, elected officials across the country are debating policy changes to address what they believe is a growing crime problem. Media coverage of the issue has focused the nation's attention on violent crime, especially violent youth crime.

Predictions of a coming crime wave are premature at best. Crime remains at or near a 30-year low. An American's chances of being the victim of a violent crime are still lower than at any point since the 1970s. According to surveys conducted by the U.S. Department of Justice, the odds of being a violent-crime victim dropped nearly 60 percent since 1994, and those odds have not increased in recent years.

Of course, there are always reasons to be concerned about violent crime. Horrific crimes continue to occur throughout the country, but the rate at which they occur has increased only slightly. The number of arrests for violent crimes grew 2 percent between 2004 and 2005. According to the most recent data released by the Federal Bureau of Investigation (FBI), arrests for several key offenses are up, including murder, robbery, and weapon offenses. Other serious crimes, however, continue to decline.

Viewed in proper perspective, the recent increases in violent crime are quite small. Compared with the scale of violent crime seen during the past 30 years, a 1-year increase of 2 percent is not enough to suggest the country is entering a new era of rising crime. America's decade-long crime decline may be coming to an end, but it is too early to predict a new surge of violent crime and it is inappropriate to imply that future increases are inevitable.

1313 East 60th Street
Chicago, IL 60637
TEL: 773-753-5900
FAX: 773-753-5940

Chapin Hall publications are available online at:

www.chapinhall.org

To learn about new publications as they appear, register on our site to receive monthly e-mail alerts.

To purchase hard copies of Chapin Hall publications, please call:

773-256-5213

The Crime Decline May Be Over

During the late 1980s and early 1990s, violent crime in the United States soared to levels higher than at any time since the beginning of modern-day crime statistics. Then, suddenly and dramatically, rates of violent crime began to descend, falling continuously through 2004.

According to national data tabulated by the FBI, 1.9 million Violent Index crimes were reported to police agencies in 1991, representing a rate of 758 crimes per 100,000 Americans.[1] By 2004, the number of Violent Index crimes dropped 28 percent to 1.36 million, for a rate of 463 crimes per 100,000.

We may never know the exact reasons for the crime decline, but researchers have tested a number of credible hypotheses. The strongest factors in the crime drop appear to be the growing prison population (accounting for about one-fourth of the total decline), improved economic conditions, greater access to housing and employment, changing cultural standards of behavior, various effects of the illegal drug market, gun laws, community policing, and other criminal justice innovations (Blumstein and Wallman, 2006). Retrospective analyses suggest that each of these factors played a part in the crime decline, but it is impossible to isolate the independent effects of such a broad array of social forces.

1. The FBI defines Violent Index crimes to include murder, forcible rape, robbery, and aggravated assault.

Growing concern about violent youth crime

Florida Searches for Root of Surge in Violent Crime
Headline in *USA Today*, November 1, 2006

Violent Crime Up in State, Especially for Kids
Headline in *Miami Herald*, October 18, 2006

"Robberies have spiked in recent years in the Washington region and many other parts of the country, as the number of juvenile offenders and the availability of guns grows, police officials said."
The Washington Post, October 13, 2006

With Arrests Way Up, Some Fear Crime Wave Among City's Youth
Headline in *New York Sun*, September 20, 2006

"So much of the uptick in crime in Minneapolis ... was among younger teenagers," said City Council Member Don Samuels, who agreed with [Police Chief Tim] Dolan's assessment that police are getting a better handle on the problem. "You have to concentrate on kids if you're going to address the crime issues."
Minneapolis-St. Paul Star Tribune, September 18, 2006

Methods

This report describes national crime trends calculated with data from the Federal Bureau of Investigation's Uniform Crime Reports (UCR). Two forms of UCR data are used in the report: the number of crimes reported to police and the number of arrests that result from those crimes. Arrest data provide the only means of analyzing crime across different age groups, as the age of an offender cannot be verified before an arrest has occurred.

National arrest estimates (as well as per capita rates based upon those estimates) are calculated using UCR data released in September 2006. The FBI collects annual information on arrests made by law enforcement agencies throughout the United States. Data are collected from jurisdictions containing a majority of the U.S. population, typically between 60 and 90 percent of residents nationwide. The primary publication of UCR data, *Crime in the United States*, is based upon data from those police agencies able to participate fully in the UCR program each year. Full participation requires that agencies submit their data to the FBI on time and their data cover all arrests for a minimum number of months during the year. For 2005, the jurisdictions that participated fully represented 73 percent of the U.S. population.

Nearly all of the arrest statistics generated by the UCR program are based on this sample. They are not national estimates. The FBI does not calculate national estimates for different age groups. To examine national arrest estimates for various groups and to calculate per capita arrest rates for those groups, this report relies on the FBI's estimate of total arrests for each major offense. It uses the data reported by UCR-participating jurisdictions to determine the proportion of arrests for each offense that involved individuals of various ages. That proportion is then applied to the FBI's national estimate for each offense. Arrest rates are determined by dividing each national arrest estimate over appropriate population estimates obtained from the U.S. Bureau of the Census.

The causes of the crime decline may be debated, but the fact of plummeting crime rates is not disputed. Americans have enjoyed good news about crime for most of the last decade. The drop in youth crime was particularly welcome. Plunging rates of youth violence fueled growing optimism about the effectiveness of youth crime policies and programs, including detention reform, family treatment, and substance abuse interventions.

The crime drop may now be ending. For the first time in a decade, several of the most serious violent crimes tracked by national crime statistics increased between 2004 and 2005. Murder arrests of adults jumped 6 percent, while robbery arrests involving adults climbed 1 percent. Among juveniles, or youth under age 18, the increase in violent crime arrests was proportionally greater.[2] Juvenile arrests for murder grew 20 percent between 2004 and 2005. Robbery arrests involving juveniles rose 11 percent in the same time period. The new crime statistics have drawn the attention of elected officials and other policymakers who are increasingly worried about youth violence.

2. This report uses the term *juvenile* as a synonym for youth under age 18. Of course, the precise legal meaning of the term varies from state to state. In Connecticut, New York, and North Carolina, juvenile court jurisdiction ends on a youth's sixteenth birthday. A dozen states—including Georgia, Illinois, Massachusetts, Michigan, and Texas — begin criminal responsibility at age 17, limiting the status of juvenile to youth age 16 and younger.

National Trends Reflect Smaller Local Changes

The 20-percent increase in juvenile murder arrests nationwide between 2004 and 2005 translates into about 200 more arrests. If this increase were distributed evenly across state and local jurisdictions according to the size of their populations, the number of additional arrests experienced by any one area would be relatively small. For example, the State of Indiana (with 2 percent of the U.S. population) could expect to see four additional juvenile arrests for murder, with one new arrest in Indianapolis. With roughly 6 percent of the population, the State of Florida could expect to see 12 new arrests overall, with Miami accounting for two of those arrests. Other areas would see comparable increases, including one additional arrest in Detroit, two added arrests in Dallas, and two new arrests in San Diego.

Violent Crime & Property Crime Rates, 1975-2005

Violent Crime Index

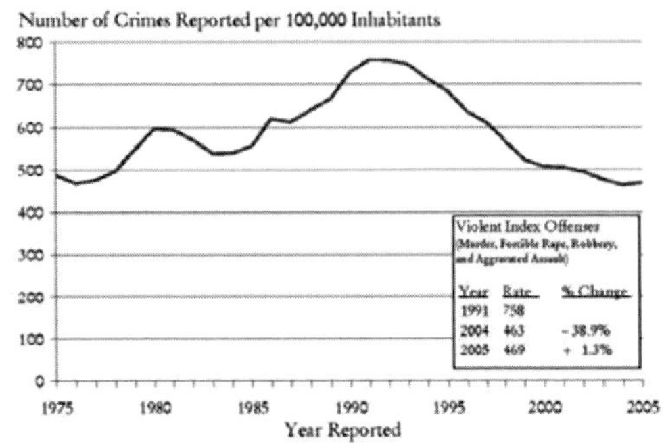

Property Crime Index

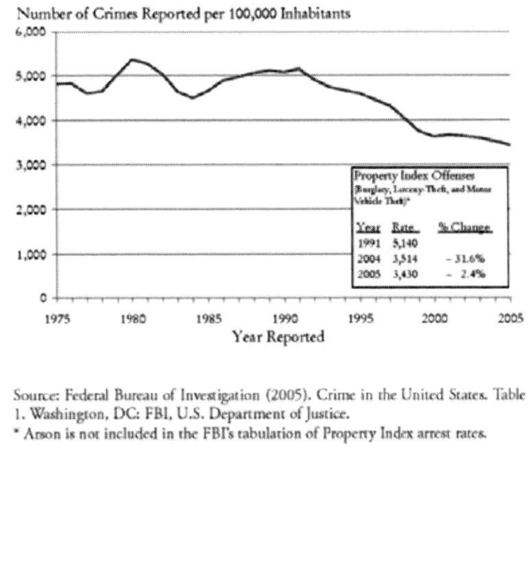

Source: Federal Bureau of Investigation (2005). Crime in the United States. Table 1. Washington, DC: FBI, U.S. Department of Justice.

* Arson is not included in the FBI's tabulation of Property Index arrest rates.

It Is Too Soon to Predict a Violent Crime Rebound

In 2005, U.S. law enforcement agencies made an estimated 14 million arrests for all types of criminal offenses. Juveniles were involved in 15 percent or 2.1 million of those arrests, which represented 3 percent fewer juvenile arrests than in 2004. Many categories of serious juvenile crime declined between 2004 and 2005. Juvenile arrests for forcible rape, for example, fell 11 percent between 2004 and 2005, while aggravated assault arrests dipped 1 percent, burglary arrests dropped 5 percent, and juvenile arrests for larceny-theft and motor vehicle theft each decreased 9 percent.

Some of the offenses included in the Violent Crime Index, however, grew between 2004 and 2005. The entire increase was attributable to two offenses: robbery and murder. The 11-percent increase in juvenile robbery arrests followed a 44-percent decline in the previous decade. Murder arrests among juveniles rose 20 percent between 2004 and 2005, after a previous drop of 63 percent. The larger number of juvenile murder arrests in 2005 was equivalent to approximately 200 additional arrests nationwide.

The recent changes in violent crime merit our attention, but it is important to consider the relative size of the changes. Between 1975 and 1987, the per capita rate of juvenile violent crime arrests remained close to 300 arrests per 100,000. In the next 7 years, from 1987 through 1994, the rate increased more than 60 percent to just over 500 arrests per 100,000. After the appearance of the crime decline in 1994, the violent arrest rate for juveniles fell to 271 per 100,000 by 2004, or roughly the level that predominated in the late 1970s and early 1980s.

Between 2004 and 2005, the violent crime arrest rate for juveniles increased 1 percent, reaching 283 arrests per 100,000. The increase of 12 arrests per 100,000 was about one-twentieth the amount it would take for the arrest rate

Violent Crime Arrests, 1995-2005

	Adult Arrests (Age 18 and Older)			Juvenile Arrests (Under Age 18)		
		Percent Change (%)			Percent Change (%)	
	2005 Arrests	1995-04	2004-05	2005 Arrests	1995-04	2004-05
All Offenses	**11,950,500**	– 1	1	**2,143,700**	– 22	– 3
Violent Crime Index:	**508,200**	– 14	2	**95,300**	– 31	2
Murder	12,800	– 25	6	1,300	– 63	20
Forcible rape	21,600	– 17	– 1	3,900	– 22	– 11
Robbery	85,700	– 14	1	28,900	– 44	11
Aggravated assault	388,100	– 13	2	61,200	– 23	– 1
Property Crime Index:	**1,190,800**	– 14	– 1	**418,500**	– 40	– 8
Burglary	220,800	– 10	3	78,000	– 39	– 5
Larceny-theft	851,800	– 16	– 2	294,900	– 38	– 9
Motor vehicle theft	109,800	– 1	1	37,700	– 53	– 9
Arson	8,400	– 23	6	7,900	– 34	1
Selected Other Offenses:						
Other assaults	1,053,500	– 7	1	247,900	8	– 1
Weapons	148,600	– 27	8	44,800	– 29	7
Drug abuse violations	1,654,600	26	5	191,800	– 4	– 2
Driving under the influence	1,354,100	– 5	– 2	17,800	20	– 9
Liquor laws	471,400	15	– 4	126,400	– 4	– 3
Disorderly conduct	476,800	– 23	1	201,400	– 2	– 1
Vandalism	175,500	– 8	1	104,100	– 32	– 1
Curfew / loitering	--	--	--	140,800	– 15	2
Runaways	--	--	--	109,000	– 46	– 5

Note: Detail may not add to totals due to rounding.
Source: Analysis and weighting of sample-specific data from the Federal Bureau of Investigation. Crime in the United States, annual. Washington, DC: FBI, U.S. Department of Justice.

to return to the level of 1994. In other words, arrests would have to grow at the same pace for 19 more years before the juvenile violent crime arrest rate would be as high as it was in 1994.

The same pattern occurred among young adults between the ages of 18 and 24. The violent crime arrest rate among young adults grew consistently between the mid-1980s and the mid-1990s, reaching a high of 849 arrests per 100,000. The rate then dropped sharply through 2004 to 575 per 100,000.

A 3-percent increase between 2004 and 2005 brought the violent crime arrest rate for young adults back up to 591 per 100,000, or roughly 6 percent of the amount that would be necessary for the rate to return to the levels of the mid-1990s. Again, these increases would have to continue beyond the year 2020 for crime rates to be as high as they were in the mid-1990s.

Similar trends were seen among all age groups in the last 30 years, but the greatest volatility in violent crime was associated with the behavior of young people between the ages of 15 and 24. Arrest rates for all youth (ages 15 to 24) were generally higher than arrest rates for other age groups throughout the period between 1975 and 2005. The increase in murder arrests, robbery arrests, and weapon offense arrests was particularly striking for offenders between the ages of 15 and 20, at least half of whom are under the jurisdiction of the adult justice system.

Recent Trends Are Not Due Only to Police Activity

Because they depend at least in part on police resources and levels of enforcement, data about the number of crimes reported and the number of arrests made are an imperfect measure of crime. Victim surveys are another important source of information, although the information they produce about offenders may be less precise. In addition, national surveys cannot measure crime trends at the state or local level.

The National Crime Victimization Survey (NCVS) has been administered by the U.S. Department of Justice since 1973. The NCVS shows no recent increase in the overall rate of violent crime in the United States (violent victimizations per 1,000). The rate of violent crimes dropped steeply after 1994 and has not increased in recent years. There was an increase, however, in the number of violent crimes in which the victim believed the offender was younger than age 18. The number of these incidents grew 57 percent between 2002 and 2005, from 278,000 to 436,000 crimes. The number of under-18 crimes in 2005, however, was still 60 percent lower than the 1.1 million reported in 1993.

Source: National Crime Victimization Survey (2006). Washington, DC: Bureau of Justice Statistics, U.S. Department of Justice. [http://www.ojp.usdoj.gov/bjs/cvictgen.htm]

Violent Victimizations, 1975-2005

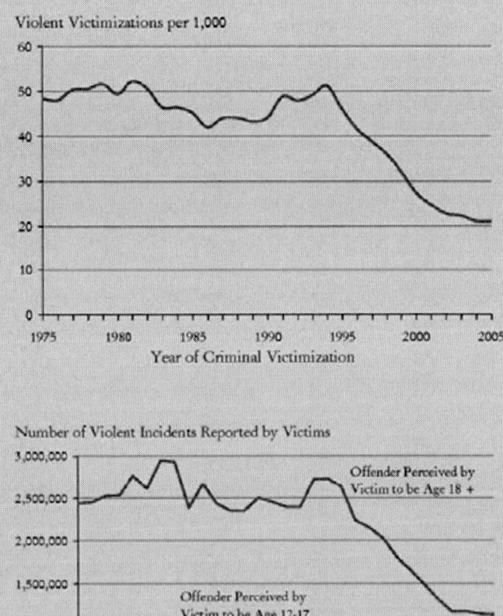

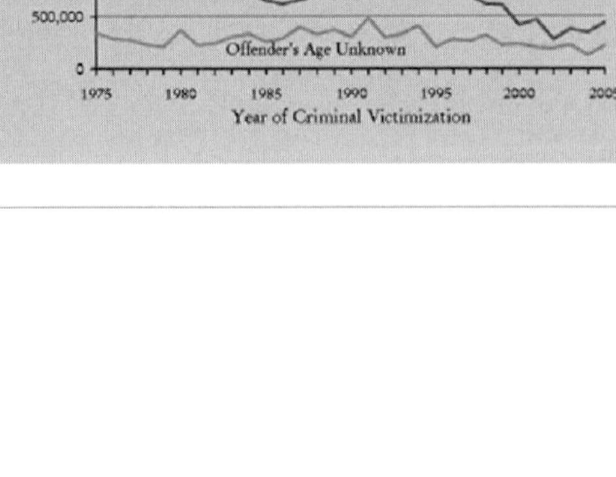

Policy Should Focus on Youth Crime, not Juvenile Crime

When policymakers turn their attention to violent crime, the discussion quickly focuses on violent youth crime. This is appropriate. Violent crime is disproportionately associated with young people, but *young* in this context means under age 20 or even below age 25. It is not accurate to describe violent youth crime as *juvenile* crime (i.e., below age 18).

Of all violent crime arrests in 2005, 16 percent (or 2 million arrests) involved juveniles under age 18, but 29 percent (or just over 3 million arrests) involved young adults between ages 18 and 24. Together, all young people through age 24

Violent Crime Arrest Rates, by Age

Violent Crime Index

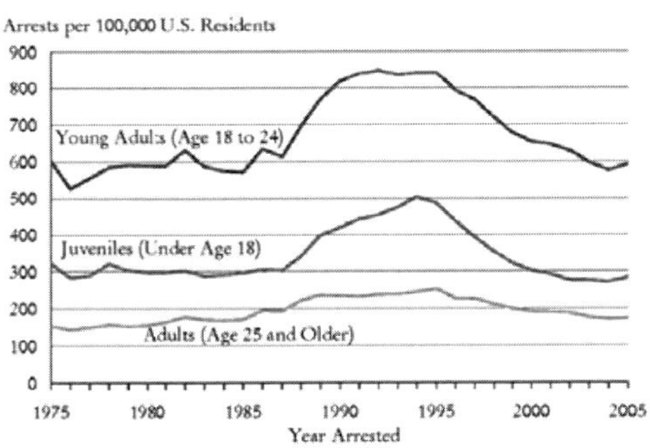

Property Crime Index

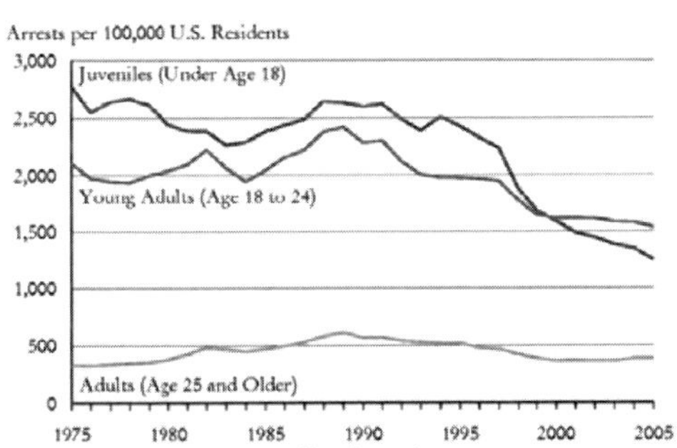

Source: Analysis and weighting of sample-specific data from the Federal Bureau of Investigation. Crime in the United States, annual. Washington, DC: FBI, U.S. Department of Justice.

Fluctuations in Arrest Rates, by Age

Murder

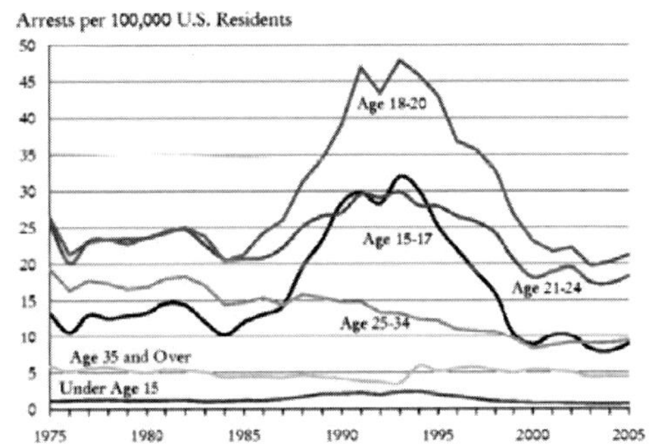

Robbery

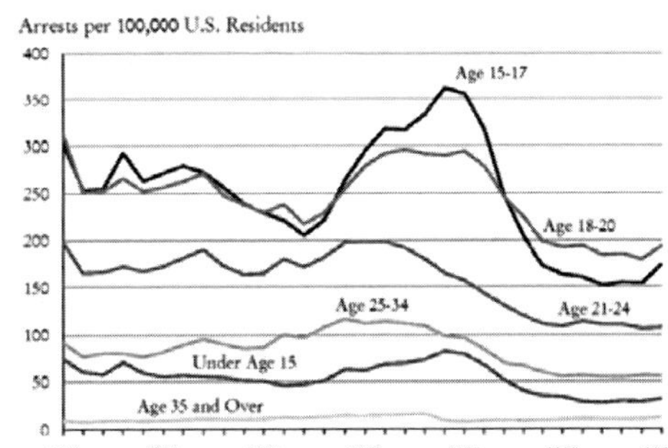

Weapon Offenses

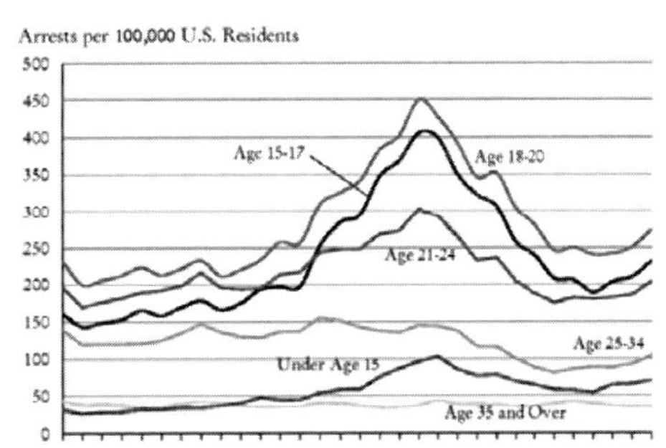

Source: Analysis and weighting of sample-specific data from the Federal Bureau of Investigation. Crime in the United States, annual. Washington, DC: FBI, U.S. Department of Justice.

accounted for 45 percent of violent crime arrests, 50 percent of murder arrests, and 62 percent of robbery arrests.

When changing crime rates are disaggregated by age, identical patterns appear among young adults (ages 18 to 24) and juveniles (under age 18). This suggests that efforts to curb violent crime should not be restricted to either the juvenile or adult justice system. Reducing youth crime requires policies and programs that cut across the legal boundaries of court jurisdiction to address all youth, those over age 18 as well as those below age 18. Furthermore, because young adults are already under the jurisdiction of the criminal (adult) court and their crime numbers tend to move in the same direction as those of older juveniles, few benefits would be gained by moving larger numbers of juvenile offenders into criminal court.

Crime Problems Are Not Shared Equally

Violent crime does not affect all communities equally. Even small increases in violence tend to have stronger effects on the nation's poorest neighborhoods and among minority communities and families. A closer look at recent trends in juvenile arrest rates reveals that this characteristic of crime is occurring today.

Violent crime arrest rates increased less for white youth than for black or African American youth between 2004 and 2005. The violent crime arrest rate for white juveniles dipped 3 percent between 2004 and 2005, but the rate for black juveniles increased 14 percent. In each of the offense categories where juvenile arrest rates increased in recent years, the increase among black youth outpaced growth among white youth.

Specifically, the murder, robbery, and weapons arrest rates for white juveniles each increased less than 5 percent between 2004 and 2005, but the same arrest rates among black juveniles increased more than 20 percent during the same period. Similarly, whereas the aggravated assault arrest rate for white juveniles fell a few percentage points, aggravated assault arrests among black juveniles increased 10 percent.

The differing rates of increase in violent crime arrests among youth of color underscore the origins of crime in social, community, and neighborhood factors. Crime-prevention efforts should focus on communities where youth are the most at-risk for involvement in crime and delinquency.

Violent Crime Arrests: Juveniles and Young Adults

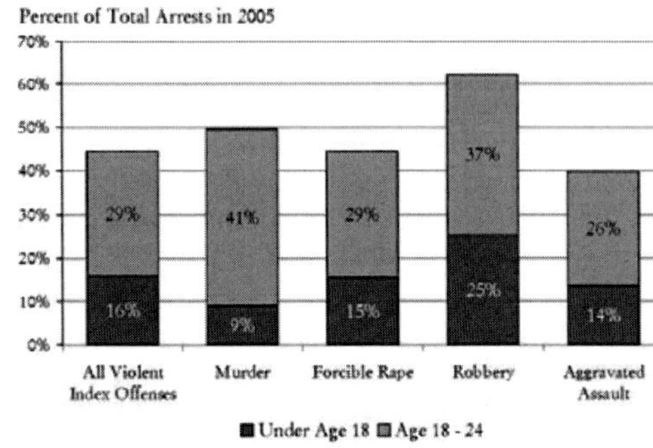

Source: Federal Bureau of Investigation (2005). Crime in the United States. Table 38. Washington, DC: FBI, U.S. Department of Justice.

Juvenile Violent Crime Arrests, by Race and Gender

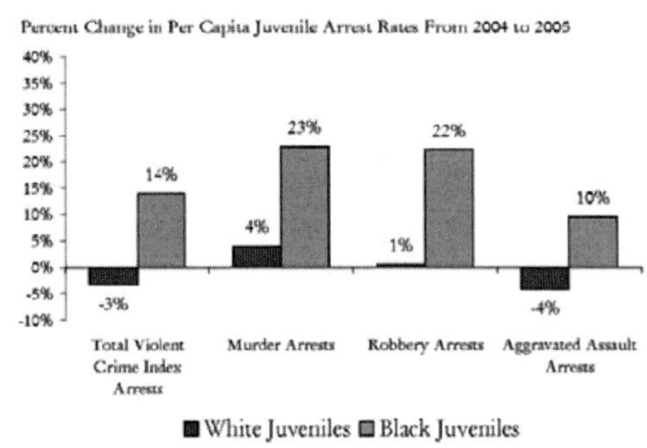

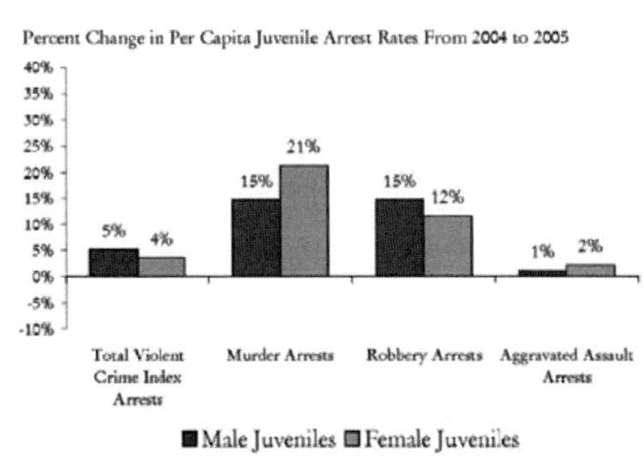

Source: Analysis and weighting of sample-specific data from the Federal Bureau of Investigation. Crime in the United States, annual. Washington, DC: FBI, U.S. Department of Justice.

Conclusion

Although violent crime rates remain at or near their lowest point since the 1970s, any increase in crime generates concern. Law enforcement organizations have expressed deep concern about a recent rise in violent crime statistics. Some of these concerns are well-founded, but others are exaggerated.

The recent changes in violent crime are small compared with the scale of shifting crime over the past 30 years. It is premature to predict a coming wave of serious violent crime after 1 year of increase. It is incorrect to assume that future increases in violent crime are inevitable, and it is inappropriate to lay the blame for any increase that does occur on "juveniles."

Crime-prevention strategies should focus on at-risk youth between the ages of 15 and 24, and most of these young people are not under the jurisdiction of the juvenile justice system. To prevent violent crime, policymakers must support community-based strategies that can reach all young people, especially those who are disconnected from school, work, and family and those who are from distressed and impoverished neighborhoods.

Analyses of Crime Trends Should Use Complete Data

The FBI's national crime information takes almost a year to compile and release. The UCR report for 2005, for instance, was released in September 2006. This means that even an expedited analysis of crime trends at the national level is based on information that is nearly a year old. It may be tempting to analyze crime trends using monthly or quarterly data from local police departments in order to report more recent information, but doing so can lead to erroneous conclusions. Violent crime occurs in intermittent and unpredictable patterns. Criminal incidents are not smoothly distributed across the calendar. Fluctuations that appear large when crime data are examined in small increments of time can turn out to be less significant when viewed over a longer period of time. Especially when crime data are released via the news media, it is always the unexpected increase that receives the most attention. If a city has more homicides than expected during the first few months of a year, the data will be covered as news. If a neighboring city has fewer murders than expected, the public is unlikely to hear about it. The best way to judge the significance of crime trends is to wait for fully processed annual data from a large number of jurisdictions.

Chapin Hall Center for Children

Chapin Hall Center for Children at the University of Chicago is a policy research center dedicated to bringing sound information, rigorous analysis, innovative ideas, and an independent multidisciplinary perspective to bear on policies and programs affecting children. Chapin Hall's focus takes in all children, but devotes special attention to children facing significant problems, including abuse or neglect, poverty, and mental or physical illness. It takes a broad view of children's needs, including their potential as well as their problems, and addresses the services and supports—public and private—aimed at fostering child and youth development.

Download Chapin Hall publications at:
www.chapinhall.org

References

Blumstein, Alfred and Joel Wallman (Editors) (2006). *The Crime Drop in America* (Revised Edition). New York, NY: Cambridge University Press.

Federal Bureau of Investigation (Annual). *Crime in the United States*. Washington, DC: U.S. Department of Justice [Internet: http://www.fbi.gov/ucr/ucr.htm].

Police Executive Research Forum (2006). *Chief Concerns: A Gathering Storm – Violent Crime in America*. Washington, DC: Police Executive Research Forum [Internet: http://www.policeforum.org/].

About the Authors

Dr. Jeffrey A. Butts is a research fellow at Chapin Hall Center for Children at the University of Chicago.

Dr. Howard N. Snyder is the director of systems research at the National Center for Juvenile Justice in Pittsburgh, Pennsylvania.

NATIONAL DISTRICT ATTORNEYS ASSOCIATION

POLICY POSITIONS ON PRISONER REENTRY ISSUES

Adopted: July 17, 2005 by the Board of Directors in Portland, Maine

National District Attorneys Association
99 Canal Center Plaza, Suite 510
Alexandria, Virginia 22314
Telephone: 703-549-9222
Facsimile: 703-836-3195

PRISONER REENTRY[1] POLICY POSITIONS

I. INTRODUCTION

STRIKING A BALANCE BETWEEN PUBLIC SAFETY AND THE REENTRY[2] AND REINTEGRATION[3] OF OFFENDERS

Policy Statement:

1. While the National District Attorneys Association believes that incarcerating criminals more frequently and for longer periods of time has significantly contributed to the lowest crime rate in decades, the National District Attorneys Association also believes that prisoner reentry has become a crucial criminal justice issue. While the NDAA recognizes that the role of prosecutors in the arena of prisoner re-entry will vary according to individual state law, America's prosecutors should, where practicable, be participants in addressing this issue in an effort to reduce recidivism and ensure the safety of victims and the community.

Commentary:

The National District Attorneys Association believes that prisoner reentry is an important consideration for the criminal justice system and society as a whole for a variety of reasons, which include:

- A record number of prisoners are being released from incarceration on an annual basis;
- The cost of housing inmates is increasing at a rapid rate; and
- The rate of recidivism among those released from confinement is high at the present time.

According to the United States Department of Justice figures, approximately 650,000 are released from incarceration annually.[4] As a result 650,000 ex-offenders reenter our

---

[1] "Prisoner reentry" as used in this document means the transition from incarceration into society for those ex-offenders (adult and juvenile) released unconditionally; those released on supervised probation/parole; and those released after re-incarceration for a violation of probation/parole.

[2] "Reentry programs," as used in this document are intended to encompass those programs or plans begun while the offender is still incarcerated. For example, literacy training, vocational education, parenting classes, substance abuse treatment and medical care fall within reentry. In addition, preparing offenders to seek housing and employment upon release may also occur at this stage.

[3] "Reintegration programs," as used in this document are intended to encompass those efforts made by the offender and the community to avoid the risk of recidivism. Obtaining employment, housing and benefits, in addition to, continued substance abuse treatment and necessary medical and mental health care are considered part of the reintegration process.

[4] "About 650,000 inmates were released from prison in 2002, up from around 150,000 in 1977." Bruce Western, *Lawful Reentry*, The American Prospect, December 2003, p. 54.

communities in need of housing, medical and mental health treatment, employment, counseling and a variety of other services. Communities are often overwhelmed by these increased demands and, due to budget constraints, unable to provide minimum services to ex-offenders. As a result, the safety of our communities and citizens is jeopardized when releasees, who are unable to acquire employment, housing and needed services, revert to a life of crime.

In addition, reports reveal that the cost of housing inmates is rapidly increasing. Direct expenditures for corrections have increased from $9,048,947,000 in 1982 to $56,956,871,000 in 2001.[5] With current economic constraints and nation-wide budget reductions, states and localities are often unable to meet the demands that the increased number of inmates place on state and local governments.

Most significant is the rate of recidivism among released offenders. It is reported that "[f]ewer than half of all released offenders stay out of trouble for at least 3 years after their release from prison, and many of these offenders commit serious and/or violent offenses while under parole supervision."[6] It is inevitable with this rate of recidivism that

---

Almost 650,000 prisoners are released from incarceration annually. United States Department of Justice, Office of Justice Programs, *Learn About Reentry*, *available at* http://www.ojp.usdoj.gov/reentry/learn.html (accessed November 24, 2004).

[5] United States Department of Justice, Office of Justice Programs, Bureau of Justice Statistics, *Key Facts at a Glance, Direct Expenditures by Criminal Justice Function, 1982-2001, available at* http://www.ojp.usdoj.gov/bjs/glance/tables/exptyptab.htm (accessed November 30, 2004).

"The average cost of incarceration for federal inmates is $22,517 a year. The annual cost of keeping inmates in a community corrections center is $17,706, according to the U.S. Department of Justice." Tresa Baldas, *Considering the Alternatives*, The National Law Journal, November 15, 2004.

[6] "Fewer than half of all released offenders stay out of trouble for at least 3 years after their release from prison, and many of these offenders commit serious and/or violent offenses while under parole supervision." United States Department of Justice, Office of Justice Programs, *Learn About Reentry*, *available at* http://www.ojp.usdoj.gov/reentry/learn.html (accessed November 16, 2004).

"Of the 272,111 persons released from prisons in 15 States in 1994, an estimated 67.5% were rearrested for a felony or serious misdemeanor within 3 years, 46.9% were reconvicted, and 25.4% resentenced to prison for a new crime." United States Department of Justice, Office of Justice Programs, Bureau of Justice Statistics, Criminal Offenders Statistics, Recidivism available at http://www.ojp.usdoj.gov/bjs/crimoff.htm (accessed November 30, 2004).

"Approximately 2 out of every 3 people released from prison in the US are re-arrested within 3 years of their release." Report Preview, Report of the Re-Entry Policy Council, Charting the Safe and Successful Return of Prisoners to the Community, The Council of State Governments funded in part by the United States Department of Justice, United States Department of Labor & United States Department of Health and Human Services available at www. REENTRYPOLICY.ORG *citing* Patrick A. Langan and David J. Levin, National Recidivism Study of Released Prisoners: Recidivism of Prisoners Released in 1994, Washington, D.C.: U.S. Department of Justice, Bureau of Justice Statistics, NCJ 193427, June 2002.

"Fully two-thirds of all those released on parole will be rearrested within 3 years. Parole failures now constitute a growing proportion of all new prison admissions." Joan Petersilia, *Prisoner Reentry: Public Safety and Reintegration Challenges*, The Prison Journal, Vol. 81, No. 3, September 2001, p. 365.

public safety will suffer unless provisions are made to assist those ex-offenders, who desire to become law-abiding and productive parts of their communities, with their transition back into society.

With more than 90 percent of inmates currently serving time predicted to one day re-enter society[7] it is important the prosecutors assist in or assume policy development roles, where permissible, in their localities and states to address prisoner reentry and reintegration into the community. This should be done to achieve a balance in the community between the public's safety, which is paramount, and an offender's reentry and reintegration into mainstream society. This balance will no doubt be difficult to predict and even more difficult to achieve. This will require the efforts and resources of both the private and public sectors.

The National District Attorneys Association recognizes that not all prosecutors will have the necessary resources to assume a key role in this endeavor. The majority of prosecutors' offices across this nation, burdened by ever-decreasing state and local budgets, in addition to continued reductions in federal grants to crucial state and local programs, are simply unable to do so. However, prosecutors cannot risk non-involvement with this issue. With the welfare and the safety of the public as their primary concerns, prosecutors should educate themselves regarding the reentry programs that are provided or being proposed in their local jails and state prisons in addition to those reintegration plans that are being supervised by probation, parole, or their local community services board and be supportive of appropriate programs and plans. It is crucial that these programs be monitored to ensure that they are genuinely aimed at reentry, the prevention of crime, and the safety of the community.

II. VICTIM REENTRY ISSUES

Policy Statements:

2(a). When addressing prisoner reentry, the National District Attorneys Association believes that the primary focus should be on providing a safe environment for the victims of crime and the community.

"67.5% of prisoners released in 1994 were rearrested within 3 years, an increase over the 62.5% found for those released in 1983." United States Department of Justice, Office of Justice Programs, Bureau of Justice Statistics, *Reentry Trends in the U.S.: Recidivism*, available at www.ojp.usdoj.gov/bjs/

According to research conducted by Gaes, Flanagan, Motiuk, and Stewart in 1999, lower recidivism results from participation in selected prison programs. James P. Lynch & William J. Sabol, *Prisoner Reentry in Perspective*, Crime Policy Report, Vol. 3, September 2001, Urban Institute, Justice Policy Center, p. 6
[7] "More than 90 percent of inmates currently serving time will one day re-enter society. On average, more than 600,000 individuals are now being released from prison each year." Prepared Remarks of Attorney General John Ashcroft, Department of Justice Offender Re-Entry Conference, September 20, 2004

2(b). The National District Attorneys Association believes that it is imperative that the needs of the victims of crime be addressed in conjunction with the development and implementation of prisoner reentry and reintegration plans.

Commentary:

While the National District Attorneys Association recognizes that ex-offenders encounter impediments to productive living, the NDAA also acknowledges that many of these impediments, such as addictions, have been self-inflicted. The focal point for reentry should be both the safety of the victim and the community. As a result, those persons and entities involved in the reentry and reintegration process must address victims concerns and needs as part of the development of the offender's program.

Victims of crime have a wide variety of concerns regarding prisoner reentry.[8] As a result, victims should be informed about the status of the offender, the offender's location, and the projected release date. Aside from being fully informed about the offender, victims should also be informed about:

- Person(s) or agency(ies) to contact if they have questions or concerns;
- Protective order application and issuance;
- Available medical and mental health services;
- Restitution
- Conditions of the offender's release

III. PRE-RELEASE PHASE (INSTITUTIONAL & TRANSITIONAL PHASES)[9]

[8] A 2000 survey conducted by the American Probation and Parole Association found that victims had concerns about the following issues (arranged in order of priority) regarding prisoner reentry:

- "Information about whom to contact if victim has concerns & Notification of offender location
- Notification of offender status
- Protective or "no contact" orders
- Input into conditons of release
- Financial/legal obligations
- Information about referrals
- Offender programming that creates awareness
- Input into interstate compact
- Input into conditions of community service
- Victim/offender programming (mediation)"

Seymour, A. K. 2000. The Victim's Role in Offender Reentry. A Community Response Manual. Washington, DC: U.S. Department of Justice, Office of Justice Programs, Office for Victims of Crime NCJ 194061.

[9] The term "transitional" in this document is intended to incorporate both the time spent incarcerated and the immediate time period following release from incarceration.

OFFENDER REENTRY OBSTACLES: LACK OF EDUCATION, UNMET HEALTH NEEDS & LACK OF SERVICES & SUPPORT UPON RELEASE

Policy Statements:

3(a) The National District Attorneys Association supports the use of educational programs, vocational training, substance abuse treatment, mental and medical health services, risk assessments, and programs which teach parenting skills and facilitate the maintenance of family relationships during the incarceration/detention of both adults and juveniles as a means of easing the transition back to productive community living. Smooth transitions will serve to reduce recidivism and increase overall public safety.[10]

3(b). The National District Attorneys Association believes that the above treatments and programs should be utilized only if such rehabilitation is used to achieve its fullest potential by those offenders who genuinely desire to become law abiding citizens and productive members of society, and who truly face substantial impediments in meeting that goal. Furthermore, rehabilitation should serve as a supplement to confinement, not as an alternative to incarceration.

Commentary:

Offenders often enter institutions with physical and chemical dependency problems and without the basic skills necessary for productive and successful living. Many lack education, vocational training, and even parenting and life skills. In addition to lacking a basic foundation offenders often have unmet medical and mental health needs as well as addictions. A lack of family or support systems, housing, transportation and even sustenance add to the list of hurdles which offenders often face as they reenter society.

Empirical evidence suggests that services such as education, job training, housing assistance, medical health care,[11] substance abuse treatment[12] provided while in prison

[10] Nancy G. La Vigne, Christy Visher, Jennifer Castro, *Chicago Prisoners' Experiences Returning Home*, Urban Institute, December 2004, p. 2. (citation omitted) "Prisoners who participate in programs and services during their incarceration are often better prepared for reintegration upon release, as evidenced by improved postrelease outcomes and reduced recidivism."

[11] "[S]oon-to-be-released offenders tend to be sicker on average than the U.S. population. The increased prevalence of infectious diseases ranges from four times greater for active tuberculosis (TB) to 9-10 times greater for hepatitis C. For chronic diseases, asthma prevalence was higher – 8.5 percent versus 7.5 percent –and while the prevalence of diabetes and hypertension is lower for prison inmates, these prevalences are relatively high given that the prison population is younger as a whole and that these conditions are typically associated with older people. Because the prison population is aging, the prevalence of chronic diseases is likely to increase." Rand Research Brief, *Prisoner Reentry: What are the Public Health Challenges?* based on Lois Davis and Sharon Pacchiana, "Health Profile of the State Prison Population and Returning Offenders: Public Health Challenges," Journal of Correctional Health Care, Fall 2003

promotes the reintegration into society and reduces recidivism, which inevitably will raise the level of public safety and lower criminal justice costs.[13]

Individual reentry plans should be created by the correctional facility as soon as is practicable and as deemed appropriate by the institution, after the inmate's entry. Such plans should require personal development in the area of education, vocational training, individual responsibility and accountability, and substance abuse treatment, where appropriate, for release into the community. Institutions should

also develop and implement objective methods for measuring the development of offenders during confinement.

Certain issues such as housing and benefits acquisition should be addressed during the latter portion of incarceration. While such provisions cannot be utilized until an offender's release, leaving such issues unresolved until the date of release will ultimately make the ex-offender's integration into society more difficult.

The National District Attorneys Association believes that the perspectives of the community and the victim(s) of crime should also be reflected in re-entry plans. Issues

---

[12] "[O]ne quarter of male and female state prison inmates fit the CAGE profile of alcohol dependence, while 83 percent of state prison inmates reported using drugs prior to their offense and 33 percent reported use at the time of their offense." *Id.*

[13] *Supra* note 6. *See also* Indiana's Allen County Reentry Court program (Fort Wayne) results indicate that "[d]uring the initial two years of the Re-entry Court's operation, offenders in the program had a recidivism rate of approximately half that of inmates released with no supervision. Within the first year, almost 50 percent of re-entry candidates were placed in full time jobs. Just as important, Fort Wayne's citizens have seen a reduction in crime while gaining a savings of almost $5 million as a result of lower law enforcement, criminal court and parole costs." Prepared Remarks of Attorney General John Ashcroft, Department of Justice Offender Re-Entry Conference, September 20, 2004.

such as the payment of restitution and provisions for victim services should always be incorporated into such plans.

IV. POST-RELEASE PHASE (TRANSITIONAL & LONG-TERM PHASES)

COMMUNITY INVOLVEMENT

Policy Statements:

4(a). The National District Attorneys Association recognizes that the lack of employment, housing, transportation, medical services and education for ex-offenders creates barriers to successful reintegration and must be addressed as part of the reentry discussion. The National District Attorneys Association supports the use of community based programs to develop and implement reintegration plans to assist ex-offenders with their transition from incarceration to productive community living upon completion of their sentence.

4(b). The National District Attorneys Association believes that it is appropriate for prosecutors, where feasible, to assume policy development or supportive roles regarding post-incarceration reintegration plans rather than active day-to-day participation in the development, implementation, and enforcement of these plans for ex-offenders.

Commentary:

In order to provide the necessary services for offenders upon release, community-based programs should be developed by utilizing resources and personnel from a variety of agencies and services in both the private and public sectors. Community-based programs should consist of those entities responsible for the formal control of offenders and capable of imposing criminal sanctions, such as the judiciary,[14] corrections, probation, parole, and law enforcement. In addition, entities with the ability to provide the offender with the necessary services, such as the departments of social services, health care providers, substance abuse counselors, mentors, faith based community members, private and public employers, housing authorities, educational institutions, policy-makers and defense counsel, should be involved.

Services to be provided by the various components

All facets of the community should be used to evaluate and provide the offender with the necessary services along with meaningful oversight and the threat of negative sanctions to assure success.

[14] This assumes that the court has continuing jurisdiction over the offender.

Correctional officers and parole boards should conduct risk assessments on offenders scheduled to be released or paroled. Risk assessments should be evaluated for efficacy and found to be reliable before their use by correctional facilities Probation/parole officers in conjunction with law enforcement and the courts should demand accountability from offenders. Supervision by probation and parole officers must be meaningful and not conducted in a cursory fashion.

With the threat of negative consequences for unacceptable behavior provided, other elements of the community from the department of social services to the local or state housing authority can intervene to provide the multitude of needed services, which often include:

- Health care (medical, dental and mental health services);
- Substance abuse treatment;
- Transportation;
- Transitional and long-term housing;
- Development of parenting and life skills;
- Educational opportunities and literacy training;
- Vocational training
- Assistance with obtaining employment
- Assistance with accessing community services and benefits

V. CONSEQUENCES OF PROBATION/PAROLE VIOLATIONS

Policy Statements:

5(a). The National District Attorneys Association believes that parolees/probationers must be held accountable for non-compliance with the terms and conditions of their probation or parole. Probationers or parolees who demonstrate that they are unwilling to live law- abiding lives should be expeditiously re-incarcerated to protect the public safety.

5(b). The National District Attorneys Association believes that parole/probation violations should never be overlooked by the criminal justice system. When appropriate, sanctions should be individually tailored to address the violation and to emphasize the importance of community-based strategies for dealing with violations of probation and parole. Progressive sanctions should be considered for successive violations of probation/parole.

5(c). The NDAA believes that a person on parole/probation charged with the commission of a new offense has demonstrated that they are a danger to society and should be held in custody, to the degree possible, until their case is resolved. If a person is convicted of a crime committed while on probation/parole the sentence should be consecutive to the sentenced offense to provide a meaningful consequence for the new offense.

Commentary:

Many in the criminal justice system have a tendency to characterize certain probation/parole violations as "technical." Typically, violations that are characterized as such include failure by a probationer/parolee to abide by his/her curfew; failure to appear for a probation/parole appointment; or failure to obtain or maintain employment. Unfortunately the tendency has been to classify any violation, with the exception of the commission of a new crime, as "technical."

The National District Attorneys Association objects to the characterization of any violation as "technical" and to the minimization of a violation of a term or condition of release. Probationers and parolees are given an opportunity to prove to authorities that they can function as law-abiding citizens by adhering to the terms and conditions of their probation or parole in lieu of incarceration. While the National District Attorneys Association recognizes that not all violations should result in the same sanction, every violation should result in a negative consequence for the probationer/parolee. Penalties should be individualized to the nature of the violation with successive violations resulting in more severe penalties for the probationer/parolee. Progressive sanctions should be considered for successive violations of probation/parole.

VI. INNOVATIVE METHODS FOR ADDRESSING REINTEGRATION ISSUES

Policy Statement:

6. The National District Attorneys Association supports the development and implementation of innovative programs to assist with prisoner reentry issues. Such programs are not intended as alternatives to incarceration. Incarceration imposed after conviction is recognized as important for punishment, deterrence, and the protection of the public.

Commentary:

Innovative solutions should be developed to deal with the myriad of prisoner reentry issues that exist upon and after release.

One such solution is the "reentry court," which is currently used in a number of jurisdictions across the country. "Reentry courts"[15] are based on the premise that the releasing correctional facility has provided the offender with a reentry plan which meets

[15] "Reentry courts" will not be appropriate in those jurisdictions where the executive branch has authority over the offender upon sentencing in lieu of the judicial branch.

his/her individual needs and has explained the plan prior to the offender's release. Upon release, the reentry court is responsible for closely monitoring the offender by arranging for regularly scheduled court dates regardless of whether the offender is succeeding or failing with his/her reentry plan. In order to provide for substance abuse treatment, medical care, literacy training, vocational training and the various other offender needs, the reentry court utilizes and manages a variety of community services. Violations of an offender's terms and conditions of release are addressed swiftly by the court and always result in negative consequences. While sanctions for violations are individualized for the nature of the violation, successive violations will result in graduated punishments. When offenders meet the expectations of the court and comply with the terms and conditions of release, positive reinforcement is provided by the court.[16]

VII. COLLATERAL SANCTIONS: Sanctions will vary depending on the individual state law but typically they include the following:

- Loss of Voting Rights -- permanent loss; temporary loss while in prison or while on probation/parole
- Ineligibility for Federal Student Loans (PELL Grants)
- Ineligibility for Federally Subsidized Housing
- Ineligibility for Licensure for Certain Occupations

Policy Statement:

7. The National District Attorneys Association believes that collateral sanctions imposed as a consequence of a conviction are an important element in protecting the public. Relief from some collateral sanctions may be appropriate if they do not relate to the conduct involved in the offense of conviction.

Commentary:

The National District Attorneys Association believes that there must be both civil and penal consequences for criminal behavior. Those consequences may and should at times involve collateral sanctions and the loss of certain civil rights. Ex-offenders must be held accountable and accept that in addition to incarceration that their illegal behavior may cause other ramifications, including collateral sanctions. While such sanctions may cause

[16] Reentry Courts: Managing the Transition from Prison to Community, A Call for Concept Papers, United States Department of Justice, Office of Justice Programs, September 1999.
The "Reentry Court Initiative" is a U.S. Department of Justice, Office of Justice Programs initiative. Additional reentry efforts include "Reentry Partnerships Project," "Intensive Aftercare Program," "Youthful Offender Demonstration Projects," "Targeted Juvenile Reintegration," "Las Vegas Weed and Seed Reentry Project," "American Probation and Parole Association Project," "Incarcerated Father's Initiative," "Redhook Community Justice Center," "Community Impact Panels," "Restitution: Promising Practices Initiative." Information about these reentry efforts is available at http://www.ncjrs.org/pdffiles1/ojp/sl000389.pdf.

additional difficulties for ex-offenders they should never be used as a justification by offenders for failing to re-enter society as productive citizens.

VIII. FUNDING

Policy Statement:

8 The National District Attorneys Association believes that increases in funding at the federal, state, and local levels are imperative to developing and implementing service plans for offenders while incarcerated; for developing and providing community resources for ex-offenders upon their release from incarceration; for providing meaningful oversight by probation and parole officers of offenders following release, and developing and implementing innovative programs such as reentry courts. Increased funding is also vital for conducting further research on prisoner reentry issues, solutions, and outcome measures.

Commentary:

Given the burgeoning numbers of prisoners being released from confinement each year, the only way that reentry and reintegration programs can achieve their goal of protecting the safety of the community while transitioning offenders back into society is through additional funding at all levels of government.

Correctional facilities will require additional funding to develop and implement appropriate reentry programs as well as provide the necessary medical and mental health care, vocational training, and development of life skills. The community and social service organizations in particular will need additional personnel and resources to provide the necessary services for reentering prisoners. The court systems, correctional institutions as well as probation and parole departments will demand additional funding in order to provide meaningful oversight of offenders and imposition of sanctions when offenders fail to comply with the terms and conditions of their release.

It is equally important that additional funding be available for long term research on issues such as the impact of reentry programs on the rate of recidivism; for developing innovative programs for dealing with prisoner release issues; for evaluating risk assessments for efficacy and reliability; and for determining those characteristics which predispose offenders to succeed or fail in these programs.

References

[1] Gottfredson, 2001.

[2] Sherman et al., 1997; Elliott and Tolan, 1999; Lipsey, 1992, 1997.

[3] Lipsey, 1992, 1997; Sherman et al., 1997; and Tolan and Guerra, 1994.

[4] See Sherman et al., 1998; Lipsey and Wilson, 1998; Aos et al., 2004.

[5] Gottfredson, 1997.

[6] http://www.ojp.usdoj.gov/nij/pubs-sum/188741.htm

[7] McGarrell, Edmund and Steven Chermak (2004) ''Strategic Approaches to Reducing Firearms Violence: Final Report on the Indianapolis Violence Reduction Partnership'' Final report submitted to the National Institute of Justice, Washington DC

[8] Wakeling, Stewart 2003 ''Ending Gang Homicide: Deterrence Can Work'' California Attorney General's Office/California Health and Human Services Agency

[9] Papachristos, Andrew V., Tracey Meares, and Jeffrey Fagan (2005) ''Attention Felons: Evaluating Project Safe Neighborhoods in Chicago'' The Law School, The University of Chicago, available at *http://papers.ssrn.com/sol3/papers.cfm?abstract—id=860685*

[10] Braga, Anthony A., Jack McDevitt, and Glenn L. Pierce. ''Understanding and Preventing Gang Violence: Problem Analysis and Response Development in Lowell, Massachusetts.'' Police Quarterly 9, no. 1 (2006).

[11] See Wall Street Journal ''Novel Police Tactic Puts Drug Market Out of Business'' September 27, 2006 http://www.publicpolicy.umd.edu/news/Kleiman% 20Reuter%20 WSJ.pdf

[12] See, for example, http://www.ojp.usdoj.gov/BJA/pdf/Offender—Notification—Meetings.pdf

[13] http://www.fightcrime.org/reports/gangreport.pdf

[14] http://www.childrensdefense.org/site/DocServer/gunrpt—revised06.pdf?docID=1761

In: Youth Gangs: Causes, Violence and Interventions
Editor: John G. Cooper
ISBN: 978-1-60692-547-8

Chapter 3

PROTECTING OUR YOUTH: PATHS TO GANG PREVENTION IN OUR COMMUNITIES

United States Government Printing Office

FIELD HEARING

Before the Subcommittee on Healthy Families and Communities
Committee on Education and Labor

U.S. House of Representatives One Hundred Tenth Congress

First Session
Hearing Held in Freeport, NY, June 4, 2007
Serial No. 110–42

PROTECTING OUR YOUTH: PATHS TO GANG PREVENTION IN OUR COMMUNITIES

Monday, June 4, 2007
U.S. House of Representatives
Subcommittee on Healthy Families and Communities
Committee on Education and Labor
Washington, DC

The subcommittee met, pursuant to call, at 10:21 a.m., at the Village Hall, 46 North Ocean Avenue, Freeport, New York, Hon. Carolyn McCarthy [chairwoman of the subcommittee] Presiding.

Present: Representatives McCarthy, Clarke, and Platts.

Staff Present: Deborah Koolbeck, Policy Adviser for Subcommittee on Healthy Families and Communities; and Kirstan Duncan, Minority Professional Staff Member.

Mr. GLACKEN. Good morning. First of all, I would like to welcome Congresswoman McCarthy, Ranking Member Platts, Ms. Clarke, Subcommittee on Healthy Families and Communities, to participate in this very important field hearing concerning a very important topic on all of our minds, and that is gang prevention, diverting our youth from the allure of gang participation, their channel, their energy, time and their efforts into a much more constructive healthy activity.

I think that as the hearing progresses it will become clear that this is not just anyone's problem, this is everyone's problem. We all have to deal with the situation because we're talking about our children and our grandchildren. So it is essential that every one of us, whether it be state officials, law enforcement officials, congressmen, senators, all the way up to federal government, we all have to deal with the situation together and we have to solve this problem working together because it is truly a national problem.

I would just like to welcome you all to Freeport and we are delighted to have the Congresswoman Clarke here. She is welcome here any time and we would be delighted to ask her to host any hearing at any time.

Without any further ado, Congresswoman McCarthy.

Chairwoman MCCARTHY. Thank you. I appreciate it.

The hearing of the committee will come to order.

Pursuant to committee rule 12(a), any member may submit an opening statement which would be made part of a permanent record.

Before we begin, I would like to remind everyone to take a moment to ensure that your cell phones and Blackberries are on Silent.

I am pleased to welcome you to the Subcommittee on Healthy Families and Communities, the hearing on gang prevention in our communities. I would like to thank Mayor Glacken and the Board of Trustees in Freeport to support us and provide a location for our hearing today. I also wanted to thank my fellow subcommittee members, Ranking Member Platts who drove down from Pennsylvania in this weather. So I really appreciate you being here. And also, Congresswoman Clarke who came in from Brooklyn this morning for examining this important issue.

Even before I was first elected to Congress, I have been working and talking about gangs here on Long Island. As we will hear today, there is no one program that will address the multiple issues that revolve around the issue of gangs in the community.

We will focus this hearing on the programs that work on preventing young people from entering gangs. However, prevention is a very complex issue. On many levels, we are failing our children.

Today we come together to examine some of these failures and learn how to educate and turn around the lives of our children.

Research reveals risk factors that lead young adults to join gangs. Poverty, poor education amongst students, jobless, unstable family structures all contribute to our children exploring the idea of joining a gang.

When a child does not see any hope for their future, namely retaining jobs, contributing to society, they do not pursue or maintain these goals. You ask these young people what their dreams are, their dreams are always the same, "I want to be a doctor." "I want to be a lawyer." "I want to be a nurse." "I want to be a teacher."

These are things that they dream about. And yet, for a reason that we don't know, a lot of them lose those dreams and end up joining gangs. That child is at risk for entering a gang.

Young people who do not believe that society has a place for them will feel that they are unable to integrate into society, will look to gangs to provide acceptance, stability, companionship and sense of identity. These children, somewhere, lost the hope that they had for the strong vision for their future.

Communities must come together to address these children. Government, law enforcement, local education agencies, businesses, institutions of higher education, service providers and concerned citizens of all ages and walks of life must collaborate to meeting the needs of our children so they do not seek what they think is the need to join or form a gang.

The people of Nassau County and across the nation need to know that we do care about them. We must invest in the young people who work to leverage community resources to serve children before and after school, as well. Children in a program at school in the morning will help to ensure that the children are going to school.

Furthermore, research shows that the hours between 3 and 6 on weekdays tend to be the hours that juveniles and gangs commit crimes. If we have a reverent, meaningful use for keeping current a school program that young people attend in a safe location, we could improve academic achievement, self-esteem and enable these children to envision their future in taking the necessary steps to achieve their goals.

We must also work to ensure to take available time in our schools. Bullying and other school violence could either leave young people in school or searching for gang protection. Children, once again, need to know that schools are safe and provide a place where they can learn and grow.

For our at-risk youth, we must not only invest in their education in making their education reverent. But we must invest in their personal development. This includes interventions for the parents, divorced parents, parents of at-risk children to strengthen families so that parents can essentially protect the lives of their young people and prevent them from the life of criminal activities, or worse, their death.

We must also draft interventions in order for our children to envision their future. Teach them employment skills and challenge them with reaching their goals, such as job training or obtaining a college degree.

Children rise to the level of expectations if we challenge our children to do the best that they can. If we expect less from them, they will give us less.

Today we will hear the role of law enforcement in gang prevention through the Nassau County District Attorney and Freeport Chief of Police. We will learn about evidence-based therapy techniques for families and children. In addition, we will learn of two organizations who work to, not only prevent children from entering gangs, but also to work with them to leave gangs and end their affiliation with gangs.

Furthermore, we will hear from a young adult who two years left a gang after five years of being in prison. I look forward to hearing each of your testimonies and learning from you.

I can tell from your testimonies, the one thing that was the common theme throughout all the testimonies is prevention. That's one thing that I certainly believe in. All of us on the committee believe in prevention because that is the key to making certain all of our children have a good chance, a fair chance and certainly for the future of this nation, a chance they all need to make.

So I want to thank you all for joining us today. And now I introduce my ranking member, Mr. Platts from Pennsylvania, for his opening statement.

Mr. PLATTS. Thank you. I have a written statement I would like to submit for the record.

I just would like to thank you for your voting this hearing on such an important issue. Some of the preparation for today is that the numbers were staggering for estimates of over 24,000 gangs in this country, over 700,000 or 800,000 members.

As the mayor pretty well stated, this is an issue all of us need to be concerned about. Federal, state, local officials, private sector, those who lived the life of a gang member, turned their lives around and now made a difference for other citizens, this is something we all need to be concerned about.

And I want to add my thanks to yours, Madam Chair, to our witnesses, a great cross section of individuals in all segments for their efforts to address this challenge for our country.

Each of your written testimonies were obviously—a lot of thought went into them, and it's very helpful in a hearing such as this one in helping to educate my colleagues and me about how to address this issue.

I will get a little better and confident about everything, and as you seek to address a specific issue you become a specialist. One of the ways to do that is to get a knowledge of those who work in whatever field you're addressing to share your knowledge, your expertise with us. And through your written testimonies, already you've done that in great form.

And Ms. Chairwoman talked about how clear it is that we know a lot about law enforcement and intervention, but the more we do on prevention in addressing the issues that are really driving young men and women into gangs, the less we'll have to worry about with intervention and law enforcement than if we do a good job up front and consult some of the social challenges of our communities that lead to that.

So I'm looking forward to all your testimony here today and we're just very grateful to each and every one of you for making an effort to be part of this hearing, for the difference you're making in your communities, for the children in your communities.

So thank you, Madam Chairwoman.

[The statement of Mr. Platts follows:]

PREPARED STATEMENT OF HON. TODD RUSSELL PLATTS, A REPRESENTATIVE IN CONGRESS FROM THE STATE OF PENNSYLVANIA

Good Morning. Thank you for joining us for this field hearing on protecting our children through gang prevention efforts. I want to thank Congresswoman McCarthy for holding this hearing to examine this important issue.

As the Subcommittee begins the process of reauthorizing the Juvenile Justice Delinquency Prevention Act, it is important that we take a comprehensive look at ways to ensure the safety of our middle and high school students. While gangs originally formed to provide immigrant students with a type of public support and a sense of community, this has all too often manifested violently for our most at-risk children.

According to the 2004 National Youth Gang Survey, there are 760,000 gang members and 24,000 gangs active in the United States. It is often said that our children are our most important resource. We must, therefore, endeavor to keep them safe from harm and prevent them from participating in those at-risk activities often connected to gang involvement.

Research shows that poverty, unstable family structures, and poor educational opportunities are just some of the factors that can motivate at-risk children to participate in gang activity. These studies have also shown that the risk of involvement in crime increases the longer a gang member remains active in his or her gang. Effective strategies for the prevention, intervention and suppression of gangs and gang violence need to be in place in order to protect those children that are most at-risk.

Many in Federal, State, and local government view gang violence as a problem faced solely by big cities. Those of us here know, however, that suburban and rural populations, including that of Freeport, New York, are also battling an escalation of gang activity.

The Federal government, through the U.S. Department of Justice, has supported grant programs to develop effective gang prevention and intervention strategies as violent crime and youth gang involvement has grown. But this must be done in close collaboration with State and local governments and law enforcement to lead prevention, intervention and suppression initiatives against gangs and gang crime. We must work together to provide alternatives for at-risk children, keeping them off the street and encouraging their involvement in a variety of educational and enrichment activities.

I look forward to receiving the testimony of today's witnesses, who have firsthand knowledge about quality prevention programs. Thank you again for joining us.

Chairwoman MCCARTHY. Ms. Clarke, would you like to say a few words?

Ms. CLARKE. Thank you very much, Madam Chair, Ms. McCarthy, Ranking Member Platts, to all assembled here.

I am delighted to bring greetings from New York's Congressional district located in central Brooklyn. I vow this opportunity to lend my voice to this very important issue of gang violence and prevention as a new member to the U.S. House of Representatives and former House member of the City of New York.

I've had an opportunity through chairing a committee called the Committee on Crime to really do an in-depth look at the conditions that basically feed in our operation in-depth, particularly in urban areas, as related to youth gangs. So this issue of prevention in how we address this growing problem in our nation, I think it's very timely.

You know, gang activity and related violence threaten public order and safety in a diverse range of communities. Historically, youth gangs were present primarily in urban areas. However, today they migrate to suburban and rural areas. It is of serious concern to all Americans, not just urban Americans.

So I think having this convention of membership here will give us an opportunity to really approach this and understanding the nuances across our nation and what each community is facing in terms of being able to address specifically how we could do prevention, what type of interventions are needed based on the climate and environment in which our young people are growing up in these days.

Madam Chair, it is my honor to face this weather. This issue is worthy of this type of attention. I want to thank you and congratulate you for bringing this to the community of Freeport.

Chairwoman MCCARTHY. Without objection, all members will have 14 days to submit additional materials for the hearing record.

We don't have a lighting system here today. So basically we would like to go with five minutes. Members will have five minutes, witnesses will have five minutes. So when you hear me tap lightly, that means try to finish up.

And with that, I'm going to be a little more relaxed than we are down in Washington because we want to hear all your testimony.

All of your testimony will be put into the record. We all have read it, so I want to start introducing the witnesses.

Today we will hear from a panel of witnesses. Your testimonies will proceed in the order I introduce you.

I would like to introduce our first witness, Ms. Kathleen Rice. Ms. Rice is the first woman to be elected to District Attorney in Long Island's history. Prior to this position, Ms. Rice served as award-winning Assistant United States Attorney in Philadelphia. Today she will describe the gang situation in Nassau County and prevention and surplus suppression in her community.

We will next hear from Mr. Michael Woodward, Chief of Police from the Village of Freeport. Mr. Woodward, native of Freeport, has been Chief of Police since 1997 and during his chamber he has maintained the availability of the Community Response Unit. The activities of this unit led Mr. Woodward to develop a Gang Awareness Suppression and Prevention Program which involves the community in addressing gang prevention and related crime. We will hear of this program by the Village of Freeport Police Department.

Now I wish to recognize the distinguished—you'll introduce. Sorry.

Next, I want to introduce Ranking Member Mr. Platts from Pennsylvania who will introduce our next witness.

Mr. PLATTS. Thank you, Madam Chairperson.

We're delighted to have with us Mr. Hayes, who served as Chief Executive Officer for Cayuga Home for Children since 1995. And under his leadership, the program under his tenure has become a multi-service provider upon counseling support facilities throughout the State of New York and in 2001 had become the first certified public provider of Functional Family Therapy in New York State and the first provider of Multi-Dimensional Treatment Foster Care in 2003.

Mr. Hayes served the local community, New York State Children and Family Services Advisory Board, and was recently elected Chair of the Board of Directors in Community Home Association for advancement of evidence-based practice, which I know we'll hear about as part of your testimony as you've submitted in your written testimony. Mr. Hayes has a bachelor of arts in education from the State University of New York. We're delighted to have you here.

Chairwoman MCCARTHY. Thank you, Mr. Platts.

Our next witness is Sergio Argueta, Executive Director of S.T.R.O.N.G. Youth, Incorporated, who will describe the work of S.T.R.O.N.G. Youth, which is dedicated to educating and empowering the youth and community on the importance of resisting gang-related violence. Regarded as one of the leading experts on gangs and youth violence through New York State who speaks through experience, he was once a gang leader himself.

I would like to ask Ms. Clarke to introduce our next witness.

Ms. CLARKE. Thank you. I have the honor of introducing Isis Sapp-Grant. I first met Ms. Sapp-Grant on a regular program and later became acquainted with her and her life's work as coach of New York City Councilwoman.

After meeting with Ms. Sapp-Grant and learning about her commitment to those who are often outcast, I am proud to have her here. Ms. Grant is the founder and executive director of the Youth Empowerment Mission. She was born and raised in Brooklyn where she still resides today with her family. As a teenager, she was the leader of one of the worst young gangs in history. During this time her boyfriend was murdered in a gang-related shooting. This dramatic incident made her realize there was only two things determining her life, incarceration or death. She made the decision to walk away from the gang.

With the help of a local police officer and certain teachers, she was able to complete the difficult process of separating from the gang. She was able to overcome pressure from the gang and many other setbacks that changed her life. She not only walked away from the gang, but finished high school on time, graduated from college and went on to earn her masters of science and social work from New York University. In 1995 she founded and monitored the Brooklyn Bedford-Stuyvesant neighborhood, and while there, sought to provide hope, vision and support to young people in high-risk situations,their families and communities. Under one umbrella, Ms. Sapp-Grant is able to bring together a diversity of individuals who believe in the organization's mission of redirecting gang membership.

As part of YEM's outreach efforts Mrs. Sapp-Grant launched the Blossom Program for Girls in 2000 to address the needs of young women ages 11 to 21. Ms. Sapp-Grant received numerous awards including the 2006 opportunity for the Boys Hope Girls Hope Organization, an award in 2004 from the Redbook Magazine and the New York Hero award in 2002 from the Robinhood Foundation and Union Square Award in 2001.

I would like to welcome Ms. Sapp-Grant.

Chairwoman MCCARTHY. Thank you, Ms. Clarke.

Our last witness is Mr. Chris Maddox. He once was an incarcerated gang member who left his gang and gang life behind him and is known from the Department of Social Services. Mr. Maddox works for the organization Help End Violence Now Families Outreach activities.

I looked forward to learning of your experiences and hearing from you what we can do to keep our young people from heading down the dangerous and terrible mountain of gang violence.

I want to thank all of you for being here today. One of the reasons we have these hearings is so that leaders and members can learn. We will be doing reorganization this year and we want to make sure that from whatever we hear from you today can be put into that reorganization.

For those of you who have not testified before, don't be nervous. We're going to be a little more relaxed today than we are down in Washington.

And I note, when we go to District Attorney Rice, that she will have to leave. She has matters that came up since we first got here.

So with that, I would like to have Ms. Rice start.

STATEMENT OF KATHLEEN RICE, NASSAU COUNTY DISTRICT ATTORNEY

Ms. RICE. Thank you. Thank you for your invitation to address the Committee on Education and for the Subcommittee on Healthy Families and Communities' interest in preventing gang proliferation and protecting our community's children.

Like many suburbs around the country, gang proliferation and gang violence are on the rise in Nassau County. Our community is feeling the effects of their violence and our children are becoming prey to their growth. Neighborhood gangs homegrown and isolated to specific streets within communities wreak havoc on innocent bystanders and contribute significantly to an area's crime rate. These gangs destroy the quality of life and make it nearly impossible for a neighborhood to embark on redevelopment or attract sustainable jobs for its families. These gangs recruit local kids and often use incredible violence to defend their turf of the image of their gang.

The answer to stopping gang proliferation is not a simple one. Many of the reasons gangs are growing in our community have regional, if not national, foundations. However, while the underlying issues may be broader than our jurisdiction, we believe we have an obligation to address their impact and an equally important obligation to develop local strategies that would protect our children.

There are some traditional methods to gang prevention through enforcement that certainly have an impact on the results of gang activity. Legislative efforts to toughen sentencing guidelines for gang related-crimes have had some impact on gang violence over the years. For instance, we have supported legislation that would enhance the penalties for carrying an illegal weapon. We know from experience where their guns, there are gangs. We are looking forward to support future efforts that target as fervently the guns coming into our communities as we have the guns in the hands of children on the street.

For some gang members, lengthy incarceration is the only option, especially in the case of a high-ranking member. This can severely disrupt, at least temporarily, the recruiting performance of the gang. Lengthy incarceration for the worst of the worst can also have a deterrent effect on those contemplating gang life or those contemplating their criminal involvement in a gang.

In addition to the traditional methods of gang suppression that I outlined above, my office has advocated for the adoption of an intelligence-led policing model in Nassau County. This is relatively new. The key to this modern proactive approach is developing, analyzing and sharing gang intelligence among law enforcement. Gangs are sophisticated and generally have a strict hierarchy that is tough to penetrate for undercover operatives.

Because of this, the gathering of information, electronic surveillance and gang debriefings, both after arrest and in jail or prison, become crucial to understanding and dismantling the core of a gang or one of its subsets.

Our office was a leader in the push for the newly created Lead Development Center, a centrally located depository designed to collect, analyze and share crime data and intelligence with law enforcement on all levels. The LDC takes advantage of some of the most advanced technology today to aggressively target gang activity and proliferation. Intelligence sharing between local, state and federal governments is as crucial in the war on gangs as it is in this country's efforts to protect itself from terrorism. While traditional enforcement strategies are essential to combating gang violence and embracing intelligence law enforcement is critical to developing successful enforcement strategies.

To curb gang proliferation, we must focus on reaching children before they join a gang. We must think outside the box and be ready to invest in children and in communities preyed upon by gang activity.

I believe a local district attorney can have an impact on gang proliferation and can do things that provide children with opportunities and alternatives to gangs. We all know that children join gangs as a last alternative. As a community and as a law enforcement agency, we have a responsibility to provide our children with education and with positive activities while they are out of school. We have a responsibility to provide them with mentors and with role models from whom they could learn. We have a responsibility as a law enforcement agency to redirect them after an initial contact—often at a very young age—occurs. As a community, we have an obligation to provide them access to work and the ability to earn a living separate and apart from a gang structure.

Finally, I believe law enforcement has a role to play when to comes to post-jail, re-entry programs for those willing to abandon the criminal life. A partnership between the communities, their stakeholders, law enforcement and private business is essential to our efforts to attack gang proliferation and to save the lives of at-risk youth in Nassau County.

My office has embarked on several gang prevention initiatives. They are aimed at reaching kids before they are entrenched in a gang and before they have a criminal history.

Through our community outreach team, we have sustained Gang Abatement Program teams in two of the five corridor towns suffering from gang and gun-related violence in Nassau County. The corridor is comprised of the Village of Hempstead, the Village of Freeport, Roosevelt, Uniondale, Westbury and New Cassel. These areas are disproportionately impacted by gun crime and gun violence. The GAP team is composed of a D.A. office, Nassau County Police Department's Task Force Against Gangs, local law enforcement, probation, local school, community and faith-based organizations, county service providers such as mental health and youth board and business owners. The idea is for at-risk youth to be identified through the people in the community. He or she is then connected to a prosecutor in my office. That attorney guides the youth to the service providers for evaluation. The hope is that the service providers determine what the youth needs in terms of education, job training, socialization skills, housing, counseling and medication.

We have also partnered with schools in Hempstead and West-bury to offer summer school programs centered on athletic activities. These summer camps for children are a safe alternative to the street and gives our office a glimpse into the life of a child possibly in need of further proactive outreach.

Our office provides mentors to at-risk children in middle school during the school year which is a program that allows a child to interact with a positive role model on a consistent basis.

Most, if not all, gang members have had contact with law enforcement at an early age. What this tells us is that in addition to our enforcement strategies and our proactive identification strategies, we must have a plan for those who have had contact with the criminal justice system.

I know my time is also almost up, but I want to talk about a program my office is looking to implement in which a youth facing jail time will have an opportunity to have his or her charges lowered or sealed if he or she finishes school and works toward their individual goals.

The contracts are structured around the needs of each individual and rely on law enforcement asking about each participant. For many kids, this is the first time they have ever been asked this question and it goes a long way towards their eventual success. The contract program has already been launched in one community here in Nassau County and it is our intention to replicate throughout the county taking advantage of the services identified by the GAP teams.

As I've said, we have taken on other projects that help the youth in the communities including job fairs where we give kids the opportunity to have work after school as a way of keeping them occupied and away from joining gangs. Traditional and increased multi jurisdictional commitment to procuring and sharing gang intelligence all play a role in disrupting gang activity and preventing inevitable violence that occurs after proliferation.

If we are serious about protecting our children from gangs, we must be willing to embark on unconventional and proactive strategies. A successful approach must include a comprehensive plan for diversion for children experiencing their first minor brush with the system. Finally, we must be willing to implement bold programs to deal with post-jail re-entry and joblessness among those young adults convicted of a crime.

As you can see, local prosecutors do have a role to play in these efforts and my administration will be committed to pushing the envelope and looking for aggressive strategies that will save the lives of our children and protect our neighborhoods.

Thank you very much.

[The statement of Ms. Rice follows:]

Prepared Statement of Kathleen M. Rice, District Attorney, Nassau County, New York

Thank you for your invitation to address the Committee on Education and for the Subcommittee on Healthy Families and Communities' interest in preventing gang proliferation and protecting our community's children.

Like many suburbs around the country, gang proliferation and gang violence are on the rise in Nassau County. Our community is feeling the effects of their violence and our children are becoming prey to their growth. Neighborhood gangs, homegrown and isolated to specific streets within communities, wreak havoc on innocent bystanders and contribute significantly to an area's crime rate. These gangs destroy the quality of life of their neighbors and make it nearly impossible for a neighborhood to embark on redevelopment or to attract sustainable jobs for its families. These gangs recruit local kids and often use incredible violence to defend their turf or the image of their gang.

Nassau County and Long Island have also seen an influx of national and international gangs. National gangs, with strongholds in nearby New York City, recruit young children from all over the county to participate in their criminal activity and to fuel their enterprise. These gangs have tentacles in most towns, villages and neighborhoods in Nassau County. Their web extends throughout the New York City region and up and down the east coast. Many of their crimes involve state border crossing and many of their members have been a part of a variety of their gang chapters since their childhood.

International gang activity has spread across Long Island like wildfire over the course of the last decade. These gangs have international origins and are usually nationality-specific.

They migrate to areas of possible recruitment and are destroying our neighborhoods and ruining the lives of the promising young children they recruit.

All of these gangs prey on our children. They use children for their most dangerous and violent acts. They prey on their innocence, on their education, and on their lack of alternatives.

The answer to stopping gang proliferation is not a simple one. Many of the reasons gangs are growing in our community have regional, if not national, foundations. However, while the underlying issues may be broader than our jurisdiction, we believe we have an obligation to address their impact and an equally important obligation to develop local strategies that will protect our children.

There are some traditional methods to gang prevention through ''enforcement'' that certainly have an impact on the results of gang activity. While these strategies do little to prevent gang growth, they are important to protecting the quality of life of a neighborhood and can result in the 'worst of the worst' being removed—temporarily or permanently—from a community.

Legislative efforts to toughen sentencing guidelines for gang-related crimes havehad some impact on gang violence over the years. For instance, we have supported legislation that would enhance the penalties for carrying an illegal weapon. We know from experience: where there are guns, there are gangs. We are looking forward to supporting future efforts that target as fervently the guns coming into our communities as we have the guns in the hands of children on the street.

For some gang members, lengthy incarceration is the only option. Especially inthe case of a high-ranking member, this can severely disrupt—at least temporarily—the recruiting performance of the gang. Lengthy incarceration for the 'worst of the worst' can also have a deterrent effect on those contemplating gang life or those contemplating their criminal involvement in a gang.

Disrupting the recruiting efforts of gangs is the only way to truly decrease their proliferation. Disrupting their recruiting efforts means not only incarcerating andinfiltrating their command structure, but limiting their ability to recruit children from our neighborhoods and families.

In addition to the traditional methods of gang suppression outlined above, my office has advocated for the adoption of an ''intelligence-led'' policing model in Nassau County. The key to this modern, proactive approach is developing, analyzing and sharing gang intelligence among law enforcement. Gangs are sophisticated and generally have a strict hierarchy that is tough to penetrate for undercover operatives. Because of this, the gathering of information, electronic surveillance, and gang debriefings—both after arrest and in jail or prison—become crucial to understanding and dismantling the core of a gang or one of its subsets.

Our office was a leader in the push for the newly-created Lead Development Center, a centrally located repository designed to collect, analyze and share crime dataand intelligence with law enforcement of all levels. The LDC takes advantage of some of the most advanced technology available today to aggressively target gang activity and proliferation. Intelligence sharing between local, state and federal governments is as crucial in the war on gangs as it is in this country's efforts to protect itself from terrorism.

While traditional ''enforcement'' strategies are essential to combating gang violence, and embracing ''intelligence-led'' law enforcement is critical to developing successful ''enforcement'' strategies, to curb gang proliferation we must focus on reaching children before they join a gang. We must think 'outside the box' and be ready to invest in children and in communities preyed upon by gang activity.

I believe a local district attorney can have an impact on gang proliferation and can do things that provide children with opportunities and alternatives to gangs.

Children join gangs as a last alternative. As a community, and as a law enforcement agency, we have a responsibility to provide our children with education and with positive activities while they are out of school. We have a responsibility to provide them with mentors and with role models from whom they can learn. We have a responsibility as a law enforcement agency to re-direct them after an initial contact—often at a very young age—occurs. As a community, we have an obligation to provide them access to work and the ability to earn a living separate and apart from a gang structure. Finally, I believe law enforcement has a role to play when it comes to post-jail, re-entry programs for those willing to abandon the criminal life.

A partnership between the communities, their stakeholders, law enforcement and private business, is essential to our efforts to attack gang proliferation and to save the lives of ''at-risk'' youth in Nassau County.

My office has embarked on several gang prevention initiatives aimed at reaching kids before they are entrenched in a gang and before they have a criminal history.

Through our community outreach team we have established Gang Abatement Program (GAP) teams in two of the five ''Corridor'' towns suffering from gang and gun related violence in Nassau County. The ''Corridor'' is comprised of the Village of Hempstead, Village of Freeport, Roosevelt, Uniondale, Westbury and New Cassel. These areas are disproportionately impacted by gun crime and gun violence. The GAP team is composed of the District Attorney's Office, the Nassau County Police Department's Task Force Against Gangs (TAG), local law enforcement, probation, local schools, community/faith based organizations, county service providers such as mental health and the youth board, and business owners. The idea is for ''at-risk'' youth to be identified through the people in the community. He or she is then connected to an assistant district attorney in my office. That attorney guides the youth to the service providers for evaluation. The hope is that the service providers determine what the youth needs, i.e., education, job training, socialization skills, housing, counseling, and medication.

It is my hope that we will soon expand the GAP program to communities outside of the Corridor and that several other programs identifying ''at-risk'' youth in the community will use GAP to address the specific needs of each child.

We have partnered with schools in Hempstead and Westbury to offer summer school programs centered on athletic activities. With the help of these school districts, and some private and charitable resources, we've been able to make these programs successful and have had hundreds of participants during what is usually the most unstructured time of the year for any child. These summer camps offer children a safe alternative to the streets and give our office a glimpse into the life of a child possibly in need of further proactive outreach. Very often ''at-risk'' children will be discovered in these programs and we can keep in touch with the child, their family and their school to provide additional assistance well after the summer is over. We anticipate that these summer camps will grow and that we will be able to expand into additional communities around Nassau County in the coming years.

Our office provides mentors to ''at-risk'' children in a middle school during the school year. This program allows a child to interact with a positive role model on a consistent basis.

Assistant district attorneys and support staff volunteer their valuable time to this mentorship program and we believe its effects are significant.

Most, if not all gang members, have had contact with law enforcement at an early age. What this tells us is that in addition to our ''enforcement'' strategies and our proactive identification strategies, we must have a plan for those who have had some contact with the criminal justice system.

These diversion efforts are crucial and require a partnership between law enforcement, private business, the child's school, community members and very often, the Department of Social Services.

Our office is looking to implement a new program in which a youth facing jail time will have the opportunity of having his or her charges lowered or sealed if he or she finishes school and works toward their individual goals. The ''contracts'' are structured around the needs of each individual and rely on law enforcement asking each participant about their personal interests and goals. For many kids, this is the first time they have been asked this question and it goes a long way toward their eventual success. This individualized attention increases the likelihood of successful diversion and fosters real trust between law enforcement, community stakeholders and community members. It is this trust that will allow this program and others to succeed.

The ''contract'' program has already been launched in one community and it is our intention to replicate it throughout Nassau County, taking advantage of the services identified by the GAP teams.

While the vast majority of our programs strive to reach kids before they have a brush with the law or before they have a criminal conviction, it is incumbent upon us to develop a strategy for those who may not be hardened criminals and who we may be able to divert from their short criminal history. The final proactive strategy to preventing children and young men and women from joining gangs focuses on reentry from jail or prison. Our office has launched an unprecedented effort to identify and target inmates eligible for this effort. The strategy partners inmates with a support network and a peer group familiar with their situation and equally eager to give up their criminal past and live a positive life.

In addition to the ''enforcement'' initiatives, the proactive identification efforts (GAP), the diversion program, and our re-entry plan, it is critical for ''at-risk'' youth to be able to find work. It is equally imperative that those eligible for the re-entry program be partnered with local employers once they are out of jail.

My office holds two job fairs per year that provide valuable manpower to local businesses and critical jobs to those looking to make an honest living and avoid the gang lifestyle. Local businesses are essential to this partnership and we're looking forward to increasing the size and the number of employers in the coming year.

As I've said, traditional ''enforcement'' strategies and an increased multi-jurisdictional commitment to procuring and sharing gang intelligence all play a role in disrupting gang activity and in preventing the inevitable violence that occurs after their proliferation.

But if we are serious about protecting our children from gangs we must be willing to embark on unconventional and proactive strategies. We must be willing to aggressively target ''at-risk'' children and provide them with education and access to a variety of work experiences and positive role models. A successful approach must include a comprehensive plan for diversion for children experiencing their first minor brush with the system. Finally, we must be willing to implement bold programs to deal with post-jail re-entry and joblessness among those young adults convicted of a crime.

As you can see, local prosecutors have a role to play in these efforts and my administration will remain committed to pushing the envelope and looking for aggressive strategies that will save the lives of our children and protect our neighborhoods.

Chairwoman MCCARTHY. Thank you, District Attorney Rice. Again, all your testimony will be put in so the committee can read everybody's testimony.

Chief Woodward.

STATEMENT OF MICHAEL WOODWARD, CHIEF OF FREEPORT POLICE DEPARTMENT

Chief WOODWARD. Thank you, Congresswoman McCarthy. Thank you, Ranking Member Platts, Congresswoman Clarke for conducting this subcommittee hearing.

Initially a West Coast phenomenon, basic street gangs have migrated throughout the United States. Once they are established in a major metropolitan area, they spread into the suburbs. Gang membership is comprised of all race, ethnic, gender and age groups. Race membership increases through the following reasons: Recruitment, peer pressure, overwhelmed with dysfunctional families, cultural differences, economic disparity, video game influence, a distorted government approach to dealing with gangs.

Many athletes and entertainers who are affiliated with gangs, they are ready to observe flashing hand signs while performing or playing professional sports, thereby offering support for embracing the gang lifestyle. Gang violence has been lavishly depicted in movies and mainstream video. Specialized magazines such as Don Diva, the ritual street fighter are dedicated to promoting the gangster lifestyle. The magazine discourages anyone for being a witness for or cooperating with police. It also is demeaning to females.

Gang members further the existence of their gang through graffiti, extortion, robbery, prostitution, drug distribution, weapons possession, assaults and murder. They have a chain of command, communication votes, dues and a charter describing their policies and procedures. They are adept at procuring the use of military weapons. They are potential for aligning themselves with terrorist organizations is a probable outcome.

The immediate focus of the Freeport Police Department is to mitigate gang recruitment and operations with a Gang Awareness Suppression and Prevention Program. The program provides gang-related information to the community for the focus on working with parents to protect their children from gangs.

The awareness information provided includes some of the symbols, colors, tattoos and codes that indicates gang involvement. Parents are requested to be observant for any substantial change in the child's behavior, academic performance or attitude towards women. Suggestions to examine their child's room, along with any drawings, writings, art, for gang symbols are all incorporated in the Awareness program.

The Freeport Police Department has its own program, which is a prevention and suppression program that works with the gang member's family. The program educates the family about their child's involvement in a gang and offers assistance or alternative programs to provide the family a social worker.

To discourage the spread of gangs, there is an urgent need for personal and governmental organizations such as the police department, prosecutor's office and school districts to partner with communities that specialize in youth outreach and development. Their resources should be used to promote sense of gang awareness and educate the public on the signs and presence of gangs. The temporary absence of gangs throughout any community does not protect that community or address gang-related crime.

The Village of Freeport has such a committee. The committee is the Officials Working Group. This group has the Gang Awareness Program to warn PTAs to all seven schools in the Freeport school district.

Our Guide to School and Community Activities; this guide provides parents with information on broad variety of supervised and structured activities categorized by their child's age and grade. The guide also includes a comprehensive list of community-based organizations along with a description for services they offer.

The Search Institute Developmental Assets Circular was conducted of students in all even grades from 4th to 12th as a means to evaluate a student's strengths and needs. The results are currently being evaluated for the development of future programs.

A parent expo was conducted. This is offered through area businesses and government agencies. The participants offered employment information and a description of available services. To prevent the growth of gangs, their recruitment efforts must be futile.

Workshops and related programs that assist parents with child development should be funded and developed. This is especially true of preschool. Social interaction needs to be based on courtesy and respect.

A common national language should be formalized to pursue a communication legislature. Many efforts were unsuccessful because of the failure to communicate. An essential component of communication that's often overlooked is to listen. As described by the Search Institute Development Asset survey, it is suggested to provide an understanding of the challenges facing the students. Every entity that has an interest in affording children an opportunity to realize their full potential free from gangs needs to have an understanding of where to focus their actions to help children the most. Youth mentoring or assistance programs sponsored by law enforcement organizations such as the Freeport Police Department, not-for-profit programs or Employment Skills Workshops should be implemented.

Other certified programs should also be created, employed and sustained. The failure to continue programs that are well-received by any student beneficiaries leaves them with a sense of abandonment. Businesses and school districts should consider holding events such as the Freeport School Advisory Council to offer its students and fund advanced learning opportunities for them.

The students of today are our hope for tomorrow. We need to invest in them now for a prosperous future free from gang violence. Thank you.

[The statement of Chief Woodward follows:]

PREPARED STATEMENT OF MICHAEL WOODWARD, CHIEF OF FREEPORT POLICE DEPARTMENT

I want to thank Chairwoman McCarthy, Ranking Member Platts and members of the Sub-committee on Healthy Families and Communities for holding this hearing to explore the gang prevention activities on Long Island to learn what might be replicated across the country. The reduction of gang recruitment efforts along with prevention of gang related crime is essential to the safety of all residents ofour country. The FBI Long Island Office reports that the Mara Salvatrucha, or MS13, gang has been deemed to be a ''High Threat'' to the northeast section of our country due to its involvement in murder, assaults with weapons, firearms possession, drug distribution, extortion from businesses, prostitution and robbery.

The immediate focus of the Freeport Police Departments efforts to mitigate gang recruitment was a Gang Awareness Suppression and Prevention Program (GASPP).The demographics of the street gang population encompass a broad spectrum of race, ethnicity, gender and age and the program provides gang related information to parents, community members, school staffs, and the work force in an effort to reduce gang recruitment

The awareness component of GASPP provides a description of various behaviors, and physical observations, which together or in some cases independently, are indicative of gang involvement. While the information provided in the GASPP brochure (attachment # 1) is representative of gang indicators, it is not all-inclusive. Symbols, colors, hand signs, clothing and gang codes consistently change due to Police awareness and fashion trends. The changes in team logos and colors of professional sports organizations are frequently the impetus for such changes.

The prevention element of GASPP encompasses many youth-oriented activities.These include mentoring programs for elementary school students, along with a guide for parents that advises them of the many programs available to their child as an alternative to gangs. Community members and businesses are requested to engage in positive interaction with adolescents to encourage appropriate social interaction. Business owners, residents, and team coaches, are all requested to actively communicate with students who are engaging in inappropriate behavior. This isdone in a manner that is courteous and provides positive instruction as a means of conveying the necessity of civil behavior and to further individual achievement. The School District Superintendent, together with high and middle school administrators, meet monthly with a Freeport Police Department command staff member to develop strategy to prevent gang activity in the schools and community based upon recent gang incidents. Informal sharing occurs between the school staff andpolice in close time proximity to any gang involved offense when students are participants. (Please see attachment #1 for detailed explanation of the GASPP program.)

The suppression element of GASPP involves various law enforcement programs that are performed independently or in conjunction with community resources to discourage gang-related activity. Suppression efforts include partnerships with federal and state prosecutors, along with a task force made up of federal, state and local law enforcement members. Participation in the FBI Gang Task Force has provided additional law enforcement resources for conducting criminal investigations of gangs with a focus on their leadership. These investigations have resulted in the arrest and successful prosecution of sixty-five members of Mara Salvatrucha, or MS-13. Other gangs that are prevalent through out Long Island such as the Latin King, Bloods, and Crips are being investigated for crimes similar to the type committed by MS-13, by both the FBI Gang Task Force and local law enforcement. The Federal Court, without a prior conviction of a predicate felony, may not prosecute individual gang members, who are seventeen years of age or less. Therefore gang members who have a defense based on their age are prosecuted locally. The MS 13 members who were arrested were involved in the commission of various violent crimes that include dealing drugs, possession of firearms, rape, robbery and murder.

Another cooperative gang suppression effort is a partnership with the Nassau County Probation Department that teams Police Officers with Probation Officers. The Probation Department Officers lead the teams that visit the residences of probationers who are gang members. These visits serve to ensure that the probationers are not in violation of any terms of their probation. This compliance program also verifies that gang members are not associating with other gang members or in possession of any firearms or drugs. It also provides a means to establish that they are abiding by curfew restrictions, thereby discouraging their participation in crime.

Supplementing traditional gang prevention techniques, the Freeport Police Department has developed and implemented a Home Visit Program (HVP). The HVP has been designed to assist the parents of gang members by helping them recognize their child's association with a gang. This usually takes place prior to an arrest of their son or daughter. After a Police Officer has confirmed that an individual is involved with a gang and the information is passed on to the Commanding Officer of the Freeport Police Department's Community Response Unit (CRU). Two Detectives are assigned to conduct a home visit of the gang member's family to discuss their child's participation in the gang and advise them of the resources available to the family to help them discourage their child's further participation in the gang. The initial reaction to the police visit is denial of their child's involvement. Only after the detectives present the parents with evidence that includes gang indicators such as tattoos, limited clothing attire restricted by color, letters or product initials, observation of hand signing, and their child or friends, are not hearing challenged, along with drawings, and gang paraphernalia in their school bags or books do, the parents realize that their child is involved with gangs. In some instances, parents have relocated their son or daughter with relatives in other states or even other countries. Other parents have expressed frustration and a lack of hope with regard to their child's future. A small percentage are currently gang members themselves or don't see a problem with their child's involved gang membership. During testimony to the Nassau County Legislation Public Safety Committee, a Roosevelt, N.Y. Community Activist testified that the gang members in her neighborhood helped her grow up and she saw no problem with them hanging out with her children. She further stated that the only gang she was afraid of was the gang dressed in blue that drive white cars with blue and orange stripes. This was a reference to the Nassau County Police Department. To make the HVP more effective, a partnership has been established with the Freeport Pride Youth Outreach organization, that has resulted in providing the parents with follow up referral services and involvement by their social workers.

School Based Programs

The Freeport Police Department Adopt-A-Cop Program is another activity that was developed to discourage youth from entering a gang. The Adopt A Cop Program was formulated to provide a positive informal interaction between students and police officers. The program requires the "adoption" of one police officer by each 4th grade class who will meet with their "adopted" Officer at the onset of the program and monthly thereafter throughout the school year. The officers who are involved in the Adopt A Cop program are volunteers. Of the ninety-two Freeport police officers, twenty-eight volunteer as Adopt A Cops.

During the monthly meeting, officers conduct an open exchange of ideas and discussions with their students that centers around the fore mentioned goals and objectives. The officers also schedule tours of Police Headquarters and attend the school trips by their respective classes. At the completion of each meeting, each student composes a letter to their police officer including any comments or questions which pertains to the prior meeting, or other police related concerns. The officer responds with a general letter to the entire class, which is read to them by their teacher in between meetings.

At the end of the school year, all of the fourth grade students, their adopted Police Officers and additional Police resources, celebrate the end of their school year together with Adopt A Cop Day. The day is filled with interactive presentations that include tours of a Police helicopter, Horse Mounted Officer, SCUBA and K-9 demonstrations. Pizza, hot dogs, soda and ice cream are enjoyed by all of the day's participants. In addition each child is also given an Adopt a Cop tee shirt.

Goals and Objectives

The goals and objectives of the Adopt A Cop program are to:

a. Encourage the mutually beneficial exchange of information and concerns between the Adopted Cop and his/her class.
b. Provide a positive police officer role model, thereby dispelling negative police stereotypes.
c. Educate children about their safety, and discuss methods which the children may use to avoid potential hazardous situations, including gang recruitment efforts.
d. Discuss projects and non-violent forms of entertainment as a positive alternative to questionable media entertainment.
e. Provide an avenue for children to discuss positive alternate means to resolve conflict, or express anger or frustration as an alternative to violence or alcohol/drug use.
f. Provide insight into the function of police officers, and encourage students to consider law enforcement as a possible career.
g. Contribute to the development of the children who participate in the Adopt A Cop program.

Each of the officers who participate as Adopt-A-Cop Program volunteers receive the Freeport Police Department Community Service Award at the bi-annual award dinner.

This program is currently in its eleventh year of operation.

The Safe Schools Healthy Students grant had funded a similar but much smaller police mentoring program that was designed for middle school students, who were recognized to be considered ''at risk'' of gang involvement. This program had been proposed by the Freeport Police Department to the Safe Schools Healthy StudentsProgram Committee Members. The committee included the Freeport School District, Nassau County BOCES, Operation Pride, Freeport Youth Outreach, and the South Shore Child Guidance Center. Middle school students were selected as the program participants due to a conscious belief by the program membership that this mentoring program would complement the Adopt-A-Cop program. Due to grant funding limitations, the program was limited with regard to the number of participants toachieve the greatest impact with limited resources. It was decided that middle school administrators and teachers would select those students they believed to be ''at risk'' of gang involvement for this program.

Ultimately the program would include this group of middle school students who the committee members believed would benefit the most from interaction with police officers. The programs six police officers would interact weekly during a sharedschool based lunch meeting. On weekends, students and police officers would jointly participate in sports, trips, and movie outings. The officers received an hourly rate, which was substantially less than their police officer salaries as per diem school district employees. Unfortunately, in spite of its success, when the grant funding expired, the school district was unable to continue the program.

Gang prevention efforts must also include educational programs that assist adolescents in achieving important developmental skills. In 2004, the Freeport Police Department introduced an employment skills workshop designed to facilitate employment opportunities for middle school students. The workshop provides these students with insight into the job application process, interview, preparation and employment expectations. The information provided affords students the opportunity to be readily prepared to seek employment opportunities, thereby offering a counter balance to the limitations imposed by gang membership. Gangs grant status to members who are violent, possess an active and lengthy criminal record and embrace a disregard of societies value on life, individual responsibility and achievement. These traits are counterproductive to being successful in seeking employment. The aforementioned gang tenets preclude a chance for a successful job interview in contrast to the Employment Skills Workshop. (Please see attachment #2, Employment Skills Workshop).

Community Partnership

The aforementioned police initiatives were presented as initial efforts to address the proliferation of gangs and related crime issues. Continuing in this vein in 2002, Mayor Glacken and the Board of Trustees with the Freeport Police Department, in conjunction with the Freeport school district, formed a consortium of various organizations and institutions that are associated with the Freeport community. The organization was formed and named the Officials Working Group (OWG) for the purpose of preventing gang related crime through the concerted utilization of new and existing resources. The main committee meets monthly, while the sub-committees meet during the month and report on their progress at the main monthly meeting.

Representation on the committee rapidly expanded to include the Nassau County District Attorney's Office, Nassau County Youth Board, Freeport Parent Teachers Association (PTA), Hofstra University Liberty Partnership, Nassau County Coalition Against Domestic Violence, Junior Achievement, Nassau County Equal Opportunity Commission, Freeport Recreation Department, Freeport Pride, Education Tutorial Services, Struggling To Reunite Our New Generation (STRONG), along with representatives of various religious clergy and community advocates. The School Superintendent chairs the committee.

In the beginning, the committee decided to focus on reducing crime by addressing street gang violence and related anti-social behavior in the schools and community. Committee members determined that the first objective would be to discourage gang recruitment efforts through community and parental awareness presentations. A revised gang awareness program was developed from the pre-existing Freeport Police Department Gang Awareness, Suppression and Prevention (GASP) program. The expanded Gang Awareness Program (GAP) is designed to inform community members, with an emphasis on parents of students, about how to determine if a person is involved in a gang through the identification of specific characteristics unique to street gang members. In addition, the presentation list the reasons people join gangs, along with a description of their rites of initiation and explanation of the types of crimes they are associated with.

The most powerful allure of a gang is the sense of power and respect that is perceived to come with membership; the power of numbers, control of a neighborhood, and fear of their potential for committing random acts of violence, that is mistaken for respect. These misplaced beliefs, in conjunction with a sense of being family or brothers or sisters against other gangs and those who they perceive as being different, creates a sense of unity. In reality, the love, power, respect, and unity ofgang membership is a path to arrest, imprisonment, injury, hospitalization, and death. A community involvement component of GAP lists the various resources available to discourage gang recruitment efforts. This includes involvement in alternative structural school activities, increased parental involvement in the education process, and access to professional counseling in schools via accredited private social outreach services. These prevention efforts, to be effective, must be in place to assiststudents as early as third grade.

One OWG sub-committee has developed a bilingual ''Guide to School and Community Activities for School Age Children.'' The guide provides parents with a broad variety of supervised and structured activities as an alternate to idle time. The activities are listed according to a child's age and grade. (Please see attachment #3 for the current guide).

A member of the OWG who was partnered with an officer from the Freeport Police Department Community Response Unit (cru) gave each GAP presentation, and by February 2004, every school PTA in the Freeport School District had a GAP presentation. Additional presentations are currently offered to any religious congregation or civic association willing to host the program. Unfortunately, most of the presentations that have taken place were poorly attended.

The expansion of Police Department school-based mentoring programs, interagency collaboration and interactive resident/police communications respective to street crime or related activity, supplement the many initiatives described above. In conjunction with these efforts, the Police Department provides an assessment of the gang issues facing village residents along with insight into existing policc-sponsored programs and enforcement operations. Group dynamics of the OWG participantshave afforded the members an opportunity to enhance existing programs. As discussed prior, the Freeport Police Department ''Home Visit Program'' (HVP) has been changed to provide an additional resource. Now when CRU officers visit the homes of known gang members to offer assistance to the gang member's parent(s), an additional service is provided. Freeport Pride, a private youth outreach program, is working with CRU officers to include their social workers in the HVP to offer theirassistance and alternate program awareness to the gang members family.

Another sub-committee is tasked with researching new programs for students as a deterrent to gang recruitment. The committee members also arrange for former gang members or other motivational speakers to address student groups. One subcommittee has the responsibility for researching new law proposals that are designed to deter gang related crime. Other members are assigned to pursue the development of new initiatives and partnerships with like organizations outside Freeport. These include the; Hispanic Counseling Center, Family and Children Associations, Nassau County Youth Board, Nassau County Department of Social Services, and the Salvation Army.

One of the new initiatives that have been implemented is a student survey. The survey was conducted in anticipation that the results would assist the committee with identifying areas of need that the committee would focus on to better assist students with meeting today's challenges. The framework of the Search Institute survey evaluates a student's sense of possessing skills or ''Developmental Assets'' in the following five categories.

1. On going relationships with caring adults.
2. Safe places and structured activities during non-school hours.
3. A healthy start for a healthy future.
4. Marketable skills through effective education.
5. Opportunities to serve.

Currently the OWG is evaluating the results of a Developmental Asset Survey that was given to even grade students from 4 to 12 grades. The Search Institute vision is to ''Have a world where all young people are valued and thrive''.

While Freeport School students offered responses that are comparable to national average results, the specific asset deficiencies were disheartening. This is especially true with regard to the following;

1. Positive family communications-only 16% locally and 28% nationally have this asset
2. Have high expectations for themselves-56% locally and 48% nationally have this asset
3. A sense of bonding to the school-38% locally and 52% nationally have this asset
4. The ability to initiate peaceful conflict resolution-21% locally and 40% nationally
5. A sense of feeling safe-42% locally and 51% nationally
6. Have and understand family boundaries-36% locally and 46% nationally
7. Experience positive peer influence-54% locally and 63% nationally
8. Use time at home constructively-43% locally and 51% nationally
9. Feel capable of exercising restraint-30% locally and 45% nationally

The above survey results, while not specific enticements to gang involvement, help explain the allure of a gang as a surrogate family. The unity, love and respect that is perceived to be, or is missing in the family, creates a void that gang membership purports to fill.

Family values once taken for granted as the foundation for child developmenthave been seriously eroded. Inappropriate societal influences including entertainment media, video games, and magazines, such as ''Don Diva'', glorify violence and misogynistic views. These sources, combined with a news media, that sensationalizes horrific acts of violence, become difficult influences for parents and schools to overcome. In addition, a confused sense as to what constitutes traditional cultural values contributes to minimizing the reservations a person may have with regardto joining a gang.

Multi-culturalism without support for the established cultural values and beliefs contributes to national confusion on how to address many of the problems facing society. A ''melting pot'' without a common language will become a ''Tower of Babble''. The ability to engage in effective communication is an essential element of any successful gang eradication effort. Confused or misunderstood communications frequently result in unattended and sometimes deadly consequences. I have witnessed native-born gang members openly discuss their distrust of non-English speaking members of opposing gangs during school gang prevention workshops.

The allure of gang membership in some cases originates from a family member. In many cases either the father or sibling is the pathway to gang membership. The family legacy road to gang membership is more common within Hispanic gangs,where two or more generations who belong to the same gang may live together. Even families without a gang member within it are experiencing difficulty with raising their children due to the outside influences.

In a recent disturbing trend, the Freeport Police Department has experienced an increase in domestic incident calls that involve parents who state that they are overwhelmed and feels incapable of dealing with the behavioral issues of their child.Most of these parents are looking for help and guidance. Others have stated that they don't care about their child and want the Police to take them and place them in jail or any place, just away from them. These children have been abandoned in place and will be at risk absent meaningful intervention by reinvigorated and accomplished government services.

The effectiveness of the programs described herein is difficult to weigh. In spiteof the efforts expended, gangs proliferate in surrounding communities, while their membership numbers remain relatively constant within Freeport. The gang recruiting that has been thwarted is due to the collective labors of the Freeport Police Department and its many partners. The total magnitude of the gang activity that has been prevented is an intangible. The obvious and consensus view is that more needs to be done on the federal, state and local levels.

The most important next step is changing the culture to restore values that incorporate and encourage a sense of unity, respect, and devotion to guarantee the rights of others to be free from threats, intimidation or harm. Free speech issues must be weighed in the context of offense it was intended to cause. Restrictions on profanity do not restrict a person's ability to communicate. Conversely, our ability to communicate would be enhanced by the expansion of vocabulary for the purpose of engaging in persuasive communication without vulgarity.

The family must plant courtesy and the skills of positive social interaction during infancy. Overwhelmingly, television has become the primary babysitter of youth. The social skills developed through this medium bare little resemblance to ''Sesame Street'' and are more representative of the "Jerry Springer Show." Parenting skill programs and related educational programs must find a way into our early child development efforts. The subsequent benefit to focusing on early development skills and communication programs will achieve benefits in reducing domestic violence, providing academic, and skills learning, all of which are measurable outcomes. They also support a cohesive family unit as the primary deterrent to gang involvement. Furthermore we must work to ensure that all people are embraced and afforded opportunity as true equals. This is a daunting task that must be implemented as soon as possible. Anything less than the timely implementation of these principles will guarantee that our gang prevention efforts will be as successful as the current "war on drugs".

Chairwoman MCCARTHY.
Thank you. Mr. Hayes.

STATEMENT OF EDWARD HAYES, CHIEF EXECUTIVE OFFICER, CAYUGA HOME FOR CHILDREN

Mr. HAYES. Thank you for inviting me.

Cayuga Home for Children is a New York State provider of services for at-risk youth and families.

As part of our commitment to be accountable to both those we serve and those who fund services, in 2001 we began providing evidence-based services. My written statement outlines these.

Our world has changed. In the past, providers of services for children and families only had faith and anecdotes to support the effectiveness of their work. Today, research such as the University of Colorado at Boulder's Blueprints for the Prevention of Violence can show if a program is effective or not; not only effective when we work with the youth and family, but effective after we finish working with the youth, effectively achieving outcomes such as avoiding out-of-home placement, avoiding arrest, avoiding gang involvement and the attending and graduating from school.

Programs such as Functional Family Therapy and Multisystemic Therapy have proven effectiveness in working with youth headed for out-of-home placement and keeping them safely living with their families in the community. In Monroe County in Rochester, New York, we work with youth who have not succeeded in prevention programs and are mired in gangs and violence. Over 60 percent of them complete these programs and in the month afterwards stayed successfully in the community.

We operate Multi-Dimensional Treatment Foster Care in both Central New York and in New York City. The youth we work with come to us as an alternative to being incarcerated in state facilities and failed a multiple, congregate care placement. 75 percent of these youth complete the program. Our limited tracking has at least two-thirds avoiding replacement, a stark contrast to the 50 percent of congregate care youth who studies show recidivate within a year of discharge.

I am not going to tell stories of youth and families, even though I could because too often providers tell stories as opposed to talking about post-end-of-intervention outcomes. The next time a provider tells you a story, ask them where the youth was one year after the provider worked with them and ask them the same question about the other youth who were in the program that they're not telling the stories about. If the youth is not living successfully in the community, what good has been accomplished?

Our need to get past stories is particularly important because, despite proven success of these programs, funders and providers have been slow to embrace them continuing with treatment as usual, even if treatment as usual is not proven effective or even proven ineffective.

In addition, all the programs promoted by the Blueprint Study are wonderful programs. They do not cover many of the issues in populations we face every day. We must find ways to increase research to increase our knowledge of what works and what doesn't work, particularly in the area of helping youth avoid gang involvement and not becoming re-involved with gangs. And we must create a culture where providers are accountable for providing programs of proving effectiveness.

To help this occur, I offer these suggestions. First, juvenile justice, child welfare, youth development, substance abuse, all of these issues are working with the same youth. Let's break down the walls or silos between these categories with hamper our work.

Second, what we are doing should be an investment, not a mere transfer of funds. As with any investment, we need to expect a return. Let's spend money on programs that research shows can produce that return, not on programs that cannot show effectiveness.

Third, give the states categorical eligibility and flexibility in using federal IV-E dollars. Currently eligibility is determined individually, dollars are tied to the 1996 definition of poverty and dollars are tied to out-of-home care. Particularly working with kids in the community that are involved in gangs, we need money that can work with these kids in the community. And let's also look at continuing funding past the age of 18. After all, you and I have supported our kids past 18. I have a 29-year-old I'm still paying.

As part of this shift, require that states use evidence-based or promising practices when they exist or programs that are working to research their effectiveness when the former does not exist. Insist all funded programs track post-discharge, real-life outcomes.

As evidence-based practice lessens of need for out-of-home care, this will save both federal and state tax dollars, will better serve our youth and families.

Finally, increase federal spending in research on child welfare and juvenile justice programs to establish whether or not these programs are effective. Look to find programs being incubated in the field to address populations and issues where there are currently no evidence-based programs.

Thank you for this opportunity and a chance to talk about this work. We have to understand doing is important but only if what we do is effective. If we could determine if what we're doing is effective, let's work effectively. Thank you.

[The statement of Mr. Hayes follows:]

PREPARED STATEMENT OF EDWARD HAYES, CHIEF EXECUTIVE OFFICER, CAYUGA HOME FOR CHILDREN

My name is Edward Myers Hayes. I am Chief Executive Officer of Cayuga Homefor Children, a New York State provider of services for at-risk youth and families.

As part of our commitment to be accountable to both those we serve and those who fund services, in 2001, we began providing evidence-based services. In 2001, we became the first New York State agency certified to provide Functional Family Therapy (FFT). In 2003, we became the first New York State agency to provide Multi-Dimensional Treatment Foster Care (MTFC). In 2005, we began to provideMultisystemic Therapy (MST)—becoming one of the first and only agencies to provide all of these Blueprint services for youth and their families.

Our world has changed. In the past, providers of services for children and families only had faith and anecdotes to support the effectiveness of their work. Today, research—such as the University of Colorado at Boulder's Blueprints for the Prevention of Violence—can show if a program is effective or not. And I don't only meaneffective while we work with a youth or family but truly effective—if the program helps the youth live more effectively and achieve outcomes that matter—such as avoiding out-of-home placement or replacement, avoiding arrest, and attending and graduating from school.

Programs such as Functional Family Therapy (FFT) and Multisystemic Therapy (MST) have proven effectiveness in working with youth headed for out-of-home placement and keeping them safely living with their families in the community. We operate FFT in five Central New York counties and operate MST in three CNY counties. In Monroe County—where Rochester is—we operate both programs and work with youth who have not succeeded in other prevention programs. Many of these youth are mired in gangs and violence. Over sixty per cent of them complete these programs and—in the months afterwards—stay successfully in the community.

We operate Multi-Dimensional Treatment Foster Care (MTFC) in both Central New York and in New York City. In New York City, the youth we work with come to us as an alternative to being incarcerated in state facilities. Upstate, we are working with youth with multiple, failed congregate care placements. 75% of these youth complete the program. While our ability to follow youth's post-discharge progress is limited due to a lack of resources for doing this, our limited tracking has two-thirds avoiding replacement—a contrast to the 50% of congregate care youth who studies show recidivate within a year of discharge.

I am not going to tell stories of youth and families even though I could because too often providers tell stories, as opposed to talking about post-end-of-intervention outcomes. The next time a provider tells you a story, ask where the youth was one year after the provider worked with them. And ask the same question about the other youth in the program. If the youth is not living successfully in the community, what good was accomplished?

Our need to get past stories is particularly important because despite the proven success of these programs, funders and providers have been slow to embrace them— continuing with treatment as usual—even if treatment as usual is not proven effective or even proven ineffective. Indeed, evidence-based is becoming increasingly watered down by providers stuck in the old and funders who accept program statistics as evidence of effectiveness.

In addition, while the programs promoted by the Blueprint study are great, they do not cover many of the issues and populations we face every day—in child welfare, in substance abuse treatment, in assisting homeless youth, in independent living, and more. We must find ways to increase research into the work being done with our children and our families to increase our knowledge of what works and what doesn't work. And we must create a culture where providers are accountable for providing programs of proven effectiveness.

To help this occur, I offer these suggestions:

- Juvenile justice, child welfare, youth development, and substance abuse are all working with the same youth. Break down the silos or walls between these categories.
- What we are doing should be an investment—not a mere transfer of funds. As with any investment, we need to expect a return. Let's spend on programs that research shows can produce that return—not on programs that cannot show effectiveness.
- Give the states categorical eligibility and flexibility in using Federal IV-E dollars. Currently eligibility is determined individually, dollars are tied to the 1996 definition of poverty, and dollars are tied to out-of-home care. And maybe even continue funding past age 18. After all, you and I kept supporting our kids past 18— didn't we?

As part of this shift, require that states use evidence-based or promising practices when they exist or programs that are working to research their effectiveness when the former does not exist. Insist all funded programs track post-discharge, real-life outcomes.

As evidence-based practice lessens the need for out-of-home care, this will both save federal and state tax dollar while better serving youth and families.

- Increase Federal spending on researching social welfare and juvenile justice programs to establish whether programs are effective. Look past the Blueprint programs to find the programs being incubated in the field to address populations and issues where there are currently no evidence-based programs.

As my staff and Board know, I can talk forever. Talking only five minutes is hard. Thank you for this opportunity. I would welcome the chance to talk more about serving at-risk children and families. Thank you for your stewardship of them.

Chairwoman MCCARTHY. Thank you.

Mr. Argueta?

STATEMENT OF SERGIO ARGUETA, EXECUTIVE DIRECTOR OF S.T.R.O.N.G. YOUTH, INCORPORATED

Mr. ARGUETA. Good morning.

I have to tell you, it's truthfully a pleasure being here this morning. Although it's cloudy outside and it's raining and I'm not very religious, I have to finally say alleluia. The reason is because if 7 years ago someone were to tell me members of Congress were to be coming to a local municipality to discuss the P word—that word prevention—I would have said it will never happen. The reason why is because way to many villages and municipalities and members of our government and school boards and local leaders were ashamed of this word gangs, and they felt it was okay so long as we never addressed it, as it was okay so long as it was only affecting or not affecting a particular segment of our community.

Nonetheless, now we know it's not only in urban settings but it's in rural areas, not just huge municipalities but also small rural areas where it's affecting anyone and everyone, as you stated.

I'm here this morning representing not only myself and my organization, but most importantly, millions of parents that cry themselves to sleep because they lost their child. I'm here representing those grandparents that actually had to deal with the horrible feelings of burying their grandchild or great-grandparents burying their great—grandchildren. It's something that really shouldn't happen. I'm also here representing the gang-involved youth who are on the streets currently because there is a serious lack of opportunity.

Today, focusing on this particular theme, thousands of kids are thirsty, thirsty for opportunity, thirsty for someone to give them a hand and guide them in the right direction. As the Congresswoman stated in her opening statement, whenever you ask a kid what do they want to be when they grow up, regardless of Hempstead, Roosevelt, or uptown, or communities with a lot of affluence, you always hear the same responses. I want to be a lawyer, I want to be a doctor, nurse, fireman, police officer. You never hear, ''I want to be dead by the time I'm 14 years of age.'' you never hear, ''I want to be incarcerated.''

So why is it we're losing so many people to this plague? We know we're losing the majority in the junior high school years. Therefore, why aren't we addressing their needs at an earlier age? Why are we not working with them in the 4th, 5th, 6th grades, bringing them closer to the realities?

Everyone wants to point the finger at hip hop. Everyone wants to point out particular magazines. This isn't something new. The modern day 50 Cent was looked at with as much disdain as Elvis Presley was in the '60s and that outlaw image of James Dean. So it's not new.

We need to understand this isn't affecting just one community. Whenever we look at the word gangs and any immigration issue, now people are quick to point to immigration. You know it what it was, it is an immigration issues. But it started back in the 1800s when these poor Irish youths were getting off these boats that arrived and then those when who arrived a little earlier and felt this was theirs.

If we know we were dealing with this plague over 200 years, why haven't we come up with some real effective strategies? That's where S.T.R.O.N.G. comes in.

I started this organization 7 years ago. The reason I started this organization is because after the death of a young lady, after the death of a relative and personally losing two friends, and a third going to prison for life I finally woke up.

It was an epiphany that happened in front of other people, dozens of television cameras and our elective speakers and elected community leaders stood up in front of these cameras, and you know what they did? They declared a war on gangs. They said we need more law enforcement, we will not be held accountable. And at that particular moment, I realized our elected officials didn't have a clue. The bars and criminal justice system had not been working. If it was effective, believe you me that the amount of money and time we have been investing in that system, we wouldn't have a problem.

So we decided to develop a counterculture to actually start addressing the needs of these youth, focus on the things previously mentioned. The family. One of the things I was able to get out of the gang life was going to a school.

I went to Nassau County Community College and I'll never forget my first experience of going to Albany for a conference. While up there, I saw something that really blew my mind.

Here I was trying to escape gang life, and I see these young brothers and sisters wearing distinct colors, throwing up hand signs and it was guys and girls and at the end of the night there was a big fight and these two different groups got into it, people were running. On my way back to the hotel one of my friends comes up to me and says, ''Sergio, what's wrong with you.''

I said, ''I can't believe there's gangs in college.'' someone takes a look at me and laughs. They told me those aren't gangs, those are fraternities and sororities. I say, ''Wow.''

So if you want to be a part of something, you go through an initiation, if you want friends in a particular place where you feel all alone. But you do it in the streets, you're considered a gang member. But if you do it in colleges and universities across this country, it's okay.

What if we provided that? What if we actually reached out to our kids and said, ''Listen, we love you, care about you, want you to succeed.''

Beyond the moving of lips, actions speak louder than words. People have the ability to put things down on paper when they have the resources. But actions speak louder than words. The fact of the matter is our kids are not hearing this. Why? Because we're not acting the way we speak.

S.T.R.O.N.G. developed a chapter and we're going to schools and we want to work with the most ''high-risk'' population. We want to work with gang members because we find that prevention programs are those that work with the honor students. Well, guess what? They don't really need us. There is a reason why those youth are already honor students. They have a system.

We need to work with those kids on the top of that list of, ''I want you out of my building'' because that kid that gets kicked out of school is not acting as bad as they are in the community, they are staying there. I want to work with that youth that's coming out of these correctional institutions and placing them in a facility with juveniles and that's what we need to work with.

This idea that working, you know, preventing these kids from further getting involved in the criminal justice system but only working with the elite, cream of the crop has not been effective.

So that's what we do. We've implemented a program where we noticed, we've traveled throughout the state, northeast region for that matter, and I can tell you that these kids learned so much and are sending us letters saying how a simple 45 minutes or an hour of assembly truly changed their lives.

Guess what? If you join a gang there are three options. Either you'll end up in prison, end up in the hospital or end up in a cemetery. And these are the realities of that lifestyle.

We bring victims, one being 19 years of age who was shot and is now confined to a wheelchair. We work with mothers who lose their children and they come and express their sorrow to these young kids who think what they see in a rap video is reality. No. It's not real.

We also have a counseling component where we actually hired a full-time therapist to work with the most at-risk kids and actually complement these same counselors that we have in the school buildings.

The best way to address these issues is a therapeutic approach. We know this. But it has to be more than just philosophy and, you know, particular specialist that comes up with it. I can take a textbook and diagnose someone but guess what? You can't diagnose the emptiness inside of a heart. No literature will tell you that. That's what we're missing in so many of these programs.

We have a girls component similar to what Ms. Isaacs does. She is one of the most amazing workers in this field. It has to do with the fact that the fastest growing prison population at this time are females, particularly African-Americans, Latinos. And we need to address their issues as gender-specific, the way they deal with those particular issues.

So we started a girls group. And we've also started S.T.R.O.N.G. University, where we've taken gang-involved individuals who served time that have been shot, that have been stabbed, that didn't get million-dollar record deals and actually know to come out and share with the same youth about the realities of that lifestyle. So there you have emerging issues of intervention and prevention.

Guess what? The real specialist on gangs are not sitting at this table. The real gang specialists are still on those street corners. That particular kid standing on that corner has the ability to pull together 30, 40, 50 individuals and get them to go do drive-by shootings and convict crimes, for that particular gang has leadership ability. How do I know? That was me.

Two years ago I lost two friends and felt I had nowhere to go. Now I have an associate's degree, I have a bachelor's degree, I have a master's degree. Now I'm a homeowner, I am the executive director of one of the leading gang-prevention agencies in this region. And I can honestly tell you, I mean, the question is where do you think I would have benefited my country or my part of the region most? Locked up in prison or actually doing what I do.

We have so much to do and although Mr. Hayes and Chief Woodward yielded their time to me, I'm going to stop just shy of Congresswoman McCarthy banging that gavel.

I will tell you this if we have so many kids we've lost to this criminal justice system, if we have so many youth who are losing to the street plague, what are we doing? We need to ask ourselves what are we doing?

Thank you.

[The statement of Mr. Argueta follows:]

Prepared Statement of Sergio Argueta, Executive Director of S.T.R.O.N.G.Youth, Inc.

Dear Honorable Congresswoman McCarthy and Members of Congress: I begin by thanking you for taking the time out to address this very important issue. The issue of gangs is one that has been devastating many of households across America, and the suburbs of Long Island are no exception.

I come to you this morning representing the countless youth lost to the plague of gang violence throughout Long Island and the United States of America. I represent the millions of mothers and fathers that cry themselves to sleep at night because they have either lost their children to the senseless gang violence or the criminal justice system as a result of gang involvement. I am here representing the countless grandparents that have had to deal with the unnatural results of buryinga grandchild due to the unprecedented accessibility to guns on the streets, while having limited accessibility to employment and alternatives to gang life. Most importantly I represent the millions of youth that are crying out, hoping to be saved from this epidemic.

I have been to hundreds of schools throughout the North East region, and no matter how hard the living conditions in that community might be, whenever a childis asked what they would like to be when they grow up, the answers are almost always synonymous. ''I want to be a lawyer * * * a doctor * * * an athlete * * * a nurse * * * a fireman * * * a police officer.'' Some of these kids have the audacity to go as far and say, ''I want to be President of the United States of America someday.'' The audacity of these young people to think they can achieve whatever they desire is something that leaves adults wishing they still had the ability to dream.

Regardless of their race, their socio-economic background, their religious background, or any other socially structured categorical framework we can place human beings under, these answers are always the same. I have never heard a child say I want to be a killer, a drug dealer, a murderer, a gang member. If this is the case, why are we losing so many children to gang involvement?

It is true that popular culture is currently glamorizing this lifestyle at unprecedented levels, but it is also true that this is not new. Although people like to point the finger at the Hip-Hop industry as the root cause for the increase in youth/gang violence and the increase in gang membership, this is not the only genre of music or entertainment that commercializes the criminal lifestyle. American pop culture as has always glamorized outlaws and that imagery as something cool. The modern day 50 Cent and Rap music is looked down upon by an older audience or those that don't listen to this genre of music with as much disdain as the parents of the 60's looked down upon Rock and Roll and Elvis Presley. The violence in our media is desensitizing to the young mind. Whether it be video games where you get more points for killing and robbing people, or popular TV Shows such as the Sopranos where a murderous mafia crime boss is often portrayed as someone with a lot of money, power, ''respect'', influence, who is a ladies man, we must look at all forms of entertainment.

We must realize the fact that this generation is seeing more violence on television, hearing more violence on the radio waves, and playing more violent video games than any previous generation in history. If you add to that the fact that more kids are being raised in single parent homes and the accessibility to guns is on the rise, in conjunction with limited accessibility to youth employment and programs that actually challenge our youth culture, we are left with a recipe for disaster.

When I decided to disengage from gang life, I decided to try the road less traveled in my neighborhood. I decided to try and further my education by enrolling at Nassau Community College. I remember attending my first collegiate state wide conference. I was dumbfounded with what I saw. I remember seeing these groups of young men and women wearing distinct colors, insignias, and throwing up hand signs. They had choreographed handshakes, and at the end of the night these twodifferent groups got into a violent altercation. Police had to be called, and people were injured. I remember looking in awe as someone asked me what was wrong and I stated that I could not believe that there were gangs in college. The person I was talking to laughed at me and said ''those aren't gangs, they are fraternities and sororities.''

That's when it all came into focus. If a young person joins a group by which theyhave to go through an initiation, and they have common colors, throw up hand signs, and do so because they want to be a part of a group or for ''networking'' purposes, and they attend a college or university, it is called a fraternity or a sorority. Yet, if youth do the same thing in the community because they don't have access to higher learning or because they come from a community with failing schools and limited resources, or broken homes looking to be a part of something, it is called a gang.

S.T.R.O.N.G.'s sole purpose is to provide alternatives to gang life in an effort to save our youth. We are not "anti-gang," we are anti gang and youth violence. We are anti drugs; we are anti illegal activity that is destroying our community. We do not have anything against the gang involved youth, but seek to address the behavior in an effort to redirect young people.

We have established STRONG Chapters in the Uniondale and Roosevelt School District. The concept aims to build a counter culture to gang life. In order to deter gang membership it is necessary to provide a positive peer groups to replace gangs. It is mandated that all youth involved in our program are identified as either gang involved or affiliated by school administrators, self identification, law enforcement, or other source of referral, or be siblings of gang involved youth. Our goal is to provide them with an alternative to the street gang.

This program focuses on discouraging gang involvement by helping to develop positive life skills and peer groups, as well as providing them with a forecast of what the future holds for them should they choose a negative lifestyle over a positive one. We currently have over 130 youth enrolled in our chapters, and many school districts are interested in implementing our program. As a result of our datacollection, this program will be evidence based by the end of the year. This program has enabled us to further develop other initiatives and strategies aimed specifically at reducing gang involvement and violent gang/gun crime. Below is a synopsis of some of our other programs.

STRONG TALK: STRONG provides workshops reaching thousands of youth, adults, and service providers throughout the North East on contemporary issues related to youth violence and gangs. We are speaking in elementary school classrooms with a focus on educating the young people on the dangers of being gang involved and following the destructive path.

STRONGIRLZ: Is an all-girls group where participants discuss gang issues and other contemporary issues as they pertain to females and violence. Females are the fastest growing prison population at this time and they have often been overlooked. The concept is to empower gang involved females with the tools, competencies and options necessary to avoid further gang involvement.

BUILDING STRONG YOUTH: Many youth find themselves feeling like there is no way out of gang life. This is an employment placement and career development program focused on intervening with youth involved in gangs. Upon intake, a psychosocial and employment assessment is implemented to determine youth needs, goals, and career and employment aspirations.

Services Provided: Job Placement and Sheltered Employment-youth are matched to employment opportunities congruent to their career interest and capacity. Some youth find it difficult to adhere to the demands of a job. Therefore sheltered employment is provided to selected participants as a bridge to other employment opportunities. Worksites are chosen to cultivate basic work ethics and skills.

S.T.R.O.N.G. University is a program that was created for the most entrenched gang involved youth who are unemployed, not enrolled in any educational or vocational program, served time in a correctional institution, and have a history of gang involvement. After undergoing a rigorous training process they design and implement presentations on youth violence and gang prevention in schools and communities throughout New York State. Participants also help STRONG develop and organize other gang prevention and intervention initiatives. Our goals it to take these current gang members that are trying to redirect their lives and use them as our ambassadors for peace and an end to violence in the community.

These young people whom have been shot, stabbed, incarcerated, kicked out of their homes, etc. serve as real life examples of what happens if you remain involved in a gang. Most importantly however, they serve as an example that change, no matter how impossible it might seem, is very much a possibility should they choose to change.

S.T.R.O.N.G. is currently looking to replicate an effective intervention model from Los Angeles California. We will be hopefully launching a STRONG SCREEN Program before the end of the summer. The introduction of the STRONG SCREEN Program will provide gang involved youth with an entrepreneurial experience that will allow them to learn tangible/marketable employment skills, expose them to a competitive vocation and viable career option, as well as provide sustainability in funding for S.T.R.O.NG. Youth, Inc.

The efficacy of this model and promotion of this type of industry cannot be overstated. HOMEBOY INDUSTRIES was developed through a screen printing business and thrives because of their Youth Enterprise Model which successfully provides gang members with the work ethic and competencies dictated by the corporate world! Founder and Executive Director Father Greg Boyle, exemplifies the type of ingenuity it will take to create programs that are effective at reducing crime and gang involvement while engaging a hard to reach population. We have hosted Father Boyle and his staff on many occasions, and have visited with them in Los Angeles. It has been a great experience to not have to recreate the wheel and have the guidance of someone who has a model that works.

As stated by OJJDP: "The most effective intervention programs use employment, training, school-to-work, access to higher educational opportunities, use of community-based organizations and consistent contact." In keeping with this framework, this initiative recognizes youth have inherent strengths to be cultivated given the appropriate approach, venue and opportunity. Integral to the services is access to support services, educational/vocational opportunities, life skills education, and career awareness. Another critical challenge factored into this model is the development of programs that prepare youth for jobs while also meeting their developmental needs.

As you can see, in an effort to truly be effective and save America's youth and communities from the devastating effects of gang involvement we need to come up with innovative ideas that merge prevention and intervention strategies. It is vital to provide youth with alternatives to gang involvement if we want to be effective in reducing gang involvement and activity.

In closing, I must emphasize the fact that it is easier to get a young person to never join a gang, than it is to leave a gang once they are already entrenched in the criminal lifestyle. Although intervention is extremely important to the success of any gang reduction program, more of our energy needs to be channeled on developing innovative gang reduction curriculums and activities aimed at educating youth in elementary schools. The days of extra home work help and sport programs are simply not addressing the needs of these youth, and as a result it is vital that we adopt new tools focused on gang prevention.

Whenever gang members tell me there gang is a family, I tell them they are right. They often look at me in shock and I continue to tell them that they are an abusive family. They are the kind of family that beats you down from the moment you join. You are abused physically, mentally, you are stripped of hope and a future, and you are raped emotionally and transformed into someone you are not meant to be.

Gangs cannot provide lawful employment, vocational programs, educational degrees, and counseling. They could never nurture and care for young people in an effort to get them to live productive lives. We on the other hand, can. Yet currently we are sending our youth to new prisons and old schools. We are providing higher salaries for law enforcement officers without bachelor's degrees, than for teachers and social workers in our schools with graduate degrees. We are expanding local county jails, but have no community centers that can keep our kids occupied in productive programs. What does it say about us as a nation, when we make accessibility to corrections so much easier than learning institutions at a higher cost?

We declared a war on poverty. That didn't work out too well. We declared a war on drugs. We have yet to win that war. Let's not declare a war on gangs. Instead, let us declare peace on our youth. After all, they are our children and they need us now more than ever.

Chairwoman MCCARTHY. Thank you. Ms. Grant?

STATEMENT OF ISIS SAPP–GRANT, DIRECTOR OF YOUTH AND EMPOWERMENT MISSION, INC.

Ms. SAPP-GRANT. What can I say? He said it all. Seriously. This is the first time I've been speechless, and blessed. It's payback. Right?

Thank you for having me here today. And I come representing Brooklyn, New York, but also representing the United States of America.

I told a group of kids the other day on Friday in Brooklyn at South Shore High School that I am the American dream. When I looked at them at South Shore High School, I realized how many of us don't feel that way. They're not feeling that. They're not feeling as though this United States of America, this country represents them.

And like you said so well, Sergio, the fact is that when they're grown up and when they come to this country because everyone comes as immigrants, there's always been gangs. Gun violence was borne out of this. Every immigrant group that came to America had their gang problems. The only way they've been able to solve that problem is by becoming a part of the greater society and by being accepted into the greater society.

So even people who are not currently immigrants who have not been accepted in that greater society are still trying to find that culture and creating cultures of their own. So you do have gang members that, young African-Americans, young Hispanic-Americans who have been here.

But as long as you take this power that you guys really have and just say, "You know what? We're going to put it into law enforcement and make it a youth problem and fight against these youths to save our community," we're always going to have a problem. You have to include young people in the process because they are hurting.

At this event I went to last week, again, the biggest issues for them are snitching. You know, we can't talk about gang violence without talking about all these other underlying issues. The fact is most young girls, for example, who are gang members, at least 75 to 80 percent of them have been sexually or physically abused. So how do we begin to talk about or lock them up for their problems when these are the issues that they're facing?

You know, what keeps coming to mind that makes me so angry, if only we gave the type of attention and saw these young people in the same way and gave the type of energy that we give to freaking Paris Hilton, we would be in a totally different situation right now. This young girl and her group of people would do whatever they want. They still find a way to treat her illness. If only looked at these issues the same way we look at anorexia, we would be dealing with a whole different—we wouldn't be sitting here right now.

You know, I was in a setting like this 5, 6 years ago and it was with one of your colleagues. Was it Roy Goodman, Senator Roy Goodman? Right? Again, very saddened at the outcome because the only thing the man could say to me after putting out these same issues was, ''Wow, you're very articulate.'' that's where he left it.

Because, again, it's sad when we talk and we see the leadership and we have to combine the leadership and we have to connect with you guys to make sure these things are put in law and that there's money coming down to these programs as service. But if you see kids as violent and that's it and if you see them as, you know, this is the end of their rope anyway or you don't see them as your children, then the conversations stop right when the door closes and we all go home and continue business as usual and I'll continue to do programs around the city and make my programs national and do it on a smaller scale. But kids will continue to die because we're not all on the same page.

So I have this whole speech written out but you guys could read it. I don't want to waste your time. But all I'm saying is, please, there has to be a way to make sure that programs that are in the community are getting some of this funding that's out there.

Millions—it breaks my heart that after doing this work for half my life we still—money is still—I look at my husband who is getting tired of supporting my organization. The money that really needs to go into these programs are going to building more jails. Everything but the right thing.

These kids are smart, they have strong hearts. They are resilient. But all they see are people who don't see them. The biggest problems are poverty and we have to deal with it by all means necessary. And it's young people who feel hopeless, powerless and invisible. Until we begin to really see these young people we will continue to have these problems.

I'm the type of person who gets on the train and when I see things that are not right I say something. If I see kids acting up on the train and say, ''I know your mama didn't raise you that way.''

People get upset, even if they're picking on somebody. I'm not going to ask everybody to do that. That's my style. But we have to continue to see young people not live on the street, carry on like crazy people and not say because they're kids. When we act scared they will become. They're kids. Plain and simple. Half the time they're looking for someone to say something.

I remember the young girl I did say something to on the train the other day and she said, ''Nobody cares.'' she turned around and all the people on the train, yes. Well, why didn't you say something? That's what our kid are saying. ''why didn't you do something, why didn't you say something?''

We have to challenge the people on the Hill to do something, take some of that money being spent for other violence and put it back into our cities where we really need it and to support the organizations on the ground.

We talked about the community-based programs, support the community-based programs. We talk about neighborhood, support them. The largest organizations, I think some of them are doing fine jobs, but kids are getting lost in these programs. They're not addressing many of the very comprehensive needs that these young people need.

The reality is that the young people need jobs, yes. The young people need to have better schooling and to be put back in school. Because by the time we get to them, they're not in school, they're truant or failing school. So a lot of our time goes to getting people back into school. They need therapy because, like I said, most of them are dealing with sexual abuse, physical abuse. They need therapy because most of them are dealing with abuse—if they're not using drugs they come from families that are abusing drugs.

We all know that if you come from a family abusing drugs you have your own set of issues that you have to deal with.

Some of these are that things that, as Americans, we are all dealing with. But other people choose to find their own way out, whether drug abuse or gang violence. They're all the same, they're all going to end in violence. So we have to address them in that way.

Thank you.

[The statement of Ms. Sapp-Grant follows:]

Prepared Statement of Isis Sapp-Grant, LMSW, Director of Youth and Empowerment Mission, Inc.

Good Morning Mr. Chairman and distinguished Members of the committee, thankyou for the invitation to appear before you today.

My name is Isis Sapp-Grant and I am the Executive Director and founder of the Youth Empowerment Mission Inc. an organization based in Bedford-Stuyvesant Brooklyn New York. YEM was founded in 1995 to meet the critical needs of young people affected by gangs, violence and delinquency. We approach this through integrated initiatives that engaged youth, their families, community-based organizations, schools law enforcement agencies and city officials. Over the years YEM has helped human service professionals and community members learn how to work more effectively with in crisis and at-risk associated with street gangs. YEM is dedicated to providing long term solutions that give young people in high risk environments real alternatives to violence and delinquency, while addressing the conditions that create these environments. We facilitate this by providing core early intervention programs like the Blossom Program for Girls (''Blossom''), the Be the Change Advocacy and Leadership Project and the Girls in Business program, these programs incorporate: educational support services and advocacy, counseling, leadership development, life skill development, mentoring, job readiness skills, and community involvement.

In 2000, YEM launched the Blossom Program for Girls (''Blossom'') to address theneeds of girl's ages 11-21 that are at high-risk or involved in gangs, violence or other self-destructive behaviors. In its five-year history, Blossom has successfully reached hundreds of girls. The Blossom Program currently serves over 70 pre-teen and teen girls. Over 90 percent of the girls we serve are African-American and 95 percent of the girls that come to Blossom are living in poverty. 90 percent come from single-mother led households. Blossom's core components prepare girls to move fromcrisis to competency by equipping them with skills and information that support their healthy development. Participants also gain an appreciation for the power they possess to advocate for changes in their lives and in their community. Participants are referred to the program by schools, detention centers, parents and other community-based organizations. In addition we offer workshops and other youth development services to schools and agencies.

Our organization is community based with national influence. We receive calls and support communities and young people around the country in the effort to aid and empower youth facing severe socie-economic difficulties, academic challenges and engagement with the juvenile justice system.

I am here this morning because the crisis facing our youth produces long term damage our communities socially, economically and morally. To many of our youth are joining gangs and in the process losing their lives to violence, losing their freedom to jails and losing their future to bad choices. Our youth can be saved The same energy and commitment that they give to their peers in the gangs can with the right strategies be refocused on changing their own lives and their communities for the better.

I have worked with gang involved and delinquent youth for nearly two decades. I have seen success in young people who were referred to me because they were designated ''delinquent'' or ''beyond help'' and I have witnessed these same youth change their lives for the better when given access to needed resources, skills and opportunities for empowerment . This is our work.

I have a vested interest in the success of these young people , I live in BedfordStuyvesant with many of the youth I work with but more important I use to be one of them and sadly the factors governing the growth of gangs has not changed;

Powerlessness, hopelessness, and feeling invisible are at the underlying feelings of most gang members. Cyclical family poverty, poor education, lack of resources, are at the root of the problem.

In the late 1990s many of the youth involved in gangs were from families andcommunities devastated by crack and HIV/AIDS. Many are young people who were raised by teen mothers or grandparents. I grew up a generation before them in the 1980's my neighborhood was ravaged by crack cocaine and the AIDS epidemic. There were no role models. The only people who weren't living in poverty were drug dealers and the gangsters who we respected out of fear. That was my world. So, as a 15 year old entering high school, the way I saw it, I had one choice—''Am Igoing to be the predator or the prey?''

I didn't set out to join, let alone start one of the most fearsome girl gangs in the city. At first we didn't call ourselves a gang. But our hopelessness and our need to survive the violence both on the streets and at home became the foundation of our bond. We protected each other and became the family that most of us didn't have. People knew that if you messed with us, we would fight back. And that's how itstarted. How does it happen? What happens to young boys and girls to make them think it's okay to knock someone out or rob them? There are a number of things but it starts out with kids in poverty feeling invisible. Kids like my friend Lisa who was born in jail and shuttled between an abusive home and foster care. If you messed with Lisa, she would hurt you without blinking. Her thought process was very simple: ''I've been hurt. I won't get hurt anymore. I'll get you first.'') Whenyou feel this vulnerable you become the most dangerous person in the world.

Some kids do it for protection Like Nelsa, whose parents were heroin addicts. She took care of her siblings from the time she was 13 by working as a stripper on her lunch break during school. And the gang protected her. We kept Nelsa safe so she could do what she had to do to take care of her little brothers and sisters.

In Bed Stuy, where our program is located crime has increased by as much as28 percent at a time when crime rates dropped in other parts of the city. And a rising number of these crimes are committed by young women who now make up 30 percent of youth gang members in New York. In most cases, these young women are perpetuating a cycle of violence that started with their own abuse—an appalling 85% of the girls who enter the prison system have been

sexually or physically abused. Once entrenched in a gang, these young women have little hope for a future. Of those that survive, over 75 percent will become pregnant or drop out of school before they're 18.

Today, All Youth are at-risk for gangs and violence, because the threat of violence is so wide spread. Those who attend school or live in a neighborhood with gangs are forced to choose membership. It is a with us or against us mentality.

The situation for girls involved in gangs and delinquency is different now. Not only have girls become more violent, they have also become more victimized. They have accepted rape as a way of showing loyalty to the gang. One girl I recently met shared her experience of being ''blessed''. She told me that she wasn't in the gang, only a gang affiliate. But she was protected because she had been forced to have sex with all the gang members. And that's what it means to be blessed.

Right now, there are girls out there, just like I was, who are counting on someone to see past the bravado. Girls who are looking for someone to listen, girls who don't know there is an alternative to pimping their bodies, who have no role models— who feel invisible. And that's where YEM comes in. We work with the young people, most of who are in crisis when they reach our doors. If you came to Blossom you would see girls in a small groups being tutored in math, a group of six girls in a sexual abuse survivors group, you would hear Jessica boasting about working at her mentors consulting firm on the weekends, you would see Girlz in Business participants creating designer pillows under their Cozy Comforts pillow business, you would see a group of ten parents in a parent support group , you will find a girl in crisis crying but coming to one of our counselors for assistance, you will hear African drums beating as 75 young women dance across the floor. You will see girls writing and performing their poetry at our Poetry cafe and if you came today you would see girls organizing for their march and speaking out against the negative impact of the media on girls and young women of color. You will see first hand what happens when we invest in our young people. YEM is genuine community empowerment.

YEM is youth empowerment. We have to stop talking about gangs it only gives it power, instead we have to address all of the bigger issues that gang involvement covers; Poverty, poor education, racism, classism, and violence. As we point the judging finger at youth we also need to look in the mirror and at our leadership for the glorified violence that our children are exposed to on the street, on television and on the radio. We live in a very violent society that forces youth to become desensitized and hardened. We send mixed messages to our children and are shocked when they express their pain and confusion by engaging in violence, promiscuity and drug abuse.

Our young people are smart and resilient if given the right academic and moral nourishment and support they need, they will succeed but if we continue to attack symptoms rather than the historical diseases of poverty, prejudice, sexism, and classism and look at the surface issue of ''gangs'' as the enemy as opposed to the real underlying factors that almost force young people to run toward gang involvement, our young people will continue to become statistics, inmates, teen parents, victims and perpetrators of violence.

Chairwoman MCCARTHY. Thank you. Chris.

STATEMENT OF CHRIS MADDOX, ASSISTANT OUTREACH WORKER, H.E.V.N

Mr. MADDOX. Good morning. Thanks for having me.

I, too, at the age of 15 joined a gang and I had an attitude like nobody ever really cared whether or not I went to prison or whether or not I succeeded in life. And when I look back at that lifestyle, now I think a lot of things like criminal activities out of misdirected anger. I didn't know how to handle the things that I was going through.

So at the age of 17, November 30, 2000, I went to prison. I did five years in prison. Then all throughout my years that I did in prison, I don't think I learned anything. I was able to read, able to sit down and get in touch with myself. But I was still bullied without substance.

I knew I wanted to be a success in life. I knew that I wanted to be, like, known by government officials. I knew I wanted to be successful. But I didn't know how to do it. I didn't know what actions to take. I was scared to sit in front of people with suits on and I was intimidated by the world.

I was intimidated and I surrounded myself around people that were just like me, that accepted poverty and we just didn't respect law enforcement. We didn't have any respect for no one other than ourselves or people that was like us.

It wasn't until 2005, March 7, 2005, that's when I came home from prison and I was talking to a friend. And I told him—and I was able to really express myself to him and tell him, like, I don't want this lifestyle no more, man. I need to get a job.

But in my heart, I knew if I got a job that that's all it was going to be, was a job. I needed somebody to help me redirect my thoughts, change my pattern, my way of thinking. And he took me to the Bishop J. Raymond Mackey and upon talking to the Bishop, he sat down and he asked me, ''Son, what do you really want to do with your life? You said you want a job. I can get you a job but you have to change the way you think in order to keep that job.''

And from that point I looked at him and I knew, I saw the sincerity that was in his heart and he let me realize that—he let me see that it was unconditional love out there other than my family. And it was a process. It was a long process that we had to go through. And I was still out there doing the things that wasn't morally—wasn't the way I was brought up.

But through consistency and through him being consistent in my life and constantly standing over me like a father—like my second father, because I did have my father, but like a second father— taught me, helped me realize that it's people out there that love you.

And this organization H.E.V.N. taught me how to be an example to others. It taught me hurt people, hurt people and heal people, heal people. I was hurt all those years. So that's all I knew, taking my anger out on others, hurting people, that I didn't have no other way to do it.

So with the Bishop, he taught me how to be a man of integrity, how to be a man of your word and how to be an asset to others and now that we have a close relationship, close bond like he's my father, I feel like I can be an asset to others.

Now, H.E.V.N., we got this program that we adopted 100 families and I have this young boy that's 13 years old and he was having a lot of problems in school. And I felt his pain. I know he was reacting because he didn't know no other way to control his anger. And he was adopted, he had a lot of issues in his life, with his mother. And I felt his pain and I'm able to be an access to his life and he's able to change his life around because somebody outside of his family showed him that they cared for him.

So we could sit here behind this desk and talk and do all these things. But the real problem is out there on the street corners. All we're seeing is consequences. Now, if we show we could go out there and reach out to somebody and adopt a family, adopt a person and let them know that you are there for them no matter what, through the good, bad and ugly, that's a major, major piece in our community.

And through the Bishop we go out there on the streets and we're involved in these gang activities. We're out there reaching out to them personally.

We can't sit back as a community and talk about it. We have to come together as components in our community and go back there and check out our streets.

So I want to end with hurt people, hurt people and heal people, heal people.

Thank you.

[The statement of Mr. Maddox follows:]

PREPARED STATEMENT OF CHRIS MADDOX, ASSISTANT OUTREACH WORKER, H.E.V.N.

Unlike most children in my community, I grew up with both parents in my life. My mom and dad divorced when I was about eight years old. It seemed as though it did not have an affect on me, but it did. I continued, however, to be an honor student for the next two years.

When I used to walk to school, I would go pass this block where there always seemed to be excitement. I was curious about what used to go on there. One day on my way home from school, my friends and I decided to walk down that block. While walking through, we saw people standing on corner, talking loud, rolling dice, selling drugs, talking to women, drinking alcohol, and countless other things. This lifestyle seemed exciting to us. We wanted to be just like them.

I held my first gun when I was in the sixth grade. I smoked my first blunt of marijuana around the same age. Slowly I was inheriting this street lifestyle that I thought was so fun. On Friday nights a group of us used to go to the train station to look for Latino men to jump and rob them. We used to steal bikes and started getting deeper and deeper into the lifestyle. But after a while, we were no longer satisfied with riding stolen bikes * * * now we were driving stolen cars.

At this point I was knee-deep in the street lifestyle. I was hanging out late nights drinking and smoking. I was basically void and without substance. I would fight in school on a daily basis, cutting classes, and leaving school when I wanted. Then in 1998, my lifestyle went to a whole different level. I was initiated as an Outlaw and went from doing petty crimes to gang banging.

There were 53 Outlaws in Hempstead. We had dreams of taking over the neighborhood. By 1999 we were recognized by all street gangs, police, and government officials. On Friday nights we use to have meetings at a local park to initiate new members and discuss things we thought need improvement within our set. We were organized criminals.

On Nov. 30, 2000 my life took another major turn. I got arrested for an armed robbery and sentenced to 5 years. This was my first time ever going to prison. There I met up with my

Outlaw brothers. It seemed almost like a disease that we all were catching and it opened my eyes. It let me see who my true friends were.

I was not really upset that I was in prison because I knew what I did was wrong. I had to handle my time. But I still was angry because the people who I thought were my friends didn't come through like I felt they should've. So I spent my whole time in prison reading and working out. I prayed at night here and there. Then when it was time for me to come home, I thought I had all the answers. I thought I knew what I wanted out of life, but something about me was still empty.

When I came home spoke to a friend and I told him that I needed a job. He took me to meet Bishop J. Raymond Mackey. From the start I saw his love and passion for saving lives. I knew it wasn't just another job for him. While talking to the Bishop, he challenged my thought process. When I strayed away, he consistently called me and did whatever it took to get me back on track. His vision for H.E.V.N. became my vision. I wanted to help save people and be a mentor to others as well. I no longer wanted to be recognized by gang bangers and street hustlers. I wanted people to see the good work I was doing in the community. Today, I sit before all as a Program Assistant Outreach Worker for H.E.V.N.

Lord Knows! [Additional materials submitted by Mr. Maddox follow:]

H.E.V.N. Coalition

Helping End Violence Now

''Our Youth Are Our Most Valued Resource''

Mission Statement: H.E.V.N. is a coalition of Faith Based Organizations/Agencies, Individuals and families.

Our goal is to preserve the quality of life for all by preventing the growth and reversing the negative influence of gang and youth violence upon communities.

What are gangs?: ''An ongoing organization, association, or group of three or more persons that have a common interest and/or activity characterized by the commission of or involvement in a pattern of criminal or delinquent conduct.''

H.E.V.N. COALITION and COUNCIL FOR UNITY PARTNERSHIP AND
H.E.V.N. HEMPSTEAD COMMUNITY CLUSTER—A CALL FOR PEACE!

Requesting All Of Hempstead CORE Gangs Members To Attend
''PROJECT PEACE TREATY''
(LET'S WORK TOGETHER TO STOP THE VIOLENCE)
Friday, December 8, 2006 10:00 AM—1:00 PM

HELD AT
All Saints Temple Church Of God In Christ 102 Laurel Avenue * Hempstead, New York
Resources will be available to address all needs!
Rev. ELIEZER REYES, H.E.V.N. Executive Board President
Bishop J. RAYMOND MACKEY I, H.E.V.N. Executive Director

Rev. LYNNWOOD DEANS, Director H.E.V.N. Hempstead Community Cluster
Mr. ROBERT DESONA, President/Founder Council For Unity

H.E.V.N. COALITION

Helping End Violence Now

"Our Youth Are Our Most Valued Resource"

Mission Statement: H.E.V.N. is a coalition of Faith Based Organizations/Agencies, Individuals and families.

Our goal is to preserve the quality of life for all by preventing the growth and reversing the negative influence of gang and youth violence upon communities.

What are gangs?: "An ongoing organization, association, or group of three or morepersons that have a common interest and/or activity characterized by the commission of or involvement in a pattern of criminal or delinquent conduct."

Tuesday, August 8, 2006.

Mr. George M. Sandas Office: 516-478-6247 Fax: 516-489-3015,

Superintendent of Parks and Recreation, Inc. Village of Hempstead, Kennedy Memorial Park, 335 Greenwich Street, Hempstead, NY 11550.

DEAR MR. SANDAS: Greetings! I appreciate your assistance in regards to 3rd Annual HEVN Hempstead Community Cluster Community Awareness Get Help Now Day.

We would like to have this event on Saturday, October 6, 2007 at Mirchelle Parkfrom 10:00 AM—4:00 PM. We are requesting the use of the village's show mobile without a fee if possible. HEVN has limited resources for this event. Last year over 250 Hempstead residents attended. They received information from our resource tables and were given free food. It was a great success!

Looking forward to hearing from you as soon as possible. You may reach me at 516-644-7801. Your continued support is greatly appreciated. Have a blessed and Wonder-FILL Day!

Yours truly,

BISHOP J. RAYMOND MACKEY SR.,

Executive Director.

H.E.V.N. COALITION

Helping End Violence Now

"Our Youth Are Our Most Valued Resource"

Mission Statement: H.E.V.N. is a coalition of Faith Based Organizations/Agencies, Individuals and families.

Our goal is to preserve the quality of life for all by preventing the growth and reversing the negative influence of gang and youth violence upon communities.

HEVN COALTION and COUNCIL FOR UNITY PARTNERS and HEVN HEMPSTEAD COMMUNITY CLUSTER PROJECT PEACE TREATY PEACE AGREEMENT FOR THE YOUTH OF HEMSTEAD

This agreement has been drawn by the Council Of Unity and HE.V.N., with the hope that a cycle of conflict will be replaced by a climate of peace and possibility for the youth of Hempstead, H.E.V.N. and Council for Unity will commit their resources and assets to support this initiative.

The Parties who sign this peace treaty agree to the following:

1. All acts of violence by opposing gangs must stop immediately.
2. Leaders from opposing gangs agree to form a H.E.V.N./Council for Unity governing body to arbitrate all disputes and settle all beefs in a fair, just and non-violent manner.
3. All individuals who appear before this group will abide by its decisions. In cases where an agreement cannot be reached, all parties can appeal to the adult H.E.V.N. and Council for Unity, Inc. for arbitration.
4. The newly formed H.E.VN./Council for Unity, governing body will plan, cultural and recreational projects for the purpose of uniting all elements of community into constructive on going relationships where a culture of conflict will be replaced by a culture of cooperation and hope.
5. The newly formed H.E.V.N./Council for Unity governing body agrees to work closely with community groups/resources and associations to further the educationalcareer possibilities of the youth of Hempstead.

By signing this agreement, I agree to accept the conditions set forth in this document and to take advantage of the second chance this arrangement provides:

(PLEASE PRINT)

Name: ---------------------Date or Year Of Birth ---------------------

Address: -- (OPTIONAL)

---------------------signature ---------------------contact phone number ---------------------date

H.E.V.N. Coalition

Helping End Violence Now

"Our Youth Are Our Most Valued Resource"

Mission Statement: H.E.V.N. is a coalition of Faith Based Ministries, Law Enforcement Agencies, School Districts/Educational Institutions, Government Officials, Community Organizations/Agencies, Individuals and families.

H.EV.N. COALITION PARTNERS

H.E.V.N. Hempstead Community Cluster Rev. Lynnwood Deans, Hempstead Cluster Director, Saturday, October 14, 2006 * 11:00 AM—4:00 PM

Place: Mirchell Park * 90 Atlantic Ave * Hempstead, NY Official Program 11:00 AM-12:15 PM Opening Prayer Greetings Rev. Lynnwood Deans Welcome Introductions Solo Statement Of Purpose/H.E.V.N. VISION, Bishop J. Raymond Mackey I Testimony/Hykiem Coney, Former Gang Leader/Member Greetings Government Officials Closing Prayer Entertainment 12:30 PM—3:30 PM The Psalms Gospel Arts Center Inc. Elder Kevin McKoy,

Founder and CEO / Tabernacle Of Joy Music Ministry Basketball Contest 12:30 PM—3:30 PM

H.E.V.N. Coalition

Helping End Violence Now

"Our Youth Are Our Most Valued Resource"
HEVN COALITION STATEMENT OF PURPOSE

- Mission Statement—HEVN is a coalition of Faith Based Ministries, Law Enforcement Agencies, School Districts / Educational Institutions, Government Officials, Businesses, Community Organizations / Agencies, Individuals and Families. Our goal is to preserve the quality of life for all by preventing the growth and reversing the negative influence of gang and youth violence upon communities.
- Plan Of Action—"A House Divided Against Itself Cannot Stand" — "A City Divided Against Itself Is Brought To Desolation"

In order to effectively address the issue of gang/youth violence there must be collaboration among the entire component of the community. Addressing not only the gang/youth violence but holistically addressing the family / community problems that are present in our communities. The gang/youth violence are the symptoms while the core of this issue traces to the problems / needs of the families of our communities which affect the community as a whole. HEVN seeks to address the social and economic issues affecting the families in order to reverse the negative influences within the community.

In order to accomplish this, HEVN is developing community clusters with a Board Of Directors and Community Cluster Partners, representing the components of the community listed above. The Board Members will be persons from the community of the cluster and as well as the partners. To identify the problems, needs, and present resources available to address the problems and network in solving them by meeting the total needs of the community. HEVN COALITION will assist in establishing the necessary assistance in addressing areas of missing gaps and links in the community in areas where services are not available. Without effective uniting, collaboration, and networking to address the concerns of the community, the greater success will not be realized.

HEVN's Coalition Partners are national, state, local, faith-alliances, government officials, law enforcement agencies, school districts, education departments, corporations / businesses, community-based organizations / agencies and personalities who will provide services in assisting HEVN's mission, vision / plan of action. The Coalition Partners will work directly with HEVN's Executive Board, Executive Director and staff. Each partner will provide HEVN a statement of services / resources they are committed to render to the Coalition.

The components of the Community Clusters and Coalition Partners will not lose their own identity, nor their present resources and or funding. HEVN is a mutual vehicle designed to organize the strongest collaboration, and networking that can exist within a community. Only together, united can we make the difference for the good of our communities.

"For United We Stand And Divided We Will Fall" * *"Let's UNITE!"*

H.E.V.N. COALITION

Helping End Violence Now

"Our Youth Are Our Most Valued Resource"

Mission Statement: H.E.V.N. is a coalition of Faith Based Organizations/Agencies, Individuals and families.

Our goal is to preserve the quality of life for all by preventing the growth and reversing the negative influence of gang and youth violence upon communities.

What are gangs?: "An ongoing organization, association, or group of three or more persons that have a common interest and/or activity characterized by the commission of or involvement in a pattern of criminal or delinquent conduct."

H.E.V.N. ACCOMPLISHMENTS/MAJOR EVENTS

* *This is not a complete list* *

1. June 1999 meeting with Nassau County Detective Corey Alleyne and Wilson Marrero and Bishop J. Raymond Mackey Sr. concerning the issues of gang/youth violence and the need for Community Awareness presentations in our local Church. June 1999-September 1999 local churches were scheduled for presentations following morning service.
2. October 1999 1st Community Leaders/Organization meeting held at Tabernacle Of Joy Church, Uniondale, NY. Gang Awareness and Planning Session to Host 1st Community Gang Awareness Workshop, over 70 persons present representing, Faith Based Ministries, Law Enforcement Agencies, School Districts, Government Officials, Community Organizations/Agencies and families.
3. December 4, 1999 1st Community Gang/Youth Violence Awareness Meeting held at Fountain Of Life Church, Uniondale, NY
4. July 1999 Hosted Boston Ten Point Executive Director, Reba Danostrog, Gang Awareness Workshop
5. January 2000 Pastors/Clergy Community Gang Awareness Breakfast held at Fountain Of Life Church, Uniondale, NY. Over 70 clergy persons in attendance.
6. March 2000 2nd Community Gang Awareness Meeting held at Grace Cathedral Uniondale, New York
7. April 2000 12 persons visited Boston Ten Point Coalition to hear their story and adopt their program as model to be brought back to Long Island and tailored to fit Long Island. A day and a half was spent in Boston as we listened and learned from each component of the Ten Point Coalition. We were told that at one time Boston Ten Point Coalition reduced their criminal gang activities from eighty six percent down to two percent. We felt that this was the model for us.

8. April 2000-August 2001 Foundational Work to Officially Establish and Incorporate H.E.V.N. Coalition
9. August 2001 H.E.V.N. Coalition Inc.
10. November 2001 501C3 status received.
11. April 2000-November 2002 Continued to host monthly Community Gang Awareness Presentations.
12. May 2000 Held anti-gang rally/march in Uniondale, NY
13. June 2000 Held a prayer vigil for Eric Rivera (who was killed by gang members coming home from Puerto Rican Parade.
14. December 2, 2000 1st Nassau/Suffolk Counties Community Gang Awareness Meeting held at Amityville Full Gospel Church, Amityville .NY
15. November 2002 Enter into a partnership with Nassau County Executive Tom Suozzi and Nassau County Task Force Against Gangs
16. October 31, 2003 Ribbon cutting ceremony of the grand opening of H.E.V.N. Executive Office 40 Main Street Lower Level, Hempstead, NY. This was a result of our partnership with Nassau County. Funding was provided for the Administrative Office. Rev. William Watson became President of Executive Board, Bishop J. Raymond Mackey Sr., Executive Director, and Elder Kevin McKoy, Program Coordinator.
17. November 2003 H.E.V.N. Hempstead Community Cluster Board of Directors was formed, with the assistance of Mayor James Gardner.
18. October 2003 H.E.VN. Roosevelt Community Cluster Board of Directors was formed.
19. January 2004 H.E.V.N. Hempstead Community Cluster held its 1st Community Partners Meeting
20. August 2004 Conducted the Funeral Service of Teddy Rainford, ninety persons attending the service came forth to give their lives to Christ and want to redirect their lives, they became clients of H.E.V.N.
21. September 2004 H.E.V.N. Hempstead Community Cluster 1st Back To School Rally,400 Back-Packs with school supplies were given out to Hempstead School District
22. September 2005 H.E.V.N. Hempstead Community Cluster 2nd Back To School Rally, 395 Back-Packs with school supplies
23. November 2004 Hykiem Coney former gang leader of Hempstead Out-Laws became H.E.V.N's Program Assistant Out Reach Worker.
24. June 2005 H.E.V.N. Westbury/New Cassel Community Cluster Board of Directors was formed with the assistance of Mayor Ernest Strada, Village Of Westbury
25. December 2005 H.E.V.N. Roosevelt Community Cluster gave one hundred and thirty eight books as Christmas gifts the Roosevelt District Pre-K School Students.
26. H.E.V.N. Community Cluster since January 2004 has been hosting Community Awareness Get Help Now Meetings. At these meetings H.E.V.N. Plan Of Action and Mission is explained, the work of the community clusters, and coalition/community partners resource tables are set up for families in need. These meetings have been held in community centers, churches, Roosevelt Centennial Park, Hempstead Mirshel Park, (at the park free food was given out cook on the grill), 100 Terance Avenue,

Hempstead, NY. Mr. Hykiem Coney and other former gang members have shared their personal testimonies at these meetings.

27. March 2006: New additional coalition partners Nassau Council Of Chambers Of Commerce, Nassau County CSEA Nassau Local 830, Council For Unity Inc.

H.E.V.N. has held several presentations concerning its vision, plan of action, and reaching youth through preventative and re-direction of the gang life style. Mr. Hykiem Coney has been a main speaking at these events. We have held these presentations at Roosevelt, Hempstead, Freeport, Far-Rockaway, Brooklyn Schools, Molly College, Rockville Centre, NY, The Holocaust Memorial and Educational Center of Nassau County, Glen Cove, NY

H.EV.N. as of April 4, 2006 has 227 clients representing 227 families. Clients needs and family need have been addressed. Housing, Clothing, Counseling, Drug and Alcohol programs, Social Service Assistance, Job Readiness programs, GED programs, assistance in enrollment in Nassau Community College, Hempstead Franklin Career Institute, Garden City Career Institute Of Health and Technology, and other areas has been addressed.

H.E.V.N. presently has two Basketball Teams ages 11-12 and 13-16. Both teamsare Hempstead Cluster Teams. The age 11-12 team February 2006 came in second place in the Hempstead P.A.L. league. It is H.E.V.N. goal to establish a Basketball League and Step Teams representing teams from each Community Cluster.

H.E.V.N. Established Project Restoration 100 Terrace Ave, Hempstead NY June 2006 Goal is to bring support and restoration to the 417 family units addressing there needs.

H.E.V.N. Roosevelt Cluster July 8, 2006 2nd Annual Community Awareness Get Help Now Day Held at Roosevelt Centennial Park. Over 200 persons were in attendance. Resources tables were set up to assist families, basketball torment for youth, barbecue cook out, free food.

H.E.V.N. Hempstead Cluster September 9, 2006 ''Festival Day'' Held at Judea United Baptist Church 83 Greenwick St Hempstead NY. Live Entertainment, FreeClothing and Food. Several hundreds attended.

Last Radio Broadcast Of Hykiem Coney with Radio Station in Chapel Hill, NC

H.E.V.N. Hempstead Cluster October 14, 2006 2nd Annual Community Awareness Get Help Now Day. Held at Hempstead Mirshell Park (Atlantic/Terrace Avenues) Over 300 persons attend, Live Entertainment, Basketball torment, Free Food given out, Resource tables to assist families in need.

H.E.V.N. Increase The Peace Rally at Hempstead School Wednesday, October 18, and Thursday, October 19, 2006 Two days presentation at Hempstead High. Last Presentation that Hykiem Coney was a part of. Wednesday, October 25 2006, Minister In Training, Hykiem Coney , H.E.V.N. Program Assistant Out Reach Worker passed.

Thursday, November 2, 2006 Funeral Service held for Hykiem Coney, Union Baptist Church, Hempstead, NY Over 3000 persons attended. Federal, State, Local Governmental Officials were present. This was the largest Funeral Service held in the Village Of Hempstead.

Monday, November 27, 2006 H.E.V.N. School Assembly Presentation PS 183 School, Far-Rockaway, NY 5th-8th Graders.

Chairwoman MCCARTHY. Thank you all for your testimony.

You know, I have a set of the testimony that we've read, and we set questions up. But after listening to all of you, I guess the questions that I have is now I am legislator. I am the one that has to back up Washington with my colleagues, with the committee and come up with how do we best help all of you to help those that we're trying to reach.

You know, we're going to have limited resources. That's always the problem. Always limited resources.

You talked about intervention and prevention, which I believe that intervention comes with the police, the Attorney General, because that means something has already gone wrong. Prevention means how are we going to reach out to our young people that we already see at risk?

You talked about groups out there to get the money. That's what I always see as the problem. You give the money to the state and then it's up to the state to decide where does the money go.

Obviously, you know, sometimes that money goes to those who have better connections than those through the programs that are actually working on the streets. And that's a shame. But I guess the question to all of you is if I take a small amount of time to answer that, how do we really resource it to make sure it gets to the groups that need it the most to reach the children? At what age? I've always said high school is too late.

Why aren't we looking at a program grade school through junior high through high school for those children at risk? For 11 years in Congress, the gang problem has gotten worse instead of better, in my opinion. You're seeing more violence on the streets than ever before, in my opinion. And we need to have a solution. We're not going to have all the winners. We're not.

But again, we have to start somewhere to show these kids they are kids, that people do care about them even if we don't know them. We want to see each and every one of our children succeed.

So, Chief, if you could start off?

Chief WOODWARD. Thank you.

First and foremost, I think we have to take control. I think for too long we've tried to be all things to all people. In doing that, I think what we've done is spread ourselves too thin. Instead of concentrating on what works—and really, that's questionable itself— I agree with you, a preschool program I think should be our main focus.

I think that every child should have the same level to start at. I believe that these preschool programs in some cases you have parents who have a tremendous amount of money. We have to put their kids in programs where they get the foundation you need to grow. Other children, because of economic disparity, fail to have that.

As you said, Congresswoman McCarthy, the initial step is preschool. It is really revitalizing the family, give the family strong foundations and strong roots in support of the government. There are so many ways to do this.

Obviously, economical is always first and foremost and it helps. But there are other ways. Faith-based organizations. These are important.

One of the things I have mentioned is communications. We have gangs from all walks of life. We have Asian gangs, Russian gangs, so many different gangs. We have to go back to our foundation that we could work with each other and understand each other.

I'll tell you, just dealing with everything in English, which is our main language, putting this report together—and obviously there's rewrites, there's grammatical errors—putting this in different languages, how to make sure we're clear, all of these things become an integral part of any successful program.

But I agree, child development first and foremost.

Chairwoman MCCARTHY. Mr. Hayes?

Mr. HAYES. I think we need to fund programs that work and stop funding programs that don't work. I think resources are taken up when we continue to put money in programs that don't work. A great example for a program that's gotten all the support but has a track record is D.A.R.E., yet D.A.R.E. Continues to be popular.

Chairwoman MCCARTHY. How do we weed that out? I know what you're saying and I agree with you, a lot of times I think that's one of the reasons we have the hearings because we have to recommend to the full committee what's working, what's not working.

Mr. HAYES. I think one of the ways you weed it out is by putting in strings that programs that are funded have to report outcomes. Programs that are funded have to have research connected with them to show results. Some of it—and as I was preparing for testimony someone was saying that's ways and means and that's this committee—the problem is we've chopped everything up so much.

I'm asking the committee to take a wide look at things. But let's influence research. There is a lot of federal dollars that go into research. How many federal dollars are going to researching gangs? Let's redirect things to needs, determine what works and put penalties where states pay back money if they're funding programs that don't work.

Change IV-E. So much of that is geared towards out-of-home placement. It's geared to help the child stay in the home, stay in the community. If a child is involved in a gang and gets moved to a facility, first of all, they're going to be with a lot of other gang members in the facility and then the facility is not going to change the way they're going and then they're going to go and come back.

Help them work through the issues while staying in the community. If you take them out of the community, use proven programs which is a non-affiliation program which is going to go and separate them and establish more positive influences on their lives.

And with agencies like Office of Juvenile Justice and Delinquency Prevention, they do a lot of work on the national level. I've probably started more programs than any other entity in the country and we're a small provider. Every time I call OJJPD they say, ''It's wonderful what you're doing. But we only help on the national level.''

Change dollars so that you help people in the trenches doing the work.

Chairwoman MCCARTHY. Thank you.

Mr. ARGUETA. One of the ways you can give assistance to us is sort of balancing that funding formula. You know, not that we're sort of at different views with law enforcement. But when we're providing billions of dollars to law enforcement and peanuts to those working in prevention and intervention, it makes it difficult to do the work that really needs to be done.

You know, I don't understand how we can invest over $60,000 a year to a correctional institution and up to a $120,000 a year for juvenile detention center and as soon as they get released they're going back to those broken neighborhoods and dilapidated communities to deal with those same exact issues.

We need to look at those national programs that are actually working. We don't need to reinvent the wheel. Theres what's called Homeboy Industries and what they've done is it started by Father Greg Boyle, Jesuit priest, and his whole motto is nothing stops a bullet like a job. It actually helps get kids the employability skills needed and provides for a nonprofit sector.

So we're in the process of trying to start a screen printing T-shirt business where we could actually hire our own youth with artistic talents to put that creativity into a positive and at the same time fulfill a funding. That's something we need to start looking at.

Again, it needs to be a local effort. We're not looking to take on the issue nationally. Because guess what? It's impossible to do so. The issues that we have here in this part of the region are not going to be identical to those being faced by others in the state.

So we need to really make this a localized issue and start working effectively with the collaborations. There has to be more collaboration between the organizations and it's more than just, you know, saying we're going to work together and share information. It's actually doing the work.

You know, I focus on one thing, Freeport does something else, Uniondale community counsel focuses on something else. Let's share those resources and work together. That's what we're doing. But those are a couple of things where you could be of assistance to us.

I need not tell you, but one is we have a problem to the accessibility of guns in our community. There's a problem where Nassau County and Suffolk County, our local county legislators have said we're not going to allow you to buy cigarettes until you're 19 years of age but any 18-year-old could walk into a sporting goods store and buy a gun. That is a serious issue and we need assistance.

Those are just a couple of ways.

Chairwoman MCCARTHY. Okay. Ms. Grant?

Ms. SAPP-GRANT. You know, we've had a lot of issues with getting support and I think, again, it really is about organizations that have been around forever who have—basically it's been monopolized by them. And I've had the experience of having, you know, people from our agencies, our city and government agencies say, ''You know what? That was the best proposal I ever read. But, you know, my hands are tied.'' heart sank.

It doesn't help the kids. But at least they're truthful and this is many years in the working. You know, when I see Ms. Clarke up there, I think about, you know, a phone call that we had some time back where she reached out and said, ''How could I help you?'' you don't hear that very often. You know, it was the first time—it gave me like a light at the end of the tunnel.

You don't have to give me a lot of money. But I am saying recognize. The same vision or the same way young people are looking at society or government and saying you know what we're here or we're trying to find a way to be. Organization is saying the same thing. So if we can't get the support, then really, young people, like, well, if you can't help us then really who will? You know, so it's really about just partner.

One of the greatest conversations I had was sitting with this woman and looking at the schools and how gang violence is affecting the schools in New York City and the fact that the biggest issue for us is the fact that nobody wants to say anything. It is the biggest secret. And going to schools around regions in the Bronx, for example, and hearing the leadership say, ''You know what? We have a big problem.'' because it's not just about the gang violence in that sort of violent way. It's about girls being raped in bathrooms in schools and we will never hear that public schools are letting this happen because everything is hush-hush and it's happening more and more.

Chairwoman MCCARTHY. I'm working on that, by the way. That's going to be in the No Child Left Behind.

Ms. SAPP-GRANT. Again, no snitching. This is not new. Again, I'm a 1980's kid in public school from the '80s and I sat and spoke from school to school to school, from leadership to police officers to anybody who would hear me, saying this is a problem now. I'm telling you what my experience is and I'm telling you who is coming from California right now and who is in the jails and it was, like, ''Shh.'' seriously. To young people.

It's frightening. But what you can do is make it a shame to ignore it. You know, bring it up and talk about it. I think the best thing, most empowering thing for people in leadership is to say something. When you say something, there's nothing for us to be fearful of. Then a lot of people could get the support that they need. And our girls don't have to walk around this shame.

The thing that hurts me the most is a young girl, 14 years old, came up to me in a school and said, ''I'm okay, nobody is going to hurt me.''

I said, ''What happened.''

She said, ''I've been blessed.''

I'm like, ''What do you mean?''

To be blessed is when you let boys gang rape you for protection. This is happening in the schools. The security knew about it and the principals know about it and nobody is saying anything about it.

You know, I don't understand. But we have to talk about it and hold these schools accountable. And we have to let them know that we know so we can solve the problem as though acting as though there's no problem.

Chairwoman MCCARTHY. Chris?

Mr. MADDOX. Like Ms. Sapp-Grant previously said, this money is being monopolized by these well-known organizations and the core problem is the failure in—we have an outreach center where we just not reach out to the gang member or a person that's in the gang, it's about the families. It's about restoring a home, bringing God back into the family and making the man head of the household, which is, like, you—it's about bringing restoration back into your household and you not—and attacking the core of the problem.

The core of the problem is the family and this person is just not going out in the streets and acting because he's just angry about his community. It's about his house. It's basically the household, basically.

Chairwoman MCCARTHY. Mr. Platts?

Mr. PLATTS. Thank you, Madam Chair and my sincere thanks for all of you, again, for your written and passionate oral testimonies here today.

Is it Argueta?

Mr. ARGUETA. Yes.

Mr. PLATTS. I appreciate what you shared today. And one of the things I think that hit home is the issue of prevention. And kind of what's setting this backward is talking about building bigger prisons.

I think one of the challenges we need to address as a nation is can we spend money on the immediate issues and problems—I'm talking about preschool or earlier intervention programs—the results, the dollar spent on those, we won't see for years. But we know they will be effective dollars spent, if we do.

And so we spend more money on what's the problem that we'll try to see it resolved instantly. And that's law enforcement dealing with it, instead of diminishing law enforcement.

One of the things I was hoping, Ms. Sapp-Grant, is your two programs, could you walk me through how you are funded, public versus private? And on the public side, from a percentage or rough share federal, state and local dollars; how do you fund your programs?

Ms. SAPP-GRANT. Private. Most of our funding is private funding. It's foundations. Our first foundation would be New York Woman Foundation. We were supported by my husband for many years, thank God. He's a lawyer so he totally understood there was a need there.

Mr. PLATTS. His personal funds?

Ms. SAPP-GRANT. Yes. We're still there.

Our board does a lot of fund-raising but most of our money is— we still have never received—besides from the Woman's Group—no funding.

Mr. PLATTS. So on an annual basis, public dollars are minimal or not at all to you?

Ms. SAPP-GRANT. Not really, unfortunately.

The other part to talk about is the fact we have to sit down and eat. Our young people are not used to that. They're used to eating, but sitting at a table and really fellowshipping around the table in the evening time before they go home. And they could eat when they go home. But we say a prayer, meditate and have a good time and eat.

So we get that through the youth program and that's about $20,000 a year. That is well used, that's part of the therapy we were all talking about at this table and it means a lot.

But most of it is private funding and we are constantly putting out, you know. And I know our proposals are great proposals, well written, and our program is also supported.

We did a lot of research through Columbia University which tracked our program over a three-year period to see what the heck are you doing and are your outcomes measured in the work that you're doing, and the fact is that we do track our young people up to two, three years afterwards.

Most of our young people now, since our organization has been around for a while, we have our older people who are now alumni coming back as mentors or who are now in college. So they're doing very well.

You have young people who even have not gone the straight and narrow who may have had young children or got into drug problems. They still come back for support. So the success is not only people that did super good, but young people learn how to reach out and help when they do stray.

So there's a difference in there.

Mr. PLATTS. Thank you.

Mr. ARGUETA. From June of 2000 to about the middle of 2004, our organization sustained—and I was running it out of my house, out of my room and we counted on volunteers. Our T-shirts is a major sort of income. For just 10 dollars, you too can be wearing one of these.

Mr. PLATTS. Do you have an extra one with you?

Mr. ARGUETA. We appreciate it. We appreciate it.

So, you know, that's basically how we were doing it.

In the last two years, we've seen a lot of growth. We had those two agencies which I previously mentioned, Uniondale Community Council and Freeport Pride served as partners where they showed up, signed on as collaborators and helped us overcome the things that I was foreseeing.

Originally, it was the Long Island Community Foundation and small foundations donating to our cause. We started a beautification project, really getting the word out on the streets, spreading the idea that we're not anti-gang, anti-gang violence. It's quite different. We're trying to rid these young people of negative behaviors.

So in the last few years, we've seen a lot of growth in regards to being able to compete for grants at the local level. We also got a little bit from republicans in the Senate and at the state level. Small $5,000 grants that really helped us that don't tie our hands to the recipe of which government—the government came up with this idea that, ''We'll tell you what we need,'' where, in reality, they don't know.

We have to tailor our programs to their recipe, where, in reality, they should propose and allow us to come up with our own recipe.

So thanks to the local level, state level and Congresswoman McCarthy was instrumental in assisting the youth board with gains and funds for employment. And so we did get a small $70,000 grant to assist in hiring a full-time job developer that also assisted these young people with counseling. That was very effective.

But, again, with what we're seeing in the nonprofit sector, there is a decrease in availability in funds. So we're looking for innovative ideas to develop funds.

Ms. SAPP-GRANT. You know what? Sergio said—one of the things that was very important was the fact when you diversify it, begin to look at the underlying issues under gang violence, I remember Ms. Clarke saying, ''Well, we need to look at monies that would support job development or therapeutic development,'' you know, getting people through counseling or through the schools.

Even if we got the support to say we will help you to find additional spaces or help you to expand the program to people who need it the most, you know, that's the access that you guys can provide that is priceless. Because a lot of times we have these programs that are phenomenal and we get calls all week from all over the country. We need Blossom here, we need Blossom there, people, individuals as well as agencies, as well as communities that are asking for it.

But if we talk to you and we're able to reach out to you and you're able to get it to the communities most in need and partner with us on that level, that will get it out there.

So it's not just single areas benefiting from it. We need to get it out to the people that really need it.

Mr. PLATTS. Thank you.

Mr. Hayes, I guess to wrap up, what I take is when we look at federal funding, the more we do on or part on a local level, where money comes down into our various not-for-profit agencies and law enforcement working together rather than us saying that we'll go for this specifically is really kind of a good focus. I want to try to get—I've got way too long a list of questions.

Chairwoman MCCARTHY. We all do.

Mr. PLATTS. Mr. Hayes, you talked about a number of the programs and therapies that you were doing and criteria. I guess one of the questions I'm going to ask is what is the right criteria to determine the program is successful?

I'll use an example. Growing up—I'm the 4th of 5 kids. My mom and dad are my heroes. The upbringing they gave us—my mom was a stay-at-home mom but worked a lot of part-time jobs that involved kids. Park director, rec center, and in that park there were a lot of kids that were, you know, on that verge of being in the juvenile detention center, right on the borderline. And my mom—I was a huge blessing to her because she was treating them as her own children. Everyone in that park was one of her children. And so she expected to discipline them the same way she disciplined us, which is, you know, to this day, 40 years later, they're individuals who will stop, visit my mom from that park who didn't go on to get a college degree, didn't maybe become a huge success in society's eyes, but they didn't go to prison and they stayed out of trouble with the law in an official capacity, and maybe did some things that they shouldn't have.

But overall, that leadership that she gave that park, I don't know how you judge that in a scientific way. So how would you say that the established criteria—one of your statements was the federal funds should be very much an outcome basis, either you're succeeding or you're not. If you're not you don't get the money. How do we know well enough.

Mr. HAYES. I think we need to look at—S.T.R.O.N.G. determines that. I think the case of your mom, and lots of good things happened while she was working with them, but she also changed the way people led their lives after she stopped working with them. And a program should work while they're in progress. The proof of the pudding is what happens afterwards?

Mr. PLATTS. What would be that criteria? That they're gainfully employed a year later, not in prison?

Mr. HAYES. Not in prison, not removed from the home, in school, finishing school, avoiding arrest, avoiding gang involvement.

Part of it, as we go in and fund things, we have to put enough money in there and also work with the universities and the likes where the universities feel a responsibility to track—just as did with Ms. Grant's program—to be able to track things and say is this a sustained determined effect.

I think if there is a sustained determined effect—the saddest thing I heard today was Ms. Grant still living with private funding. There's something wrong about that.

The other thing I want to say—and block grants are simplified— but let's avoid the problem of block grants in the past. Usually when we put together block grants in the past, we looked at federal funding and cut it.

The block grants only make sense if we do it in a way where it becomes a tool to produce results. If you want to look at some of the Washington Policy Institute studies, dollars spent on effective prevention today save many tax dollars in the future. We're talking about $60,000 a year to keep somebody in prison, 120,000 to keep youth in youth detention.

Having the cost of domestic violence, cost of substance abuse, if we look at all those costs, we have to see that we're making an investment and let's make an investment to reduce those future costs.

Mr. PLATTS. Thank you, Mr. Hayes.

Thank you, Madam Chair.

Chairwoman MCCARTHY. From Brooklyn, Ms. Clarke?

Ms. CLARKE. Thank you, Madam Chair. Thank you to all our witnesses here today as well.

This has been a very informative, reaffirming, quite frankly, to me, type of hearing because I think this is an issue that we must confront and give life. It's just time, Madam Chair.

This subcommittee, I'm so glad I was able to come on it. I'm one of the newest members. So I am glad I am able to get on Healthy Families and Communities because that's what many municipalities are seeking right now.

We've heard conversations here from the law enforcement and the intervention provider end. What I see, what happens over time is the misdiagnoses have been very costly to us. Costly not only in the tax dollars that we have put into the system, which is multifaceted, but also costly to the lives of the people who we live with. These are our neighbors.

We are manufacturing a lot of this behavior in our community right before our very eyes. Until we put the resources into community-based prevention strategies and look at the formulas and re-engineer them, because as Mr. Hayes stated, I see this as a local official, when you get a block grant there are these giant organizations that need to be maintained. That is their main focus and purpose at a certain point in time. They have to be maintained. So right away their application is re-supported.

That doesn't leave any room for any new innovation in support, particularly when we're cutting a lot of grants. Either we're going to look at new methodology for addressing these organizations, which means that some of the organizations that traditionally been funded will have to lose some funding, or we continue as business as usual.

And I think this is really a very critical time for us to really re-engineer how we're going to address the methods that are really dealing with and managing this issue properly.

The criminal justice system, the law enforcement that takes place in communities, in urban areas and other places are heavily vested with regard to funding. On the other end, our children are being exposed to the criminal justice system and law enforcement a lot earlier in life than they have ever before.

When you think about the fact that in most of the public high schools in New York City you already have police officers stationed there. Behaviors that should get you in the principal's office can now land you in central booking. And so that begins a process of exposure, of alienation, that when we start stalking about families—you know, everyone has a vision of family in their heads. I heard the chief say family and then I heard the folks on the other side of the table say family. The problem is that we're not talking about the same types of families. Families range.

Some families are very high functioning and produce some crazy kids. Some families are poorly functioning and produce crazy kids.

Grandparents are raising very young children; foster care is raising children.

So all of these nuances, Madam Chair, have to be addressed if we're going to get to why we can get alienated so quickly in our society in gang-related violence, in gang related activities.

I want to ask a couple of questions. All of this is wrapped up in my brain and I want to get to the root of what has to be focused on in our nation with real, practical solutions and not in a one-sizefits-all type of way. We have to change that mindset as well.

We talked about the criminal justice system and kind of brushed it over. I wanted to get to juvenile detention and what happens in terms of interventions to address that whole juvenile detention piece. I'm aware of the alternative to incarceration and alternatives to detention, but what kind of discharge planning are we talking about here?

We have young people that are incarcerated, they become professional gang members. Now that they're locked up and we say, ''Okay, you've done your time, go back to your neighborhood,'' we're sending back professional gang members back to the neighborhood.

There's been nothing in between that time they've been incarcerated and when they end up back in the hood. And I'm saying, what types of things are we seeing or hearing about discharge planning for young people? That's my first question. And I'll stop there for right now because I've said a lot.

Chief WOODWARD. Congresswoman, I would speak to the D.A., she's not here.

They have a program in Nassau County called Rising Star. Rising Star, when an individual is incarcerated with a charge through the system, it's alternative sentencing. And she had mentioned that briefly. The individual in that case does not get a criminal record, they are screened by the District Attorney's office to determine what the offense is.

Obviously, different levels of offenses are going to be handled in a disparate manner. You will have a situation, relatively minor type of offense, once the individual crosses over into the area of a violent felony, the Rising Star program is no longer available. And that would probably indicate, for all intents and purposes, a lengthy detention, sentence.

The lesser offenses, through Rising Star there's actually a program, an educational component where the person has to fill that component to successfully complete the Rising Star program, complete the program where they obtain no criminal record, there is criminal disservice. This is a chance for the child to return to the community without being involved.

But if I may, also, one of the more disturbing trends that we're seeing now is where a police officer is called quite commonly to intervene in domestic situations involving young children and their parents. And, again, we're bringing law enforcement into the family household. It's not really our role, but we—unfortunately, society has given us that role because Child Protective Services is inaccurately funded, other social programs that are available are minimal, at best.

So we need to intervene in that case and it's important for us to assist the family. And more than that, give referrals to organizations such as Pride, other outreach organizations to get the family the help and assistance necessary so it does not become a reoccurring problem to both law enforcement and the family.

I also believe that we're very serious about crime prevention, that the way is not the traditional law enforcement approach. To make the houses fortresses, talk to people how to be safe every time to go out publicly, it's to start to intervene at earlier ages, as said earlier by Congresswoman McCarthy and others on this committee. That is the true step, true direction we have to take because that's the only way we'll make a better tomorrow.

Ms. CLARKE. Thank you, Chief.

Mr. ARGUETA. Congresswoman Clarke, here in Nassau County, I can honestly tell you we have not been serious about re-entry and it's not a priority whatsoever. What we're finding is that the discharge planning is non-existent and it consists of actually referring those same kids to these same small not-for-profit organizations and that's the discharge plan.

We've been looking at it as something that we would like to focus on. We've partnered with the Uniondale agency who just submitted an application in regards to seeing if we could fund, get the funding with those individuals who are already working in this particular arena to see if we could further develop these plans.

You know, a lot of these kids unfortunately, or even adults, have it better while incarcerated than they do out in the world. They're able to excel so much in regards to the programs and institutions because all of their needs are being met. Yet, upon discharge plan there is no plan there. So that's why we have a 70, 80 percent resistance rate throughout the entire country. So that's definitely something that needs, you know, much more attention. To tell you the truth, it's minimal at best in many municipalities.

Ms. CLARKE. Mr. Hayes?

Mr. HAYES. In the Bronx we're operating a multidimensional treatment foster care program. And it's one of the programs that has been studied by the University of Colorado at Boulder. Instead of going to upstate juvenile jail facilities, youth are placed without program, we place them in community homes with trained people in the community that live in the community home for 6 to 12 months.

The host parents, as we call them, are particularly trained in a behavioral approach. They're supported by 24 hours on-call by our program staff. Each of the youth has an individual therapist that works with the youth weekly. Each of the youth have a family therapist that works with the family and bio-family to help the bio-family learn to be stronger parents. There is also a skills trainer involved in the model, we have a nurse.

So we're updating medical needs. It is a different kind of program. A lot of times we feel more comfortable with youth being away in jail. Our youth stumble, get into problems. While in the program, we review problems as an opportunity to build skills and to learn.

We recognize that we could help kids succeed in the community. As they go back to their families, there is a greater chance succeeding than if they're sent away upstate.

In Monroe County, the state operates industry, a large facility of the Office of Children and Family Services where youth are traditionally placed through the year. We use Functional Family Therapy.

Another blueprint program, to begin working with families a month to six weeks before discharge to bring the youth and family together, working on relationships, working on family assistance and improving that so that as the family goes back, we just can't take youth away and leave families in the same shape.

Also in Monroe County youth are arrested and they're placed in detention while awaiting disposition. We have introduced Multi Systemic Therapy. The third blueprint program is aimed at adolescence and their families.

And our workers have four families that they're working with in the home every day. And if we look at many of the problems is the influence circle. Ideally the influence circle should be the family. In a lot of these cases the family circles get broken down. What we're doing is working to rebuild the family, working to bring in community organizations, like the church that the youth belongs to and the like, to rebuild the circles of support around the youth to give them a chance to go and to learn and to practice more normal behavior.

Ms. CLARKE. Mr. Hayes, what is the average cost per child that would come into your program?

Mr. HAYES. Well, if you look at our residential program, the multi dimensional treatment foster care costs about $70,000 a year, still less than prison. If you look at, you know, Functional Family Therapy, probably costs about $5,000 for the intervention, Multi-systemic Therapy about $7,000 with the intervention.

FFT is lasting three months roughly to 4 months; Multi Systemic Therapy group would be 4 to 6 months for the family and youth.

Ms. CLARKE. That says something right there when we start looking, Madam Chair, at how we're going to approach this in the reorganization of No Child Left Behind.

Thank you.

Chairwoman MCCARTHY. Thank you, Mr. Hayes.

One of the things from listening to all of you—if you don't mind, I don't know the time constraints you may have. But some of us have one or two more question, if you can stay with us.

In July, I believe it was you that brought up that we were going to be talking about, you know, sometimes there's a cross in jurisdictions. We're going to have a hearing with the judiciary committee in July, because they have jurisdictional programs, whether it's incarceration or some of the other programs. So we're going to work together on that.

We have done that also with our—we were trying to do it but it didn't work out this year—on the agricultural committee, mainly because one of my other subcommittees that we're on, we're looking at children and obesity. So we're trying to convince people that we could still make money but you can put an apple in the machine instead of having some of these other particular foods that they put in there.

But I guess the question that I would like to ask, especially with you, Chris, being that you came out of prison. I hear from correctional officers all the time, services that—especially young people in prison—that they need.

But, you know, in this country some complain that if you try to help those in prison, you were soft on crime. You are going to be out of prison one day. There has to be jobs out there, there has to be a way of coming back into society. There has to be educational opportunities as well as in prison.

That's something that I happen to think that if you really talked about it instead of having a ten-second sound byte, you're actually trying to improve the communities that they're going back to. It has nothing to do with being soft on crime.

I do believe that when we have those that are incarcerated, whether it's in juvenile detention center or prison, we have the opportunity that particular time to give the services.

Let's face it. If somebody doesn't want to take them, you can't do anything about them. You have these people that need help. Some can't be helped but I do believe if we try, they can be. This is one of our chances.

So I was wondering, did you receive services? And also, what kinds of services are needed when somebody is incarcerated, when they come back out.

Mr. MADDOX. Well, some of these services go inside prisons and talk, instill in their heads that this lifestyle is like a dead end. And the process is renewing your mind.

We need things that's going to challenge the way we look at things. We're going to have organizations out there to get you a job. But if you don't know how to keep that job, you will not succeed in life.

We need organizations that will judge the way you think. We need organizations that's not afraid to come into these prisons, that are not afraid to make contact.

We need organizations that's right there in the core of the problems. And H.E.V.N. is right there at the core of the problems and on the streets. Right there.

We need organizations that's going to challenge the way we live.

Mr. ARGUETA. Like I said, we're been working a lot with these organizations out on the West Coast. One of the most effective programs that they have institutionalized within the prison walls is called Criminal and Gang Members Anonymous. Basically a 12step approach, same way you would to a drug, to alcohol.

The criminal lifestyle and gang life is a serious addiction. And what these individuals came up with is a curriculum, a 12-step program developed by an inmate who is serving a lifetime sentence alongside his own child. And it's basically looking at the law, the look of the streets, and it's a self-help initiative.

In other words, I always say S.T.R.O.N.G. does not get kids out of gangs. All we do is provide assistance. If a gang member has not hit rock bottom and says, ''I want to change my life,'' there is no program or religion in the world that can get you out of a gang. This program has been very effective.

One of the things we're doing in the same process, the re-entry application, developed this self-help model to put out in the street.

Individuals from the Nassau County Probation Department are actually looking to implement this program themselves and unfortunately, the funding just isn't there.

That's where you have an excellent opportunity for collaboration between law enforcement and organizations to attack an issue.

Just my view on what you previously stated. What you're doing is being tougher than anyone else on crime, by talking about prevention and intervention, because you're going beyond the barrel of a gun and a handcuff in a prison cell. You're actually saying, ''I am really going to be tough on crime and make sure that we nurture you and take care of you to realize how that how special and unique each one of my community is.''

So I just wanted to share that with you.

Chairwoman MCCARTHY. Thank you.

Chief, I was wondering, because obviously, you've been in the Village for a long time, you've worked on this issue for a long time. You've seen some that have gone to Nassau County jail, prison.

When you see them come back to the community, where is their stance? Do they go back to the gangs because of the services we're not providing? What happens when they do come back into the community.

Chief WOODWARD. More often than not, resume where they left off. One of the things we've seen is when you are a gang member, the gang membership solidifies your position in the jail system. Our prison system is actually a gang incubator.

If fact, if we look at the Mexican Mafia, which was one of the primary gangs that really started to spread in this system of embracing a gang presence within the penal system, we look at the fact that our own system of justice allowed it to spread nationally.

When the Mexican Mafia was first in the California federal prison system, they felt that by moving them and separating them throughout the country, they would alienate their influence. Instead, what we did was facilitate growth. Because what we permitted is we permitted that when you want to process an appeal, you haven't had the record of assistance in the way of witnesses and we actually then flew all of them together and allowed them to perpetuate the system.

Only now, we've actually supported these gatherings that allowed the Mexican Mafia to become one of the most powerful prison gangs in this country.

Chairwoman MCCARTHY. Mr. Platts, do you have any more questions.

Mr. PLATTS. Thank you, Madam Chair.

Mr. Hayes, in your written testimony you mention and we talked about those who have participated in various therapy programs and that 60 percent complete the programs and show the results about the program.

Is there a single or acute factor that you identify as the biggest difference between those who do complete the programs and are successful and those who don't? Is there a family issue, is it drug related; anything that jumps out and distinguishes the groups?

Mr. HAYES. I think that what would distinguish would be evidence-based and non-evidence based treatment. I can talk about that. Those who succeed and those who don't succeed. We're still looking for more common denominators.

Sometimes it looks if the factors are there, you can expect success and you don't see it and other times you don't.

I think that one of the things we have to understand is while these approaches are better approaches, there's no silver bullet. That a lot of the people we've worked with have been trapped into negative behavior, poverty, there's been a tremendous amount of trauma for a long period of time.

And I think the encouraging thing is we could work with about 60, 70 percent of the people who have failed in other programs, we can go and turn around. We still need more effort to see how we reach the others and turn them around.

I do want to support what everyone here has talked about, about poverty being one of the underlying issues. And if people are in bad housing and bad jobs, we're going to keep people like me in business because there's going to be lots of social problems, lots of victims of society who are going to be damaged.

We have Chris Maddox before who talked about hurt and heal. We have to do things that are going to lessen the hurt and promote more healing.

Mr. PLATTS. Thank you.

Ms. SAPP-GRANT. One of the things that we have to look at is post traumatic stress syndrome. This is something that affects most people.

I remember, you know, just thinking as a younger person, dad, "Why doesn't everybody see this? Why isn't this quite obvious to people."

But having a young gentleman talk about the fact that even after he got out of the gang, he still can't sleep with his little daughter because he's not used to being out of the violence because it's so real.

But if you live in a community where people are being shot, and if you even watch television for too long or even the news, you get those same feelings. I imagine if you're around that 24/7 every day, you're dealing with it and you need a counselor, you need a therapist in order to deal with it. And in most cases you need medication.

So these are very real issues, they are medical issues that a lot of our young people are dealing with. So we have to end depression.

Again, they can deal with alcohol or there are so many cases. But in this case we're talking about gang violence.

Mr. PLATTS. I think it goes to the complexity and issue of challenge. There's no simple solution, it's going to take a very coordinated, organized effort.

We talked about prevention. Our colleagues Dan Davis from Illinois, he and I are sponsors of the organization called Home, and it's not trying to reinvent the wheel. But it's taking effective programs that help mostly low-income families, single-parent families to be a better parent for children to help them get on track in the beginning.

I count my blessings because I say, "Hey, I'm a product of my mom and dad." that example that I had, I had that benefit and I seem to give that to now my children. It's societal changes today, both parents are working because of economic necessity. No matter how loving or devoted a parent you are you're working two jobs just to put food on the table or pay bills.

The preschool studies that are now 30 years strong show that every dollar we invest today down the road, the return is many, many more dollars, more productive workers.

So I hope that as we move forward from this hearing what each of you brought to us is an important piece to this puzzle of what we need to do in prevention, in intervention, in law enforcement. We certainly need to protect or citizens as well. But at least we're confident in that approach.

I want to thank you again, Madam Chair, for supporting this and having diverse testimony. Actually, that made me think of one last question actually.

Ms. Grant, you mentioned about one of the challenges of immigration, we seem to have more individual groups, and that language issue the Chief mentioned about common language of the past, do you think that the issue of more promotion of funding, as it relates to No Child Left Behind, in schools as English as a second language where more and more students of which English is not their first language, maybe we're not doing enough to help the child learn to break out of that community, and better assimilate it to the broader community.

Ms. SAPP-GRANT. I don't think that's it. It's classes. It's still property. It's still a different color, unfortunately, trying to become part of the mainstream.

Mr. PLATTS. My question is, is that one of the barriers, the language barrier.

Ms. SAPP-GRANT. Language is a part of it but it's also acceptance. You know, when I think about it, I don't want to stigmatize or point out a group of people, but in order to give an example, when you talk about Mexicans and all of the Mexican people who have come here and built this country and brought such a piece of the American—we've separated, we've stigmatize them, labeled them, then we wonder why gangs then separate and take over their children. We give them the ammunition to say, ''You know what? Look at the way they treat you. Be a part of this, we will build a culture.''

It's the same with any other people. You are going to be a part of your people. But there are people that are just evil. But if we give them the energy and the tools to do that, to do those things, then we're part of the problem. We have to embrace them in the same way we embrace Italians, Irish, we have to embrace all people and we haven't done a very good job at that.

Mr. ARGUETA. Congressman, one of the things we need to do is develop inclusion programs. By that, I mean when you walk in a school and speak a different language you're placed in an ESL classroom and receiving services is like a breeding ground for this because ESL students are treated differently, they're made fun of. Because you dress a certain way, you're not part of the popular culture. You get bullied a lot. As a result, these students are joining gangs as means of protection.

The minute you come in as an ESL student, you have the head of the cheerleading squad, head of the chess club or math club welcome you, embrace you and introduce you to an entire group of friends, positive peers, I can honestly tell you that we are light years behind in regards to addressing the gang epidemic.

And if you really look at the ESL population, we're twice that behind, scraping the services of the means of that population. I'm not talking about the undocumented population. I'm talking about those that are legally here. We need to get to the core of that.

Here on Long Island we're regarded as the most segregated suburb of the entire country. So our belief, and we've talked about it even through our own chapter, starting this year we'll provide counselors and start an ESL S.T.R.O.N.G. chapter to address the needs of those kids in their own native language. So for us, it's inclusion in making them feel they're part of us.

Gang members often say gang life is a family. We agree with that. But the fact is it's an abusive family. It's one that beats you from the moment you get in. It rapes you physically, emotionally and destroys you. That's your community, those are your parents, you know, your religious leaders, that's what we want to focus on, inclusion.

Mr. PLATTS. Your testimony makes the point as one of the challenges. Thank you, again.

Chairwoman MCCARTHY. Ms. Clarke, would you like to ask one question?

Ms. CLARKE. I am very conscious of the time. I'll make it very short. But I wanted to respond to the last statement.

I think one of the things that America has to realize is that human beings are human beings. The issues are in the values that we share. If we don't have shared values, and there are some in our society who value themselves less than others, and we reinforce that and everything else, then we helped create that climate. If we begin to share our values in a way that people recognize that they can be, as you would say, Mr. Platts, assimilated and they're not giving up anything of themselves in doing that, but they're enhancing and enriching who we are as a nation, we would be going a very long way.

I want to focus on gender specificity here and put that on the record, Madam Chair, because I think what is more shocking to me is the level of participation we see of girls now in gang activity. I'm sure it existed for quite some time. But I'm noticing having visited many facilities who house women that are incarcerated, that they're growing, children are actually having children while incarcerated in the facilities with them. And I think we need to put on the record some of what could be done to address that.

So I want to put my question out there for everyone, but in particular Ms. Sapp-Grant.

There seems to be a significant increase of girl gangs. It is my understanding that your program is one that develops a sense of self-worth and will to make positive changes in their lives in the communities. Can you describe what your program does, just a synopsis because we're short on time.

Ms. SAPP-GRANT. What we're seeing—and throughout my career I used to work in locker facilities in group homes and juvenile justice facilities and these facilities that took our young people off the street—people who needed supervision and we get young people who come in as gang members or, you know, who are at risk of becoming gang members, when they come to our program we have an assessment that's done, yet we do the piece that Mr. Hayes is talking about where you really set up those goals.

Those goals are not developed by us saying, ''These are the things we need to accomplish.'' it is about creating a system with that young person and finding out what they want to do in their lives. Our goals for a young person may not be the same as yours. ''I don't want to argue so much with my parent. I know I don't want to be with this group of people but I don't know how.''

You know, they're not going to come with the same things. So we're learning also not to push all our ideas on that young person. In order to keep them out of trouble, they're going to develop over a period of time.

Our program is three tiered. The first part is getting them to a place of safety, getting to know that person. The second phase involves getting them involved with a mentor, making sure they're in school, making sure they get the clinical support that they need. The program is very comprehensive.

So it's a clinical piece where, you know, each person does have a therapist. There's an educational piece. Each person is back in school or getting their GED. Because, again, everybody is not going to college. Everybody is not interested in that. If you come to us and say, ''You know what? I want to go here.'' then we'll do our best to help you, support you in getting to your dream. Not our dream but your dream. It's about advocacy and leadership.

A lot of these youth are smart, brilliant. Getting them to talk to the people, to learn how to access the services that they need, because part of it is just the fact that we're not addressing our needs.

So if you're saying, ''You know what? I'm hurting.'' and nobody, your teacher is not listening to you, or your guidance counselor is not listening to you, you're going to turn to something else.

A lot of time it's just frustration. It's about getting them back into the school or changing schools, or special ed if they need it. Because a lot of times they're not getting what they need in schools. Sometimes people need a different school setting.

The other part is the mentoring. We make sure every one of our girls has a one-on-one mentor based on what they want to do in their lives. One who wants to go into law, which a lot do, we have school lawyers we find, constantly recruiting mentors to make sure our girls have access to mentors.

The advocacy and leadership is crucial because these are girls that go out and march against—again, they all develop their other political minds. It's letting them understand they have the power to speak and they begin to use that, which, again, alleviates the anger. Because now we're learning how to talk.

We do anger management, we do family counseling which is crucial because we have a lot of girls that come to us because their parents say, ''Fix her. She's broken. And it has nothing to do with me.''

So I would think, no, we will help your family. We won't fix her so she could go into your house. So let's work together as a family. It's about bringing the whole family to the table.

And sexual abuse, which is, again, a critical issue. 75, 85 percent of our girls. You just can't change it. It keeps coming over and over again. We have to address those issues and help them to address it in a meaningful way.

The last piece is jobs. We have a program called Girls in Business. So they create their own things. It's not about waiting for employment to roll around because a lot of them don't get. Cozy Comfort pillows, they create pillows, they create stabs, carbon stabs that are very decorative. And then whatever it is they want to do, because that's what it is about, being an American child, that we as adults are out there to help them realize their dream and to realize how important they are to society.

So as an organization, we help the community understand, again, how important it is to help support our young children in realizing their dream.

It's not brain science or anything like that. It's about being human, being a community. If we do those basic things it doesn't cost $170,000, as it does to lock up a young person for a year. It costs very minimal to just be involved in a child's life and teach other people how to do it in a meaningful way.

Chairwoman MCCARTHY. Ms. Clarke.

Ms. CLARKE. Thank you, Madam Chair.

Chairwoman MCCARTHY. You're welcome.

I'm going to do my closing statement. I want to thank each and every one of you. You really have given us an awful lot of information.

We have probably gone over a little bit in our time. But we, as members, I'll be very honest with you, when we do a hearing down in Washington there are probably about 30 or 40 of us sitting there. So we'll give an opportunity to ask a second round of questions or even allow to take the time to get questions out and then have you come back without, you know—in five minutes, let's face it, five minutes is not much time really but we have a luxury to be able to be here a few more minutes.

The complexities that you all brought out, those are things that we will go over. Everything has been taken down so we could go over it and see how to integrate that with other programs that we have out there.

You're absolutely right. It was brought up a number of times. We have to figure out how to make sure that money is available for those programs, to go back to the communities on a community level.

One of the things I found is there's a lot of repeating on programs even here in my own district when we fight to get grants back into our district. And you might have 5 or 6 programs in the district doing what they say they're going to be doing as far as working with gangs and other issues.

There's only one goal that we're all looking for. How are we going to help our young people? How are we going to make sure they have a productive life, to live their dreams? I think that's what we all feel strongly about.

Again, I thank you all for your testimony. At this time, we have to go through the formality of closing the hearing.

As previously ordered, members will have 14 days to submit additional materials for the hearing record. Any member who wishes to submit follow-up questions in writing to the witnesses should coordinate with the majority staff with a request of time.

Without objection, this hearing is adjourned.

[The prepared statement of Jane Bender follows:]

Prepared Statement of Jane Bender, Committee Chair, Gang Prevention/ Intervention Programs

Background

The City of Santa Rosa, California (pop. 157,983) is located 50 miles north of San Francisco in the heart of the Sonoma Wine Country. Our median income is over $75,000. The average home price is over $500,000. It seems like an unlikely place for gangs to breed and grow, but they have. For the past several years, the gang violence in our community has continued to escalate to a point where the community finally said...enough!

In 2004, the citizens passed a quarter-cent sales tax measure that would provide funding for fire stations, gang prevention/intervention, and gang enforcement. We receive $7 million annually which is used to address these important community issues.

After researching successful models in cities throughout California we took the best of San Jose and Fresno and formed the Mayor's Gang Prevention Task Force (MGPTF) and the Mayor's Advisory Board. From the beginning, there was an understanding that we could not "arrest" our way out of this critical problem. Gangs are a community-wide issue and need to be addressed with a community-wide response.

The MGPTF is divided into two major sections:

- A policy team that represents probation, the courts, schools, business, and law enforcement. The highest officials of these agencies sit at the table and get updates on the gang issues facing our community. They hear first hand what is going on in our city. They are the policy makers that can help reshape the way we respond to the crisis. It is working. The group has developed a sense of trust with each other and is finding ways to work effectively to change the way we work. They set the goals for our community to reduce the number of gang related violent crimes and the level of gang members; provide opportunities that assist young people in making healthy lifestyle decisions; and create and maintain safer schools and neighborhoods.
- An operational team is composed of Police, Probation, Recreation and Parks, the District Attorney, non-profit community group, neighborhood associations, and individuals who are directly involved with youth. They are representatives who bring the knowledge, expertise, and resources to the table. They work in a confidential manner to help focus on specific areas of prevention and intervention.

Recreation and Parks took the leadership role in developing the prevention and intervention programs. They receive about $1.4 million per year that provides critical after-school programs at school and community sites. Over $800,000 has been awarded to non-profits that work with gang-affiliated or at-risk of being involved youth through our Community Helping Our Indispensable Children Excel (CHOICE) program. The CHOICE program includes targeted funding for at-risk youth; outpatient counseling for youth and their families that are exhibiting pre-gang or gang lifestyles; parent and family support programs to help develop parenting skills; and job readiness training for gang involved youth.

After-School Programs

We believe that a critical component to any gang prevention program is having a place where young people can be safe after school and where they can get tutoring and mentoring to help them be successful in school. Our Recreation and Parks Department, with the help of the tax money described above now offers after-school programs in almost 20, out of 34 elementary schools throughout the city. We hire people from the neighborhood that have an investment in the youth in the area and individualize the programs, depending on the needs of the students at the program. Because the program is still so new, it is difficult to measure how successful the Task Force is; however, we have found with the survey information that young people love the programs and are taking advantage of the opportunities they present and feel better about them, based on the Asset Model. We expect more definitive results within the next month that we would be happy to share with the committee.

Summary

We believe that Santa Rosa has served as a model that could be used by other (small and mid-sized) communities to help young people succeed and stay out of gangs. The keys to the model are:

1. Commitment from the policy makers that things will change
2. Commitment from organizations and individuals that they will work together to develop programs that address a specific gang issue
3. Ongoing funding source that is supported by the community.
4. A commitment to evaluate and measure success and make the necessary adjustments

We are happy to provide further details to the committee or address any questions that you might have about this program.

[Whereupon, at 12:38 p.m., the subcommittee was adjourned.]

INDEX

9

9/11, 20, 41, 61

A

abusive, 120, 208, 212, 237
academic, 36, 179, 190, 199, 212, 213
academic performance, 190
academics, 4, 107
access, 84, 85, 94, 96, 185, 188, 189, 196, 206, 208, 212, 215, 228, 238
accessibility, 205, 206, 209, 225
accountability, 52, 83
accounting, 53
achievement, 48, 179, 192, 195
acute, 235
adaptability, 104, 106
addiction, 233
adjudication, 61
administration, 49, 186, 190
administrative, 82
administrators, 46, 60, 192, 195, 207
adolescence, 232
adolescent behavior, 57, 59
adolescents, 24, 118, 134, 192, 195
adult, 6, 14, 16, 31, 33, 34, 37, 46, 50, 54, 58, 60, 61, 100, 118, 119, 128, 131, 139, 179, 218
adulthood, 14
adults, 5, 6, 10, 11, 14, 31, 32, 34, 38, 46, 62, 94, 95, 118, 123, 127, 128, 141, 178, 186, 190, 197, 206, 207, 231, 238
advocacy, 27, 137, 211, 238
African American, 14, 15
African-American, 104, 107, 127, 139, 205, 209, 211
afternoon, 94, 100, 101, 138
after-school, 20, 35, 141, 240
age, vii, 1, 10, 14, 21, 31, 35, 36, 38, 47, 57, 59, 61, 62, 100, 101, 107, 126, 128, 138, 185, 188, 189, 190, 191, 192, 193, 196, 200, 202, 203, 204, 214, 215, 222, 223, 225
agent, 106
agents, 22, 24, 26
agricultural, 233
aid, 30, 212
AIDS, 212
AIM, 103
alcohol, 3, 48, 53, 126, 194, 215, 233, 235
alcohol use, 3
alien smuggling, 4
alienation, 4, 35, 230
alternative, 27, 32, 95, 135, 185, 188, 190, 192, 194, 196, 199, 201, 207, 213, 230, 231
alternatives, 20, 27, 32, 37, 93, 123, 126, 128, 135, 139, 141, 181, 185, 187, 188, 205, 207, 208, 211, 230
ambassadors, 207
amendments, 34, 42
American culture, 104
American Revolution, 3
analysts, 22
anger, 57, 59, 78, 82, 123, 125, 126, 129, 194, 214, 238
anger management, 57, 59, 238
anorexia, 210
anthropology, 49
anti gang, 207
anxiety, 62
anxiety disorder, 62
application, 82, 123, 141, 195, 230, 231, 234
appropriations, 24, 26, 31, 32
arbitration, 218
Arizona, 42, 135
Arkansas, 42, 131
armed robbery, 215
Army, 49, 108, 197

arrest, 16, 20, 28, 33, 55, 57, 58, 59, 61, 81, 84, 85, 100, 120, 122, 126, 131, 132, 134, 184, 187, 192, 193, 196, 199, 201, 229, 240
arson, 9
ART, 85
artistic, 225
Asian, 14, 15, 80, 108, 223
assault, 9, 12, 13, 103, 128
assaults, 4, 18, 80, 190, 192
assessment, 13, 14, 21, 39, 83, 196, 207, 237
assets, 57, 58, 60, 218
assignment, 31, 81, 101
assumptions, 52, 120
ATF, 19, 22, 26, 98, 105
athletes, 190
Atlantic, 218, 222
atmosphere, 25
attachment, 25, 192, 195, 196
attacks, 20, 24, 96
attempted murder, 19, 61, 62
attitudes, 3, 108
Attorney General, 31, 32, 43, 121, 135, 176, 223
Australia, 46
authority, 19, 31, 122
availability, 16, 100, 182, 228
aversion, 52
awareness, 26, 190, 191, 192, 196, 197, 208

B

background information, vii, 2
barrier, 236
barriers, 3, 16, 236
basketball, 139, 222
batteries, 128
beating, 213
beautification, 228
beef, 139
behavior, 4, 20, 25, 36, 48, 52, 57, 59, 94, 95, 120, 121, 125, 134, 137, 141, 190, 192, 196, 207, 230, 232, 235
behavioral problems, 3
beliefs, 85, 97, 99, 196, 198
benefits, 25, 31, 48, 51, 55, 58, 60, 119, 131, 142, 199
benign, 4
bilingual, 132, 196
bipartisan, 46
Black students, 17
block grants, 229
board members, 60
boats, 203
bonding, 58, 60, 197
boot camps, 53
border crossing, 186
borderline, 229
boredom, 93, 95
Boston, 3, 28, 36, 49, 78, 80, 81, 107, 119, 135, 220
bounds, 10
boys, 101, 212, 226
brain, 230, 238
breast cancer, 82
breeding, 236
broad spectrum, 46, 192
Bronx, 225, 232
Brooklyn, 85, 178, 181, 183, 209, 211, 222, 229
brothers, 196, 204, 212, 216
buildings, 123, 204
bullying, 85, 134
Bureau of Alcohol, Tobacco, Firearms and Explosives, 13
Bureau of Alcohol, Tobacco, Firearms and Explosives (ATF), 13
burglary, 9
burning, 108
Bush Administration, 81
buyer, 104
by-products, 104

C

Cambodian, 129
Cambodians, 3
campaigns, 26
Canada, 46
capacity, 23, 52, 53, 80, 82, 94, 96, 207, 229
carbon, 238
career development, 207
carjacking, 101
cartels, 132
Caucasian, 14, 15
cell, 29, 101, 135, 141, 178, 234
cell phones, 178
Census, 6
Census Bureau, 6
Central America, 18, 19, 40
CEO, 219
chain of command, 190
child abuse, 134
child development, 191, 198, 199, 224
child welfare, 200, 201, 202
childcare, 84
childhood, 27, 31, 53, 85, 186
children, 18, 20, 21, 24, 27, 55, 93, 95, 97, 100, 101, 104, 107, 123, 141, 142, 178, 179, 180, 181, 184, 185, 186, 187, 188, 189, 190, 191, 193, 194, 198,

199, 201, 202, 204, 205, 206, 209, 210, 213, 215, 223, 227, 229, 230, 231, 233, 235, 236, 237, 238
China, 46
chocolate, 107
Christmas, 221
cigarettes, 225
Cincinnati, 78, 81, 124, 142
citizens, 54, 55, 101, 105, 179, 180, 236, 239
civilian, 101
classes, 32, 194, 215, 236
classification, 54
classroom, 236
classrooms, 25, 207
clients, 54, 221, 222
clinical psychology, 62
clinical trial, 53
clinical trials, 53
Clinton Administration, 81
clusters, 219, 221
coaches, 192
Coalition for Evidence-Based Policy, 54
cocaine, vii, 1, 2, 13, 21, 100, 103, 123, 212
codes, 190, 192
coercion, 126
cognitive, 27
cognitive development, 27
cohort, 118
collaboration, 13, 51, 96, 130, 181, 196, 219, 225, 234
Collaboration, 54
college campuses, 14
colleges, 117, 204
Colorado, 48, 50, 140, 199, 201, 232
colors, 14, 101, 103, 190, 192, 204, 206
Columbia, 78, 80, 81, 83, 93, 94, 95, 96, 97, 98, 100, 227
Columbia University, 80, 227
commerce, 5, 21
Committee on the Judiciary, 45, 99
communication, 23, 28, 39, 48, 96, 132, 190, 191, 198, 199
Community Oriented Policing Services, 21
Community Oriented Policing Services (COPS), 21
community service, 32
community support, 79, 82
compassion, 137
competency, 211
complement, 195, 204
complexity, 35, 37, 235
compliance, 126, 193
components, 22, 25, 84, 120, 121, 211, 215, 219
composition, 4, 40
computer mouse, 102
confidence, 53, 101
conflict, 20, 25, 32, 107, 194, 197, 218
conflict resolution, 25, 32, 197
confrontation, 122, 129
confusion, 51, 54, 198, 213
Congress, iv, vii, 1, 2, 5, 20, 21, 23, 24, 26, 30, 32, 33, 35, 36, 37, 40, 41, 42, 46, 47, 85, 93, 97, 98, 104, 106, 108, 138, 140, 177, 178, 180, 202, 205, 223
Congressional Record, 43
consciousness, 94, 96
consensus, 36, 198
consent, 136
Consolidated Appropriations Act, 22, 23
conspiracy, 19, 26, 34, 81
constraints, 233
consulting, 213
contracts, 186, 189
control, 25, 27, 36, 51, 52, 53, 54, 55, 79, 118, 120, 123, 138, 196, 214, 223
control group, 25, 118
controlled substance, 5
convergence, 20
conviction, 30, 43, 61, 134, 189, 193
Cook County, 104
coordination, 96
COPS, 21, 28
corporations, 219
correlation, 16
cost benefits, 142
cost-effective, 51, 58, 60, 85, 134
costs, 31, 33, 34, 51, 53, 142, 229, 232, 238
counsel, 225
counseling, 20, 27, 33, 36, 93, 95, 182, 185, 188, 196, 204, 208, 211, 228, 238, 240
counterterrorism, 24
courts, 27, 29, 61, 240
CPR, 108
crack, vii, 1, 2, 20, 21, 100, 103, 118, 123, 212
creativity, 225
credibility, 126
credit, 14, 138
credit card, 14
criminal activity, 2, 4, 5, 9, 13, 17, 22, 37, 93, 95, 96, 99, 128, 186
criminal acts, 4, 14, 26
criminal behavior, 4, 22, 52, 53, 85
criminal gangs, 38
criminal justice, 12, 105, 185, 189, 203, 204, 205, 230
criminal justice system, 185, 189, 203, 204, 205, 230
criminality, 141
criminals, 4, 33, 57, 60, 84, 93, 95, 189, 215

criminology, 49
criticism, 34
cross-sectional, 25
CRS, 1, 10, 11, 15, 39, 40, 41, 42, 43
crying, 205, 213
cultural differences, 190
cultural values, 198
culture, 13, 79, 102, 118, 198, 200, 201, 206, 207, 209, 218, 236
curriculum, 24, 25, 233
cycles, 142

D

danger, 134
DARE, 50, 54
data collection, 5, 37
data mining, 61
database, 32
death, 30, 34, 46, 127, 139, 179, 183, 196, 203
death sentence, 30
deaths, 82
decisions, 82, 97, 126, 128, 218
defendants, 26, 100
defense, 193
deficit, 57, 59
definition, vii, 1, 4, 5, 28, 30, 33, 35, 36, 38, 62, 200, 202
delinquency, 3, 21, 25, 35, 50, 52, 85, 120, 211, 213
delinquent acts, 4
delinquent behavior, 25, 52, 53, 120
delinquent friends, 25, 85
delinquent group, 53
delinquents, 4, 125
delivery, 25, 43, 52
demand, 51, 79, 82, 104
democracy, 107
demographic data, 15
demographics, 16, 192
denial, 193
Department of Education, 22, 54, 117
Department of Homeland Security, 19
Department of Justice, 4, 7, 9, 21, 38, 39, 40, 41, 43, 48, 54, 55, 58, 99, 118, 181
Department of Justice (DOJ), 4
depressed, 119
depression, 62, 119, 235
desire, 104, 137, 206
detection, 13, 34
detention, 141, 211, 224, 229, 230, 231, 232, 233
deterrence, 26, 33, 105, 125, 127
direct observation, 4
disappointment, 123
disaster, 206
discipline, 125, 229
discretionary, 122, 128
discriminatory, 118
diseases, 213
disorder, 119
dispersion, vii, 1
disposition, 141, 232
disputes, 98, 218
disseminate, 24, 32
distribution, 10, 13, 14, 103, 104, 190, 192
District of Columbia, 94, 96
diversity, 53, 183
division, 23
doctors, 107
dogs, 127, 194
domestic violence, 199, 229
dominance, 57, 59
doors, 213
draft, 179
dream, 107, 178, 206, 209, 238
drinking, 215
dropouts, 21, 124
drug abuse, 211, 213
Drug Enforcement Agency, 19, 22
Drug Enforcement Agency (DEA), 19, 22
drug offense, 21, 106, 141
drug smuggling, 4
drug trafficking, 4, 14, 21, 22, 24, 28, 34, 37
drug treatment, 57, 59, 85, 126
drug use, 21, 25, 50, 51, 52, 120, 194
drug-related, 32
drugs, 3, 13, 20, 21, 22, 38, 53, 98, 100, 102, 123, 137, 193, 199, 207, 209, 211, 215
duplication, 23

E

ears, 203
eating, 227
Education, 21, 22, 24, 32, 41, 54, 177, 184, 186, 196
educational attainment, 33, 35
educational programs, 93, 95, 195, 199
educators, 35, 107
El Salvador, 13, 18, 37
elderly, 12
election, 140
electronic surveillance, 105, 184, 187
elementary school, 18, 192, 207, 208, 240
emerging issues, 205
emotional, 141
employability, 33, 225
employees, 60, 195

employers, 189
employment, 27, 31, 32, 35, 36, 37, 94, 95, 179, 191, 195, 205, 206, 207, 208, 228, 238
employment status, 94, 95
empowerment, 212, 213
energy, 178, 208, 209, 212, 236
engagement, 212
England, 46
English as a second language, 236
enrollment, 222
enterprise, 2, 24, 53, 101, 186
entertainment, 194, 198, 206
environment, 104, 108, 127, 181
environmental factors, 3
epidemic, vii, 1, 2, 21, 101, 205, 212, 236
equipment, 22, 31
ESL, 236, 237
ethics, 50, 207
ethnic groups, 3, 121
ethnic minority, 34
ethnicity, 14, 15, 35, 192
evening, 227
evidence-based policy, 52
evidence-based program, 51, 54, 55, 200, 202
evil, 104, 236
evolution, 37
exclusion, 16
execution, 37, 101
expenditures, 52, 53
expert, iv
expertise, 52, 105, 180, 240
exposure, 25, 52, 230
extortion, 4, 190, 192
eyes, 216, 229, 230

F

failure, 28, 53, 191, 226
faith, 23, 27, 118, 120, 185, 188, 199, 201, 219
familial, 3
family, 3, 27, 36, 47, 52, 57, 59, 60, 79, 82, 85, 93, 94, 95, 96, 118, 121, 125, 126, 129, 134, 142, 178, 181, 183, 188, 190, 193, 196, 197, 198, 199, 201, 203, 208, 211, 212, 214, 215, 219, 222, 223, 226, 230, 231, 232, 235, 237, 238, 240
family development, 93, 95
family structure, 3, 178, 181
family support, 36, 240
family therapy, 57, 59, 85, 121, 134
family units, 222
FBI, 6, 9, 10, 11, 12, 13, 19, 22, 23, 24, 32, 34, 40, 41, 49, 55, 58, 98, 134, 192
fear, 29, 57, 59, 82, 101, 130, 134, 137, 196, 212
February, 20, 40, 45, 196, 222
Federal Bureau of Investigation, 6, 39, 41
federal criminal law, 33
federal felonies, 5
federal funds, 229
federal government, 20, 32, 84, 178, 184, 187
federal law, 2, 5, 21, 22, 26, 105
fee, 217
feelings, 203, 212, 235
felony, 5, 21, 31, 99, 103, 193, 231
females, 101, 190, 205, 207
FFT, 85, 201, 232
fidelity, 52, 53
field agents, 24
fines, 38
fire, 99, 103, 239
firearm, 21, 43, 139
firearms, 3, 4, 13, 14, 21, 22, 26, 99, 192, 193
first language, 236
FL, 26
flare, 96
flexibility, 37, 96, 106, 200, 202
focusing, 31, 96, 119, 199, 203
food, 123, 124, 217, 221, 222, 236
foreclosure, 104
foreign policy, 37
foreign travel, 31
forfeiture, 38
France, 46
franchise, 48
fraud, 104
freedom, 28, 212
friction, 122
Friday, 209, 215, 216
frustration, 193, 194, 238
fuel, 2, 186
funding, 8, 21, 22, 23, 24, 26, 31, 32, 34, 35, 46, 47, 50, 51, 52, 53, 54, 84, 85, 101, 106, 108, 118, 119, 129, 135, 141, 195, 200, 202, 208, 210, 219, 224, 225, 227, 228, 229, 230, 231, 234, 236, 239, 240, 241
funds, 22, 27, 50, 101, 129, 200, 202, 227, 228
futures, 118

G

games, 139, 198, 206
gang crimes, 33
gender, 14, 35, 190, 192, 205, 237
generation, 206, 212
genre, 206
Georgia, 42, 106, 124
gifts, 221

GIP, 93, 94, 95, 96, 135
girls, 204, 205, 207, 209, 211, 212, 213, 225, 226, 237, 238
goal setting, 25
goals, 25, 94, 96, 126, 178, 179, 185, 189, 194, 207, 237, 240
God, 216, 226, 227
going to school, 139, 179, 204, 225
government, vii, 1, 20, 22, 23, 27, 32, 36, 37, 84, 96, 120, 122, 132, 178, 181, 187, 190, 191, 198, 202, 214, 215, 219, 223, 225, 228
grades, 35, 191, 197, 203
graffiti, 4, 13, 28, 29, 102, 190
grandparents, 203, 205, 212
grants, 5, 21, 28, 30, 31, 32, 35, 41, 61, 62, 106, 120, 126, 135, 228, 229, 230, 239
graph, 62, 130
groups, 3, 4, 5, 6, 13, 16, 19, 20, 23, 25, 36, 38, 47, 80, 81, 83, 84, 107, 118, 119, 121, 122, 125, 142, 190, 204, 206, 207, 213, 218, 223, 235, 236
growth, vii, 1, 13, 16, 34, 38, 184, 186, 187, 191, 212, 216, 217, 219, 220, 227, 228, 234
Guatemala, 18, 37
guidance, 125, 137, 198, 208, 238
guidelines, 101, 184, 187
guns, 26, 100, 107, 119, 125, 184, 187, 205, 206, 225
gymnasiums, 122, 123

H

hands, 184, 187, 225, 228
handshakes, 206
hanging, 103, 122, 193, 215
harm, 50, 78, 82, 119, 181, 198
Harvard, 40, 49, 108
hate, 5, 6
HE, 218
healing, 235
health, 27, 134, 141
Health and Human Services, 54, 176
health care, 27
health services, 141
hearing, 19, 24, 45, 46, 47, 48, 77, 79, 81, 86, 97, 99, 119, 124, 127, 132, 137, 140, 142, 178, 179, 180, 181, 183, 190, 192, 193, 204, 206, 217, 225, 229, 231, 233, 236, 239
heart, 204, 210, 214, 225, 239
height, 123
heroin, 100, 212
heroin addicts, 212
high risk, 94, 95, 119, 211
high school, 35, 100, 119, 123, 127, 180, 183, 212, 223, 230
higher education, 179, 208
high-level, 19
high-risk, 27, 32, 35, 58, 60, 85, 126, 183, 204, 211
hip, 103, 203
hiring, 22, 31, 100, 228
Hispanic, 13, 14, 15, 17, 18, 80, 99, 104, 132, 133, 135, 197, 198, 209
HIV, 212
HIV/AIDS, 212
Hmong, 101
holistic, 94, 95, 96
holistic approach, 94, 95
homeland security, 47
Homeland Security, 19, 41, 45, 84, 140
homeless, 27, 201
homeowners, 123
homicide, 8, 9, 11, 13, 61, 62, 78, 80, 81, 84, 85, 94, 96, 102, 106, 107, 124, 126, 129, 133
homicide rate, 11, 62, 81, 84, 85, 124, 126, 133
homicide rates, 11, 85
Honduras, 18
hopelessness, 212
hospital, 82, 204
hospitalization, 196
host, 178, 196, 221, 232
House, 40, 41, 45, 46, 177, 181, 219
household, 16, 226, 231
household income, 16
households, 12, 205, 211
housing, 33, 100, 101, 103, 122, 123, 124, 136, 185, 188, 235
human, 55, 62, 206, 211, 237, 238
human resources, 55
humans, 20
husband, 210, 227
hybrid, 14

I

ice, 40, 194, 215
ICE, 19, 20, 40, 41, 98, 105, 106
id, 176
identification, 4, 5, 23, 31, 33, 131, 185, 189, 196, 207
identity, 3, 4, 14, 179, 219
ideology, 6
Illinois, 42, 49, 98, 99, 126, 235
imagery, 206
images, 4
immigrants, 3, 13, 18, 19, 209
immigration, 3, 19, 20, 203, 236
Immigration and Customs Enforcement, 19
Immigration and Customs Enforcement (ICE), 19

implementation, vii, 1, 27, 32, 54, 82, 83, 84, 199
imprisonment, 5, 19, 21, 28, 30, 33, 34, 104, 196
incarceration, 20, 28, 29, 46, 62, 78, 79, 80, 82, 93, 95, 104, 139, 141, 183, 184, 187, 230, 233
incentives, 33
incidence, 16, 130, 134
inclusion, 236, 237
income, 4, 14, 16, 23, 32, 104, 227, 235, 239
India, 46
Indian, 14, 34
Indiana, 42
indication, 11
indicators, 192, 193
industry, 206, 208, 232
infancy, 198
infants, 27
information sharing, 23
infrastructure, 32, 108
initiation, 196, 204, 206
injunction, 29, 130
injury, iv, 119, 196
inmates, 189, 213
innocence, 187
innovation, 34, 230
insecurity, 93, 95
insight, 10, 194, 195, 196
Inspector General, 24, 41
institutionalization, 78, 81, 83
institutions, 4, 57, 142, 179, 195, 204, 209, 231
institutions of higher education, 179
instruction, 192
insults, 99, 100
intangible, 198
integration, 3
integrity, 214
intelligence, 19, 22, 23, 24, 28, 33, 37, 94, 95, 106, 107, 184, 186, 187, 189
intelligence gathering, 28, 94, 95
interaction, 191, 192, 194, 195, 198
interference, 130
internet, 102
Internet, 102, 108
interstate, 5, 21, 31
intervention, 18, 20, 22, 25, 27, 28, 30, 31, 32, 34, 36, 37, 52, 53, 54, 55, 57, 58, 59, 60, 79, 85, 94, 95, 97, 119, 127, 134, 139, 140, 141, 142, 180, 181, 198, 199, 201, 205, 207, 208, 211, 223, 224, 226, 230, 232, 234, 236, 239, 240
intervention strategies, 20, 94, 95, 141, 181, 208
interview, 195
intimidation, 13, 97, 98, 106, 130, 134, 198
Investigations, 24
investigative, 23, 24
investment, 27, 51, 52, 55, 200, 202, 229, 240
Iraq, 108
isolation, 11

J

JAG, 41
jails, 209, 210, 212, 226
January, 1, 23, 83, 220, 221
Japan, 46
Japanese, 108
job skills, 126
job training, 36, 122, 124, 179, 185, 188
jobless, 178
jobs, 27, 85, 93, 95, 118, 122, 123, 135, 178, 184, 186, 189, 208, 210, 229, 233, 235, 236, 238
Jordan, 122
judge, 49, 125, 229, 233
judges, 35, 46
judgment, 127
judiciary, 36, 233
Judiciary, 23, 41, 47, 130
Judiciary Committee, 23, 47, 130
junior high, 203, 223
junior high school, 203
jurisdiction, 6, 8, 16, 33, 97, 98, 99, 184, 187
jurisdictions, 6, 7, 8, 16, 20, 25, 29, 78, 81, 82, 83, 96, 97, 106, 233
justice, 12, 21, 27, 43, 48, 57, 58, 59, 60, 62, 85, 93, 95, 105, 141, 142, 200, 202, 212, 230, 234, 237
Justice Assistance Grant, 41
Justice Assistance Grant (JAG), 41
Justice Department, 78, 83, 117, 118
juvenile crime, 35, 46, 47, 84, 120, 140
juvenile delinquency, 20, 22, 25, 32, 34, 37
juvenile delinquents, 4
juvenile justice, 21, 27, 43, 48, 57, 58, 59, 60, 62, 85, 93, 95, 141, 200, 202, 212
juveniles, 3, 5, 10, 11, 14, 21, 26, 31, 34, 37, 46, 54, 57, 59, 84, 85, 100, 101, 118, 128, 132, 139, 141, 179, 204

K

killing, 119, 206
King, 137, 193
knees, 129

L

land, 34, 230

language, 3, 16, 99, 120, 125, 135, 191, 198, 223, 236, 237
language barrier, 16, 236
Latin America, 3, 37, 40, 41, 49, 93, 94, 95, 135, 140
Latin American countries, 37
Latino, 2, 18, 19, 20, 38, 93, 94, 95, 96, 99, 132, 133, 215
Latino gangs, 2, 18, 19, 20, 38, 99, 133
Latinos, 16, 141, 205
laundering, 2, 4
laws, 2, 19, 20, 26, 28, 32, 33, 34, 42, 46, 126, 132, 141
lawyers, 136, 238
lead, 28, 33, 84, 94, 95, 98, 105, 178, 180, 181, 193
leadership, 19, 47, 48, 94, 95, 135, 140, 182, 192, 205, 210, 211, 213, 225, 226, 229, 238, 240
learning, 25, 57, 60, 123, 179, 183, 191, 199, 206, 209, 237, 238
Lebanon, 107
legislation, vii, 1, 2, 20, 21, 22, 33, 34, 35, 36, 37, 42, 46, 47, 61, 85, 97, 184, 187
legislative, 2, 47, 104, 128
lien, 4
life style, 118, 222
lifestyle, 189, 190, 204, 205, 206, 207, 208, 214, 215, 233, 240
lifestyle decisions, 240
lifestyles, 240
lifetime, 142, 234
likelihood, 10, 12, 25, 53, 62, 119, 121, 189
limitations, 195
lingual, 95
links, 27, 219
listening, 108, 130, 223, 233, 238
literacy, 31
living conditions, 27, 205
local community, 26, 182
local government, 22, 27, 181
location, 4, 54, 118, 178, 179
long period, 235
longitudinal study, 25
long-term, 23, 25, 37
Los Angeles, 8, 13, 18, 19, 26, 28, 29, 39, 42, 78, 81, 104, 122, 123, 127, 129, 130, 208
Louisiana, 42
love, 82, 107, 125, 133, 136, 137, 196, 198, 204, 214, 216, 240
low-income, 14, 23, 32, 235
low-level, 13, 137
loyalty, 18, 213

M

magazines, 190, 198, 203
magnetic, iv
mainstream, 190, 236
major cities, 45, 140
males, 14, 101, 122
management, 57, 59, 238
Manhattan, 49, 93, 95
manpower, 189
manslaughter, 9, 10
manufacturing, 230
Mara Salvatrucha (MS-13), 1, 13, 18
marijuana, 13, 14, 100, 215
market, vii, 1, 55, 103
marketing, 98
markets, 80, 98
Maryland, 46, 49, 93, 95, 130, 131
Massachusetts, 28, 49, 80, 176
maximum penalty, 5
meanings, 101
measurement, 36
measures, 12, 25, 29, 32, 33, 34, 35, 37
media, 4, 52, 102, 121, 194, 198, 206, 213
median, 239
medication, 185, 188, 235
melting, 198
membership, vii, 1, 4, 5, 6, 8, 22, 25, 42, 94, 96, 134, 135, 181, 183, 190, 193, 195, 196, 198, 206, 207, 213, 234
men, 102, 103, 119, 180, 189, 206, 215
mental health, 119, 129, 141, 142, 185, 188
mentor, 58, 60, 137, 216, 237, 238
mentoring, 27, 32, 33, 141, 191, 192, 195, 196, 211, 238, 240
mentoring program, 27, 192, 195, 196
mentorship, 189
messages, 213
methamphetamine, 14
metropolitan area, 19, 190
Mexican, 13, 23, 100, 136, 234, 236
Mexico, 18, 100, 102, 132
Miami, 19, 26
Middle East, 102
migrant, 3
migrant population, 3
migrant populations, 3
migration, 1, 2, 9, 13
military, 190
Millennium, 38, 39, 42
mimicking, 103
mining, 61
Minnesota, 42

minority, 10, 34, 136, 140, 142
mirror, 213
misleading, 134
Mississippi, 42
Missouri, 49, 84, 99
modeling, 134
models, 3, 27, 53, 85, 119, 136, 137, 185, 188, 189, 212, 213, 240
money, 2, 4, 50, 51, 52, 57, 59, 100, 104, 106, 108, 119, 120, 122, 123, 124, 127, 135, 142, 200, 203, 206, 210, 223, 224, 225, 226, 227, 228, 229, 233, 239, 240
money laundering, 2, 4
Monroe, 199, 201, 232
Montana, 42
morning, 45, 55, 58, 93, 97, 98, 107, 108, 122, 123, 126, 178, 179, 202, 203, 205, 212, 214, 220
mortgage, 104, 126
mothers, 25, 119, 123, 131, 132, 134, 204, 205, 212
motor vehicle theft, 9
mountains, 4
movement, 9, 16
multicultural, 93
multidimensional, 85, 133, 232
murder, 4, 10, 34, 61, 62, 100, 101, 102, 119, 126, 128, 190, 192, 193
music, 58, 60, 102, 103, 206

N

narcotics, 14, 26
narratives, 81
nation, 4, 16, 22, 35, 84, 126, 132, 141, 179, 181, 209, 226, 230, 237
national, vii, 1, 5, 6, 7, 12, 13, 19, 20, 21, 22, 23, 24, 25, 26, 32, 33, 37, 39, 40, 48, 50, 52, 54, 55, 57, 58, 59, 83, 84, 120, 132, 178, 184, 186, 187, 191, 197, 198, 210, 212, 219, 224
national community, 83
National Crime Victimization Survey, 9, 12, 34
National Science Foundation, 118
National Strategy, 23
nationality, 186
Native American, 14, 98, 103
Native Americans, 14
natural, 83
NC, 222
NCVS, 9, 12, 34, 39
needles, 61
negative attitudes, 25
negative influences, 52, 136, 219
network, 80, 103, 133, 189, 219
networking, 102, 206, 219
Nevada, 42
New Jersey, 103
New Orleans, 100, 102, 131
New York, 3, 21, 38, 39, 49, 77, 80, 100, 101, 131, 177, 181, 182, 183, 186, 199, 201, 207, 209, 211, 213, 216, 220, 225, 227, 230
No Child Left Behind, 226, 232, 236
non-English speaking, 198
non-profit, 240
non-violent, 194, 218
normal, 232
norms, 53
North Carolina, 16, 48, 78, 80, 124
Northeast, 13
Norway, 134
not-for-profit, 191, 228, 231
nurse, 134, 178, 203, 206, 232

O

obesity, 233
obligation, 184, 185, 187, 188
observations, 192
occupational, 126
offenders, 10, 22, 24, 28, 29, 31, 36, 37, 46, 55, 57, 58, 59, 60, 61, 62, 78, 79, 80, 81, 82, 84, 85, 118, 121, 125, 131, 141
Office of Justice Programs, 5, 38, 39, 40, 41, 43, 49
Office of Justice Programs (OJP), 5
Office of Juvenile Justice and Delinquency Prevention, 4, 6, 38, 99, 224
Office of Juvenile Justice and Delinquency Prevention (OJJDP), 4, 6
Ohio, 48, 124
OJJDP, 7, 8, 16, 21, 26, 34, 36, 38, 39, 40, 41, 43, 208
OJP, 21, 24, 34, 41, 42
older people, 227
online, 39, 102, 103
on-line, 99
opposition, 137
oral, 226
Oregon, 48
organization, 4, 5, 19, 28, 32, 34, 84, 132, 133, 183, 193, 195, 203, 210, 211, 212, 214, 216, 217, 220, 227, 235, 238
organizations, 5, 13, 20, 21, 23, 24, 26, 35, 98, 179, 185, 188, 190, 191, 192, 195, 197, 208, 210, 211, 219, 223, 225, 226, 230, 231, 232, 233, 234, 241
organized crime, 13, 19, 23, 34
outpatient, 240
oversight, 120

P

Pacific, 42
pain, 108, 213, 214
paper, 204
Paper, 43
parental involvement, 3, 196
parenting, 85, 240
parents, 3, 18, 27, 35, 79, 80, 93, 94, 95, 100, 107, 119, 125, 130, 141, 179, 190, 191, 192, 193, 196, 198, 203, 206, 211, 212, 213, 215, 223, 231, 232, 235, 237, 238
Paris, 209
parole, 19, 24, 35, 54, 61, 130, 131, 138
parole board, 61
partnership, 78, 79, 80, 82, 107, 125, 185, 188, 189, 193, 221
partnerships, 62, 94, 95, 97, 104, 142, 192, 197
pathology, 57
pay off, 60
peace treaty, 218
peanuts, 224
peer, 52, 62, 79, 82, 94, 95, 121, 189, 190, 197, 207
peer group, 52, 79, 121, 189, 207
peer influence, 197
peer relationship, 95
peers, 137, 212, 236
penalties, 5, 20, 21, 28, 30, 33, 34, 46, 184, 187, 224
penalty, 2, 21, 28, 30
Pennsylvania, 49, 61, 126, 140, 178, 179, 180, 182
Pentagon, 108
per capita, 46
perception, 8, 29
perceptions, 12
performance, 134, 184, 187, 190
permit, 30, 31, 32, 33, 34, 43
personal, 25, 103, 179, 189, 191, 222, 227
Philadelphia, 3, 42, 61, 62, 107, 119, 125, 126, 131, 182
philosophy, 49, 107, 204
Phoenix, 42
phone, 29, 101, 135, 218, 225
physical abuse, 211
pilot programs, 108
plague, 203, 205
planning, 36, 230, 231
play, 3, 18, 119, 185, 186, 188, 189, 190
pleasure, 50, 94, 202
police, 4, 5, 21, 25, 27, 28, 29, 35, 36, 37, 39, 49, 79, 81, 84, 85, 93, 94, 95, 99, 100, 101, 102, 104, 106, 107, 122, 124, 125, 126, 127, 128, 129, 130, 132, 135, 138, 139, 183, 190, 191, 193, 194, 195, 196, 203, 206, 215, 223, 226, 230, 231
policy makers, 2, 5, 36, 240, 241
policymakers, 12, 18, 59
poor, 3, 52, 58, 60, 123, 124, 141, 142, 178, 181, 203, 212, 213
population, 8, 12, 15, 16, 39, 57, 59, 99, 103, 106, 121, 192, 204, 205, 207, 208, 236
population density, 8
porous, 19
portfolio, 51, 55
positive attitudes, 25
positive influences, 136, 224
positive reinforcement, 53
post-traumatic stress, 62, 119
post-traumatic stress disorder, 62, 119
poverty, 3, 35, 181, 200, 202, 209, 210, 211, 212, 213, 214, 235
power, 123, 126, 196, 206, 209, 211, 213, 238
prayer, 221, 227
predators, 93, 95, 125
predicate, 34, 193
prediction, 61, 62
predictors, 61
pre-existing, 196
pregnancy, 134
pregnant, 213
prejudice, 4, 25, 213
prenatal care, 134
preschool, 27, 191, 223, 226, 236
president, 49, 99, 135
President Bush, 23
pressure, 28, 183, 190
pretrial, 61
preventive, 134
prices, 98, 103
printing, 208, 225
priorities, 24, 26
prisons, 53, 55, 85, 209, 226, 233
private, 18, 51, 53, 120, 180, 185, 188, 189, 196, 197, 227, 229
private sector, 120, 180
proactive, 23, 98, 106, 137, 184, 185, 186, 187, 188, 189
probability, 53, 54
probation, 24, 35, 36, 37, 50, 53, 54, 61, 62, 80, 94, 95, 119, 125, 126, 131, 185, 188, 193, 240
probation officers, 35, 37, 94, 95, 126
problem behavior, 48
problem solving, 84
production, 104
productivity, 23
profanity, 198
profit, 53, 104, 191, 228, 231, 240
profits, 240

proliferation, 2, 35, 184, 185, 186, 187, 188, 189, 195
promote, 13, 22, 24, 26, 54, 191, 235
property, iv, 22, 25, 104, 236
property crimes, 25
prosecutor, 93, 95, 97, 101, 103, 104, 106, 132, 185, 191
prostitution, 190, 192
protection, 42, 47, 53, 94, 96, 101, 106, 134, 137, 139, 179, 212, 226, 236
protective factors, 27, 57
psychiatrists, 57, 59, 119
psychologist, 142
PTA, 196
public, vii, 1, 4, 5, 18, 20, 26, 29, 32, 49, 53, 54, 57, 58, 59, 60, 85, 97, 99, 100, 101, 103, 122, 123, 130, 135, 138, 142, 180, 181, 182, 191, 225, 226, 227, 230
public administration, 49
public awareness, 26
Public Health Service, 48
public housing, 100, 101, 122, 123
public policy, vii, 1, 5
public safety, 20, 57, 59, 85, 97, 99
public schools, 18, 225
public service, 26, 142
public support, 53, 54, 180
Puerto Rican, 3, 221
punishment, 57, 59, 125, 127
punitive, 33, 37, 141

Q

qualifications, 127
quality control, 52, 120
quality of life, 184, 186, 187, 216, 217, 219, 220
questioning, 33, 117
questionnaire, 13

R

race, 14, 15, 35, 78, 190, 192, 206
racism, 4, 213
racketeering, 19, 23, 26, 30, 34
radio, 104, 206, 213
radio station, 104
random, 54, 78, 81, 107, 196
range, vii, 1, 4, 20, 32, 36, 37, 83, 101, 119, 181, 230
rape, 9, 12, 193, 213, 226
reading, 216
real assets, 124
real time, 23
reality, 141, 196, 204, 210, 228
rearrest, 34
recall, 127
recidivate, 199, 201
recidivism, 34, 53, 105, 134
recidivism rate, 34
recognition, 48, 135
recollection, 12
reconciliation, 82
recreation, 27
recreational, 27, 94, 95, 96, 218
recruiting, 184, 187, 198, 238
redevelopment, 184, 186
reduction, 26, 35, 51, 55, 62, 117, 118, 133, 192, 208
refugees, 18
regional, 13, 36, 184, 187
regular, 123, 182
rehabilitation, 33, 123
relationship, 214
relationships, 57, 60, 78, 80, 94, 95, 197, 218, 232
relatives, 129, 193
religion, 234
rent, 124
repair, 85
replication, 23
research, 3, 4, 5, 20, 21, 22, 26, 27, 34, 35, 47, 48, 50, 51, 57, 58, 59, 60, 83, 84, 85, 108, 117, 118, 119, 120, 123, 133, 142, 179, 199, 200, 201, 202, 224, 227
research and development, 21
researchers, 3, 4, 5, 18, 35, 36, 37, 38, 46, 78, 81, 82, 83, 108, 134
resentment, 122, 125
residential, 93, 95, 232
resistance, 231
resolution, 20, 25, 32, 105, 197
resources, 23, 27, 32, 33, 37, 52, 55, 57, 59, 78, 79, 80, 82, 84, 97, 98, 101, 105, 106, 120, 133, 134, 135, 139, 141, 179, 188, 191, 192, 193, 194, 195, 196, 201, 204, 206, 212, 217, 218, 219, 223, 224, 225, 230, 240
responsibilities, 25, 105
retaliation, 101, 102, 106
retirement, 48, 108
retribution, 102
returns, 53, 121, 134
Rhode Island, 42, 49, 80, 103, 107
RICO, 19, 23, 34, 40, 43
rings, 26
risk, 3, 4, 10, 18, 20, 25, 27, 31, 32, 35, 52, 58, 60, 62, 79, 80, 82, 85, 94, 95, 96, 118, 119, 126, 131, 134, 141, 142, 178, 179, 180, 181, 183, 185, 188,

189, 195, 198, 199, 201, 202, 204, 211, 213, 223, 237, 240
risk factors, 52, 178
robberies, 80
robbery, 4, 9, 12, 26, 190, 192, 193
role playing, 123
rolling, 215
RP, 26
rural, 2, 3, 6, 7, 8, 9, 14, 15, 16, 17, 18, 39, 40, 103, 181, 203
rural areas, 2, 3, 8, 9, 15, 16, 181, 203
rural communities, 14, 16, 18
rural population, 181
Russia, 46
Russian, 13, 223

S

safety, 18, 27, 29, 93, 95, 99, 101, 105, 123, 180, 181, 192, 194, 237
salaries, 142, 195, 209
sales, 239
sample, 6, 8, 12, 16, 35, 36, 39, 40, 62
sampling, 8, 27
San Salvador, 135
sanctions, 36, 46, 82, 85, 126, 133
Saturday, 43, 217, 218
saving lives, 216
savings, 51, 55, 142
scarce resources, 105
school activities, 196
school performance, 134
schooling, 210
scientists, 12
SCUBA, 194
searching, 179
Seattle, 48
second language, 236
secondary schools, 16
secret, 225
Secret Service, 98, 105
Secretary of the Treasury, 21
secular, vii, 1
secular trend, vii, 1
security, 2, 18, 20, 32, 47, 85, 93, 94, 95, 96, 105, 226
seed, 106
seeding, 83
selecting, 52
self-destructive behavior, 211
self-esteem, 25, 179
self-help, 234
self-improvement, 120
self-report, 25
self-worth, 237
Senate, 23, 30, 41, 99, 228
senators, 178
sensitivity, 25
sentences, 28, 30, 33, 34, 38, 46, 93, 95, 126, 141
sentencing, 33, 38, 103, 142, 184, 187, 231
September 11, 24
series, 5, 32, 50, 54, 57, 59, 83, 100
service provider, 78, 79, 80, 81, 83, 94, 95, 179, 182, 185, 188, 207
services, iv, 27, 36, 46, 52, 61, 62, 80, 84, 85, 93, 95, 96, 122, 124, 141, 186, 189, 191, 193, 196, 198, 199, 201, 208, 211, 219, 233, 234, 236, 238
sex, 213
sexism, 213
sexual abuse, 211, 213, 238
sexual assault, 12, 128
shame, 223, 226
shape, 132, 232
sharing, 23, 37, 184, 186, 187, 189, 192
shelter, 27
shock, 50, 53, 54, 208
shoot, 81
short period, 51
short run, 126, 142
short-term, 42
shy, 205
sibling, 198
siblings, 207, 212
sign, 5, 218
signs, 4, 18, 103, 190, 191, 192, 204, 206
silver, 52, 235
sites, 26, 83, 93, 98, 102, 103, 240
skills, 27, 57, 60, 126, 179, 185, 188, 195, 197, 198, 207, 208, 211, 212, 225, 232, 240
sleep, 203, 205, 235
slums, 3
smoking, 215
smuggling, 4, 20, 40
social activities, 119
social assistance, 27
social behavior, 196
social context, 52
social institutions, 16, 60
social problems, 37, 235
social services, 36, 124
Social Services, 183, 189, 197
social skills, 198
social structure, 3
social support, 4
social welfare, 202
social work, 48, 57, 59, 107, 183, 190, 193, 197, 209

social workers, 57, 59, 107, 193, 197, 209
socialization, 18, 185, 188
socioeconomic, 3, 4, 128
socioeconomic background, 128
socioeconomic status, 3
solutions, 20, 25, 108, 211, 230
South Carolina, 83, 98, 100
South Dakota, 42
specificity, 237
specter, 20
spectrum, 20, 46, 192
speculation, 20
speech, 198, 210
spiritual, 125
sports, 58, 60, 190, 192, 195
St. Louis, 99
stability, 3, 179
stakeholders, 185, 188, 189
standardization, 36
standards, vii, 1, 79, 82
State of the Union, 23
State of the Union address, 23
statistics, 9, 13, 36, 201, 213
statutes, 19, 23, 34, 40, 43
stereotypes, 194
strategic, 26, 29, 36, 41, 84
strategies, 18, 20, 22, 24, 28, 33, 34, 35, 36, 37, 54, 55, 78, 81, 82, 83, 85, 94, 95, 97, 98, 105, 119, 141, 181, 184, 185, 186, 187, 189, 190, 203, 207, 208, 212, 230
strategy use, 28
strength, 105
stress, 119, 235
strikes, 137
student group, 197
students, 17, 18, 25, 32, 35, 100, 106, 178, 180, 191, 192, 194, 195, 196, 197, 204, 236, 240
substance abuse, 52, 54, 57, 60, 93, 95, 141, 200, 201, 202, 229
substance use, 51
suburban, 2, 3, 7, 8, 9, 17, 18, 39, 181
suburbs, 14, 19, 46, 103, 108, 184, 186, 190, 205
success rate, 142
suffering, 62, 185, 188
summer, 80, 96, 105, 185, 188, 208
Sunday, 101, 102
supercomputers, 61
supervision, 36, 54, 61, 80, 85, 93, 95, 119, 125, 126, 131, 237
suppliers, 26
supply, 26, 103
support services, 208, 211
support staff, 22, 189
suppression, 18, 20, 22, 27, 28, 29, 36, 37, 181, 182, 184, 187, 190, 192, 193
Surgeon General, 48
surplus, 182
surveillance, 105, 130, 184, 187
survivors, 213
suspects, 19, 131
suspensions, 94, 96
sustainability, 78, 79, 81, 83, 208
switching, 102
symbolic, 4
symbols, 4, 190
sympathy, 129
symptoms, 142, 213, 219
syndrome, 235
systems, 35, 82, 119, 141

T

tactics, 13, 20
talent, 48
tangible, 53, 208
task force, 2, 21, 23, 24, 31, 36, 46, 127, 192
taxpayers, 53
teachers, 183, 195, 209
technical assistance, 83, 84, 97
technology, 22, 31, 98, 102, 103, 104, 105, 184, 187
teens, 20, 85, 102
telephone, 123
television, 124, 198, 203, 206, 213, 235
tension, 78, 129
tenure, 182
territory, 123
terrorism, 24, 47, 184, 187
terrorist, 20, 24, 32, 43, 190
terrorist attack, 20, 24
terrorist groups, 20
terrorist organization, 32, 190
terrorists, 20, 102
Terrorists, 41
testimony, 19, 23, 24, 47, 48, 50, 55, 58, 60, 84, 94, 97, 99, 101, 104, 117, 118, 120, 121, 122, 130, 131, 132, 133, 138, 140, 180, 181, 182, 190, 193, 222, 223, 224, 234, 236, 237, 239
Texas, 102, 138, 139, 140
theft, 4, 9, 12, 14
theory, 57, 59, 81, 125
therapists, 57, 59
therapy, 57, 59, 62, 85, 126, 179, 211, 227, 234
thinking, 78, 79, 104, 214, 235
threat, 2, 4, 13, 16, 18, 19, 20, 23, 29, 33, 39, 57, 59, 97, 98, 101, 128, 139, 213
threatened, 102, 137

threatening, 119, 122
threats, 13, 19, 33, 98, 106, 138, 198
time constraints, 233
time frame, 61
title, 46
tobacco, 53
tolerance, 28, 37
torture, 102
toxic, 78, 79
tracking, 199, 201
trade, 38, 132
trading, 99
traffic, 22, 101
training, 22, 26, 27, 31, 32, 36, 37, 53, 57, 59, 93, 95, 98, 108, 119, 122, 123, 124, 179, 185, 188, 207, 208, 240
training programs, 26, 123, 124
traits, 195
trajectory, 78, 79, 118, 119
transactions, 124
transfer, 31, 43, 128, 200, 202
transformation, 41
transition, 36
transnational, 20
transport, 14
transportation, 13, 31
trauma, 235
travel, 48, 103
Treasury, 21
treatable, 62
trend, vii, 1, 7, 9, 10, 11, 42, 57, 59, 104, 198
triage, 126
trial, 53, 62, 101, 131
tribal, vii, 1, 32, 41
tribes, 98, 103
truancy, 126
trust, 101, 123, 130, 189, 240
tutoring, 93, 95, 240

U

UCR, 9, 10
uncertainty, 11
unemployment, 134
unemployment rate, 134
uniform, vii, 1, 20, 107
Uniform Crime Reports, 11, 12, 34
United States, vii, 1, 3, 6, 7, 12, 16, 18, 19, 24, 35, 37, 38, 39, 46, 47, 81, 93, 95, 99, 106, 121, 130, 132, 138, 180, 182, 190, 205, 206, 209
United States Attorneys, 81
United States Marshals Service, 106
universities, 204, 229
updating, 232
urban areas, 2, 3, 14, 15, 181, 230

V

validity, 12
values, 198, 237
vandalism, 4, 13
variability, 8
variable, 16
vein, 103, 195
venue, 208
victim advocates, 12
victimization, 6, 12, 16, 55, 58, 118, 128
victims, 12, 25, 61, 84, 94, 98, 105, 129, 131, 204, 213, 235
video games, 198, 206
Vietnam, 107
Vietnam War, 107
village, 196, 217
violent arrests, 57, 59
violent behavior, 94, 95
violent crime, vii, 1, 2, 5, 9, 10, 11, 12, 20, 21, 23, 29, 30, 31, 33, 34, 45, 55, 57, 58, 59, 80, 85, 97, 98, 100, 130, 140, 141, 181, 193, 240
Violent Crime Control and Law Enforcement Act, 21, 38
violent crimes, 5, 9, 10, 20, 21, 30, 33, 34, 45, 100, 140, 141, 193, 240
violent offenders, 12, 31, 55, 85
viruses, 102
visible, 13, 103
vision, 179, 183, 197, 216, 219, 222, 225, 230
vocabulary, 198
vocational, 54, 207, 208
voice, 55, 58, 60, 78, 79, 80, 81, 82, 125, 129, 181
voids, 23
voting, 180

W

walking, 100, 129, 215
Wall Street Journal, 176
war, 23, 184, 187, 199, 203, 209
warehousing, 85
warfare, 99, 129
Washington Post, 43
weapons, 13, 20, 21, 102, 190, 192
wear, 101, 103
web, 102, 103, 186
web sites, 103
websites, 83, 102

welfare, 200, 201, 202
Western Hemisphere, 40, 41
wheelchair, 204
white women, 82
wildfire, 186
wind, 108
winning, 182
winter, 80
Wisconsin, 98, 99, 103
witnesses, 46, 47, 48, 50, 61, 98, 101, 106, 117, 124, 127, 132, 138, 140, 142, 180, 181, 182, 229, 234, 239
women, 12, 82, 180, 189, 190, 206, 213, 215, 237
work ethic, 207, 208
workers, 79, 80, 107, 108, 119, 129, 138, 205, 232, 236
workforce, 93
World War I, 107
World War II, 107
worry, 180
writing, 83, 121, 128, 213, 239

Y

yield, 127, 131, 142
young adults, 5, 6, 10, 32, 178, 186, 190
young men, 102, 103, 119, 180, 189, 206
young women, 183, 212, 213
younger children, 100